Notes on Genesis and Exodus

Notes on Genesis and Exodus

Novitiate Conferences on Scripture and Liturgy 2

Thomas Merton

EDITED WITH AN INTRODUCTION BY
Pauline F. O'Connell

FOREWORD BY
Pauline A. Viviano

CASCADE Books • Eugene, Oregon

NOTES ON GENESIS AND EXODUS
Novitiate Conferences on Scripture and Liturgy 2

Copyright © 2021 Thomas Merton Legacy Trust. All rights reserved. Except for brief quotations in critical publications or reviews, no part of this book may be reproduced in any manner without prior written permission from the publisher. Write: Permissions, Wipf and Stock Publishers, 199 W. 8th Ave., Suite 3, Eugene, OR 97401.

Cascade Books
An Imprint of Wipf and Stock Publishers
199 W. 8th Ave., Suite 3
Eugene, OR 97401

www.wipfandstock.com

PAPERBACK ISBN: 978-1-7252-5315-5
HARDCOVER ISBN: 978-1-7252-5316-2
EBOOK ISBN: 978-1-7252-5317-9

Cataloguing-in-Publication data:

Names: Merton, Thomas, 1915–1968, author. | O'Connell, Patrick F., editor and introduction. | Viviano, Pauline A., foreword.

Title: Notes on Genesis and Exodus : novitiate conferences on scripture and liturgy 2. / Thomas Merton ; edited and introduction by Patrick F. O'Connell; foreword by Pauline A. Viviano.

Description: Eugene, OR : Cascade Books, 2021. | Includes bibliographical references and index.

Identifiers: ISBN 978-1-7252-5315-5 (paperback). | ISBN 978-1-7252-5316-2 (hardcover). | ISBN 978-1-7252-5317-9 (ebook).

Subjects: LCSH: Bible. Genesis—Criticism, interpretation, etc. | Bible. Exodus—Criticism, interpretation, etc. | Merton, Thomas, 1915–1968.

Classification: BS1235 M43 2021 (print). | BS1235 (ebook).

"As a Cistercian, Merton's life was shaped by the scriptural basis of the monastic offices. Patrick O'Connell's honest, critical introduction and exacting editing of Merton's notes for talks to his novices on Genesis and Exodus provide fresh insight into the monk's pre-Vatican II thought and fill in a missing piece of the puzzle of his theological development. Merton readers and admirers owe O'Connell a debt of gratitude for his impressive editing of the massive body of Merton's heretofore unpublished notes for monastic conferences."

—BONNIE THURSTON, author of *Shaped by the End You Live For: Thomas Merton's Monastic Spirituality*

"Patrick O'Connell continues his remarkable project of publishing Thomas Merton's work as a teacher in this edition of his notes for courses given to Gethsemani Abbey novice monks on the books of Genesis and Exodus. Meticulously edited and annotated, these notes reveal a discerning teacher who provides not just exegetical commentary but connections to liturgy, preaching, and theology, and the ongoing formation of his student monks. Impressive work that gives a fascinating vision of Merton on the Scriptures."

—MICHAEL PLEKON, author of *Saints As They Really Are: Voices of Holiness in Our Time*

"In this book we see Thomas Merton doing exegesis of Scripture in his novitiate classes. While he lay no claim to being an expert in Scripture, this book shows him as being certainly very competent. Yet he does exegesis in a way that is thoroughly in accord with monastic *lectio divina*. He develops it by making full use of early monastic writers as well as fathers of the church to show how the texts serve as profound means of prayer, in a way that is of benefit not only to monastics, but to anyone desiring to approach these early scriptural texts as truly leading to God and to prayer. Patrick O'Connell's introduction situates these classes in relation to other books of Merton written both before and after the date of these conferences. It serves to give a more comprehensive picture of Merton's writings. We can be very grateful to the editor for his work."

—JAMES CONNER, OCSO, Abbey of Gethsemani

"This book is priceless for two major reasons: it offers a window into Merton's contemplative biblical spirituality that he shared with the Trappist novices; and these insights are buttressed by the meticulous editing of O'Connell—his rich interpretive introduction, extensive explanatory notes, and cross references to Merton's journals, letters, and poetry."

   —MONICA WEIS, SSJ, author of *The Environmental Vision of Thomas Merton*

CONTENTS

Foreword by Pauline A. Viviano | vii

Introduction | xi

Notes on Genesis | 1

Notes on Exodus | 135

Textual Notes | 193

Bibliography | 207

Scripture Index | 213

General Index | 227

FOREWORD

THE FIRST BOOK I read by Thomas Merton was *Seeds of Contemplation*. I was only ten years old, and I must confess I didn't understand a word of it, but I knew I was in the presence of someone who had a profound spiritual depth. Over the years I moved from art to philosophy to biblical studies, but I continued to read Merton. I marveled, not only at the depth of his understanding of spiritual matters, especially prayer, but also at his prophetic insight into American society and his challenge to that society with respect to racial injustice, the proliferation of nuclear arms, the horror of war, and the deadening impact of consumerism on the human soul. Lately I have learned to appreciate Merton as an artist, a poet, and a photographer. With this volume of Merton's novitiate conferences on the books of Genesis and Exodus I must add teacher and biblical interpreter to my list of what I admire most about Merton.

This edition of Thomas Merton's class notes brings us into the workings of a great spiritual leader's mind as he reflects upon Scripture. His notes on Genesis are well-developed; regrettably those on Exodus are incomplete. His audience consists of the novices at the Abbey of Gethsemani in Kentucky, but all who are on a spiritual journey can gain from his insights and the lessons he draws from Scripture. Even contemporary biblical scholars who take a very different approach to Scripture can benefit from engaging Merton's perspective.

Biblical interpretation has been spoken of as a science in the past two centuries—not a science in the sense in which biology and chemistry are sciences, but a science in the sense of employing a rigorous method with the expectation of agreed-upon, well-grounded results. It may be debated as to how successful this approach has been, but it is clear that this modern venture into interpretation of texts moved away from more traditional methods of interpretation that have dominated for more than two thousand years. Thomas Merton's unraveling of the meaning of Genesis and Exodus takes place at the point of transition within Catholicism between the use of traditional methods of interpretation and adoption of the more recent historical and literary critical approaches that insist on the necessity of understanding texts from within their historical and literary contexts.

At the risk of oversimplifying the history of two millennia of Christianity, we may say that the search for meaning in the biblical text has been concerned with two senses of the text: the literal and the spiritual. The literal sense focuses on the meaning of the words, that is, the surface meaning of the text. This became the dominant focus of the nineteenth and twentieth centuries with the rise of historical and literary-critical methods of interpretation. Merton is conversant with the adoption of historical and literary criticism by Catholic biblical scholars of the late 1940s and early 1950s and often makes reference to their work. Contemporary biblical scholars will find this aspect of Merton's notes dated and superseded by the work of later scholars, but they can nevertheless appreciate how aware Merton was of the biblical scholarship of his day.

Where Merton excels is in his treatment of the spiritual sense of the text. The spiritual sense is concerned with a presumed deeper meaning hidden within the text, now revealed to those of faith. The spiritual sense has been divided into several subcategories, but by the end of the medieval period biblical interpreters had settled on three: the allegorical/typological sense, the tropological or moral sense, and the anagogic sense. The moral sense focused on the lessons drawn from the text that guided the Christian in living a Christian life; the anagogic sense focused on the heavenly goal of Christian life and afterlife issues.

The allegorical/typological interpreters sought to discover a deeper meaning that allowed ancient, and sometimes obscure or offensive texts, to have meaning for readers of later centuries. Biblical characters were identified with virtues to be pursued or vices to be avoided. Names, numbers, measurements, and mundane details were given a significance far removed from their original context. We tend to distinguish allegory from typology, but this was not done until the early twentieth century. The deeper meaning we label typology has to do with the relationship between the Old Testament and the New Testament. The persons and events that preceded Christ in the Old Testament are seen as "types" which anticipate or foreshadow the "antitypes" later found in the New Testament.

Merton sees the Scriptures as "letters from God in which He awakens in us love for our homeland" (35). He characterizes every person's life "as an apostolic journey. To be called by God is to start on [that] journey" (41). Thus, it is not surprising that he often draws moral lessons and speaks of the goal of human life as he works his way through the narratives of Genesis and Exodus. The lives of biblical characters (e.g., Adam, Eve, Noah, Abraham, Sara, Lot, Jacob, Joseph, Moses) become exemplars of various behaviors, such as obedience or disobedience, recklessly moving forward or patiently waiting, an ordinary spirituality or a spirituality guided by God. Merton reveals a profound understanding of human nature in his treatment of Adam's and Eve's sin, of Cain's murder of his brother, and of the flood narrative, to mention but a few examples. Time and again Merton leads us through these biblical narratives, calling our attention to what can serve us on our own journey back to God.

It is with Merton's focus on the allegorical/typological sense of Scripture that the depth of his understanding of Christianity comes to the fore. Of many examples, one in particular comes to mind: Abraham's suffering in offering his beloved son Isaac becomes a template of God's experience in offering his beloved Son. Merton connects Abraham's longing for his son with God's longing for sinful humanity and his desire to recover them through Christ (see 73). Over and over again Merton leads us through his analysis of the narratives of Genesis and Exodus into the depth of the mystery of redemption in Christ.

Allegorical/typological interpretation of the Bible continues today in the Mass, for the Old Testament and Gospel readings are regularly set in typological relationship. It is visually represented in stained-glass windows and in great works of Christian art. The church affirms the value of this particular form of patristic interpretation for the service that it has provided and continues to provide to the church, but it has been largely abandoned. Indeed the church acknowledges that such interpretation "runs the risk of being something of an embarrassment to people today."[1] It becomes an embarrassment when it disregards the literal sense of the text. Without a firm grounding in the literal sense there are no controls over flights of fancy in the discovery of meaning in texts. Merton's discovery of deeper meanings is well-grounded in the literal sense of the text. He makes a seamless movement from literal sense to hidden meaning, building upon what the text actually says. The breadth and depth of his

---

1. Pontifical Biblical Commission, *Interpretation of the Bible in the Church*, #173 (*Bible Documents*, 175).

understanding of Christian reality and spiritual life are interwoven into his spiritual interpretation of Genesis and Exodus. We find in Merton's notes the best of spiritual interpretation. There is much in these notes to meditate upon and much that can be used to guide us on our own spiritual journey. Beyond this, Merton's notes stand as a challenge to biblical scholars to remember that the Bible is a living text; it is a sacred text. Thus, biblical scholars have a responsibility to make their research accessible to the "people in the pew" and meaningful for their lives.

We are indebted to Patrick O'Connell for his expertise and meticulous work in bringing us this edition of Thomas Merton's notes on the Books of Genesis and Exodus. I am personally grateful to him for inviting me to write this foreword, for it has led me to appreciate even more Thomas Merton's legacy.

Pauline A. Viviano, PhD

INTRODUCTION

WHEN HE BEGAN HIS decade-long term as master of novices at the Abbey of Gethsemani in October 1955, Thomas Merton included weekly conferences on Scripture, along with classes on monastic history, practices, and spirituality,[1] as part of the regular instruction given to the prospective monks entrusted to his charge.[2] Initially, he recycled a set of lectures entitled *A Monastic Introduction to Sacred Scripture*, originally composed for the newly professed monks whom Merton taught during his tenure as master of scholastics between 1951 and 1955, which focused mainly on standard theoretical topics in Scripture studies, including inspiration; the biblical canon; textual matters; and hermeneutics, principles of interpretation. After completing this introductory overview on May 10, 1956, the Feast of the Ascension,[3] he turned his attention and that of his audience to the opening books of the entire Bible, which presented what he called "the first act in the great drama of salvation" (1). The two sets of conferences included in the present volume, a thorough, comprehensive course on the book of Genesis that began sometime in the summer of 1956 and concluded on June 9, 1957, the Feast of Pentecost (134),[4] and

---

1. See Merton, *Cassian and the Fathers*; Merton, *Pre-Benedictine Monasticism*; Merton, *Rule of Saint Benedict*; Merton, *Monastic Observances*; Merton, *Life of the Vows*; Merton, *Charter, Customs, and Constitutions*; Merton, *Cistercian Fathers and Their Monastic Theology*; Merton, *Medieval Cistercian History*. Though presented during the period of his mastership, the conferences in Merton, *Introduction to Christian Mysticism* were not given to the novices but to recently ordained professed members of the Gethsemani community.

2. See also Merton's undated 1956 letter to Jean Leclercq, OSB in which he refers to his early sets of conferences on monastic material but does not mention the scripture courses that he was also giving at the time (Merton and Leclercq, *Survival or Prophecy?*, 75–76).

3. See Merton, *Monastic Introduction*, 142.

4. It is uncertain how soon after completing the introductory Scripture course

a considerably less detailed, more diffusely organized series of classes on the book of Exodus that probably ran from midsummer 1957 through the early spring of 1958,[5] make up the only major surviving teaching notes on Scripture dating from the years when Merton was in charge of the novitiate.

Merton began the conferences on Genesis, but a reference to "mosquitoes" on the verso of page 9 of Merton's own typescript of his Genesis notes (page 20 of the present edition) suggests that he had reached that point sometime during the summer, so any delay between the conclusion of the former set and the beginning of the latter could not have been very long. By the First Sunday of Advent, the epistle and gospel of which are mentioned on page 35v of the typescript (page 71 of the present edition), Merton had reached about the halfway point in his text, his discussion of Genesis 22, the sacrifice of Isaac. A reference to "Lenten reading" on page 52v (page 105 of the present edition) indicates that at this time he has just begun discussion of the material on Joseph, the last major section of the book of Genesis (cc. 37–50). His concluding discussion (133) of the appropriateness of considering the final chapters of Genesis on the Feast of Pentecost not only provides the *terminus ad quem* for this particular series of conferences but indicates that they had evidently been delivered on Sundays.

5. It is not clear whether the conferences on Exodus began immediately after the Genesis series had concluded, though there is one possible indication that there may have been a pause of a few weeks between them. On the verso of the fourth page of his Exodus notes (page 146 of the present edition), Merton had written a note, somewhat obscured by its subsequent cancellation, that looks like it may read: "Mass 18th Sun—Peace"; the gospel for the Ninth Sunday after Pentecost, celebrated in 1957 on August 18, is Luke 19:41–47, the passage in which Jesus weeps over Jerusalem and addresses the city with the words: "If you had known . . . the things that make for your peace!" It seems somewhat unlikely (though not impossible, given his customary procedure of using his written notes only as a general guide for his oral presentations) that it would have taken Merton more than two months to proceed through the first three chapters of the book of Exodus, so he may have begun this second series after a brief hiatus. More certain, though still somewhat approximate, is the chronological information provided by Merton's brief note "Hospital? Return?" written on the verso of a page completing his outline of the stages of the Israelites' passing through the desert as found in Exodus and Numbers (page 165 of the present edition). This was probably a note for his conference on or about Sunday November 17, since in his journal entry for that day he wrote: "Tomorrow to Doctor in Bardstown to get my guts looked at. Perhaps an operation" (Merton, *Search for Solitude*, 139). He was in fact hospitalized for surgery from November 18 through November 26 (Merton, *Search for Solitude*, 141–43). There are no further indications of dating, other than the fact that the article by Louis Bouyer that Merton summarizes at length in subsequent pages (169–74), about two-thirds of the way through his written notes, appeared in the December 1957–February 1958 issue of *Bible et Vie Chrétienne*. Thus it seems plausible that Merton may have begun the conferences on Exodus sometime in late June or July 1957, and ended them, even though he had not completed a discussion of the entire book, in the late winter or early spring of 1958.

Merton's intention, as indicated in a one-page typed outline headed "Scripture Seminar—Program" (135), had been to consider in sequence each of the five books of the Pentateuch, to be followed by Joshua, Judges, and Ruth, the first of the Old Testament historical books, but it is unclear to what extent he pursued this ambitious plan beyond the materials included in the present edition. Though there is no extant documentary evidence from this period that indicates Merton undertook any extensive systematic explication of other scriptural material, either from the Old Testament or the New,[6] in his recent memoir Br. Paul Quenon, who entered Gethsemani in 1958 and spent the following two years as a novice under Merton, writes of Scripture conferences he particularly remembers: "Fr. Louis taught scripture with the kind of literary-analytic skill he most likely learned while studying at Columbia University. His commentaries on the book of Job and the two books of Samuel are most vivid in my mind because he simply traced out the narrative line and drew our interest to what many of us had never paid much attention to."[7] In the absence of actual texts, it is uncertain whether conferences on Samuel followed sets on the intervening books mentioned in Merton's outline, or were stand-alone presentations as, presumably, were those on Job. In any case, Merton's teaching notes on Genesis and Exodus provide the only extended purview of how he introduced his novices to the contents of specific biblical books and to the intellectual, and particularly the spiritual, contexts in which they should be read, understood, and appreciated.

Merton begins his "Notes on Genesis" with an introduction to the Pentateuch as a whole, providing a brief description of each of the five books (as well as of the book of Josue [Joshua][8] that completes the story of the

6. The only other surviving conference material on Scripture from the novitiate period is a three-page handwritten text entitled "The First Epistle of St. John" that was apparently presented in early 1958, since in his journal entry for December 29, 1957, Merton wrote: "Preparing notes on first epistle of St. John for the novices' conference" (Merton, *Search for Solitude*, 150); these notes were preserved with the typescript of Merton's conferences on "The Life, Works and Doctrine of Saint Bernard" and are transcribed in Appendix A of Merton, *Cistercian Fathers and Their Monastic Theology* (414–18).

7. Quenon, *Useless Life*, 24.

8. Merton almost always follows the spelling of proper names as found in the Douay–Rheims translation of the Bible, based on the Latin Vulgate, rather than the

entrance of the chosen people into the promised land). He refers to Moses as the author, the standard Catholic position in the mid-1950s, but immediately nuances this statement as not to be taken as meaning simply that Moses sat down and wrote out the Torah as it exists today, and he goes on to give a tentative but positive evaluation of the Documentary Hypothesis, which assigns various passages in these books to Yahwist, Elohist, Priestly, and Deuteronomic authors, and as the conferences progress he will occasionally mention with no apparent reservations that a particular pericope belongs to one or another of these sources. Thus the text exemplifies the transitional state of Catholic biblical studies at the time of its writing, making clear both Merton's awareness of current positions and his openness to new developments that will largely transform the framework of biblical exegesis in the Catholic community in the decade to follow.

Merton then turns to the "prehistory" presented in the first eleven chapters of Genesis, leading up to the call of Abraham that initiates the story of the patriarchs, the forebears of Israel, that will be the focus of the rest of the book. In his discussion of the two opening chapters, there is an unquestioning acceptance of the presence of two distinct creation stories, and of the first (1:1—2:4a) as the product of the Priestly source. Rather surprisingly, Merton gives little explicit attention to the sequence of God's creative acts over the course of the six days, pointing out only the common pattern found at each stage. His focus is rather on the liturgical aspects of the account, the element of "worship, praise, adoration" that is the proper response to the divine gift of life and order, and its contemporary implications, especially for monastic life: "Our liturgical life should be impregnated with this spirit—kinship with creatures and with God. We are the natural mediators between God and the rest of His creation. {This is} our key position—our dignity. Love is the answer" (3). These verses are seen as providing a pattern of life for the child of God, in which the mysterious presence of the Holy Spirit hovers not only over the abyss of the waters but over the abyss of the soul as well, a source of continuing vitality and creativity in both the outer and inner world. He goes on to touch upon the patristic teaching of the divine image, always present in the very structure of the human person, and the divine likeness, capable of being lost through sin and recovered through redemption;[9] on the

---

more familiar versions universally used today.

9. Merton discusses this image-likeness theology in detail in the third chapter of *New Man*, 49–68; this book, originally titled *Existential Communion*, was written

importance of marriage and fecundity as a participation in God's creative activity; and on the Sabbath as a foreshadowing of the ultimate rest in God in the new creation. He finishes up this discussion with references to relevant psalms that celebrate the creation, to links with baptism as a new creation, and to the prayer for the dying that explicitly refers to God as Creator. These initial reflections exemplify the approach that will characterize Merton's methodology throughout these conferences—making connections with later scriptural passages, as well as ecclesial texts and practices, that will provide commentary on and amplification of the original material in Genesis, and inviting his audience to consider the personal, experiential implications of the word of God. He is interested less in objective exegesis, though he does not neglect this dimension, than in exploring the biblical text as a resource for spiritual formation.

The discussion of the second creation account (2:4b–25), while somewhat more circumstantial, omits completely any account of the creation of Adam—perhaps considered so well-known to his audience that it needs no explicit attention. Instead Merton discusses at some length the setting in paradise, a garden that is the oriental image of perfection, touching on commentators' various suppositions, both literal and figurative, as to its location, and likening the Genesis presentation of paradise as the scene of intimate encounter with God to the traditional perception of the "appropriateness of gardens and woods for contemplation" (5)—again giving a spiritual and monastic nuance (one very meaningful to himself personally[10]) to the scriptural detail. Mention in the text

---

substantially during the five weeks of the fall vacation in 1954 (see Merton's journal entry for November 23, 1959 [Merton, *Search for Solitude*, 348]), though not published until more than six years later. It includes Merton's most extensive discussion of the spiritual and theological significance of the early chapters of Genesis. In a journal entry for February 1, 1959, Merton wrote: "After dinner . . . thought of finally writing up some of the material on Genesis. This will have to be done, but when?" (Merton, *Search for Solitude*, 254). It is likely that this is a reference to *The New Man*, which he was revising for publication at the time of his November journal entry, rather than to the novitiate conference notes, for which there is no evidence of any further work.

10. The symbolism of paradise, its loss in the fall and its recovery through the death and resurrection of Christ, is one of the most central and powerful elements in Merton's spiritual teaching; see for example Merton, *New Seeds*, 290–91, where he describes the opening chapters of Genesis as "a poetic and symbolic revelation, a completely *true*, though not literal, revelation of God's view of the universe and of His intentions for man. The point of these beautiful chapters is that God made the world as a garden in which He himself took delight. He made man and gave to man the task of sharing in His own divine care for created things." For an overview of this theme, see O'Connell, "Paradise," in Shannon et al., *Thomas Merton Encyclopedia*, 349–51, and in

of "every kind of tree" (6) leads to citations of various passages on trees elsewhere in the Bible, the association of trees with the fruit of wisdom, and especially to the trees of life found in the New Jerusalem in the final book of the Bible. More particularly he notes Saint Augustine's comment that the tree of life (associated with Christ himself) feeds the spirit with the mystery of divine presence as the other trees feed the body with their fruit, and then turns to the meaning of the tree of knowledge, an image of profound significance for Merton's spiritual teaching on the true and false self.[11] Following Saint Bernard,[12] he sees the fruit of the tree of knowledge as the source of division, destroying the unitive knowledge of the good by providing an experiential knowledge of evil, and so bringing about the loss of an intuitive awareness of reality through love, introducing the illusion of autonomy and the spurious perception of the self as independent arbiter of what is good and evil, and leading human beings to become in effect one's own (false) god,[13] as the serpent had insidiously promised. Merton will expand on this insight in his discussion of the fall in the following chapter, but first he touches on the four rivers of paradise, two real and two legendary and thus perhaps symbolic, and then on Adam's naming of the beasts,[14] with its profound implications for "the mystery of language: 'What man calls each thing, that it is'"; in the face of the "modern devaluation of language," he proposes that "Trappists above all should have respect for the value of words" (12)—precisely because of their tradition of not using them promiscuously. Finally he considers the creation of Eve from the side of Adam, who is described in the Greek of the Septuagint and in the writings of Saint Bernard as being

---

more detail, O'Connell, "Awakening in Eden."

11. See for example Merton, *Inner Experience*, 112: "we notice a deep symbolic wisdom in Patristic interpretations of the story of the Fall in Genesis. This indeed is the forbidden tree: this tree of self, which grows in the middle of Paradise, but which we ourselves are not supposed to see or notice. All the other trees are there, and they refresh us with their fruits. Of them we can be aware, and they are there to be enjoyed for the love of God. But if we become aware of ourselves, turn back too much upon ourselves, and seek to rest in ourselves, then we take the fruit that was forbidden us: we become 'as gods, knowing good and evil,' for we find division within ourselves and are cut off from external reality at the same time."

12. See Merton, *New Man*, 104–12; and Merton, *Spirit of Simplicity*, 92–93, 106–7.

13. Merton repeatedly returns to this central insight throughout his writings. See for example Merton, *Disputed Questions*, 100: "the fundamental temptation, the one to which Adam owes his fall, is the temptation to be 'like unto God.'"

14. See Merton, *New Man*, 81–86.

in ecstasy; the story reflects the equality of man and woman, the foundations of the family, and above all the mystery of love, a reflection of the mystery of divine, Trinitarian love and the foundation of all the nuptial imagery for the mutual love of God and humanity throughout the rest of the Bible, climaxing in the image of the New Jerusalem "prepared as a bride adorned for her husband" (Rev 21:2) in the final chapters of the book of Revelation.

The discussion of the fall[15] that follows is probably the most powerful section in this entire set of notes, expanding upon what had already been said of the tree of knowledge. Prompted by the serpent, the diabolic agent of division, the fall is described by Merton as entailing a loss of authentic relationship with God, with creation, and with one's own genuine self. It is the reduction of illumination to the light of one's own mind, the pursuit of superficial desires as illusory sources of meaning and fulfillment, a substitution of self for God as the center of life. The inevitable result is self-deception and frustration, as the world refuses to conform to one's own demands and fantasies. Merton sees in "the nakedness . . . of which they are afraid" an awareness of "their own nothingness, their helplessness, their frailty, their propensity to fall into folly and death," and that "the knowledge of their nakedness is the knowledge of their conflict, of the division that is in them between a flesh that can overwhelm the spirit and a spirit which struggles vainly to control the flesh"; this results in a profound ambivalence toward their own bodies, an alienation between spirit and flesh that "keeps them convinced of their 'nothingness'" (15). God is considered as a rival, the destroyer of (false) projections. Creation is no longer a place to encounter God but somewhere to hide from God, no longer a sign of divine love and care but something to be controlled, exploited, and feared as a threat. Likewise the inner self is no longer perceived as a manifestation of the divine image and likeness but as an abyss of uncontrollable and unrealizable desires and passions. Yet, Merton emphasizes, "Nothing has changed but man, who now sees only creatures, mirrors of his own desires and interior states, instead of going through their transparency to see the infinite reality of God" (16). But set in the larger context of the biblical revelation as a whole, Merton maintains that the story of the fall is ultimately one of hope in the divine

---

15. Merton repeatedly discusses the fall and its consequences throughout his writings; see in particular the chapter titled "Spirit in Bondage," in Merton, *New Man* (99–128); for an overview, see O'Connell, "Fall," in *Merton Encyclopedia*, 153–54.

mercy,[16] the intimation of a deeper truth than sin and punishment, a promise to fallen humanity that wisdom ultimately overcomes malice. He finds in God's words to Adam and Eve an anticipation of the good news of redemption, the traditional "protoevangelium" that interprets the "seed" of the woman in conflict with the serpent as ultimately to be recognized as Christ himself.

The immediate consequence, however, is the further extension of the power of evil as presented in the Cain and Abel story. But Merton first calls attention to the haiku-like gnomic pronouncement of Eve that it is "through God" that she has borne a son, an expression of her "humility and wisdom" (18) that certainly suggests a process of maturing that she has undergone since the expulsion from paradise. The contrast between Cain and Abel is presented by Merton as the first instance of the divine favor falling on the younger, the weaker, the less significant in worldly terms. In sacrificing the fruit of his own toil, Merton suggests, Cain may be asserting his sense of his own self-sufficiency; in his anger at being rejected he reflects a magical rather than a truly religious attitude, an expectation that the correct performance of certain ritual actions "should have *obliged* God to be favorable" (19)—an expectation that God can be controlled. Abel's sacrifice on the other hand is the gift of a life that is first God's gift to him, a free act of love, a disinterested expression of his purity of heart. Yet the Lord has not abandoned Cain but still "speaks in the intimacy of his heart" (19), reminding him that he is free not to give in to selfish impulses. Merton suggests that the situation poses a test as to whether actual sin will be added to original sin—a test which of course Cain fails spectacularly, in his murder of his brother and in his arrogant and contemptuous response to God's question "where is thy brother?" (in which Merton hears an echo of the earlier question "Adam, where art thou?"): Cain's response implies a conscious attempt to usurp the divine prerogative over life and death and over one's own destiny. But even here, Merton finds evidence of divine condescension: as Cain's attitude turns from pride to despair, an existential awareness of his own estrangement from others and alienation from himself, the Lord's protection is given to him.

As he does when discussing the first creation account, so here as well Merton cites later scriptural references to Cain and Abel that develop the foundational story further, particularly the "magnificent passage" in

---

16. See the references to the "happy fault" (*felix culpa*) of Adam in Merton, *New Man*, 95, 245.

Hebrews 12 in which he discovers the "idea of Abel entering by the sacrifice of his life into the eternal and immovable riches of God's mercy, and Cain by his crime being cast out into the shifting, unstable, unsubstantial desert of time, to end in nothingness" (22). Likewise, after a brief look at some of the descendants of Cain, particularly the "tough-guy" warrior figure Lamech, with his boastful proclamation of seventy-seven-fold vengeance (contrasted by Merton with Christ's command to forgive a like number of times in Matthew 18), the line of Seth is traced to the mysterious figure of Enoch, whose reappearance elsewhere in the Scriptures and even in the apocryphal books in which he is the central figure is witness to the fascination he continued to exert to the very end of the biblical era.

After briefly considering the various hypotheses as to the identities of the "sons of God" and "daughters of men" whose coupling exemplified the corruption and degeneration of humanity that led up to the deluge, Merton recounts the story of Noe (Noah) in some detail, including explicit references to both the Priestly and Yahwist contributions to the final text; a verse-by-verse exegesis of 7:17–24; the linking of Noe's climactic sacrifice of thanksgiving with God's "alliance" (covenant) with all creation, the renewed promise of fertility, and the reiterated command to "increase and multiply"; and once again an extensive examination of the ways later texts of both Old and New Testaments have further elaborated the spiritual significance of the flood story in various ways, whether eschatological (Matt 24), ethical (Heb 11), or sacramental (1 Peter 3). Particularly noteworthy is Merton's "contemplative" reading of the scene in the ark as a kind of cosmic dark-night experience, in which *"all life is gathered around Noe in the darkness of the ark*, where they have gone by the command of God . . . all life, hidden in the ark with Noe, is *abandoned to the mercy of God in complete darkness*; God Himself has shut the door from the outside, emphasizing the fact that His mercy and Providence have shut them in, and they depend entirely on Him," eventually emerging, purified and renewed, from this immersion in chaos into a new creation (29). Merton articulates in this context the important exegetical principle that "the spiritual truth of the narrative is first of all contained in the *literal* meaning" (30), not something extrinsic to it (as was frequently the case in the fanciful allegorical applications devised in much patristic biblical commentary). Thus the personal appropriation of the message of the flood story that Merton proposes to his audience is discovered through prayerful reflection on the text itself, a characteristically monastic way to respond to the word of God:

> Abandonment to the mercy and providence of God is an essential part of our penance, our transformation. God is the One Who must transform all. Our function is to let Him do so, and to rest in the night of faith with "all life," gathered in the mystery of life into which we withdraw, leaving God to work what we do not know. We are content to "be" and God works. {In the} mystery of silence, abandonment, faith, hope, rest, humility, {we are} *waiting* for God. Waiting is of the very essence of penance—patience, remaining enclosed, silent, in hope. (31)

Likewise Noe's sacrifice, made not on his own initiative but at the time and in the manner designated by the Lord, is a reminder that in order for genuine fruitfulness, true creativity to develop, "we must wait God's time, the right day, the day appointed by Him. Then, at His command, we come forth and produce—but not before. Our sacrifice is then offered in the days of fertility, not in the days of darkness, as a recognition that God has done the work" (31) and that true creativity depends on and flows from a relationship of intimacy with God and a complete reliance on divine mercy and grace.

This "prehistory" section of Genesis reaches its climax with the story of the tower of Babel,[17] another manifestation of the human "desire to be equal to God" (35) that recurs in different forms following its initial appearance as the cause of the fall, the essence of original sin. The figure of Nemrod (Nimrod), descendant of Cham (Ham), another "tough guy, self-sufficient, strong in human means" (34), founder of Babylon, archetypal City of Man from Genesis to Revelation, prepares the ground for the building of the tower. Merton draws on Augustine's distinction between the two cities: Babylon and Jerusalem—the City of Man, built on *cupiditas* and exhibiting a pretense of unity, and the City of God, motivated by *caritas* and forming authentic community.[18] The tower, constructed as an expression of pride in human strength, is therefore inevitably destined to fall, a victim of its own illusions, above all the illusion that its builders are truly able to comprehend one another, that their words are vehicles of genuine communication. In a rare contemporary reference, Merton

---

17. See Merton's verse play, *The Tower of Babel* (first published in 1955), in Merton, *Collected Poems* 247–73; for an overview, see O'Connell, "Tower of Babel," in *Merton Encyclopedia*, 490–91.

18. In *Tower of Babel* (Merton, *Collected Poems*, 247–48), Merton uses as an epigraph the passage on the two cities and their respective types of love from Augustine's *City of God* (14.28); in these conference notes, he cites the similar passage from Augustine's *Commentary on Psalm 64* (34–35).

compares Babel to his former home, New York City.[19] He remarks: "There is something very American about the Tower of Babel—an underlying false optimism based on a very fragile unity, an appearance of having one mind and one heart—{but} only an appearance. Men {are} united by pride and self-interest; they hold together as long as there is prosperity" (35)—but hardship reveals the fault lines that were already there. Merton brings this section of his conferences to a close by contrasting this earthly city with "the monastic 'city' built in the presence of God," whose "foundation is humility" (36), a participation in "the heavenly Jerusalem" described in its fullness in the final chapters of the book of Revelation, but already established at Pentecost with its "gift of tongues to heal the division caused at Babel and proclaim {the} *wonderful works of God*" (36). This, Merton suggests, is the ultimate purpose that draws people to the monastery—to witness to the eschatological reality of authentic communion with God and with others through the grace of God, in the midst of the conflict and disunity symbolized by the story of the tower and its disintegration.

Before beginning his chapter-by-chapter discussion of Abraham, whom he calls "the Father of the People of God, one of the most monumental figures in the Old Testament" (36), Merton provides a brief overview, following the identification of Jesus as "Son of David, Son of Abraham" in the very first verse of Matthew's Gospel, of the *"Importance of Abraham in the New Testament"* (36–37), noting the distinction between physical and spiritual descent from Abraham made in the preaching of John the Baptist (Matt 3:9); citing Jesus' parable of the eschatological banquet in which Abraham and the patriarchs share the feast with righteous Gentiles, exemplified by the centurion whose faith in the healing power of Jesus (Matt 8:5–13) reflects that "by which Abraham was able to believe in God's promises and hope against hope"; referencing Paul's teaching in Romans 4 on the justification that comes through faith "not just in the promise made to Abraham but *in Christ as the fulfillment of that promise*" (38), and that is brought to completion (Merton remarks in a distinctly nonecumenical tone) by the works of charity (Gal 5:6); and

---

19. See the similar perspective in part 6 of Merton's long poem "Figures for an Apocalypse" (1947), titled "In the Ruins of New York" (Merton, *Collected Poems*, 143–46), in which he describes the aftermath of apparent atomic warfare: "How are they down, how have they fallen down / Those great strong towers of ice and steel, / And melted by what terror and what miracle? . . . / The ashes of the leveled towers still curl with tufts of smoke" (ll.19–21, 32).

discussing Christ's debate in chapter 8 of John's Gospel with those who renounce their own identity as children of Abraham by rejecting the One who is not simply the son of Abraham but the son of God. Thus Merton takes pains to situate the Abraham story as it is told in Genesis within the broader context of the significance of that story in relation to the history of salvation that reaches its fulfillment in the person and work of Christ.

This same strategy is immediately in evidence once again in Merton's comments on the very first mention of Abraham in Genesis, his removal from Ur to Haran that is the initial stage of his journey to Canaan (11:31), a detail cited by Stephen in his sermon in Acts 7 and explicitly mentioned in the commendatory prayer for the dying in the Cistercian *Ritual*, which asks that the soul be liberated as Abraham was liberated from Ur, as well as in the prayer for travelers, the *Itinerarium*, which likens the journey to be made to that of Abraham from Ur (40), identified by Merton as "the center of the highest civilization at this time" (40), so that Abraham's withdrawal from what is secure and familiar can be likened as well to what Saint Benedict called for in his *Rule*. The call of Abraham as related in the following chapter is presented specifically as a paradigm for the vocation of religious life, which is also a journey into the unknown, and in fact it provides a pattern for every authentic Christian life, which has the apostolic task of witnessing to and working for the reunification of divided humanity, begun with the call of Abraham and completed in the death and resurrection of Christ. Implicitly looking ahead to Abraham's encounter with the three travelers in chapter 18, Merton proposes that the "heart of this mystery of travelling is that God Himself is hidden in those He calls and sends; it is He, in them, Who seeks to bring back to unity the scattered family of man; hence the mystery of the stranger, of hospitality, the guest {as} an 'angel' or messenger of God" (42), a mystery obscured in contemporary society where the stranger is typically regarded either as a consumer, a potential customer, or else as a potential threat. It is once again evident here that Merton's consistent intention is to highlight the relevance of the scriptural texts for the lives of his novitiate audience in particular and for the church, the People of God, as a whole.

Continuing with the remainder of chapter 12, Merton considers the blessings, both temporal and spiritual, that are connected with the promise made to Abram, above all that "the knowledge of the true God was to be communicated to the whole world by the seed of Abraham" (44), and the journey from Haran to Sichem (Shechem) and into Egypt, where the fulfillment of the promise is threatened by the attraction of Pharaoh to Sarai. The separation of Abram and Lot in the following chapter is marked by Lot's choice of the superficially attractive site of the Jordan valley around Sodom, whereas Abram is divinely directed to go and dwell in the place God has chosen. Again Merton sees the application to the life of the disciple: "Lot just looked straight ahead to the Jordan valley and went to dwell there among others. With the saints it is different—they suddenly awake and find that all around them in every direction has been given to them by God. {An} application of the two cases to the spiritual life {can be made}: Lot {has} an ordinary spirituality that gets nowhere, Abram a spirituality guided by God, on an entirely different level" (46). Chapter 14 tells the story of Abram's rescue of Lot, which Merton recognizes as an insertion that serves to connect Abram with Jerusalem, represented by the mysterious figure of Melchisedec, "King of Salem (Jerusalem—City of Peace) . . . priest of the most High God" (47), who offers a sacrifice of bread and wine and blesses Abram, an encounter that is already seen to have profound messianic significance in Psalm 109[110] and in Hebrews 7 is interpreted as anticipating the appearance of the true King of Justice (*tsedeq*) and King of Peace, the unique High Priest in the Order of Melchisedec.

The discussion of chapter 15, the renewal of the promise that contains the key declaration of Abram's faith being "*reputed unto justice*" (49) (or reckoned to him as righteousness), notes his surrender of intellect, will, and life itself to God and God's plan. The words "pact" and "contract" are used by Merton here (49), but surprisingly he does not refer to this encounter as a covenant (or "alliance," the favored term at the time of writing), reserving this for the discussion of chapter 17 where it is again explicitly found in the text (as it is in vs. 18 here). Despite the Lord's reassurance, the promise of descendants as numerous as the stars in the sky, the focus of Merton's comments here is largely on the darker elements of the episode: the birds of prey attacking the ritually split carcasses are interpreted as "signify[ing] the enemies of Abraham and his sons" (49) and foreboding the exile and oppression in Egypt to come that the Lord now predicts.

Merton actually gives considerably more attention to the chapter that follows—the conflict between Agar (Hagar), who flaunts her fertility after becoming pregnant with Ishmael, and Sarai, whose resentment of her slave leads her to "beat her so much that Agar fled into the desert" (50), which of course for Merton is the locus par excellence for the contemplative experience of the presence of the living God, as Agar discovers in the apparition of the Angel of the Lord, the "Mal'akh Yahweh." The question posed to her—"Where are you coming from, whither are you going"—is seen by Merton as one with universal application: "the Lord speaks to us and immediately brings us face to face with the actual reality of our life, not in a static way, but dynamically, a sudden consciousness of our life in its 'becoming,' its tending, its development, its meaning, its value. This {is} typical of true religious experience" (50–51). The subsequent directive to return prompts both the general observation that "[w]e cannot find our reality, our true self, our place in the world, by merely running away aimlessly from suffering and persecution," and a specific recognition that even though Agar's child is not the child of the promise he, and she, still have an integral place in the divine plan. Merton finds in Agar's simple statement "I have seen Him Who sees me" (an explanation of her name for God: El Roi, "God sees") "a perfect expression of the deepest experience of God, an expression of the soul's meeting with His infinite Truth in mystery, {with an} emphasis on the concreteness, the personality of God" (51) that corresponds to the focus on the divine presence found in Saint Benedict's *Rule*. It is quite remarkable that Merton finds in this relatively minor incident in the Abraham story evidence for Genesis being "one of the great source books for Christian mystical theology" (52).

The definitive identification of the child of promise with the offspring of Abram and Sarai (now to be known as Abraham—"Father of multitudes"—and Sara) comes in chapter 17, the covenant of circumcision, in which, as Merton circumspectly notes, the organ of the propagation of the race is consecrated to God, a symbol that contrasts with pagan fertility rites, a visible sign of the new peoplehood that continues until this communal identity is no longer based on physical kinship, already foretold in chapter 4 of Jeremias (Jeremiah) and effected by the coming of Christ and the institution of baptism. Once again Merton calls the attention of his audience to the importance of a personal appropriation of the message of the passage. The gradual unfolding of the meaning and accomplishment of the promise first given at the very beginning of the Abraham story provides a pattern for Christian spiritual growth:

> So too in our own lives, God's plan and His promises are fulfilled by degrees. He subjects us to a long preparation, gradually revealing to us the magnitude of His gift (sanctity—salvation) and the greatness of Him Who gives it to us. The longer and more completely this preparation goes on, the better and holier

we will be for it. We should learn seriously to see our own lives in the light of Abraham's life—the child of the promise, Christ, is to be manifested in us. We already possess Him in hope, from the baptismal font, but our life is a gradual growth to the clear vision of Him living in us. (53)

Likewise the command "*Walk in my presence and be perfect*" (17:1) is to be understood not merely as pertaining to the practice of piety and virtue, the pursuit of moral perfection, but as a transformation brought about by the intimate personal experience of the divine presence, which "is not known except by love. Love gives us the contact by which we are *aware of His sanctity and power*" (54). Abraham's relationship with God becomes a kind of template for all those who have become children of Abraham through Christ, who is "the child of the promise" in the full sense, the perfect realization of the redemptive process set in motion with the conception and then the birth of Isaac (whose name, meaning "laughter," is recognized as connoting "a very human reaction to wonder and joy . . . the laughter of a mystical liberation" [56–57]).

Before the actual birth of Isaac, of course, comes the apparition of the three mysterious figures at Abraham's encampment by the terebinth of Mambre (Mamre) and the destruction of Sodom and Gomorrah that follows, which Merton calls "one of the most impressive passages in Genesis," with its stark drama, the suspense of Abraham's (ultimately fruitless) intercession and its foreshadowing of both the definitive appearance of God in space and time through the incarnation and of the definitive eschatological reckoning at the final judgment. But Abraham's response to this unprecedented event is completely consistent with his manner of behaving in much more ordinary circumstances, and as such is exemplary for others, monks in particular. "Abraham's hospitality, offered in a spirit of faith, is a classic example of supernatural charity which attains directly to God in and through the neighbor" (59). His care for his guests is simply an expression of his habitual sensitivity to all those he encounters. "The lesson in all this is the incomparable solicitude and politeness and piety of Abraham toward the Lord in all this—his love of God needs no higher expression, ordinarily, than the perfect performance of the customary duties practiced among his own people" (60). Even the extraordinary conversation in which Abraham bargains for the survival of the city, in which "the tone of confident pleading and reproachfulness mingles with respect" (62), is consistent with the rapport which had been established as soon as the visitors appeared. Merton finds the same attitude "of *respect coupled with realism*" rather than "a lot of grandiose and dramatic considerations without foundation in the affections of the heart" to be characteristic of Benedictine spirituality (60–61), in which each visitor is received as Christ, and the duty "to intercede for sinners" is an integral part of "our own vocation" (62). At the same time, the situation of Lot in the midst of the arrogance, lust, and sacrilegious insolence of the Sodomites, the monstrous inverse of Abraham's hospitality, is a lesson in the necessity for monastic detachment:

> We must certainly work and live ordinary lives . . . but in such a way that we are completely detached and ready to let go of what we have at any moment. . . . Our "contemplative" life is not a matter of sitting in the middle of Sodom thinking about divine things. It is a going forth from this world which passes away to seek and find God we know not where. While we are in this life, we continue to work and to live as other people do—without of course the evil that they do!—but we are living in heaven . . . by hope, and we are ready to leave all things behind at a moment's notice in order to follow Christ wherever He may lead us. (64–65)

After a brief look at chapter 20—which Merton rightly recognizes as a somewhat more morally elevated doublet of the Yahwist story of Abraham, Sara, and Pharaoh (Abimilech in this version) in chapter 12 (the only time in these conferences a passage is explicitly attributed to the Elohist source)—he reaches chapter 21, the birth of Isaac, whose name once again is perceived as symbolic, as Sara is filled with laughter, no longer the skeptical laughter of her reaction to hearing the prophecy of the visitor at Mambre (18:12), but a "pure cry of joy" that "has reached the mystical quality of the laughter of Abraham" (66). It is, Merton suggests, the same joy experienced at another, greater birth that can also be seen as fulfilling the promise to Abraham, "the quiet, supernal laughter we feel in our hearts on Christmas night . . . reproduced more perfectly in the simple hearts of the shepherds," expressed by the angels in "their song of joy . . . on a higher and more eminent level. It is the laughter of the created world which wakes up to discover that its God and Creator has become part of it, has taken flesh and lives in the midst of the works of His own hands!" (66–67). This scene of exultation, however, is immediately juxtaposed with the passage on the casting out of Agar and Ishmael, which Merton characterizes as a "deeply touching narrative" (67) that is in its own way a story of salvation, of providential care for the one whose rejection was nevertheless part of the working out of the divine plan. Merton goes on to reflect on the Pauline application of this story in Romans and Galatians—in which the literal descendents of Isaac are ironically identified with Ishmael, and the apparently excluded Gentiles with Isaac—as well as on the interpretation of the passage by John of the Cross, in which the desire for "carnal" liberty, for temporal success ("prelacy"!) and worldly satisfactions, is in fact an enslavement that precludes true sonship and authentic freedom.

The climactic, though not quite the final, episode in the saga of Abraham is of course the sacrifice of Isaac, which Merton calls "the high point of the book of Genesis, one of the most important passages of the Old Testament and one of the keys to the meaning of Christian revelation" (69), and to which he devotes the most detailed discussion of his entire text. He repeatedly emphasizes that it is the story not only of Abraham's total loyalty and obedience to God but of a faith in God's promise even in the face of apparently incomprehensible contradiction, including an awareness that human sacrifice is itself an abomination to God, "a mark of pagan degeneracy" (70). Abraham's willingness to follow God's instructions without question, "believing that this is the way to the fulfillment of the promise, *believing firmly that Isaac will not be lost to him but will somehow be recovered*" (69–70), even though he cannot understand how this can be so, is an expression of total self-surrender, submission of both will and mind, a journey into the darkness of unknowing, the darkest of the dark nights of the soul. He lets go of what is most precious to him in all creation; he chooses God over God's own greatest gift.[20]

As such, Merton tells his audience, the "application of this to us is obvious." Abraham is the model par excellence of "the soul perfectly consecrated to God," whose life of fidelity ultimately must go beyond the trust that marked its earlier stages when he steadfastly believed, despite his age and that of his wife, that God would honor his pledge to make of him a great nation. Merton clearly conceives of this trial as exemplifying that final death to self that leads to union with God, "the greatest trial, when *all that has been acquired* through the grace and mercy of God

---

20. See Merton's comments on Abraham in *Inner Experience*, 29: "The religion of Abraham indeed was primitive, and it hovered, for a terrible moment, over the abyss of human sacrifice. Yet Abraham walked with God in simplicity and peace, and the example of his faith (precisely in the case of Isaac) furnished material for the meditations of the most sophisticated religious thinker of the last century, the father of existentialism, Søren Kierkegaard" (a reference to Kierkegaard's *Fear and Trembling*).

must also be sacrificed. We must rise above it to God alone—in doing so, however, *we recover all*. In losing all we gain all, and we must have Abraham's faith and courage to do this. Only then can God fully manifest Himself in our lives, in the great darkness like that which came upon Abraham" (70).

Such a reading of the Abraham and Isaac story certainly seems incompatible with the traditional typological reading that Merton also provides, in which the sacrificial rite involving father and son is seen as foreshadowing the sacrificial death of Christ the Son in total acceptance of the will of his Father; and on a strictly logical level it is evident that they cannot be reconciled. But this divergence provides a salutary warning against constructing a simplistic one-to-one correspondence between type and antitype—after all the ascent of Moriah has a quite different outcome from the ascent of Calvary: a symbolic death and rebirth should not be equated with actual death and resurrection, which is redemptive in a way that the sacrifice of Isaac, even if carried out, could never have been. The value of viewing the two events in tandem, Merton suggests, is to allow them to cast light on one another: to discover in Abraham's seemingly impossible commitment of unconditional love at once for his God and for his child some intimation of the ultimately incomprehensible mystery of the Father's love for his Son that nevertheless gives him up to a full participation in the human lot of limitation, rejection, suffering, mortality—a sign of the divine compassion (however that be understood) for a broken world that is made whole only by being brought, through Christ, into the experience of God himself. As Merton says, "as a manifestation of the loving mercy hidden in the bosom of the Father, this passage is scarcely surpassed by any other in the Bible except the great manifestations in the New Testament: the Baptism of Jesus, the Transfiguration, Calvary and the Resurrection" (70).

Merton then develops both of these perspectives through a phrase-by-phrase commentary on the text of the chapter, which includes such traditional elements as associating the wood for the sacrifice carried by Isaac with the cross, along with some applications that are apparently original with Merton, as when he wonders if it might be "permissible to push this a little far" and liken the fire carried by Abraham to the Holy Spirit, who can be described as "fire that consumed the Victim on Calvary" (73–74); or the attractive suggestion that Abraham's words to Isaac that God will provide the victim might be considered as true not only in the immediate context of the ram caught in the bushes but in the accommodated sense of the Lamb of God whose life is a sacrificial offering for not just a single individual but for the entire world, so that "we can see in the mystery of Abraham and Isaac the longing of the heavenly Father for sinners, His prodigal sons, and His desire to offer even His only-begotten Son to recover them." Here, Merton declares, is "depth beyond depth of mystery" (73). He concludes by finding in Abraham's willingness to leave "the destiny of the chosen people entirely in the hands of God" and "to act in all humility as a perfectly obedient instrument of the divine will" a model for a religious life of interior poverty that recognizes and accepts the inadequacy of one's own limited perspectives, and of unquestioning obedience that trusts God's will is being realized even when *"human standards of judgement and comparison"* (75) seem to indicate otherwise.

Except for a brief look at the death and burial of Sara in the following chapter, featuring a rather juridical but "very lively" account from the "levitical" author of Abraham's bargaining for a burial place, the first property in the promised land actually owned by the patriarchs, Merton's discussion of the first of these patriarchs is now virtually complete. (He does not explicitly mention Abraham's own death, related in chapter 25.) Abraham does make an appearance in chapter 24, but only to set in motion the lovely story of the journey of his servant back to the "old country" to find a wife for Isaac, which is clearly a favorite passage for Merton, who refers to the "beauty and simplicity" of the narrative (76), the "charm and reality" of the scene (77). He points out the mystery of journeys such as this, which result in providential encounters and witness to a longing for unity and peace in God through union with other people, and refers as well to "the mystery of hospitality" (77) already seen in the story of Abraham and his guests and now displayed by the family of Rebecca, Abraham's kinsmen. Merton stresses once again the important exegetical principle of the *"spiritual value of the simple literal sense"* (78) as exemplified in this narrative, in which key spiritual insights are intrinsic to the story itself, not just fanciful applications devised by an inventive commentator.

Having said this, however, Merton immediately goes on to present a rather extensive section on "REBECCA AND ISAAC IN THE FATHERS" (78–84), in which the ingenious allegorical interpretations of Origen and Ambrose have only the most tenuous connection to the literal sense but nevertheless possess a spiritual wisdom of their own that Merton is not willing simply to exclude from his own commentary. Building on the identification of Isaac as a "type" of Christ, even a "sacrament" of Christ for Abraham in that he is a visible sign of a still invisible reality, Origen then turns to the scene of Rebecca at the well as an image of the patient, simple soul who comes to draw sustenance from the "well" of Scripture, the living water given by Christ to the Samaritan woman in John 4 and identified with the Holy Spirit (in John 7:37–39), and who at the right time encounters the servant who has come to reveal Christ's desire to espouse her to himself. Merton extends this "sacramental" perspective to apply to the experience of his novices, suggesting that "our monastery, the community, the abbot, the brethren" can and should function as Isaac does for Abraham, as signs of Christ, "capable of being vehicles and containers of grace" (78). For Ambrose, the story of the marriage of Isaac and Rebecca serves as the occasion for developing "a brief treatise on mystical theology" in which "the union of Christ with the Church and . . . of the Word with the individual soul" (80) is described in four successive stages, drawing not from the Genesis text itself but from the Song of Songs. The first degree identifies the "kiss of the mouth" (Song 1:1) with the enlightenment of wisdom, and the ointments of the following verse with the experiential perception of divine goodness and mercy through the spiritual senses; in the second degree the soul enters into the inner chamber of the Word (the "*cubiculum*") and recognizes both her own radical insufficiency and her intrinsic dignity and potential for union with the Word, now experienced as absent and the object of her search; the third degree is that of mystical rest and silence, after encountering the Word unexpectedly; the fourth and final degree, when "I sleep and my heart wakes" (Song 5:2), is the full conformity of wills in spiritual marriage, in which the soul becomes fecund, spiritually fruitful, and Christ is "placed on the soul like a 'seal'" (Song 8:6) signifying "perfect transformation" (84).

Compared with his father and his son, of course, Isaac receives relatively little attention in Genesis, at least as a principal character, so these patristic amplifications of this love story (in which the initiative is still not his own) do go some way to redress the balance. The brief details of his activities found in chapter 26—another iteration of the patriarch and his wife motif (in which Abimilech is now attracted to Rebecca rather than Sara), the conflict with the Philistines over wells, eventually resolved, the renewal of the promise made to his father and the construction of an altar at Bersabee (Beersheba), and the dissatisfaction of the parents at their son Esau's marriages to local women—are all mentioned by Merton, but with little interpretive comment.

In the intervening chapter, however, the birth and preliminary rivalry of Jacob and his slightly older twin are related, so that the considerably more intriguing figure of the third patriarch has already begun to overshadow his father. After noting the (fanciful) etymology of Jacob's name and pointing out that the enmity between Jacob and Esau foreshadows the future relationship between their descendants Israel and Edom, Merton comments that modern readers tend to sympathize with Esau, "the rough-and-ready, impulsive, simple, even crude, but basically sincere countryman—outwitted by a city-slicker" (84), but that his casual relinquishing of his birthright for the proverbial "mess of pottage" makes clear his inadequacy as a bearer of the divine promise. The story conveys the "very important spiritual point" that "what matters above all is not our skill and our activities, which wear us out and weaken us, sometimes to no purpose whatever, but our birthright—our vocation—God's love for us" (85): the bustling, busy Esau is much less capable of perceiving the divine presence and the divine plan than the quiet, reflective Jacob, even if at this point he is simply exploiting his brother's flaws for his own advantage with no awareness of how even this manipulative behavior can serve the divine plan. As Merton notes in beginning his discussion of the Jacob story proper (chapters 27–35), his trickery is not to be approved or imitated, but understood and recognized as evidence that God's freedom of choice is not conditional even on moral rectitude, though Jacob will certain mature ethically and spiritually as his story progresses. But from the outset he is presented as a prime example in the series of unlikely divine instruments, "the *younger son*, the little one, the one who seems to be handicapped" (88), apparently weaker in worldly terms, who turns out to be "the man of God, the ancestor of the chosen race in whom the alliance with Abraham is confirmed and definitively established" (86). The same pattern is observed in his deceptive appropriation of his blind father's deathbed blessing (though in fact Isaac actually dies only in chapter 35, after Jacob's return from Mesopotamia!), at the instigation of Rebecca his mother, whose favorite he clearly is. The traditional association of Rebecca with the Blessed Virgin Mary in this context ("one thinks immediately of Rebecca as a type of Our Lady"[88]!) is perhaps more shocking than Jacob's own behavior, but Merton provides a plausible explanation in Mary's mediation on behalf of sinners who receive the undeserved "divine inheritance," not simply disguised as the legitimate heir (Esau as Christ?!) but in fact "transformed, sanctified and divinized" (88) through the passion, which unites them to the true heir, not by duplicity but by repentance, analogous to that of the Samaritan woman at Jacob's well and that of the prodigal son.

Obeying his parents' wishes that he, like his father, find a wife among his kinfolk (as well as removing himself from Esau's wrath, not explicitly mentioned by Merton here), Jacob sets out for Haran and the house of Bathuel (Bethuel) and Laban, stopping on the way at Bethel, where he has his famous dream of the ladder reaching to heaven and traversed by angelic intermediaries,[21] the "great revelation of the intimacy of God with man and man with God" (90) being reestablished after the expulsion from paradise, that will reach its culmination in the incarnation. Jacob's consecration of this sacred site serves as a reminder, Merton indicates, that while God is omnipresent, there are places of divine encounter, churches in particular, that are marked by "a special 'religious' presence, in which He makes Himself known and disposes man to receive His messages, and to reply with the offering of his whole being" and which "are therefore necessary for our special religious contact with and worship of God. . . . They call for special consecration on our part and are the proper place for sacrifice and for the *consecration of ourselves*" (91). This particularity is not a substitute for the awareness of the divine presence within the heart or throughout all creation, but provides a salutary counterweight to "a vague, impersonal sort of presence" and to any tendency toward an "identification of the being of God with my own being" that "in the end is *no presence at all*" (92). This theophany, then, is a revelation of "the God of Jacob" spoken of in the Psalms, who "is our God, and we have only to listen to Him and receive the same blessings in evidence of His power" (93).

The subsequent chapters, recounting Jacob's adventures in Mesopotamia and eventual return to the land of promise are dealt with by Merton in rather summary fashion, providing the salient details without much commentary or spiritual application to his audience. Merton seems rather dismissive of the "pious" interpretation found in the *Catholic Commentary on Holy Scripture* that "regards Jacob's sufferings and toil with Laban as a punishment for his trickery in getting the blessing from Esau" (93), but one might consider Laban's clever deception in substituting his plain elder daughter Lia (Leah) for the beautiful and beloved Rachel, her sister, as Jacob's bride, to be less a matter of piety than of irony, an example of

---

21. See Merton's use of the terms "House of God" and "Gate of Heaven" from this passage in Part II of his poem "Elias—Variations on a Theme" (Merton, *Collected Poems*, 242).

the venerable topos of "the trickster tricked." (Nor does Merton note that the same Laban who was lauded for his hospitality to Abraham's servant in chapter 24 shows a considerably less noble motivation in his welcome of his nephew Jacob here.) Merton provides a preliminary list of Jacob's twelve sons and one daughter and their respective mothers, details the diverse stratagems employed by the two sisters, along with their maids, that result in the various births; he particularly notes that of Joseph, the first child of Rachel, with a reference to that of his full brother Benjamin back in Canaan that will result in the death of Rachel. Merton points out that these facts "have to be remembered in order fully to understand the story of Joseph, the enmity of Joseph's brethren, and Joseph's special love for Benjamin—also Jacob's special love for those two" (93). Merton does emphasize that the relationship between Jacob and Rachel, particularly his willingness to work an additional seven years to marry her as well, exhibits "a profound sense of the value of his love, rather than an eagerness to enjoy its possession—a homage to the reality and goodness seen in Rachel. {This is an} important note in the psychology of mature love!—a real expression of the homage and respect which characterize *amor amicitiae*"—the "love of friendship" (94).

Jacob's scheme to get a flock of his own, with its folktale motif of "causing variegated sheep to be born from white" (95–96) after he contracts with Laban to work an additional seven years in exchange for what would be expected to be the relatively few offspring in the former category (after Laban's surreptitious removal of any spotted potential parents), becomes one more episode in the battle of wits between uncle and nephew, and leads to Jacob's secret departure from Haran with his flocks and large family. His reconciliation and subsequent treaty with Laban is merely a prelude to the more fraught meeting to come with his brother Esau, whose continued enmity he fears. Merton relates these developments briskly, spending little time even on the great scene of Jacob's wrestling with the mysterious figure on the banks of the Jabbok before his return to the land of promise, a story of "great antiquity" that results in his being blessed and given a new name (not actually specified as Israel by Merton at this point), and leads to his astonished realization "that he has fought with God" yet "is still alive. The whole thing," Merton concludes, "is a renewed promise of victory and a pledge of God's favor" (97). Rather surprisingly, however, there is no consideration of the spiritual or mystical implications of this enigmatic confrontation with God in the darkness, a "homecoming" encounter that matches the dream at Bethel at Jacob's departure some two decades earlier.

The subsequent events of the Jacob saga are then quickly summarized: his meeting with Esau, who turns out to hold no grudges and in fact "admires Jacob's achievement" (98); his settlement at Sichem (Shechem) and the grisly tale of the rape of Dina (Dinah) and the subsequent revenge of her full brothers; his burial of the idols and removal to Bethel; a new theophany there and repetition of the new name (now explicitly mentioned); the birth of Benjamin and death of Rachel (and of Isaac!); and the final separation of Jacob and Esau, who decamps for Edom. Merton concludes succinctly: "end of the Jacob story—Joseph now begins" (99). One gets the definite sense at this point that he is looking forward to bringing the Genesis conferences to a swift conclusion.

Nevertheless, he follows this announcement with a very thorough survey of Egyptian geography, history, and culture, presumably drawn from some (unidentified) encyclopedia (supplemented by details taken from the article on Egypt in *The Catholic Encyclopedia*[22])—explicitly identified as background material not only for the Joseph story but also for the book of Exodus, which he evidently is already intending to discuss after Genesis. He provides extensive information on the principal locations and events of Old, Middle, and New Kingdoms; the social strata of Egyptian society during its various periods; its agricultural products; the status of its rulers; the development of its religious system—animistic, polytheistic, pharaoh-worshiping; its cult of the dead that resulted in pyramids and mummies and esoteric texts; and its moral code that enshrined justice and hospitality and honesty and probably influenced the biblical book of Proverbs. One might wonder how much of this plethora of detail found its way into the conferences as actually presented; it was in any case available for consultation in the written version made available for distribution to the novices.

Turning to the account of Joseph and his brothers that makes up the final segment of Genesis (chapters 37–50), Merton begins by providing an overview of the main events and highlights the three aspects of the material that he finds most significant. The first, the major religious lesson of the whole story, expressly declared by Joseph himself, first in 45:5 and definitively at the very end of the book in 50:19–20, is the "teaching

---

22. All the details from this source (Hyvernat, "Egypt," in *Catholic Encyclopedia*, 5.329–63) are found as handwritten additions on the typescript, listed in the textual notes.

of the dogma of *Divine Providence*, . . . in which the inscrutable wisdom and love of God triumphs over all apparent obstacles, . . . and the *problem of evil* is also luminously solved here, for even evil enters into God's plan for the greater good of His elect" (105); this divine care is revealed not through the direct revelation of theophanies as with the previous generations of patriarchs but through the agency of dreams communicating the divine will and through the interior action of God within the human heart. The second is that the style of the narrative is significantly, and appropriately, different, marked by "greater psychological realism and detail, closer to the style of the novel" (106) both in its complicated plot twists and in its implicit and explicit consideration of the motivations of its characters' actions. Third, Joseph's role as a redeemer figure, whose sufferings at the hands of his own family lead to unexpected salvation even for his oppressors, is seen as suggestive of the role to be played by the Messiah to come. These motifs will continue to be emphasized in the more detailed commentary on the individual chapters that follows.

Thus in discussing the initial plot against Joseph and its execution (c. 37), Merton points out the "psychological finesse" of the narrative, with its depiction of the brothers' resentment of Joseph for his reporting of their misdemeanors to their father and his ingenuous recounting of his prophetic dreams in which symbolically they (and even their father) do homage to him, and their jealousy at their father's preference for this child of his old age and of his beloved Rachel, signified by his fancy tunic with its long sleeves. The stripping of this tunic, to be dipped in goat's blood, is then likened to the scene of Christ's passion, in which he is stripped of his seamless tunic, "a striking foreshadowing," as is the price of twenty pieces of silver for selling their brother into slavery ("close enough," Merton says, to "the price paid to Judas" for betraying Christ). He also points to the irony that Jacob, who had once deceived his father, is now deceived by his own sons, and in both cases the "result of the deception" is that "the chosen one of God goes away to prepare the further history of the chosen people" (109).

The chapter on Juda (Judah) and Thamar (Tamar) that follows, which serves to build suspense by postponing the recounting of Joseph's earliest days in Egypt, is itself also a story of deception, as Thamar tricks her father-in-law into having a child with her (two in fact), so that his line will continue, a righteous act as Juda himself acknowledges, "for he had gone back on his promise to give her Shela, and she was justified in wanting a child from her husband's blood" (110). Thamar's daring ruse is memorialized by the explicit mention of her as one of only five women included in the genealogy of the Messiah in Matthew, though Merton is mistaken in saying that Zara, "the one who put his hand out first and had a red thread tied to his wrist, but was born second," is "the one mentioned in the genealogy of Jesus" and is "the 'younger' [who] supplants the elder as {the} ancestor of {the} Messias" (110); in fact both the twins are named in Matthew 1:3, but it is Perez, not Zara, who is in the ancestral line of Jesus.

After this interlude the focus returns to Joseph, where it remains throughout the subsequent chapters of Genesis. The purchase of Joseph by Putiphar (Potiphar), his outstanding competence due to the power of God, quickly recognized by his master, and the growing obsession of Putiphar's wife with Joseph, her unsuccessful attempt to seduce him, and her vengeful accusations of attempted rape that land Joseph in prison are all vividly told "with color and drama" and "much living psychological detail," exemplifying the "novelistic" quality of the account that Merton had earlier pointed out. Here he also emphasizes the motivation of Joseph as centering "on justice and loyalty first of all, on not betraying a trust," rather than being presented primarily as resisting sexual temptation. He comments:

> This is important. Justice is a higher virtue than temperance. It is objective. We in our day seem to retain a preference for the subjective virtues. {It is} good to have a greater appreciation of *justice*, of the reality of obligations, and the homage we offer to God by living up to them. This has many subjective advantages. Among others, we are saved from the error of making everything stand or fall by our own subjective feelings. To keep an objective obligation is a great thing, even if it does not make us feel anything special. (110–11)

Merton recognizes the same literary skill, the same "beauty and vividness of the narrative," in the following episode, in which Joseph interprets the dreams of his fellow prisoners, Pharaoh's butler and baker, destined for restoration and execution respectively. "Elements in the beauty of the narrative {include} *balance*, contrast, movement, leading to a result and a final surprise—a perfect part of a greater whole, a moment of excitement and hope for Joseph, ending in a disappointment which prolongs the suspense" (112) when the butler fails to inform his master of the powers exercised by Joseph and he spends two more years as a prisoner, albeit as one whose organizational skills have brought him to the point where "he practically runs the prison" (111). Merton points to the spiritual lesson in all this, the need to be patient and to allow God's will to unfold according to God's own time:

> Divine Providence gets him out not when it is convenient for Joseph himself, but when it is for the good of all. . . . God does not merely consider our own interests, in answering our prayers. Our desires, however good, inspired by Him, always fit in with the needs and interests of someone else, and, in fact, of the whole. Their fulfillment must also fit in with the whole plan of God. Our happiness is subordinated to His whole plan—or rather, more accurately, is incorporated in that plan. We have no real hope of fulfillment and happiness merely in the line of our own personal and individual perspectives. (113)

It is only when Pharaoh himself is in need of Joseph's ability to interpret dreams that the butler recalls his experience in prison and Joseph is summoned to court. Again the basic message of the whole story, that injustice and suffering can eventually serve the greater good, is at the heart of the events related, as Joseph now not only predicts the coming famine but suggests a plan to deal with the crisis that he himself is appointed to implement, placing him in a position to encounter and to save his own family—a result that would not have been possible had Joseph been freed from prison under different circumstances and at a different time.

Merton calls Joseph's elaborate testing of his brothers in the chapters that follow, marked by the "dramatic irony" of their ignorance of the identity of the Egyptian official on whom their very survival depends, "by far the most developed and sophisticated story yet told in the Bible, and perhaps the most marked by these qualities in the Old Testament" (115). Joseph takes his revenge, says Merton, using a Pauline image, "by heaping coals of fire upon their heads with goodness," by a sublimation of violence that "makes clear that his motive is to 'get even' in a spiritual and innocent way" (115), but which also forces the brothers to demonstrate their probity by their behavior toward their youngest brother. The crisis provoked by Joseph's permission to return only if accompanied by Benjamin, his profound emotion at seeing his full brother, and the special treatment accorded him at the banquet, all reveal "the intensity of the passions and the feelings involved" and contribute to "the heightened tension of the plot" (116); "the effectiveness of the irony" (116) continues with details such as Joseph's seating of the brothers at the banquet according to their birth order, an indication of "inside knowledge" they fail to notice. The climactic event of the "framing" of Benjamin when Joseph's silver "divining cup" is discovered in Benjamin's sack is considered by Merton a "perfect narrative" (117) and is followed by Juda's offer to sacrifice his own freedom for that of Benjamin, above all for the sake of their father, Jacob, at which point Joseph can no longer conceal his true identity; and the deeply emotional recognition scene follows. The spiritual and theological insight into "the mystery of divine Providence" that Joseph now expresses to his brothers, "that nothing happens but for the good of those loved by God" and that "even sins fit in to the providential plan for the good of all" (118–19), is at the heart of the Joseph story. Merton also finds in the revelation of Joseph's identity a foreshadowing of the final judgment in which the same Jesus now enthroned in glory is discovered to be identified with the least of these, the poor, humble, unknown, and rejected, and what has been done to them was done to him. But the mildness of Joseph toward his guilty brothers, Merton suggests, promises a similar mildness on the part of Christ, "an unexpected solution that is kept hidden in the Gospel story" (119). Jesus will not be less merciful toward his erring brothers and sisters than his predecessor Joseph has been, an encouraging and comforting elaboration on the reconciliation scene found here:

> For as Joseph is not harsh to his brethren but receives them to himself with tears, so Jesus will receive to Himself all who have not made it absolutely impossible for Him to do so. He will go out of his way to circumvent their wickedness with His love and mercy, so that as far as possible no one shall be able to escape from His forgiveness—yet escape will always be possible because freedom will always remain freedom. But only the most deliberate malice and hardness of heart will be able to refuse Him: this no doubt {is} the "sin against the Holy Ghost." (119)

Merton concludes his commentary on this chapter with the observation that for Jacob the news that his lost son is not only alive but the instrument of his family's rescue is experienced as though by "one waking out of a deep sleep" (119), a striking image for a story in which dreams have been the means of revelation for both father and son.

At this point in the conferences, rather than proceeding directly to a discussion of the final five chapters of Genesis, Merton unexpectedly inserts a rather extensive discussion of the first Easter sermon of the celebrated twelfth-century Cistercian abbot Guerric of Igny, based on Genesis 45:26-28, the verses just read.[23] It is almost as if with the end in sight, Merton feels able to make a "side trip" in the company of one of the principal early figures of his own and his students' particular monastic tradition. Merton makes it clear from the very outset that Guerric's allegorical reading of the account of "Jacob's reaction to the news that Joseph is alive," which the abbot defends as an appropriate and revelatory text for the celebration of Easter, is what he refers to elsewhere as an "accommodated" sense of Scripture,[24] principally dependent on the imaginative ingenuity of the preacher, who in this case equates Jacob with the college of the apostles in the upper room on Easter Sunday night, who like the patriarch "believed slowly, 'as though waking from a deep sleep'" (120). Though properly recognized as an "application, not true spiritual interpretation," Guerric's homily serves as a vehicle "to display the depths of his thought on the subject" (120), on what it means to encounter the resurrected Christ. Guerric's message to his monks is that they too are called to wake up to the central message of new life received through union with Christ in the paschal mystery:

> the Apostles came to know the risen Jesus by the fact that He gave them the Holy Spirit—they knew Him, in other words, by the effects of the Resurrection in their own souls, that *is, in their own spiritual resurrection*. This applies to all of us: it is the Holy Spirit within us Who testifies to the truth of the resurrection, and without Him we cannot know the Risen Christ. The grace of Easter is then the gift of the Holy Spirit, in an inchoate way leading up to the fullness of His coming at Pentecost. Hence the Paschal season is a season of new life in the Spirit of the Risen Jesus. (120-21)

The joy of this experience of love in Christ is presented by Guerric as the consummation of the monastic life: if Christ truly lives, nothing else, not even one's own life, matters. This is the perfection of love in total self-forgetfulness, which is at the same time total self-fulfillment, since the true self is the self in Christ. "That is to say, since our love has entirely gone out to Him, we truly live in Him and no longer need to live in and for ourselves. This is the true consummation of the monastic life, the real

---

23. A transcription of a pair of later conferences on this sermon, presented April 6 and 7, 1963, is found in Merton, *Cistercian Fathers and Forefathers*, 186-215; a condensed and rearranged version of these conferences had appeared earlier as the posthumously published article: Merton, "Guerric of Igny's Easter Sermons."

24. See Merton, *Monastic Introduction*, xxxi, 112, 117.

summit of Cistercian prayer and spirituality" (122). Merton identifies this understanding of pure love, *amor castus*, as "traditional Cistercian doctrine, true to the spirit of St. Bernard" (122), but it can also be recognized as an expression of his own central teaching on the meaning of the true self, with its deep roots in Cistercian spirituality. While Guerric's particular applications may not be intrinsic to the biblical passage which has prompted them, the scriptural text, as is so often the case with patristic and medieval exegesis, has provided a starting point for insights that are valid and valuable in their own right.

After this substantial excursus, Merton returns to the text of Genesis itself to trace the final scenes that bring the book to its conclusion—the reunion of Joseph with his father, the settlement of the children of Israel in the land of Gessen (Goshen), the adoption by Jacob of Joseph's children, his final testament, his death, and his burial in Canaan, the promised land. Merton calls attention to the events marking Jacob's departure from Canaan, particularly the dream at Bersabee (Beersheba) that reiterated the Lord's continuing presence and fidelity and thus provided Jacob with the reassurance that was "necessary because he was after all *leaving the land* which God had promised to Abraham and he might have been deeply troubled over this possible defection" (123). Surprisingly little notice is taken of the "affectionate greeting" (124) that marks the meeting of Jacob and Joseph; in fact Merton gives considerably more consideration to the "moving little document" recounting Jacob's encounter with Pharaoh, as it witnesses to Jacob's "greatness and simplicity"—the spiritual maturity of his humble acceptance of the insignificance of his achievements, a sign of true nobility and magnanimity, marked by a "wonderful sense of proportion and of the meaning of life" as he looks toward its end (125). Merton notes that the practical reasons for settling in Gessen (Goshen) are a bit hazy, both in the text itself and in commentaries, but points out that the theological significance is clear enough: "that the Israelites might be *left alone* and not absorbed into the Egyptian nation, but might retain their own independence and character, on the border, ready to move out when God's will is signified. *The passage must be interpreted in the light of the Divine Promise*" (124).

The dramatic power of Jacob's penultimate act, the adoption of Joseph's sons Ephraim and Manasses (Manasseh), is dependent on its connection both to the central thematic motif of the election of the younger son and to its reminiscence of the scene of Jacob's own blessing by his father Isaac. Though Joseph places his father's right hand on Manasses, the elder son, and his left on Ephraim, Jacob reverses the order to give the younger son the primary blessing. "Joseph, intensely put out by the whole affair, tries to move his father's hands by force, but Jacob resists and explains, evidently under the impulsion of divine prophecy" (126) that foresees the rise of the family of Ephraim to predominance in the nation of Israel. There follow the deathbed blessings—or more properly, prophetic oracles—concerning the future role of each of the tribes descending from Jacob's sons, indicating "in what way each tribe will participate in the divine promises" (126). The three oldest children—Ruben (Reuben), Simeon and Levi—are each "demoted": the first for incestuous relations with his father's concubine Bala (Bilhah) (cf. 35:22), the other two for their savage revenge for the violation of their sister Dina; thus the fourth son, Juda, is elevated to the first position, and the future of his descendants is filled with messianic intimations that make this passage, in Merton's words, "the culmination of Genesis . . . supremely important as well as beautiful . . . the fulfillment of all that had been narrated and the foundation of all that followed" (126). The subsequent predictions of the future of the remaining tribes are more succinct both in the text and in Merton's summary, except of course for the "double tribe" of Joseph's sons, recipients of a "special blessing: to him that hath it shall be given" (132). Merton expresses some disappointment with what he considers a "minimizing approach" (126) to this passage taken by the *Catholic Commentary on Holy Scripture* (and by most other modern commentators), which distances these prophetic predictions from the historical Jacob and so tends "to water everything down and to seek as far as possible to find a prosaic common-sense and 'reasonable' explanation for everything," which "may in many cases completely empty a real mystery of all its content" (127). While willing to grant the likelihood of later reshaping of the blessing, Merton is clearly uncomfortable with what he perceives to be a despiritualizing of the text: "one sees no earthly reason why the substance of the *poetry*, and of the *prophecy*, should not be attributed to Jacob himself" (128–29), a position that even in the mid-1950s was rapidly losing adherents even among Catholic Scripture scholars, and which Merton himself would perhaps be less inclined to maintain as his own familiarity with and appreciation of critical biblical scholarship continued to evolve in the years to come.[25]

25. See the discussion of this topic in the Introduction to Merton, *Monastic Introduction*, xli–li.

Merton treats the final scenes of the Genesis story succinctly—the death of Jacob, the embalming of his body "in the Egyptian manner" and its transport back to the promised land for burial, even "the moving and definitive reconciliation" of Joseph with his brothers, his "charity and his sense of the divine plan" (132–33), his restatement of the key lesson of the mysterious power of divine providence ultimately to transmute even evil into an instrument of a greater good. The book ends with Joseph's reassuring deathbed prophecy that the sons of Israel will one day return to their true homeland, and his command that his body be brought with them when they leave—with no indication that more than four centuries will pass before this prediction is fulfilled.

In his final comments Merton points out the appropriateness of concluding this series of conferences on the Feast of Pentecost, as the blessing of the twelve sons of Jacob is seen as a remote preparation for the gift of the Holy Spirit descending upon the twelve apostles, and the twelve gates of the new Jerusalem represent both the patriarchs and the apostles. All this, Merton tells his novices, has a particularly monastic resonance and can be applied especially to the monastic vocation: "The 'twelve tribes' dwell mystically in our monastic church; they are very close to us" (133). It is this closeness, to the twelve tribes and their immediate and remote ancestors, that Merton has certainly tried to encourage in this series of conferences on "the first act in the great drama of salvation" (1).

It is clear almost from the outset that, at least in their written form, Merton's conferences on the book of Exodus, which he himself labeled "incomplete" on their title page, are going to be considerably less detailed, less comprehensive, and less exclusively focused on the scriptural text than the "Notes on Genesis." Contrary to his usual practice, Merton did not type up his working copy of these lectures, nor were typed stencils of the text prepared to be multigraphed and distributed to the novices, as was the case with the Genesis notes and most of Merton's other novitiate courses. Aside from the one-page outline of his projected "scripture seminar" on the Old Testament from Genesis through Ruth that prefaces these notes, the text is entirely handwritten, a total of twenty-seven pages (with further material, amounting to 2–3 more pages of text, found on numerous verso pages), along with a title page and a hand-drawn map of the Sinai Peninsula tracing the route of the Israelites' journey through the desert. The difference in focus, as well as in length, between this pair of documents may of course be largely due to a change in the purpose of the text itself, which in the Exodus notes could simply be intended to function more as a sort of outline, an aide-memoire for Merton himself, notes in a stricter sense to be expanded upon in the actual oral presentations, than would be the case if, like the preceding set of conferences, at some point they were going to be reproduced and made available to his students. On the other hand, the frequent resort to rather bare-bones summaries in the Exodus set may stem from the realization that to proceed at the same leisurely pace as with the Genesis conferences, which required an entire year to present, would entail an extensive multiyear commitment if he were to complete the entire program proposed in his Scripture seminar outline, which after all encompassed only the earliest books of the Old Testament.

Since no recordings of the actual conferences were being made during this period,[26] it is impossible to determine to what degree the written material corresponded to the oral presentations. But it is quickly evident that the scope and even the tone of the two series diverge substantially. Here there are frequent directives to read extensive passages of Scripture, often with little if any accompanying commentary. Aside from a couple brief comments on the French *Bible de Jerusalem* translation of terms relating to Pharaoh's hardness of heart, there are virtually no references to exegetical resources, such as the *Catholic Commentary on Holy Scripture*, frequently mentioned in the Genesis notes (though occasionally the information Merton provides can be traced to that volume). No notice is taken of the different sources (Yahwist, Elohist, Priestly) that continue into Exodus from Genesis, where they had been pointed out occasionally by Merton. On the other hand, fully one-third of Merton's text is not directly engaged in summarizing and interpreting Exodus itself but introduces supplementary discussions of topics that are related in some way to the scriptural material currently being considered, but which often receive more sustained attention and insightful analysis than the passages from Exodus they are ostensibly intended to illuminate.

These characteristics are immediately evident in Merton's discussion of the opening chapters of Exodus, climaxing with the theophany at the burning bush in chapter 3. The notes originally began by identifying

---

26. Recordings of Merton's actual conference presentations began to be taped in late April 1962 so that the brothers could listen to them while at work in the abbey kitchen; for details, see Merton, *Cassian and the Fathers*, xlvii.

the first fourteen chapters as the "exodus" proper, the series of events culminating in the actual departure from Egypt, but Merton then added two brief preambles that provide orientation for what is to follow. The first (written on the opposite page) is a patristic citation, advice from Origen on how to read Exodus: one should avoid a "small and petty" approach to the text and "ask Jesus to show us all that is sublime and great in Moses" (136). The biblical text, Merton thus suggests, is to be approached primarily as a source of edification and inspiration—not as an alternative to study, but as its appropriate result when undertaken in a spirit of prayer. The second of these preliminary guidelines (added in the upper right-hand corner of the first page) is based on reflections on the exodus event in later passages of Scripture, which recognize it as "the *great work of God*, the great sign of His fidelity and mercy" and find in it a revelation of "*how God saves*"—a paradigm that extends beyond Israel to "Jesus" and "ourselves" and teaches the fundamental lesson (conveyed, as Merton will repeatedly point out, by both positive and negative examples) to "trust in God and obey Him" (136). Thus Merton is indicating that what is to follow is not to be regarded as a purely academic undertaking but as an intrinsic component of the program of monastic formation that has been entrusted to him as master of novices. Merton certainly intends to familiarize his audience with the key components of the exodus story, but he wants his students to recognize the relevance of that story for their own spiritual lives, their own journey through the desert to the promised land. It is important to keep this purpose in mind even when the written text itself consists largely in synopses of scriptural passages, as in the significantly compressed summary of the opening chapters of Exodus that immediately follows.

The persecution of the Israelites described in chapter 1 is simply indicated in the brief phrases "hard labor" and "killing the firstborn," with no mention of the dramatic dialogue between Pharaoh and the clever Hebrew midwives that takes up most of the latter part of this chapter. More attention is given to situating the events to follow in their proper historical setting, noting that the thirteenth century BCE is a more likely date than its principal alternative, two centuries earlier. Merton does briefly point out the "internal contradictions" in Pharaoh's attitude toward the Hebrews—the desire to eliminate them while continuing to depend on their labor—and refers to the "demoniacal" character of the tyranny he exemplifies—thematic elements that will recur later in these notes, though not explicitly mentioned in the biblical text itself (136).

Moving on to the birth of Moses and the events of his early life (relatively speaking) as recounted in chapter 2, Merton immediately identifies him as a contemplative and as an answer to prayer (the first an extrascriptural conception and the second an anticipation of the people's pleas that are not explicitly mentioned until the following chapter). Merton will develop this "spiritual" approach to Moses's character in subsequent comments and quotations. He briefly notes, but does not feel any need to elaborate on, Moses's adoption by Pharaoh's daughter, presumably taking for granted that his listeners are familiar with the tale of "Moses in the bulrushes," though missing the opportunity to point out, for example, that the same word found in Genesis for Noah's ark is used here to describe the basket in which Moses floats in the Nile—a fact he might have noted had he continued to provide the same level of detail in this set of conferences as in the last. The episode of Moses slaying the oppressive Egyptian does elicit a comment—it is "*his attempt to take matters in hand*" himself that is actually evidence of "*his failure*—the anger of man does not work the justice of God" (137). Then suddenly Moses is in Madian (Midian), coming to the aid of the daughters of Jethro at the well and marrying one of them (the unnamed Sephora [or Zipporah]); no notice is taken of the fight between the two Hebrews that alerts Moses to the fact that his secret is known and causes him to flee Egypt. Instead, Merton supplies brief details supporting his initial description of Moses—his "*forty years of preparation* in solitude" in the desert before his call, and the declaration that the (still unmentioned) "prayer of Israel is heard" (137) and answered through that call, in the encounter with the Lord in the burning bush at the foot of the mountain of God that opens the next chapter.

After pointing out the two principal elements of this central episode, the theophany itself and the revelation of the divine name, Merton takes a step back to consider the communal implications of what is about to happen, the fact that the events of Exodus are a revelation of God's plan not just for an individual but for a people (the vocation that of course will be disclosed later in the book when Moses returns to Sinai with the entire community of Israel—a connection implied but not explicitly made by Merton here). Turning back to the mysterious manifestation of the divine presence in the unconsumed bush, Merton follows tradition in seeing it as a symbol of transcendence within the world of space and time, first manifested in creation itself and to be brought to fulfillment in "the new creation, all transfigured in Christ" (139), but recognized as well in the Incarnation and identified specifically with the virginal conception of

Mary's child. This figural reading of the burning bush story is then amplified by the first major example of Merton's supplementary comments, an entire page devoted to the reflections on Exodus 3 by one of Merton's favorite patristic theologians, Saint Gregory of Nyssa, clearly a principal source of the characterization of Moses not only as a "lover of justice" but as a contemplative, "a lover of solitude, having retired to the innermost desert" (139); Gregory is also a major interpreter of the burning bush as imaging "the *Epiphany of the Word*" (139). Merton goes on to draw multiple lessons from Gregory's commentary, concluding a reflection far more extensive than anything directly said about the corresponding passage from Exodus itself. The story becomes a paradigm for the encounter with truth and with the fullness of being through renunciation of worldly knowledge and of sensuality, a transformation that empowers one to lead others to salvation as well. Merton finds in Gregory's *Life of Moses* a classic expression of the "*traditional doctrine on action and contemplation*" (140).[27]

After a couple of Latin quotations from Saint Bonaventure and Saint Augustine on the divine presence within the self, Merton's second extensive "interpolation" follows: "thoughts from St. Thomas" (141) on the divine name, drawn from the first part of his *Summa*, that actually precede any discussion of the scriptural verses on this topic. Thomas emphasizes the ultimate inadequacy of any name for the infinite God, but goes on to point out how the terms "*qui est*" ("He who is"), with its implication of absolute Being,[28] "*theos*," connected with the divine operation of seeing and governing, and the Tetragrammaton of Exodus 3 (YHWH), which "signifies the incommunicability of {the} divine nature" (142), all provide insight into the divine reality. Only after this theological exposition does Merton turn back to the Scriptures, but rather than focusing exclusively on Exodus 3 he surveys the various names given to God in the Old Testament generally, culminating with "*Yahweh* . . . the 'ineffable' word used to express God's revelation of Himself to Moses" (142),[29] so sacred that it was never pronounced aloud. Merton then concludes this entire opening

---

27. See Merton's discussion of Gregory in Merton, *Cassian and the Fathers*, 52–60; and Merton, *Introduction to Christian Mysticism*, 72–96.

28. This of course is very closely related to the scholastic understanding of God as "*Ens a se*" that played so essential a role in the initial stages of Merton's conversion: see Merton, *Seven Storey Mountain*, 171–75.

29. See Merton's 1962 essay "The Name of the Lord," in Merton, *Seasons of Celebration*, 183–203.

section of his text with the reminder that "God has revealed His Name in Jesus" and the exhortation to "say this Name in the depths of our heart!" (143)—thus situating all that has been said thus far in an explicitly Christian context that should culminate in prayer.

At this point Merton provides a succinct overview of chapters 4–18, surveying the entire sweep of the story of the deliverance of Israel from the point of Moses's departure from Sinai for Egypt to his return to the mountain accompanied by the entire community, with particular mention once again of the "demoniacal resistance" (143) of Pharaoh and of various figural interpretations of the events to be recounted: the plagues as foreshadowing the final judgment, the passage through the sea as an image of baptism, and of course the celebration of the Passover as an anticipation of the liberating sacrifice of Christ the paschal Lamb. Mention of the "struggle between grace and the heart of Pharaoh, who 'will not *see*'" (145) prompts Merton to turn again to Thomas Aquinas, summarizing his teaching on the relationship of the divine will and human freedom, and on necessary and contingent effects and their causes, in order to provide a philosophical and theological context for the references to the hardening of Pharaoh's heart, attributed now to God, now to Pharaoh himself. This is followed by a summary of a contemporary Dominican's ideas concerning divine providence, which maintain that "God's first causality *takes away nothing* from my causality" (150) and that complete submission to the will of God is paradoxically an exercise of the most complete freedom, the full realization of the true purpose of human life.

Only after these rather extensive abstract ruminations does Merton return to the foot of Mount Sinai to pick up the thread of the scriptural narrative, mentioning but not commenting on Moses's reluctance to respond to God's call, his reception of the gift of miraculous powers, the circumstances of his return to Egypt and his initial confrontation with Pharaoh, then coming full circle to apply the teachings of Thomas Aquinas and Thomas Philippe to the circumstances described in Exodus: "God hardens Pharaoh's heart as {the} primary cause; Pharaoh hardens his own heart as {the} secondary cause—moderns emphasize this last element" (151). This observation immediately precedes discussion of the plagues, including Pharaoh's fluctuating responses to the successive manifestations of God's power, which Merton describes in some detail, pointing out their distinctive elements as well as their common and cumulative witness to the divine sovereignty that Pharaoh ultimately refuses to recognize and accept, with dire consequences.

Merton considers the social and religious implications of the prescriptions for the paschal meal as contained in the text of Exodus itself—its status as a family feast, the importance of the purity of the victim ("And it shall be a lamb without blemish" [12:5]), the involvement of the entire community in the rite, and its function as a sacrifice of reconciliation. Similarly, the connotations of the unleavened bread, associated with a weeklong "Sabbath" and with the haste needed to be prepared to embark on a journey on short notice, are seen as filled with deep spiritual significance. But he is especially eager to alert his readers to subsequent elaborations of the paschal pattern, to the richness of the Passover rituals for comprehending the mystery of redemption as found in New Testament texts and in the liturgy, so that the liberation of Israel from bondage becomes in the fullness of time a template for the ultimate liberation effected by the cross, expressed in the words of the Exultet chanted at the Easter vigil.[30] ("This is the paschal festival, in which that true Lamb is slain, with Whose blood the doorposts of the faithful are consecrated" [157].) Likewise the passage through the sea, the liberation from bondage,[31] becomes a paradigm for the experience of conversion and the discovery of vocation,[32] and the instruction to remain silent and allow the Lord to fight on his people's behalf is identified as "an important Old Testament theme" found in the prophets as well, while the image of the dark cloud that nevertheless illumines the night becomes an icon of faith for mystics like Saint John of the Cross, echoing the simple declaration "they believed" (14:31) in which Merton finds "the grand finale to the whole plague sequence" (161).

30. See Merton's discussion of the *Exsultet* as revealing "the true significance of the paschal Lamb, and of the night in which the Children of Israel escaped from Egypt," in the concluding pages of Merton, *New Man* (244–48).

31. See Merton, *Conjectures of a Guilty Bystander*, 76–77: "the promise to Abraham is a promise of freedom, of independence under God, and the passage through the Red Sea was the passage out of Egyptian slavery into the liberty of the people God had formed and chosen for Himself, to be His own people, to live in fidelity to a covenant, which is a free agreement and a bond of liberty and love. The fidelity of Israel to the covenant meant refusing to be enslaved by the fascination and lure of the cosmic nature cults, refusing to surrender to the blind cycle of nature and to the domination of the forces of the earth. What did the prophets protest against more than the infidelity by which Israel forfeited her freedom and her espousal to Yahweh in liberty and in love?"

32. Merton himself describes his baptism in his autobiography in terms of the exodus and the journey to the promised land: see Merton, *Seven Storey Mountain*, 226–32, 255.

After a brief mention of the Canticle of Moses, sung in triumph on the far shore of the sea after Israel's miraculous escape, there is an equally brief typological application of the first episode in the desert, in which the bitter waters of Mara, sweetened by the immersion of the wood as directed by the Lord, becomes a figure of the spiritual life: "the Cross of Christ must 'sweeten' our trials" (161). Then follows an outline (accompanied by a hand-drawn, labeled map) of the entire period of forty years in the desert, including not only the itinerary for chapters 16–19 of Exodus that brings the children of Israel to the holy mountain but the subsequent journey from Sinai to the borders of the promised land as found in the book of Numbers, with a final notice of the death of Moses as related in the closing chapters of the book of Deuteronomy. At this point one might begin to wonder if Merton is having second thoughts about his original intention to produce a complete set of notes on the book of Exodus, much less on the later books of the Pentateuch and beyond, as this synopsis of the passage through the desert, perhaps still intended as a preview, eventually functions as a substitute for a full-dress treatment of the "stations" of Israel's pilgrimage.

It is somewhat ironic, then, that the next two pages of Merton's handwritten notes are both focused on the same incident, the gift of the manna, and actually overlap to a certain extent, suggesting they were composed independently and never integrated with one another. (Merton notes twice that Exodus 16:6–7 is used in the Christmas Eve liturgy, and twice gives instructions to read the first eighteen verses of chapter 16; the second time he directs that the remaining eighteen verses of the chapter be read as well.) The initial discussion emphasizes the desert as a place of testing and training, cites the passage from Deuteronomy 8 about not living by bread alone that Jesus will quote when tempted by Satan in the desert, and refers to various passages elsewhere in Scripture about spiritual hunger that bear witness to this truth. References to "murmuring" and to the need for trust in God are given a specifically monastic resonance by reminders of similar themes in the Benedictine *Rule*. The page that follows identifies the text as one of obedience and trust, considers the various ways the Israelites try to manipulate the gift of the manna to their own advantage, and refers to the application of the Exodus text in the Bread of Life discourse of John 6, where manna is first presented as a symbol of Jesus himself, then of the Eucharist, an identification also made in the various eucharistic hymns found in the liturgy, which of course his listeners themselves would periodically sing. It is clear that

1   INTRODUCTION

Merton was continually aware of the importance of connecting the topics of his conferences with the lived experience, particularly the (still not completely familiar) monastic experience of his audience.

Rather than commenting further on the subsequent episodes on the way to Sinai, already briefly mentioned in the journey outline, Merton summarizes at length an article by Louis Bouyer on the shekinah, the immanent glory of God, that by remarkable happenstance had just appeared in a French journal.[33] Merton himself had already introduced the term in relation to Exod 16:10 ("Behold the glory of the Lord appeared in a cloud" [166]), and now he follows Bouyer's lead closely in the longest of his supplementary passages. This divine presence is first associated with both the fire and the revelation of the name of God in Exodus 3; the divine glory is encountered at the sea in chapters 13 and 14, on the mountain in chapters 24 and 34, in the luminous cloud that descends on the tabernacle throughout the journey of Israel in the Pentateuch, and is likewise found in the temple in the first book of Kings and in the inaugural vision of Isaias (chapter 6)—only to depart at the time of the Babylonian captivity due to Israel's infidelity, as described in the visions of Ezechiel (Ezekiel). It is identified with the inner wisdom of the faithful Israelite in Ecclesiasticus (Sirach) and in postbiblical Jewish sapiential and mystical writing. Finally it is fully identified in Christian tradition with Jesus, Wisdom incarnate; with the church; and even with the individual Christian, temple of the Holy Spirit, transformed "from glory to glory" through love; and with the Eucharist, the visible, tangible manifestation of the glory of God, the body and blood of Christ crucified, resurrected and glorified, who "is the true and eternal temple of God" (174). This synopsis enables Merton to trace this central image all the way from Exodus through key texts of Old and New Testaments, arriving finally at the New Jerusalem of the final chapters of the Apocalypse, in which "there is no temple . . . since the Lord God Almighty and the Lamb were themselves the temple" (21:22).

Drawing on another favorite continental theologian, Romano Guardini, Merton then provides an introductory overview of the law about to be received at Sinai, which is considered both as "reflect[ing] deep wisdom and insight into human nature" and as "a tremendous burden" (174) that, as Saint Paul recognized, "was meant . . . to *convince man utterly of his failure* and thus strip him of all his illusions and make him turn to

33. Bouyer, "La Schékinah: Dieu avec Nous."

God" (174)—yet it could be and was, in Guardini's words, transformed into a way of "reducing God and His will to a guarantor of the glory of human law. . . . a documented charter of rights and demands" (174).

These prefatory comments are followed directly by a listing of the two versions of the Decalogue, as recorded in slightly different form in Exodus 20 and in Deuteronomy 5, sources of the two different enumerations made by the Latin and Greek Churches (and adopted respectively by Lutherans and Calvinists)—though Merton fails to point out that it is actually the Deuteronomic phrasing, which mentions the neighbor's wife first (Deut 5:21) rather than the sequence house, wife, servants, livestock, as in Exodus 20:17, that makes possible the Western distinction between the ninth and tenth commandments—coveting thy neighbor's wife and coveting thy neighbor's goods (treated as a single final commandment in the Eastern tradition, which considers the first commandment of the Latins as two).

Before turning to a discussion of individual commandments, Merton takes another brief look back at the journey through the desert thus far, finding an analogy with the early stages of religious life that his students are currently experiencing: leaving Egypt and passing through the desert is equated with leaving "the world" and becoming novices, with the Canticle of chapter 15 and the Mara incident likened to initial consolations and the sweetness of the Cross, the springs of Elim (15:27) with a love of the scriptures, the manna with living in total reliance on God, the battle with Amalek (17:8–16) with trust in the power of prayer, and the creation of judges (18:13–27) with "learning to share responsibility" (176). This is hardly an example of objective exegetical interpretation but rather an informal homiletic application that encourages his charges to make the story their own.

Merton then calls attention to the initial divine declaration of the vocation of Israel to be the People of God, "*a kingdom of priests, a consecrated nation*, His own property, sacred and set apart for Him alone" (176), a calling that is at the heart of the covenant about to be made, "compared to an ESPOUSAL" by the prophets, but one to which Israel will not be consistently faithful. As usual Merton presents this relationship of intimacy between God and God's people as finding its deepest expression in the church of the New Covenant, "the new People of God, built on Christ" (178). Following a quick consideration of the preliminaries that precede the meeting of Moses with the Lord on the mountain, Merton focuses on the commitment of love and fidelity that the covenant requires, violated by idolatry but also trivialized by allowing the encounter with the Word of God in Scripture to be reduced to an "external and verbal" level, the repetition "of a few catchwords—Law and alliance" and the like, that can easily substitute for a genuine relationship and can even degenerate into contemporary forms of idolatry—"magic thinking . . . pathological rituals . . . guilt complexes" (179).

This brings Merton to the point of considering the commandments themselves, first noting the two groupings that correspond to the two great commandments of love of God (1–3) and love of neighbor (4–10). He then provides for the first of these divisions what constitutes the most developed commentary on scriptural passages in the entire set of these conferences on Exodus. The first of the commandments, of course, enjoins faith in and worship of "the true and living God" (179), directed against the temptation to idolatry that will become particularly acute when the Israelites come into contact with the "fertility cults *which kept man {a} prisoner of nature*" (181). The prohibition of images is not to be regarded as absolute but applies only to images that represent false gods and become objects of worship: though with regard to the true God there is "no need of intermediaries" (180)—images included—since God is immediately present "in His people" (n.b. not just "to His people," which suggests both the relationship and the distinctiveness of the transcendent God and humanity, but a Presence which has identified itself intimately with the community of faith). Citing passages from Deuteronomy as explanatory glosses on this first of the commandments, Merton notes the command to reject even the places connected with pagan shrines, dangerous because of their traditional associations, in favor of "the place, which the Lord your God shall choose" (Deut 12:5), though in the New Dispensation "worship in spirit and in truth" (John 4) will transcend the limitation of worship to a single place, even the temple, as Stephen proclaims in the speech just before his martyrdom (Acts 7). The prohibitions of this commandment extend to divination—the attempt to control the supernatural for one's own ends (as Saul tries to do with the Witch of Endor) and to "superstition and vain observance . . . *serv[ing] Yahweh as one would serve an idol*" (181-82) (Saul again). The refusal to treat "the world" and its "POWER" as an object of worship has as its positive correlative the "duty to believe in God's word and trust in Him alone" (182), in his mercy and love.

Merton finds in the second commandment, prohibiting the misuse of God's name, a fruitful paradox that recalls his discussion of the divine name revealed at the burning bush in chapter 3, a recognition of "the inadequacy of any Name for God, but the fact that His Name really represents His Nature, His true identity" (183). The commandment forbids both attempts to control events for one's own ends through manipulation of the power of the Name, and blasphemy, which invokes the Name of God while ignoring or rejecting the Reality it represents. It is significant that Merton extends this prohibition of taking the name of the Lord in vain to a sense of profound respect, even reverence, for language as a vehicle of meaning generally: "*words are not to be treated as meaningless*" (183). The creative word of God brought all things into being and sustains them in being. "Our words for things," therefore, "try to grasp and identify His will as expressed in that thing" (183). To describe things accurately is ultimately to recognize and honor God as the source and end of every creature, including one's own unique self, "our own identity, in itself inexpressible but expressed to some extent by our 'name'" (184), not simply used as an arbitrary label but as a way of affirming the divine image that is the deepest dimension of each one's own being. Once again Merton concludes his discussion of the commandment by drawing out the positive implications of the negative prohibition, clarifying what the proper use of the divine name involves: "{the} first positive obligation {is} to *praise the Name of God* by confessing Him before men, especially by confessing Christ our Savior, {and} by loving His word and meditating on it and seeking to do His will, {by} thanking Him in all things" (185). This characteristically (but not exclusively) "monastic" devotion to the Name of God finds expression in the regular communal recitation of the "divine praises" ("Blessed be God, Blessed be His holy Name . . ."), traditionally considered as a way of making "reparation for infidelity and blasphemy" and so counteracting the violations of both first and second commandments.

Merton's discussion of the third commandment, on keeping the Sabbath, is the most extensive, emphasizing that it indicates that work is not an end in itself, that God has a right to all our time, that the injunction is positive, not negative, setting aside a time for leisure and repose as a way of honoring God and providing "*liberty* from pressing obligations" (186). He notes that whereas Exodus 20 associates the Sabbath with creation—God's own rest on the seventh day (Gen 2:3), the parallel passage in Deuteronomy 5 links it with liberation from enslavement in Egypt, a reminder not to fall under the tyranny of the "Pharaoh within us" (186). The weekly Sabbath is in turn connected to the sabbatical year, in which the land is allowed to rest, to lie fallow; to the annual Sabbath of weeks that leads from Passover and the feast of unleavened bread to Pentecost, commemorating the end of the wheat harvest as well as the giving of the law; and to the observance of the Jubilee, the fiftieth year, the Sabbath of Sabbaths. Merton points to the Sabbath as both a foreshadowing of the messianic age of peace and an expression of the "deep mystery" of care for the poor, with its implications of "freedom, economic independence, mercy and charity" (187).

He then turns to a brief consideration of 1 Corinthians 10 as the great "exodus" text in the New Testament, in which Paul finds in the cloud and the sea a figure of baptism, and presents the temptations and struggles of the Israelites in the desert as a warning to the new People of God not to fall into the same evil desires, murmuring, idolatry, and tempting (i.e. testing) Christ himself—"all these things," writes Paul, having been "written for our instruction, living in the last times" (189). With this Pauline application of the lessons of the Israelites' paradigmatic journey, Merton's commentary on the book of Exodus comes to a sudden, abrupt, unexpected conclusion. Before the text itself actually ends, he appends some brief remarks on the image of the spiritual Sabbath as found in Aelred of Rievaulx's *Mirror of Charity*, with its focus on the links between *labor* and *cupiditas*, *requies* and *caritas*; a set of brief descriptions of seven of the ancient peoples of Palestine (which overlaps with but is not identical to the traditional seven tribes of Canaan repeatedly mentioned in the later books of the Pentateuch and the book of Joshua); and finally a single-page summary of the entire book of Leviticus that immediately follows Exodus: while this book "takes us down to {the} erection of {the} Tabernacle" (192), it is Leviticus, "the book of the Levites' duties," that explains the sacrificial rituals performed in the tabernacle (as later in the Temple), as well as the duties of the priests and their assistants, the laws of purification and holiness, and various feasts including the Day of Atonement and the sabbatical and jubilee years mentioned a short time before.

Here Merton stops. There has been no discussion of the last seven commandments; no discussion of the Covenant Code of chapters 21–23; no discussion of the covenant ratification ceremonies in chapter 24; no discussion of the instructions for building the tabernacle in chapters 25–31 or the accomplishment of this task in chapters 35–40; no discussion of the golden calf, the breaking of the tablets, the request of Moses to "see God" and its paradoxical fulfillment. What has happened? It may seem as though Merton simply couldn't bring himself to proceed through the rather pedestrian moral demands of the remaining commandments, and of the detailed legal regulations to follow. But this would not explain the omission of any consideration of the key events of chapters 24 and 32–34, certainly among the most significant and most fascinating sections of the entire book, as they bring to a climax much of what has preceded. The decision to forgo further consideration of the final chapters of Exodus remains an enigma that probably has something to do with Merton's feeling overextended after almost three years of preparing nearly constant weekly conferences on the Bible while simultaneously preparing numerous series of classes on more directly monastic topics required as part of his duties as master of novices.

The copy text for the "Notes on Genesis" material is Merton's own seventy-one-page typescript,[34] with numerous handwritten additions and corrections, that he had before him as he presented these conferences to the novices. There is also a second version of this material, a seventy-eight-page "spirit master" copy[35] that was retyped on stencils, presumably by novices assigned by Merton, as for other series of conferences, to be reproduced and distributed to the novices before the conclusion of the course. Since it was simply copied from the original typescript, this second version has no independent textual authority and therefore has no contribution to make to the text found in the present edition. For the Exodus material the sole textual witness is the thirty-page set of notes,[36]

---

34. The typescript begins with a handwritten title page, followed by: one typed page of general introduction to the Pentateuch; one handwritten page headed "GENESIS—I. The Creation & Fall"; one typed page headed "Genesis—contd."; twenty-two typed, numbered pages headed "Genesis 3/24"; one handwritten numbered page headed "Gen 25"; fifteen typed, numbered pages headed "Genesis 26/40"; three typed pages on "REBECCA AND ISAAC IN THE FATHERS," the first unnumbered, the second and third headed "Rebecca 2/3"; a handwritten page of preliminary notes headed "*Jacob + Esau*" (not included as part of the critical text); twenty-three typed, numbered pages headed "Gen[esis] 41/63"—the running head on the final page added by hand; two handwritten pages, the first numbered "Genesis 64." and the last unnumbered.

35. This version is completely typed except for the handwritten running heads reading "Genesis 2" "Genesis 4/78" (only "Genesis 3." is typed) and handwritten notes on page 28 reading "(Go to p. 31)" and on page 31 reading "—(Insert pp. 29 and 30)"—indicating that the intervening pages headed "*The Renewal of God's Promise—the Ominous Sacrifice* (ch. 15)" (pages 48–49 in the present edition) should be transposed to follow ". . . packed into such an incident" (as in the typescript).

36. This material consists of the title page, twenty-eight pages of text, unnumbered except for the running head "Exod 2/4" on the first three pages of handwritten text, plus the title page and the hand-drawn map of the route through the desert from the

all but one handwritten, that Merton would have had before him as he presented this series of conferences, which therefore serves as the copy text for this section of the present edition.

All substantive additions made to the text, in order to turn elliptical or fragmentary statements into complete sentences, are included in braces, so that the reader can always determine exactly what Merton himself wrote. No effort is made to reproduce Merton's rather inconsistent punctuation, paragraphing, abbreviations, and typographical features; a standardized format for these features is established that in the judgment of the editor best represents a synthesis of Merton's own practice and contemporary usage: e.g., all Latin passages are italicized unless specific parts of a longer passage are underlined by Merton, in which case the underlined section of the passage is in roman type; all other passages underlined by Merton are italicized; words in uppercase in the text are printed in small caps; periods and commas are uniformly included within quotation marks; patterns of abbreviation and capitalization, very inconsistent in the copy texts, are regularized. All references to primary and secondary sources are cited in the notes, which also include all passages from Scripture or other sources that Merton has marked "read" in his text. Untranslated Latin passages in the original text are left in Latin but translated in the notes; unless otherwise noted, the translations are by the editor. Scripture passages are quoted from the Douay–Rheims version customarily used by Merton at the time these conferences were given.

The textual notes record all alterations made by Merton in his two sets of conferences, both those made online as he was writing and those added subsequently. They are followed by a bibliography including full information on all materials cited in the Preface, Introduction, text proper, and notes.

Red Sea to the promised land. Though the typed outline of "SCRIPTURE SEMINAR—Program" that follows the title page is not part of the "Notes on Exodus" proper, the fact that handwritten notes on the "Preamble from Origen" (page 136 of the present edition) are found on the verso side of this page indicates that it was not inserted later but had its present position from the outset of this series of conferences, and it is therefore included in the text of the present edition.

In conclusion I would like to express my gratitude to all those who have made this volume possible:

- to the Trustees of the Merton Legacy Trust, Peggy Fox, Anne McCormick, and Mary Somerville, for permission to publish the *Notes on Genesis and Exodus* conferences and for their consistent support in this and other projects;
- to Scripture scholar and longtime Merton reader Pauline A. Viviano, for graciously providing the insightful foreword for this volume;
- to Paul M. Pearson, director and archivist of the Thomas Merton Center, Bellarmine University, Louisville, KY, and Mark C. Meade, assistant director, for their hospitality and valued assistance during my research visits to the Center;
- to Brother Gaetan Blanchette, OCSO, librarian at the Abbey of Gethsemani, and Father Lawrence Morey, OCSO, monastery archivist, for their deeply appreciated aid and support in locating and making available relevant materials in the abbey's collections;
- to the Gannon University Research Committee, which has awarded a generous grant that allowed me to pursue research on this project at the Abbey of Gethsemani, at the Merton Center and at various libraries;
- to Mary Beth Earll and Betsy Garloch of the interlibrary loan department of the Nash Library, Gannon University, for once again providing invaluable assistance by locating and procuring various obscure volumes and articles;
- to all those at Wipf and Stock who have brought this volume to publication with grace and efficiency, particularly K. C. Hanson, editor; George Callihan, editorial administrator; Jeremy Funk, copy editor; Mike Surber, designer; and Heather Carraher, typesetter.
- to library staff of the Hesburgh Library of the University of Notre Dame, the Latimer Family Library of St. Vincent College, and the Institute of Cistercian Studies Collection at the Waldo Library of Western Michigan University, for assistance in locating important materials in their collections;
- again and always to my wife, Suzanne, and our children for their continual love, support, and encouragement in this and other projects.

NOTES ON GENESIS

Choir Novitiate—Gethsemani

1956—1957

THE PENTATEUCH, or five books of Moses—the Torah ({a} book composed of five rolls [*teuchos*]) contains the book of the Law (including Josue, which is inseparable—really makes six books): Genesis—the beginning, the Patriarchs; Exodus—the going-out from Egypt to {the} desert, Sinai, the Law; Leviticus—priestly prescriptions (no action); Numbers (because beginning with a census)—from Sinai to Jericho; Deuteronomy—the second Law (recall and reaffirmation, re-promulgation of the Law). {This is} the first act in the great drama of salvation. God creates the world, gives the initial promises of salvation, creates a Chosen People and gives them the law which they must keep in order to fulfill their divine mission. The destiny of mankind will depend on the conduct of the Chosen People. {It covers the period} from Creation to {the} death of Moses and {the} entry of the Chosen People into the Promised Land.

Moses is the author of the Torah, with due allowance for additions and modifications: (1) he summarized early oral or written tradition concerning what went before him; (2) later writers added to his main contribution; (3) he did not write them systematically as we have them—he put things down as they happened and they were later collected, edited {and} organized by later writers. Note the Wellhausen Theory,[1] {which}

---

1. For critical discussions of the Documentary Hypothesis of Julius Wellhausen (1844-1918), in his *Composition des Hexateuchs*, see Dyson and Mackenzie, "Higher Criticism," 61-64 [nn. 44a-45g]; and Sutcliffe, "Introduction to the Pentateuch,"

attacked Mosaic authorship of the Pentateuch, (1) traces the Pentateuch to four sources: (a) the Yahwist writers used J from {the} beginning (about {the} ninth century); (b) the Elohist writers (eighth century); (c) the Priestly writers (in Babylonia); (d) the Deuteronomical writers ({the} time of Josias—seventh century). (2) {The} Wellhausen theory {was} rejected in substance by theologians. At present, some Catholics hold (with Cardinal Suhard[2]), that though Moses is {the} principal author, there are still writers of Yahwist, Elohist and Priestly traditions, but they form more of a unity, and the Torah did not have to wait until {the} seventh century before being formed. Most agree it is not safe to be too categorical about {the} ancient origin of Deuteronomy, but that much of the legislation is substantially ancient—okay, {there was} probably a new edition, with additions, in {the} seventh century.

Conclusion (from {the} *Catholic Biblical Commentary* 135{t}):

> The Catholic scholar should keep in mind the directives of *Humani Generis*. At the same time, there should be no biased censure of the exegete who, while conforming in all docility to the magisterium, abandons a purely defensive attitude and looks squarely at the difficulties raised by Wellhausen. The progress of critical studies has clearly shown that certain conclusions of the new criticism, removed from all compromise with rationalistic evolution, can, without danger and even with profit, be incorporated into Catholic science. On the other hand, a good number of independent critics no longer assigns a recent date for the composition of the *corpus* of legislation in the Pentateuch; they admit the reality of the Sinaitic legislation and recognize a Mosaic nucleus in the Pentateuch. One must admit that, without Moses, the law of Israel is inexplicable; on the other, that no legislator would give a law that would remain unchanging through the centuries. (Fr. Dyson, SJ)[3]

172–74 [nn. 135b–h].

2. Cardinal Emmanuel Suhard (1874–1949), archbishop of Paris, had written to the Pontifical Biblical Commission to inquire about the acceptability of the Documentary Hypothesis, and the Commission's reply of January 16, 1948, 45–48, responded along the lines Merton summarizes here; see Crehan, "Inspiration and Inerrancy," 51 [nn. 37g–i]; Sutcliffe, "Replies of Biblical Commission," 74–75 [nn. 53l–m], which quotes much of the reply; Dyson, "Some Recent Catholic Viewpoints," 174 [n. 135k].

3. Dyson, "Some Recent Catholic Viewpoints," 176 [n. 135t (misnumbered "135s" by Merton)], which reads: "... must keep ... of the Encyclical *Humani* ... to the guidance of the 'magisterium ecclesiasticum' ... raised by the theory of Wellhausen ... assign ... of the whole *corpus* of ... Sinaitic tradition and ... recognize in the law-code

Genesis—I. The Creation & Fall

I. The two creation narratives:

a) Chapter 1 to 2:4 {is} a sacerdotal narrative {with} emphasis on the work of God bringing forth creatures or their hierarchies. At the summit {is} man, the image of God, the king and high priest of creation; all creation {is} given into the hand of man (cf. Psalm 8). At the end, God rests from His work—the Sabbath. The tone {is} liturgical, {with a focus on} worship, praise, adoration—"Cosmic Liturgy." The creatures come forth in an ordered procession, entering, by man, into the Temple of the Godhead, the divine rest. Our liturgical life should be impregnated with this spirit—kinship with creatures and with God. We are the natural mediators between God and the rest of His creation. {This is} our key position—our dignity. Love is the answer.

Verse 1–2: In the beginning—{note the} mystery: before the beginning only God existed. God creates "heaven and earth"—empty and deserted. The ABYSS {is} full of darkness. The Spirit of God {is} hovering over the abyss like a mother bird. This "hovering" of the Spirit of life {is} important, not only at the Creation but at all times. *Emitte Spiritum tuum et creabuntur.*[4] {This is} the Spirit of inexhaustible life—also in the abyss of our soul. {Note the} pattern of each creative act: God said . . . God separated . . . God called . . . God saw . . . This is the pattern of life for the Child of God—the idea, the execution, the witness, rest and fulfillment. Like Jesus, we must do what we see the Father doing—{the} alternation of action and rest.

Verse 26: *Faciamus*[5]—{this is the} interior council of God—Elohim (plural)—with the angels? the interior richness of God? the Holy Trinity? *Hominem* {is} a *collective name*—image and likeness? {Note} the Fathers' interpretation: image {is} nature: freedom; likeness {is} grace.

27 is really a short poem {with an} added solemnity {through} repetition: man {is} made by God; man {is} made in the image of God; man and woman {are} created by God ({note the} suggestion that marriage

---

of the Pentateuch a Mosaic, or even pre-Mosaic, nucleus. On the one hand, one must admit . . . unchangeable through . . ." *Humani Generis* was an August 12, 1950, encyclical of Pope Pius XII on issues including human origins, evolution, polygenism, and the historicity of the Old Testament narratives.

4. "Thou shalt send forth thy spirit, and they shall be created" (Ps 103[104]:30, which reads: "*Emittes* . . .").

5. "Let us make [man to our image and likeness]" (Gen 1:26).

and fecundity {are} necessary to bear witness to the divine image in humanity).

28: {the} divine command to man to multiply. God blesses His creation.

2:1–2: God blesses the seventh day. *This Sabbath will be replaced by the first Day of the New Creation.*

In connection with the creation narrative, {see}: (1) the *Adjutorium nostrum in nomine Domini—qui fecit coelum et terram.*[6] (2) Psalm 8; Psalm 103; Psalm 135—comment {on vv.} 1–9: creation as evidence of God's everlasting mercy. (3) Baptism: {at the} font, *Spiritus Dei ferebatur super aquas.*[7] (4) *Proficiscere, anima Christiana, in nomine Dei Patris omnipotentis qui te creavit* . . .[8]

Read Genesis 2—man in Eden:[9]

2:8: And the Lord had planted a paradise of pleasure, etc. Paradise {is} from {the} Septuagint *Paradeisos*—originally from Persian, meaning

---

6. "Our help is in the name of the Lord, who made heaven and earth" (Ps 123[124]:8).

7. "the spirit of God moved over the waters" (Gen 1:2).

8. The opening words of the prayer for the dying in their final agony, which reads in full: "*Proficiscere, anima Christiana, de hoc mundo, in nomine Dei Patris omnipotentis, qui te creavit: in nomine Jesu Christi Filii Dei vivi, qui pro te passus est: in nomine Spiritus Sancti, qui in te effusus est: in nomine Angelorum et Archangelorum: in nomine Thronorum et Dominationum: in nomine Principatum et Potestatum: in nomine Cherubim et Seraphim: in nomine Patriarcharum et Prophetarum: in nomine sanctorum Apostolorum et Evangelistarum: in nomine sanctorum Martyrum et Confessorum: in nomine sanctorum Monachorum et Eremitarum: in nomine sanctarum Virginum, et omnium sanctorum et sanctarum Dei: hodie sit in pace locus tuus, et habitatio tua in sancta Sion. Per eumdem Christum Dominum nostrum. Amen*" ("Go forth, Christian soul, from this world, in the name of God the Father Almighty who created you, in the name of Jesus Christ the Son of the Living God who suffered for you, in the name of the Holy Spirit who was poured out upon you, in the name of the angels and archangels, the thrones and dominions, the principalities and powers, the cherubim and seraphim, in the name of the patriarchs and prophets, the holy apostles and evangelists, the holy martyrs and confessors, the holy monks and hermits, the holy virgins and all the saints of God. May your place today be a place of peace, and may your dwelling be in holy Zion, through the same Jesus Christ Our Lord. Amen") (*Rituale Cisterciense*, 194–95 [Bk. 5, c. 5, n. 5]).

9. "So the heavens and the earth were finished, and all the furniture of them. And on the seventh day God ended his work which he had made: and he rested on the seventh day from all his work which he had done. And he blessed the seventh day, and sanctified it: because in it he had rested from all his work which God created and made. These are the generations of the heaven and the earth, when they were created, in the day that the Lord God made the heaven and the earth: And every plant of the

an enclosed park.¹⁰ When the ancient Orientals wanted to think of something that included within itself all joys, they thought of a beautiful garden with many shady trees and all kinds of flowers and shrubs, and traversed by cool breezes, spreading on all sides the sweet odor of flowers and spices (cf. Dan.13)—hence the appropriateness of gardens and woods for contemplation. God came and walked with Adam and spoke with him in the evening, or the cool time of the afternoon, when he rested.

Where was Paradise? "Paradise in Eden" (LXX)¹¹—in the Babylonian plain? at any rate an oasis in the midst of an arid steppe or desert, watered without rain by springs and rivers. Modern commentators insist that Eden must have had a precise locality on earth. The Fathers tend

---

field before it sprung up in the earth, and every herb of the ground before it grew: for the Lord God had not rained upon the earth; and there was not a man to till the earth. But a spring rose out of the earth, watering all the surface of the earth. And the Lord God formed man of the slime of the earth: and breathed into his face the breath of life, and man became a living soul. And the Lord God had planted a paradise of pleasure from the beginning: wherein he placed man whom he had formed. And the Lord God brought forth of the ground all manner of trees, fair to behold, and pleasant to eat of: the tree of life also in the midst of paradise: and the tree of knowledge of good and evil. And a river went out of the place of pleasure to water paradise, which from thence is divided into four heads. The name of the one is Phison: that is it which compasseth all the land of Hevilath, where gold groweth. And the gold of that land is very good: there is found bdellium, and the onyx stone. And the name of the second river is Gehon: the same is it that compasseth all the land of Ethiopia. And the name of the third river is Tigris: the same passeth along by the Assyrians. And the fourth river is Euphrates. And the Lord God took man, and put him into the paradise of pleasure, to dress it, and to keep it. And he commanded him, saying: Of every tree of paradise thou shalt eat: But of the tree of knowledge of good and evil, thou shalt not eat. For in what day soever thou shalt eat of it, thou shalt die the death. And the Lord God said: It is not good for man to be alone: let us make him a help like unto himself. And the Lord God having formed out of the ground all the beasts of the earth, and all the fowls of the air, brought them to Adam to see what he would call them: for whatsoever Adam called any living creature the same is its name. And Adam called all the beasts by their names, and all the fowls of the air, and all the cattle of the field: but for Adam there was not found a helper like himself. Then the Lord God cast a deep sleep upon Adam: and when he was fast asleep, he took one of his ribs, and filled up flesh for it. And the Lord God built the rib which he took from Adam into a woman: and brought her to Adam. And Adam said: This now is bone of my bones, and flesh of my flesh; she shall be called woman, because she was taken out of man. Wherefore a man shall leave father and mother, and shall cleave to his wife: and they shall be two in one flesh. And they were both naked: to wit, Adam and his wife: and were not ashamed."

10. See Sutcliffe, "Genesis," 184 [n. 143e].
11. That is, the Greek Septuagint translation of the Old Testament.

rather to hold it was allegorical, spiritual, not geographical in the strict sense; v.g. {the} apocryphal Jewish tradition says Paradise was made before the earth. Jerome adopts from this "*quam plantaverat a principio*" and explicitly states his belief that Paradise was made before the earth.[12] Evidently Paradise was made before the ordinary trees and vegetation of the earth: cf. verse 5—plants were created in a seminal manner but had not yet grown. Two points must be noted: Luke 23:43—*Hodie mecum eris* in Paradiso[13] (why not literally?); 2 Corinthians 12:4—*Raptus est in paradisum*[14] (probably a figure of speech).

Description of Paradise:

1. *The Trees*: the Lord brought forth from the earth every kind of tree, beautiful to look at and having good fruit to eat. {With regard to} trees, note Ezechiel {31}:8 ff.,[15] in {a} parable against the King of Assyria, whom he compares to a tree—{the} tree being {a} symbol of power and fruitfulness and long life (*justus ut palma florebit*[16]) —{writes}: "The cedars in the paradise of God were not higher than he" etc.; {he} also mentions fir trees and plane trees (like sycamores) (Read Ezech. 31:8 ff.;[17] Read Daniel 4[18]). Note how wisdom is compared to various trees in

---

12. "*Necnon quod sequitur, contra orientem, in Hebraeo* MECEDEM *scribitur, quod Aquila posuit* απο αρχης; *et nos, ab exordio, possumus dicere. Symmachus vero,* εκ πρωτης, *et Theodotion,* εν πρωτνοις, *quod et ipsum non orientem, sed principium significat. Ex quo manifestissime comprobatur, quod priusquam coelum et terram Deus faceret, paradisum ante condiderat, sicut et legitur in Hebraeo: Plantaverat autem Dominus Deus paradisum in Eden, a principio*" (*Quaestiones Hebraicae in Genesim*, 2:8 (Migne, PL 23, cols. 940B—941A) ("Also what follows, '*contra orientem*,' is written MECEDEM in Hebrew, which Aquila interpreted as απο αρχης; and we can say 'from the beginning.' Certainly Symmachus translated it εκ πρωτης and Theodotion εν πρωτνοις, because it means not 'the east' but 'the beginning.' From this it is very clearly proved that before God made heaven and earth he had previously established paradise, as is written in Hebrew: 'For from the beginning the Lord God had planted paradise in Eden'").

13. "This day thou shalt be with me in paradise" (Luke 23:43).

14. "he was caught up into paradise."

15. Copy text reads: "21."

16. "The just shall flourish like the palm tree" (Ps 91[92]:8).

17. "The cedars in the paradise of God were not higher than he, the fir trees did not equal his top, neither were the plane trees to be compared with him for branches: no tree in the paradise of God was like him in his beauty. For I made him beautiful and thick set with many branches: and all the trees of pleasure, that were in the paradise of God, envied him" (vv. 8-9).

18. "This was the vision of my head in my bed: I saw, and behold a tree in the midst of the earth, and the height thereof was exceeding great. The tree was great and strong, and the height thereof reached unto heaven: the sight thereof was even to the

Ecclesiasticus 24 (cf. Proverbs 3:18): 24:17—I was exalted like a cedar in Libanus and as a cypress tree on Mt. Sion, as a fair olive in the plains etc. (*read Eccli. 24:17-32*[19]). In this passage Wisdom herself is compared to a

---

ends of all the earth. Its leaves were most beautiful, and its fruit exceeding much: and in it was food for all: under it dwelt cattle and beasts, and in the branches thereof the fowls of the air had their abode: and all flesh did eat of it. I saw in the vision of my head upon my bed, and behold a watcher, and a holy one came down from heaven. He cried aloud, and said thus: Cut down the tree, and chop off the branches thereof: shake off its leaves, and scatter its fruits: let the beasts fly away that are under it, and the birds from its branches. Nevertheless, leave the stump of its roots in the earth, and let it be tied with a band of iron and of brass, among the grass, that is without, and let it be wet with the dew of heaven, and let its portion be with the wild beasts in the grass of the earth. Let his heart be changed from man's, and let a beast's heart be given him: and let seven times pass over him. This is the decree by the sentence of the watchers, and the word and demand of the holy ones: till the living know, that the most High ruleth in the kingdom of men: and he will give it to whomsoever it shall please him, and he will appoint the basest man over it. I, king Nabuchodonosor, saw this dream: thou, therefore, O Baltassar, tell me quickly the interpretation: for all the wise men of my kingdom are not able to declare the meaning of it to me: but thou art able, because the spirit of the holy gods is in thee. Then Daniel, whose name was Baltassar, began silently to think within himself for about one hour: and his thought troubled him. But the king answering, said: Baltassar, let not the dream and the interpretation thereof trouble thee. Baltassar answered, and said: My lord, the dream be to them that hate thee, and the interpretation thereof to thy enemies. The tree which thou sawest, which was high and strong, whose height reached to the skies, and the sight thereof into all the earth: And the branches thereof were most beautiful, and its fruit exceeding much, and in it was food for all, under which the beasts of the field dwelt, and the birds of the air had their abode in its branches. It is thou, O king, who art grown great, and become mighty: for thy greatness hath grown, and hath reached to heaven, and thy power unto the ends of the earth. And whereas the king saw a watcher, and a holy one come down from heaven, and say: Cut down the tree, and destroy it, but leave the stump of the roots thereof in the earth, and let it be bound with iron and brass, among the grass without, and let it be sprinkled with the dew of heaven, and let his feeding be with the wild beasts, till seven times pass over him. This is the interpretation of the sentence of the most High, which is come upon my lord, the king. They shall cast thee out from among men, and thy dwelling shall be with cattle, and with wild beasts, and thou shalt eat grass, as an ox, and shalt be wet with the dew of heaven: and seven times shall pass over thee, till thou know that the most High ruleth over the kingdom of men, and giveth it to whomsoever he will. But whereas he commanded, that the stump of the roots thereof, that is, of the tree, should be left: thy kingdom shall remain to thee, after thou shalt have known that power is from heaven. Wherefore, O king, let my counsel be acceptable to thee, and redeem thou thy sins with alms, and thy iniquities with works of mercy to the poor: perhaps he will forgive thy offences. All these things came upon king Nabuchodonosor" (vv. 7-25).

19. "I was exalted like a cedar in Libanus, and as a cypress tree on mount Sion. I was exalted like a palm tree in Cades, and as a rose plant in Jericho: As a fair olive tree in the plains, and as a plane tree by the water in the streets, was I exalted. I gave a sweet

paradise (not explicitly stated) in which we are nourished by fruits of love and truth. Cf. Apocalypse 2:7—To him that overcometh I will give to eat of the tree of life that is in the Paradise of my God (one of many promises, made to each of the Churches, all roughly equivalent—a new name, crown of life, white garments, manna to eat, to sit in the same throne with Christ, to have power over the nations, to be a pillar in the temple of God). {See also} Apocalypse 22:1–3 (READ[20]): the river of {the} water of life, {with} the tree of life "on both sides of the river," yielding its fruits every month, {with} leaves for the healing of the nations. We *must* pay attention to these texts from {the} Apocalypse in trying to understand whatever is said about the trees of the earthly paradise. This brings us to the *Tree of Life*, which we must now consider. (Note: *Paradise as a type of Our Lady*: her soul {is} compared to paradise—{see the} lessons {of the} Feast of {the} Immaculate Conception (As a garden enclosed in which God takes His pleasure[21]); cf. St. John {of the} Cross, *Spiritual Canticle*;[22] St. Bernard, lessons {of the} votive office of Our Lady[23]).

---

smell like cinnamon and aromatical balm: I yielded a sweet odour like the best myrrh: And I perfumed my dwelling as storax, and galbanum, and onyx, and aloes, and as the frankincense not cut, and my odour is as the purest balm. I have stretched out my branches as the turpentine tree, and my branches are of honour and grace. As the vine I have brought forth a pleasant odour: and my flowers are the fruit of honour and riches. I am the mother of fair love, and of fear, and of knowledge, and of holy hope. In me is all grace of the way and of the truth, in me is all hope of life and of virtue. Come over to me, all ye that desire me, and be filled with my fruits. For my spirit is sweet above honey, and my inheritance above honey and the honeycomb. My memory is unto everlasting generations. They that eat me, shall yet hunger: and they that drink me, shall yet thirst. He that hearkeneth to me, shall not be confounded: and they that work by me, shall not sin. They that explain me shall have life everlasting. All these things are the book of life, and the covenant of the most High, and the knowledge of truth."

20. "And he shewed me a river of water of life, clear as crystal, proceeding from the throne of God and of the Lamb. In the midst of the street thereof, and on both sides of the river, was the tree of life, bearing twelve fruits, yielding its fruits every month, and the leaves of the tree were for the healing of the nations. And there shall be no curse any more; but the throne of God and of the Lamb shall be in it, and his servants shall serve him."

21. "*Hortus conclusus, soror mea sponsa, hortus conclusus, fons signatus, Emissiones tuae paradisus, o Maria!*" ("My sister, my spouse, is a garden enclosed, a garden enclosed, a fountain sealed up. Thy plants are a paradise, O Mary") (Song 4:12–13; ninth responsory of the first nocturn) (*Breviarium Cisterciense, Hiemalis*, 496).

22. John uses the image of the garden for the soul of the Bride (First Redaction: stanza 26; Second Redaction: stanza 17) and for God himself (First Redaction: stanza 27; Second Redaction: stanza 22) in *The Spiritual Canticle*, but does not liken it to Mary (Peers, *John of the Cross*, 2:133–38, 2:281–86; 2:138–43, 2:306–11).

23. "*Altius intuemini, fratres mei, quanto devotionis affectu a nobis Mariam voluerit*

The Tree of Life and the Tree of Knowledge of Good and Evil: read vv. 16–17[24]—{the} command not to eat {from the} tree of knowledge. {This is} not merely an arbitrary command—the tree would be bad for man.

1. Some authorities hold that these were really one and the same tree. But there is no possibility of finding out if this is correct. On the contrary it makes more sense to suppose that there were two trees as the text says.

2. The Tree of Life: in Genesis 3:22, after the expulsion from Paradise for eating of the tree of knowledge, God decrees to close Paradise lest "perhaps he put forth his hand and take also of the tree of life and eat, and live forever"; and in 3:24 the explicit purpose of the cherub with the flaming sword is to "keep the way of the tree of life." Hence this is a different tree with a fruit that confers immortality, while the fruit of the tree of knowledge conferred death. The Fathers see in the Tree of Life a type of Christ, and St. Augustine says[25] that this tree was placed in Paradise to feed man's spirit with mystery, while the others nourished his body with their fruits.

---

honorari, qui totius boni plenitudinem posuit in Maria: ut proinde si quid spei in nobis est, si quid gratiae, si quid salutis, ab ea noverimus redundare, quae ascendit deliciis affluens. Hortus plane deliciarum, quam non modo afflaverit veniens, sed et perflaverit superveniens auster ille divinus, ut undique fluant et affluant aromata ejus, charismata scilicet gratiarum" ("Consider more deeply, my brothers, with how much feeling of devotion he who has placed the fullness of all good in Mary has willed her to be honored by us: since if there is anything of hope in us, anything of grace, anything of salvation, we know it streams forth from her, who rose up flowing with delights. Clearly a garden of delights, whom that divine south wind not only came and breathed upon, but overcame and breathed through, so that on all sides its fragrances, that is, the gifts of graces, flow and overflow") (*Officium Beatae Mariae in Sabbato, Lectio 2: Ex Sermone 2 de Virgine Deipara, alias, de Aquaeductu* [*Breviarium Cisterciense*, 175–76*]).

24. "And he commanded him, saying: Of every tree of paradise thou shalt eat: But of the tree of knowledge of good and evil, thou shalt not eat. For in what day soever thou shalt eat of it, thou shalt die the death."

25. "*nec sine mysteriis rerum spiritualium corporaliter praesentatis voluit hominem Deus in paradiso vivere. Erat ei ergo in lignis caeteris alimentum, in illo autem sacramentum; quid significans, nisi sapientiam, de qua dictum est, Lignum vitae est amplectentibus eam*" (*De Genesi ad Litteram*, 8.4.8 [Migne, *PL* 34, col. 375]) ("God did not wish man to live in paradise without mysteries of spiritual things presented in bodily form. Therefore, on other trees there was food for him, but in that one a sacrament; and what does it signify but wisdom, of which it is said: she is a tree of life to them that lay hold on her [Prov 3:18]").

3. *The Tree of the Knowledge of Good and Evil*: {among the} exegetes, some say it is the tree of discernment, the use of reason (v.g. Fromm, {a} psychoanalyst, says the Adam story is that of man's "punishment for {the} autonomous use of his own reason"[26]). But this view is not correct. Adam already knew good. For him to know evil, which he could know by inference from good, was also possible and legitimate. But this tree was the tree of the *experience of evil*, and it led to a *division in man*: (1) by disobedience to God, man becomes himself the arbiter of good and evil; that is to say: (2) having forfeited the right to light, by which one always knows the will of God, and having claimed the privilege of knowing good and evil by himself, apart from the divine light, he is no longer led exclusively by the single light and unction which teaches all things (*unctio ejus docet vos de omnibus*[27]); (3) man forfeits the "one thing necessary,"[28] the privilege of being guided and formed by the Holy Spirit, to do what love indicates, without thought whether it be good or evil, prompted only by unitive love with God and by the movement of His Spirit (*ama et quid vis fac*[29]—in the correct sense); (4) he falls into a state of conflict and uncertainty in which he is constantly faced with the possibility of sin, and actually falls into sin, doing what divides him still more from God and from himself; (5) this is the fruit of death, which brings what St. Bernard calls "*sapor mortis*"[30] (from {the} *De*

---

26. The exact source of this quotation is unidentified, but in *Psychoanalysis and Religion*, Fromm distinguishes between the authoritarian and the humanistic strands of biblical religion, contrasting the authoritarian impulse as seen in the fall story, in which "man is forbidden to know good and evil and his position toward God is that of submission—or sinful disobedience" with the humanistic strain, in a story about rabbinic decision-making from the Talmud, which "emphasizes the autonomy of man's reason with which even the supernatural voices from heaven cannot interfere. God smiles, man has done what God wanted him to do, he has become his own master, capable and resolved to make his decisions by himself according to rational, democratic methods" (45, 47). For Merton's letters to Fromm, see Merton, *Hidden Ground of Love*, 308–24.

27. "his unction teacheth you of all things" (1 John 2:27).

28. See Luke 10:42.

29. Properly "*Dilige, et quod vis fac*" ("Love, and do what you will"): Augustine, *Homilies on I John*, 7:8 (Migne, PL 35, col. 2033); see also Augustine, *Commentary on Galatians*, 57: "*Dilige, et dic quod voles*" ("Love, and say what you will") (Migne, PL 35, col. 2144).

30. "taste for death": see Merton, *New Man*, 108: "Now St. Bernard puts this *sapor mortis*, this taste for death, at the very heart of original sin. It is the exact opposite of

Gradibus Humilitatis et Superbiae—St. Bernard addresses Eve: "If the other trees are all good, and taste good, what is the use of eating of a tree which has the taste of evil [*quod sapit etiam malum*]";[31] this is indeed "tasting by experience more than we should experience": *sapere plus quam oportet sapere* [Rom. 12:3]. SAPERE ENIM MALUM SAPERE NON EST, SED DESIPERE. . . . STA IN TE NE CADAS A TE SI AMBULAS IN MAGNIS ET IN MIRABILIBUS SUPER TE[32]). The fruit of this tree gives *experience of evil, experience of sin*, separation from God, {a} plunge into unreality; one has to be one's own God, an impossible and unbearable situation.

The Rivers of Paradise: one river goes out "from the place of pleasure"[33] {and} waters Paradise, which when it leaves Paradise is divided into four rivers. {As this is} a geographical impossibility, hence this also seems to need to be taken mystically. Phison flows through Hevilath, {in} northern Arabia, where there is no river (bdellium[34] {is} a yellow aromatic gum); Phison has also been identified with the Phase, which flows from the foot of Ararat through Colchis, the land where the Argonauts went to get the golden fleece; {it is} also thought by some to be the Indus. Gehon "flows about all the land of Kush,"[35] which came to be identified with Ethiopia, so Gehon came to be identified with the Nile. Tigris and Euphrates represent these true rivers. Hence {there are} two real rivers and two perhaps legendary rivers. What are we to conclude? Whatever may be the solution, the author of Genesis was probably trying to locate Paradise according to tradition, and located it somewhere in Chaldea, probably. What does the Holy Spirit want us to get from these rivers??? Here read

---

the wisdom, the *sapida scientia* or existential ('tasting') knowledge of the divine good. The two are incompatible with one another. They cannot exist together. Consequently, having acquired the one, Adam necessarily lost the other."

31. "*Si enim caetera bona sunt, et sapiunt bonum, quid est opus edere de ligno, quod sapit etiam malum?*" (*De Gradibus Humilitatis et Superbiae*, c. 10, n. 30 [Migne, *PL* 182, col. 958D]).

32. "[I say] not to be more wise than it behoveth to be wise [Rom 12:3]. For to taste evil is not to be wise but foolish. . . . Stay within yourself lest you fall from yourself, if you walk in great and marvelous matters beyond yourself (Ps 130[131]:1)" (c. 10, nn. 30, 31 [cols. 958D, 959B]).

33. Gen 2:10.

34. Gen 2:12.

35. Gen 2:13.

Ecclesiasticus 24:35–37:³⁶ literal investigation beyond a certain point is utterly fruitless. What about something else: spiritual realities?

The Creation of Eve: 15–17—God places man in Paradise to keep it (not to guard it—it did not need to be guarded). Man is commanded not to eat of the fruit of the tree of knowledge, because he will die. {In} 18 ff., companions for man {are made}; here the animals are supposed to be created *after* man and are brought to him so that he may name them. {Note} the mystery of language: "What man calls each thing, that it is."³⁷ Trappists above all should have respect for the value of words—{note the} modern devaluation of language. Man named all the animals, but not one of them was a helper appropriate to him. {Here follows} the mystery of the creation of woman, and of human society in its fundamental cell, the family. The sleep of Adam {is} ecstasy, according to St. Bernard³⁸—in other words here too we are dealing with a mystical reality ({the} LXX {reads} *ekstasis*; the Hebrew word signifies an extraordinary sleep produced by the Lord). The meaning of the story of Eve's formation from the side of man {is that} she is really his equal in everything (Orientals thought she was less than man, {an} inferior species, halfway between man and the animal). Refer back to {the} earlier verse where the creation of man and woman forms the "image of God."³⁹ WHAT IS THE MYSTERY HERE? IT IS THE MYSTERY OF LOVE: human love is the image of divine love. In the mystery of human society is reflected the mystery of God; in the union of souls, the union of men with God, and of the Divine Persons within the Trinity. READ EPHESIANS 5:22 to the end,⁴⁰ especially 31–32,

36. "Who filleth up wisdom as the Phison, and as the Tigris in the days of the new fruits. Who maketh understanding to abound as the Euphrates, who multiplieth it as the Jordan in the time of harvest. Who sendeth knowledge as the light, and riseth up as Gehon in the time of the vintage."

37. Gen 2:19.

38. "*Immisit Dominus soporem in Adam. Immisit et in se ipsum, factus nimirum secundus Adam; sed est distantia forte non parva. Ille enim soporatus videtur prae excessu contemplationis; Christus miserationis affectu: ut in illum soporem immiserit veritas, in hunc charitas, cum utraque sit Dominus. . . . Adam soporatus est in contemplatione*" (*Sermo 2 in Septuagesima* [Migne, *PL* 183, cols. 166B, 168A]) ("The Lord cast a deep sleep upon Adam [Gen 2:21]. Of course he sent the same upon himself, having become the second Adam; but the difference is in fact not small. For the former is seen to have been put to sleep for the sake of a contemplative ecstasy, Christ, for the sake of compassionate feeling, so that in the former truth sent the sleep, in the latter, charity, since the Lord is both. . . . Adam slept in contemplation").

39. Gen 1:27.

40. "Let women be subject to their husbands, as to the Lord: Because the husband

where Paul reveals that the mystical meaning of the creation of Eve is that she is a type of the Church. Here we have the germs of the Canticle of Canticles, of the whole New Testament, of the nuptial theme in the prophets, etc. This mystery manifests God's love for us and the plan of His love for us, made clear in the Apocalypse (read Apoc. 21:1–4[41]).

THE FALL (C. 3)

1. Outline of the scripture text: *The Fall and its consequences* (vv. 1–11)—{first comes the} introduction of the "serpent," a symbolic being, a "mask" of the devil, the "opposer," characterized by his craftiness. He raises a question, a doubt, as to the wisdom of the order established by God. Eve replies to the question first with a simple statement of fact— what they have been told. The serpent then questions and contradicts this, denies that they will die, makes a contrary promise of his own: their eyes will be opened; they shall be as gods, knowing good and evil. The work of the serpent is *to divide* man—from God, from other men, from himself—by doubts, opinions, etc., embraced as supreme knowledge, as ultimate standards of "good and evil." If man eats of the fruit of this tree, in order to have a higher illumination, he will find himself in fact left to the light of his own mind which is limited and weak. He will be divided against himself in the search for truth—accepting now this opinion and now that; he will be at odds with other men, bickering and fighting with

---

is the head of the wife, as Christ is the head of the church. He is the saviour of his body. Therefore as the church is subject to Christ, so also let the wives be to their husbands in all things. Husbands, love your wives, as Christ also loved the church, and delivered himself up for it: That he might sanctify it, cleansing it by the laver of water in the word of life: That he might present it to himself a glorious church, not having spot or wrinkle, or any such thing; but that it should be holy, and without blemish. So also ought men to love their wives as their own bodies. He that loveth his wife, loveth himself. For no man ever hated his own flesh; but nourisheth and cherisheth it, as also Christ doth the church: Because we are members of his body, of his flesh, and of his bones. For this cause shall a man leave his father and mother, and shall cleave to his wife, and they shall be two in one flesh. This is a great sacrament; but I speak in Christ and in the church. Nevertheless let every one of you in particular love his wife as himself: and let the wife fear her husband" (vv. 22–33).

41. "And I saw a new heaven and a new earth. For the first heaven and the first earth was gone, and the sea is now no more. And I John saw the holy city, the new Jerusalem, coming down out of heaven from God, prepared as a bride adorned for her husband. And I heard a great voice from the throne, saying: Behold the tabernacle of God with men, and he will dwell with them. And they shall be his people; and God himself with them shall be their God. And God shall wipe away all tears from their eyes: and death shall be no more, nor mourning, nor crying, nor sorrow shall be any more, for the former things are passed away."

them over their partial viewpoints. He will be divided against God, and will try to divide God Himself, putting God on one side or the other in these futile controversies. In reality, God is above all these divisions. In Him there is no division between truth and falsity, good and evil. What is, is. All in Him is pure being, reality, goodness and truth. Evil and error are outside of Him—that is, they "are not." To be divided between what is and what is not—this is the illumination promised by the devil. In addition, man will pay for his rebellion against reality by tending, with his will, to embrace what is false, and to love what is the illusory and the apparent good, rejecting what is true. When this promise has been made, and accepted by the woman, she gets a new outlook on the tree. Before, it had been simply the tree of which they were not to eat. Now it acquires a special attractiveness. Like all things God has created, the tree is good and beautiful, but she sees in it an exaggerated and illusory goodness and beauty, magnified by the lying promise of the devil. It appears to her in a sense more beautiful and desirable than the other trees because of the vain hope of fulfillment which she conceives to be possible there. Thus we have the basic attitude which allows of sin: on the one hand, a clear knowledge of the will of God, on the other a fatal attraction for what is contrary to the will and word of God, *a propensity toward illusory good*, to which we are impelled by the coloring our own subjective desires give to it. In other words, here is a new illumination: *the light projected on things by our own will and our own desire*, the transforming action of our own illusory hopes and ambitions. ("Delightful to behold"[42] [Douay] is in {the} *Bible de Jerusalem* "desirable for the sake of acquiring understanding."[43]) Eve eats the fruit, gives it to her husband {and} he eats also. Their eyes are opened {and} they recognize their nakedness. This means: (1) the awakening of concupiscence: sex existed before the fall and was something good, subjected to man's reason; now the order is inverted—illusory wishes and desires invest the object of love with powerful dynamic attractions which overwhelm reason; man is afraid of this overwhelming power and has to defend himself against it; (2) consequently the nakedness which is revealed and of which they are afraid is their own nothingness, their helplessness, their frailty, their propensity to fall into folly and death; (3) the knowledge of their nakedness is the knowledge of their conflict, of the division that is in them between a flesh that can

---

42. Gen 3:6.

43. "désirable pour l'entendement" (de Vaux, *Genèse*, 46).

overwhelm the spirit and a spirit which struggles vainly to control the flesh, and this keeps them convinced of their "nothingness." So they make aprons with fig leaves—that is to say, they conceal the real state of affairs from themselves. Whereas God had created them naked and simple, and their happiness had consisted in simply accepting themselves as they were and loving God, now they rebel against their nakedness and say, in effect, "we are not naked." In this question of nakedness we immediately see the development of the knowledge of good and evil. Before, they did not care whether or not they were naked. The fact simply was that they *were*. Now there is ambivalence: from the point of view of the lost spirit, it is good to be not naked, and evil to be naked; from the point of view of the unruly flesh it is good to be naked and evil to be clothed. Ultimately all kinds of strange things come from this conflict. Man remains both naked and clothed. But sometimes he uses clothes to convince himself that he is not and cannot be a mere naked being. On the other, clothing can be used lasciviously to enhance the attraction of nakedness which it does not altogether hide. Man's original nakedness, from being a simply matter-of-fact reality, now becomes an immensely complicated problem for him—a typical effect of the fall—a source of ambivalence. Man fell not only into sin but into mental sickness—not that all men are insane, but the division that is in man by virtue of the fall, and the dialectic of falsity and reality that goes on within him all the time, sets the stage for mental sickness as well as for moral degeneration.

Then the Lord walks in the garden and they hide from Him. {Here is} the loss of *parrhesia*.[44] In his original innocence, without divisions or schisms in his being, man enjoyed the privilege of perfect intimacy and union with God. There were no questions, no hesitations, no fears, no problems. God, Who spoke to man in the depths of his own being and in the nature all around him, could reach everything in man because man was simple and perfectly attuned to reality, whether within himself,

---

44. See *New Man*, 72: "The concept of man's intimacy with God in work as well as in contemplation was sometimes rendered by the Fathers in the Greek word 'parrhesia' for which perhaps the most convenient translation is 'free speech.' The word represents, in fact, the rights and privileges of a citizen in a Greek city state. This 'free speech' is at once the duty and the honor of speaking one's own mind fully and frankly in the civil assemblies by which the state is governed. The Genesis story tells of Adam's 'freedom of speech' with God not so much by directly describing it as by saying what replaced it when it was taken away. The Parrhesia of Adam in Eden is known by inference, by implication. We see it by the contrast of his state after the fall with what is implied to have gone before."

outside himself or above himself. Now man is no longer attuned to reality with the same simplicity: (1) *in himself*, man is a helpless, doubting and hesitant being, elevated to the rank of a god and supreme arbiter of good and evil; (2) *outside himself*, man sees reality as something to be dominated and controlled, for his own purposes, something to be feared in so far as it menaces his own security; (3) *within himself*, man faces conflict and turmoil: there are vast areas within himself which he cannot fully know and which he fears, for in these depths lurk the passions which have become hostile (yet he loves them more than himself) and which threaten his balance and sanity; (4) *above himself, and within*, is the even more terrifying unknown—God; man no longer enjoys free, direct contact with God at will; God will continue to speak, but now His voice inspires terror, because it is the voice of One at once supremely powerful and supremely unknown, Who has been offended with an infinite offense. They hide from God in the trees of the garden. *Creation is no longer a place in which to meet God, but a place in which to hide from Him*—yet they are identically the same creatures. Nothing has changed but man, who now sees only creatures, mirrors of his own desires and interior states, instead of going through their transparency to see the infinite reality of God.

God calls Adam (v. 9): *Adam, ubi es?*[45] God is not separated from Adam, but Adam is separated from God. Adam cannot exist without God, and God's knowledge of Adam sustains Adam in existence. Therefore God does not need to ask where Adam is, for Adam is in God, and God, as Creator, is in Adam. But Adam is separated from God, and although God is intimately present to him, Adam is far from God, divided from Him by the illusory "divinity" which he has taken upon himself as arbiter of good and evil. Adam has become his own god, his own judge, his own master. Consequently, the voice of God is the voice of a rival, of an enemy to be feared (from Adam's own subjective viewpoint). God has only to speak, and Adam must hide; he cannot bear the sound of a voice which shatters all his illusions and destroys his whole new moral universe. Adam explains, with a trace of naïve sincerity—he has not yet completely learned to be an expert in all guile, as will his descendants—"I was naked, and I was afraid"[46]—what volumes in this! Man cannot bear the sight of his own insufficiency when he is separated from God. It becomes an "evil" which the goodness of God is bound to reproach. Yet when man

---

45. "Adam, where art thou?" (Gen 3:9).
46. Gen 3:10.

was united to God his nakedness was no evil and his insufficiency in himself was no reproach. Perfectly in accord with reality, he had all that he needed both in himself and in God and in all the other creatures of God, for all was united in perfect harmony. He did not have to worry about not being a god. He did not expect to be. When once he has set up the claim to divine omnipotence, then his insufficiency (symbolized by the nakedness which leaves him at the mercy of incontrollable passions) becomes an unbearable reproach and source of internal contradiction. (Note how this process operates in neurotics.) God then tells Adam frankly what the reason for all this is.

The Defense of Adam and Eve—The Sentence of Banishment (vv. 12–24): Adam puts the blame on Eve, Eve on the serpent. God condemns the serpent, but in His condemnation of the serpent is the Proto-evangelium, the original promise of the Redemption: the serpent is cursed; man shall be at enmities with the serpent, {in a} constant struggle; the seed of the woman shall crush the serpent's head. Note the points contained in this: (1) God's mercy—at the very moment when sin has first been committed, He announces that the effects of sin shall be annulled, and declares that He will send a Redeemer; (2) He takes the initiative—His original plan for man to be united to Him will not be frustrated; God does not prophesy merely; His word is creative (*vivus et efficax*[47]): what He says here is a divine *fiat*; He is not merely taking the part of man against the serpent; as ever, He is saying what IS; (3) this is the first promise made by God to men, immediately after man's sin; it contains God's whole intent to overcome evil with good, to overcome malice with wisdom[48] (not that He is immersed in the struggle, but His reality working down into the unreality and nothingness of man will assert itself and rescue what is its own); the promise is collective, and each individual must strive by the efforts of his own freedom to make the promise good in his own life; the serpent can still wound, but final victory belongs to man, by the promise and the grace of God; (4) later revelation makes clear that the "seed"[49] who will crush the head of the serpent is Christ, and us in Him: "For this purpose the Son of God appeared, that He may destroy the works of the devil" (1 Jn. 3:8; cf. Heb. 2:14).

---

47. "[the word of God is] living and effectual" (Heb 4:12).
48. See Wis 7:30.
49. Gen 3:15.

CAIN AND ABEL (ch. 4): This is the immediate consequence of the sin of our first parents in Paradise. It gives evidence of the reign of sin, an advance of the kingdom of evil. There has been a lapse of time since Eden, in which Cain and Abel are born and grow up, a lapse of time in which there is a kind of lull while evil gathers strength to begin its terrible course through the history of man. There are no doubt other sins committed (cf. 1 Jn. 3:12:[50] Cain was jealous because his works were wicked and his brother's just). The sin now breaks out and asserts itself definitively, and it becomes clear that the history of man will be, among other things, a history of sin.

1. The birth of Cain: {note} the humility and wisdom of Eve, her poetic memorial of the birth of her first child, a phrase which sums everything up: "I have begotten a man through God."[51] The custom of these gnomic poetic utterances in primitive peoples {is such that} they will be common in Genesis—{they are} brief poetic statements that "fix" definitively the meaning of an event (cf. Japanese poems). The birth of Abel {follows}: he is the younger son, the lesser. His name means "breath," and therefore what is "weak" and "evanescent."[52] Here we see the beginning of a struggle in the Bible between the elder, the stronger, who is "in possession," who is smarter and more crafty in the natural order, but who is not *chosen by God*, and the younger, the weaker, the poorer, who has nothing, yet whose weakness becomes the vehicle of God's strength. The first line leads to antichrist, to the Kingdom of the World. The second line leads to Jesus, the Victim and Savior, and to those redeemed by Him—the Kingdom of God.

The two ways of life {are in contrast}. Abel is a shepherd, the nomad without fixed abode, less dependent upon skill and civilization, {living a} simpler life, the life Israel will lead in the desert, directly cared for by God (n.b. {the} Nazarites[53] and Rechabites[54] drank no wine to recall nomadic days). Cain is a farmer, under the curse laid upon the labor of man by God. He has roots, is sedentary, close to the soil, and therefore earth gods and their religion will spring up around his descendants—when Israel was settled in Canaan, religion became infected with paganism because

---

50. "And wherefore did he kill him? Because his own works were wicked: and his brother's just."
51. Gen 4:1.
52. See Sutcliffe, "Genesis," 188 [n. 146a].
53. See Num 6:1–21.
54. See Jer 35:2–19.

of {the} cult of fertility, or productiveness, inseparable from dependency on crops, etc. The two sacrifices {likewise contrast}: Cain presents the fruit of his own toil and ingenuity; Abel presents living beings that had been given by God—the firstlings of his flock. The sacrifice of Abel is an effusion of blood, a greater deprivation for himself and {one which} costs more. As a reward he himself becomes a victim of {a} bloody sacrifice, prefiguring Jesus. However, the important thing is that Abel's sacrifice is *accepted by God*—not for a special worth in the sacrifice only but because of God's special love. God accepts the sacrifice of Abel, not that of Cain. How does He accept? perhaps by some sign. The important point is that this acceptance is a *free act* of God. Cain is angry because his attitude is already magical—he feels that his offering should have *obliged* God to be favorable. Therefore he was trying to bind God, to force Him to give good things. Hence in the very nature of his sacrifice (selfish, centered on himself, etc.), he was rejected by God. God answers the sacrifice that is already prompted by love and purity of heart for His own glory, disinterested, etc.

Cain's sorrow and the Lord's warning {follow: note} the brevity and force of the description of Cain. The Lord, always at hand, speaks in the intimacy of his heart, showing him exactly what the situation is, what he is about to do, and that he does not have to do it. Cain's freedom is shown to him. It is the state of man after the fall. One feels however that it is something in the nature of a test. Here man falls further into sin. He deliberately adds actual sin of his own to original sin. God tells Cain: (1) if you do good you will lift up your head (see Pirot[55]); (2) if you do evil, "sin will immediately be present outside your door"[56]—{a} powerful image!—sin as a mysterious, inscrutable being that sits outside your door and looks at you (*peccatum meum contra me est semper*[57]); (3) Cain is inclined to sin, but he can still master the inclination. Note that God has by no means abandoned Cain, but loves him and guides him.

Cain's sin: Cain does not master the hatred in his heart; he yields to it deliberately without answering God. Note again the stark brevity of the narrative. {There is} no pause, no transition between God's warning and Cain's invitation to come out into the field. ({Consider} how a hammy modern writer might put it—perhaps find some example of bad

---

55. "Si tu agis bien ne peux-tu lever (ton visage)?" (Pirot and Clamer, eds., *Sainte Bible*, 1:157).

56. Gen 4:7.

57. "my sin is always before me" (Ps 50[51]:5).

writing in a modern narrative of a similar situation.) Cain "rises up"[58] against Abel—since people can be killed in the pulling of a trigger we have lost this image of a man "rising up," gathering up all his force for the single blow that must not miss. {Then follows} God's question and Cain's answer: "Where is Abel thy brother?"[59] (cf. the question in Eden—Adam, where art *thou*? In Eden it was Adam himself that was dead; God had to seek him, for Adam was not "in God" as before—God had to look outside of Himself to seek Adam, who was lost.) Here God "looks for" Abel who has departed from life—this for Cain's benefit, for Abel has returned, really, to the bosom of God. Hence God does not call Abel, but He asks Cain, "Where is Abel?" Cain's answer is arrogant and nasty. Sin has progressed. {He shows} contempt for God and for his brother {with} the answer of pride and hatred that seeks to defend itself in sin. Cain is saying in effect, "Mind your own business." This flows logically from the fact that by sin man has become "as a god,"[60] knowing good and evil. Cain claims the right to be the arbiter of his own fate. This he can be in the sense of choosing or rejecting God—not in the sense of determining, at pleasure, what is good and evil for himself. {In} verse 10–11, the voice of Abel cries out from the earth: Cain is cursed by the earth drenched in the blood of Abel (not "upon the earth"). There is an additional curse then in the earth tilled by man: it is watered by the blood of fratricidal wars and bears witness against man, while providing nourishment for him. It will no longer be so generous in its gifts to him. {Verse} 13 {tells of} Cain's despair: Cain falls from pride into despair (the sin of the proud) and feels himself driven out from the face of God and man. Terrified of becoming a wanderer and exile, he feels that everyone will be his enemy—but no, as soon as he himself becomes poor and weak, the sign of the Lord is upon him to protect him. Cain then flees to the east side of Eden (?).

Cain and Abel in the New Testament:

1. Read Luke 11:47 ff.:[61] Woe to you who build the monuments of the prophets, etc.

---

58. Gen 4:8.
59. Gen 4:9.
60. Gen 3:5.
61. "Woe to you who build the monuments of the prophets: and your fathers killed them. Truly you bear witness that you consent to the doings of your fathers: for they indeed killed them, and you build their sepulchres. For this cause also the wisdom of God said: I will send to them prophets and apostles; and some of them they will kill and persecute. That the blood of all the prophets which was shed from the foundation

God will send prophets to Jerusalem, and in rejecting them Jerusalem will reject the wisdom of God and "the blood of all the prophets that was shed from the beginning of the world shall be required of this generation, *from the blood of Abel*" etc. Then read the same passage in Matthew 23:29–{39}[62] and note the desolation of Jerusalem, which is the desolation of Cain. Jerusalem in respect of the gentiles is the "elder son," rich and strong, deprived of inheritance for the weak and despised. Yet the Jews wander over the face of the world, protected, as was Cain, by God's mark upon their foreheads, killed by everyone and never extinguished, and those who kill them receive sevenfold punishment.

2. Read Hebrews 11:1–5:[63] Abel's sacrifice was a sacrifice of faith, {and so} pleasing to God for that reason. Cain {was} rejected because he trusted not in God but in himself. The author of Hebrews loves to think

---

of the world, may be required of this generation, From the blood of Abel unto the blood of Zacharias, who was slain between the altar and the temple: Yea I say to you, It shall be required of this generation. Woe to you lawyers, for you have taken away the key of knowledge: you yourselves have not entered in, and those that were entering in, you have hindered" (vv. 47–52).

62. "Woe to you scribes and Pharisees, hypocrites; that build the sepulchres of the prophets, and adorn the monuments of the just, And say: If we had been in the days of our Fathers, we would not have been partakers with them in the blood of the prophets. Wherefore you are witnesses against yourselves, that you are the sons of them that killed the prophets. Fill ye up then the measure of your fathers. You serpents, generation of vipers, how will you flee from the judgment of hell? Therefore behold I send to you prophets, and wise men, and scribes: and some of them you will put to death and crucify, and some you will scourge in your synagogues, and persecute from city to city: That upon you may come all the just blood that hath been shed upon the earth, from the blood of Abel the just, even unto the blood of Zacharias the son of Barachias, whom you killed between the temple and the altar. Amen I say to you, all these things shall come upon this generation. Jerusalem, Jerusalem, thou that killest the prophets, and stonest them that are sent unto thee, how often would I have gathered together thy children, as the hen doth gather her chickens under her wings, and thou wouldest not? Behold, your house shall be left to you, desolate. For I say to you, you shall not see me henceforth till you say: Blessed is he that cometh in the name of the Lord" (copy text reads: "29–29").

63. "Now faith is the substance of things to be hoped for, the evidence of things that appear not. For by this the ancients obtained a testimony. By faith we understand that the world was framed by the word of God; that from invisible things visible things might be made. By faith Abel offered to God a sacrifice exceeding that of Cain, by which he obtained a testimony that he was just, God giving testimony to his gifts; and by it he being dead yet speaketh. By faith Henoch was translated, that he should not see death; and he was not found, because God had translated him: for before his translation he had testimony that he pleased God."

of the eloquence of Abel's blood: read Hebrews 12:22-29,[64] a magnificent passage which sees the Blood of Christ as God's voice moving both heaven and earth at the end of the world. {There is a} return here to the idea of Abel entering by the sacrifice of his life into the eternal and immovable riches of God's mercy, and Cain by his crime being cast out into the shifting, unstable, unsubstantial desert of time, to end in nothingness. This then is the "way of Cain" (read Jude 7-11[65] against the leaders of the Gnostics).

Cainites and Sethites: 4:17 ff.—Cainites: Cain begets Henoch and *builds a city*; {he} calls it after the name of his son. {This is the} beginning of the self-sufficient city, {the} civilization of man. {There are} other contributions of the Cainites: Jabel is the father of tent-dwellers and herdsmen (20); Jubal, {the} brother of Jabel {is the} father of harpers and musicians (21); Tubal Cain {is the} "hammerer and artificer in every work of brass" (22). Note verse 23-24: Lamech, the tough-guy, {the} fighter, sings a savage song of triumph. He has slain two men, a man and a stripling, who had injured him. He is proud of his strength and his ability to take revenge, and he boasts that while Cain is revenged seven times, he, Lamech, will be revenged seventy times seven (cf. St. Matthew: forgive

---

64. "But you are come to mount Sion, and to the city of the living God, the heavenly Jerusalem, and to the company of many thousands of angels, And to the church of the firstborn, who are written in the heavens, and to God the judge of all, and to the spirits of the just made perfect, And to Jesus the mediator of the new testament, and to the sprinkling of blood which speaketh better than that of Abel. See that you refuse him not that speaketh. For if they escaped not who refused him that spoke upon the earth, much more shall not we, that turn away from him that speaketh to us from heaven. Whose voice then moved the earth; but now he promiseth, saying: Yet once more, and I will move not only the earth, but heaven also. And in that he saith, Yet once more, he signifieth the translation of the moveable things as made, that those things may remain which are immoveable. Therefore receiving an immoveable kingdom, we have grace; whereby let us serve, pleasing God, with fear and reverence. For our God is a consuming fire."

65. "As Sodom and Gomorrha, and the neighbouring cities, in like manner, having given themselves to fornication, and going after other flesh, were made an example, suffering the punishment of eternal fire. In like manner these men also defile the flesh, and despise dominion, and blaspheme majesty. When Michael the archangel, disputing with the devil, contended about the body of Moses, he durst not bring against him the judgment of railing speech, but said: The Lord command thee. But these men blaspheme whatever things they know not: and what things soever they naturally know, like dumb beasts, in these they are corrupted. Woe unto them, for they have gone in the way of Cain: and after the error of Balaam they have for reward poured out themselves, and have perished in the contradiction of Core."

seventy times seven[66]). With Lamech and the Cainites, man is travelling directly away from the ways of the Lord into self-sufficiency, craftiness, pride, violence. {Verses} 4:25 ff.—*Sethites*: Adam has another son, Seth, to replace Abel, who was killed (compare Genesis 4:{25}[67] and Isaias 1:9[68]—the necessity of "a seed"). Seth's son *Enos* (man in his weakness) {is} the first to call upon the name of Yahweh. {Here is an} interesting contrast with the strength and pride of Lamech, praising himself. {This is the} beginning of religion *as we know it*, calling upon the Lord through a *Name*, suggesting that Adam had known Him before without name, as it were, immediately. This could not go on—God had to be known by a Name, although He had no name. {Note the} importance of this idea of a NAME for God. *Enoch* {is} a striking figure among the descendants of Seth. He lives less than the others, but his life attains a perfect mystical number.[69] He walked with God (this is said twice[70]); GOD TOOK HIM. Dom Damasus says:[71] he lives as many years as the sun has days; his name means beginning or initiation; it points mysteriously to the dawn of a new day; he walks with God after the birth of his first son; it is not said of him, as of the others, "and he died"; {this is a} prophecy of the mercy of Christ and life in God. {See} two texts on Enoch from Ecclesiasticus: Eccli. 44:16: Henoch pleased God and was translated *into paradise*, that *he may* give repentance to the nations; 49:16: no man was born on the earth like Henoch, for he also was taken up from the earth. (See also WISDOM 4:7–14, {which} speaks of Henoch again, without naming him.) {In} Hebrews 11:5, by faith Henoch was translated, that he should not see death, and he was not found because God had translated him, for before his translation he had testimony that he had pleased God. {In} Apocalypse 11:3 ff., read the passage about the "two witnesses,"[72] the *duae olivae*—

66. Matt 18:22.

67. "Adam also knew his wife again: and she brought forth a son, and called his name Seth, saying: God hath given me another seed for Abel, whom Cain slew" (copy text reads: 4:26).

68. "Except the Lord of hosts had left us seed, we had been as Sodom, and we should have been like to Gomorrha."

69. "And all the days of Henoch were three hundred and sixty-five years" (Gen 5:23).

70. Gen 5:22, 24.

71. Winzen, *Pathways*, 1.5.

72. "And I will give unto my two witnesses, and they shall prophesy a thousand two hundred sixty days, clothed in sackcloth. These are the two olive trees, and the two candlesticks, that stand before the Lord of the earth. And if any man will hurt them,

Elias and Henoch—cf. their translation in v. 12. {In} Jude 14–15, Henoch prophesies the Last Judgement (according to Jewish tradition—{a} quote from {the} apocryphal books of Henoch[73]). The fascinating mystery of Henoch {is also evident elsewhere}—note the apocalypses of Henoch:[74] {In} 1 Henoch[75]—the *Ethiopic Henoch*, written after 200 B.C. {and} before 1 B.C.—Henoch intercedes[76] for the "angelic watchers" who fell because of their love for the daughters of men (Gen. 6:1–4). {There are} messianic prophecies and {a} prophecy of judgement—quote from this.[77] See

---

fire shall come out of their mouths, and shall devour their enemies. And if any man will hurt them, in this manner must he be slain. These have power to shut heaven, that it rain not in the days of their prophecy: and they have power over waters to turn them into blood, and to strike the earth with all plagues as often as they will. And when they shall have finished their testimony, the beast, that ascendeth out of the abyss, shall make war against them, and shall overcome them, and kill them. And their bodies shall lie in the streets of the great city, which is called spiritually, Sodom and Egypt, where their Lord also was crucified. And they of the tribes, and peoples, and tongues, and nations, shall see their bodies for three days and a half: and they shall not suffer their bodies to be laid in sepulchres. And they that dwell upon the earth shall rejoice over them, and make merry: and shall send gifts one to another, because these two prophets tormented them that dwelt upon the earth. And after three days and a half, the spirit of life from God entered into them. And they stood upon their feet, and great fear fell upon them that saw them. And they heard a great voice from heaven, saying to them: Come up hither. And they went up to heaven in a cloud: and their enemies saw them" (vv. 3–12).

73. See Willmering, "Epistle of St Jude," 1192 [n. 961e]: "The prophecy of Henoch is not contained in Scripture, but is found almost verbatim in the apocryphal *Book of Henoch*, I, 9."

74. See Foster, "Apocrypha," 122 [nn. 92h–j].

75. Charles, *Apocrypha and Pseudepigrapha*, 2.163–277.

76. 1 Enoch 12–16 (Charles, *Apocrypha and Pseudepigrapha*, 2.195–99).

77. "And I saw till a throne was erected in the pleasant land, and the Lord of the sheep sat Himself thereon, and the other took the sealed books and opened those books before the Lord of the sheep. And the Lord called those men the seven first white ones, and commanded that they should bring before Him, beginning with the first star which led the way, all the stars whose privy members were like those of horses, and they brought them all before Him. And He said to that man who wrote before Him, being one of those seven white ones, and said unto him: 'Take those seventy shepherds to whom I delivered the sheep, and who taking them on their own authority slew more than I commanded them.' And behold they were all bound, I saw, and they all stood before Him. And the judgement was held first over the stars, and they were judged and found guilty, and went to the place of condemnation, and they were cast into an abyss, full of fire and flaming, and full of pillars of fire. And those seventy shepherds were judged and found guilty, and they were cast into that fiery abyss. And I saw at that time how a like abyss was opened in the midst of the earth, full of fire, and they brought those blinded sheep, and they were all judged and found guilty and cast into this fiery

CBC: "And before the sun and the heavenly signs were created, before the stars were made, his [i.e. the Messias] name was named before the Lord of spirits. He shall be a staff for the just, that they may lean upon him and not fall: *he shall be the light of the peoples, and he shall be the hope of those who suffer in their hearts.* All those who dwell upon the dry land shall prostrate themselves and adore him, and they shall bless and sing praises to the Lord of Spirits."[78] Other matters {are also found} in 1 Henoch: {a} vision of the flood, of {the} future history of Israel, etc. etc. 2 Henoch[79]—the *Slavonic Henoch*—deals mostly with his assumption, his

---

abyss, and they burned; now this abyss was to the right of that house. And I saw those sheep burning and their bones burning. And I stood up to see till they folded up that old house; and carried off all the pillars, and all the beams and ornaments of the house were at the same time folded up with it, and they carried it off and laid it in a place in the south of the land. And I saw till the Lord of the sheep brought a new house greater and loftier than that first, and set it up in the place of the first which had been folded up: all its pillars were new, and its ornaments were new and larger than those of the first, the old one which He had taken away, and all the sheep were within it. And I saw all the sheep which had been left, and all the beasts on the earth, and all the birds of the heaven, falling down and doing homage to those sheep and making petition to and obeying them in every thing. And thereafter those three who were clothed in white and had seized me by my hand [who had taken me up before], and the hand of that ram also seizing hold of me, they took me up and set me down in the midst of those sheep before the judgement took place. And those sheep were all white, and their wool was abundant and clean. And all that had been destroyed and dispersed, and all the beasts of the field, and all the birds of the heaven, assembled in that house, and the Lord of the sheep rejoiced with great joy because they were all good and had returned to His house. And I saw till they laid down that sword, which had been given to the sheep, and they brought it back into the house, and it was sealed before the presence of the Lord, and all the sheep were invited into that house, but it held them not. And the eyes of them all were opened, and they saw the good, and there was not one among them that did not see. And I saw that that house was large and broad and very full. And I saw that a white bull was born, with large horns, and all the beasts of the field and all the birds of the air feared him and made petition to him all the time. And I saw till all their generations were transformed, and they all became white bulls; and the first among them became a lamb, and that lamb became a great animal and had great black horns on its head; and the Lord of the sheep rejoiced over it and over all the oxen. And I slept in their midst: and I awoke and saw everything. This is the vision which I saw while I slept, and I awoke and blessed the Lord of righteousness and gave Him glory. Then I wept with a great weeping and my tears stayed not till I could no longer endure it: when I saw, they flowed on account of what I had seen; for everything shall come and be fulfilled, and all the deeds of men in their order were shown to me" (1 Enoch 90:20-41 [Charles, *Apocrypha and Pseudepigrapha*, 2.259-60).

78. 1 Enoch 48:3-5 (Foster, "Apocrypha," 122 [n. 92i], which reads: ". . . light of peoples . . ." [emphasis added]).

79. Charles *Apocrypha and Pseudepigrapha*, 2:425-69.

passage through the angelic choirs, and the fallen angels asking him to pray for them (probably written {in the} first century of our era). Henoch {was} the great-grandfather of Noe.

Noe and the Deluge

Preamble: the state of mankind in Noe's time (Gen. 6:1–4): *the "sons of God and the daughters of men."*[80] {This is a} mysterious text, {intended} to explain a race of "supermen" before the deluge—giants, *nephilim*, born of the union of angels and men—taken up from pagan mythology? (cf. {the} Titans). Some Fathers thought the "sons of God" were angels—fallen angels; others thought sons of God were Sethites, sons of men Cainites. *CBC* thinks it just means that "men," the "sons of God," indiscriminately took to wife anyone they felt like—"the daughters of men."[81] In a word, it is a problem without {a} full solution. God limits the age of man to 120 years; or (*CBC*[82]) He gives them 120 years to repent before the flood. ({For} Nephilim, check {the} cross-references given in {the} Douay Bible.[83])

The corruption of mankind (Gen. 6:5 ff.): READ 5–7,[84] one of the most moving descriptions of sin and its consequences, moving precisely because {it is} anthropomorphic. God does not "regret" the creation, but there is something about sin and about God that we cannot understand unless we see it as it is expressed in verses 5–7 here. Man, completely turned away from God, "thinking of evil at all times," has become in fact "nothing," yet thinks himself to be something. God, "touched inwardly with sorrow" ({this} indicates the separation of man from reality, which is in God and the will of God), meditates the extinction of man. Return to the picture of the desert tribe telling this story—it is necessary for us to think of One, beyond the emptiness of the desert, Who feels a cosmic

---

80. Gen 6:2.

81. Sutcliffe, "Genesis," 189 [n. 146j].

82. Sutcliffe, "Genesis," 189 [n. 146j].

83. Bar 3:26, Amos 2:9, Wis 14:6; Sutcliffe, "Genesis," 189 [n. 146k] refers to Num 13:34; Wis 14:6; Eccli [Sir] 16:8; Bar 3:26–28.

84. "And God seeing that the wickedness of men was great on the earth, and that all the thought of their heart was bent upon evil at all times, It repented him that he had made man on the earth. And being touched inwardly with sorrow of heart, He said: I will destroy man, whom I have created, from the face of the earth, from man even to beasts, from the creeping thing even to the fowls of the air, for it repenteth me that I have made them."

sorrow at our separation from Him (yet is not man, does not feel as man, is within us, etc.; yet we cannot do without occasional recourse to this way of looking at things).

{Thus the importance of} *Noe*: everything depends on him, for while all the world is "corrupting its way,"[85] Noe is a just man and has found favor in the eyes of God. *God consults Noe* (13): "The end of all flesh is come before me." But there *is* an end of all flesh, and it *will be*. Noe then is Christ, in figure and in mystery. Something is to be enacted here that refers to our own life and death, our own fate before God, and the fate of the whole world. {It foreshadows} baptism, judgement, also the death of Christ {and} the exodus of the Chosen People. So God commands that Noe build the ark (*arca*—box). {Verses} 14–22 {describe} the construction of the ark. {There is the} problem of the dimensions: Origen thought it was forty miles long.[86] {There is} one window and one door—more exactly, a door in the side and a trap door in the roof. It is not a ship that can be maneuvered—only a floating crate. {Verse} 19 {specifies} two of every living creature (cf. 7:2–3, evidence of a second narrative in which seven of each clean creature and two of each unclean {are brought aboard}: a Levitical author[87]).

Read 7:1–6:[88] {note the} *question of the universality of the flood*: (1) geographical universality is no longer insisted upon ({it} would have had

---

85. Gen 6:12.

86. According to Origen, in the second of his *Homilies on Genesis*, the numbers of the cubits given as the dimensions for the ark were intended by Moses to be squared, in conformity with an ancient Egyptian system of computation, yielding a length of 90,000 cubits, a width of 2,500 cubits and a height to 900 cubits (Migne, *PG* 12, cols. 165B–168A). See also Origen, *Contra Celsum* 4:41: "Should we not rather admire a construction which resembled a very large city? For when we square the measurements, the result is that it was ninety thousand cubits long at the bottom, and two thousand five hundred broad" (Origen, *Contra Celsum*, 217; Migne, *PG* 11, cols. 1095A–1098A).

87. See Lev 11:47 for the distinction between clean and unclean animals; by "Levitical author" here Merton is evidently referring to the Priestly source.

88. "And the Lord said to him: Go in thou and all thy house into the ark: for thee I have seen just before me in this generation. Of all clean beasts take seven and seven, the male and the female. But of the beasts that are unclean two and two, the male and the female. Of the fowls also of the air seven and seven, the male and the female: that seed may be saved upon the face of the whole earth. For yet a while, and after seven days, I will rain upon the earth forty days and forty nights; and I will destroy every substance that I have made, from the face of the earth. And Noe did all things which the Lord had commanded him. And he was six hundred years old, when the waters of the flood overflowed the earth."

to cover Mt. Everest, etc.); (2) Many authors also insist that it was not anthropologically universal ({the} Chinese, Japanese, etc. have no deluge story—{descended} from other sons of Adam). Non-biblical flood stories {such as the} Babylonian and Hindu include {the} idea of an ark in which the animals are saved; other flood stories {are} found in Siberia, Germany, Australia.

Chapter 7: *the Flood* (read here Wisdom 14:1–7,[89] especially verse 6–7: "this wood by which justice cometh"). God again gives warning—seven days (v. 4). Read ch. 7:7 ff.:[90] verses 7–16 {present} the solemnity of the entry into the ark. Two narratives {are} mixed together: {in the} first narrative (7–10), the Yahwist attributes the deluge to a forty-day rain; read 11–16:[91] the Priestly writer attributes it to the breaking of the dike which holds back the upper and nether abyss, resulting in a return to chaos, or an abolition of the separation God made on the second day (v.12 {is an} insertion of Yahwist {material} in {the} sacerdotal). Note {the} special solemnity of verses 11–16: {the passage} opens with a solemn announcement of the exact *day* (*Dies Domini!*[92]); 13: "that very day,

---

89. "Again, another designing to sail, and beginning to make his voyage through the raging waves, calleth upon a piece of wood more frail than the wood that carrieth him. For this the desire of gain devised, and the workman built it by his skill. But thy providence, O Father, governeth it: for thou hast made a way even in the sea, and a most sure path among the waves, shewing that thou art able to save out of all things, yea though a man went to sea without art. But that the works of thy wisdom might not be idle: therefore men also trust their lives even to a little wood, and passing over the sea by ship are saved. And from the beginning also when the proud giants perished, the hope of the world fleeing to a vessel, which was governed by thy hand, left to the world seed of generation. For blessed is the wood, by which justice cometh."

90. "And Noe went in and his sons, his wife and the wives of his sons with him into the ark, because of the waters of the flood. And of beasts clean and unclean, and of fowls, and of every thing that moveth upon the earth, Two and two went in to Noe into the ark, male and female, as the Lord had commanded Noe. And after the seven days were passed, the waters of the flood overflowed the earth" (vv. 7–10).

91. "In the six hundredth year of the life of Noe, in the second month, in the seventeenth day of the month, all the fountains of the great deep were broken up, and the floodgates of heaven were opened: And the rain fell upon the earth forty days and forty nights. In the selfsame day Noe, and Sem, and Cham, and Japheth, his sons: his wife, and the three wives of his sons with them, went into the ark. They and every beast according to its kind, and all the cattle in their kind, and every thing that moveth upon the earth, according to its kind, and every fowl according to its kind, all birds, and all that fly, Went in to Noe into the ark, two and two of all flesh, wherein was the breath of life. And they that went in, went in male and female of all flesh, as God had commanded him: and the Lord shut him in on the outside."

92. "the Day of the Lord" (see Amos 5:18; Is 13:6; Jer 46:10; Ezek 30:3; Zeph 1:14; Joel 1:15).

Noe etc. entered into the ark"; 14: the list of all the creatures "according to its kind" entering into the ark; 15: "went in to Noe into the ark"—{a} picture of all living things gathered around Noe in the darkness of the ark—all life, all male and female; 16: And God shuts the door from the outside. This is a tremendous picture, and in mystery we must seek its meaning. Let us recapitulate: (1) *the chaos has returned*: the separation of abyss from abyss by God is abolished {and} all life, all the known world, is in chaos—one element, water, invades everything else and takes over; (2) *all life is gathered around Noe in the darkness of the ark*, where they have gone by the command of God; (3) there is only one window, no decks, no nothing—no bridge, no steering gear—all life, hidden in the ark with Noe, is *abandoned to the mercy of God in complete darkness*; (4) God Himself has shut the door from the outside, emphasizing the fact that His mercy and Providence have shut them in, and they depend entirely on Him. What is the great dogmatic truth that is thus taught? {Now comes} *the Deluge*—17: the waters swell and the ark begins to float; 18: the waters overflow exceedingly and the ark floats away, abandoned to the waters; 19: the highest mountains are covered; 21: then every living being "that has breath" perishes; 23: {there is a} solemn announcement of the death of everything that was not with Noe in the ark; 24: the "waters prevail" {for} 150 days.

The Flood recedes (c. 8)—1: "Then God remembered Noe" again—note the force of this anthropomorphic expression. It tells a spiritual truth that could not have been otherwise rendered—for instance by something abstract. He remembers not only Noe, but all the beasts huddled around him in the ark—a marvelous sentence! It implies that in the darkness of the deluge, Noe was "forgotten" by God, not left alone, but forgotten, because he was enclosed as it were in the inmost heart of God's Providence. 2: He closes up the fountains of the deep; He stops the rain; the waters dry up. 4: The twenty-seventh day of the seventh month, the ark rests on the mountains of Armenia. Three months pass; the tops of the mountains appear. Forty days later Noe opens the trap door in the roof of the ark and sends forth the crow; then the dove (v. 9)—she does not find anywhere to land (as opposed to v. 5, when the mountain tops have appeared); she returns and Noe "put forth his hand and caught her and brought her in into the ark"—a beautiful touch ({the} Yahwist writer). Seven days later the dove returns at evening with the olive branch, sign of vegetation—another seven days and she does not return at all (11–12). {In} verse 13 {is the} final, solemn announcement of the end of it all—again the precise day. Noe opens up the roof of the ark and looks out ({the} first time he has really looked out himself) and sees that the earth is dry.

Noe's sacrifice and the alliance (8:20–22): the end of the story, *the most important part, is the reconciliation of God with man by Noe's sacrifice.* God orders Noe to come forth (he waits for God's order!). God orders all the living beings to increase and multiply—therefore this is a new creation. They all emerge in an orderly procession, Noe and his wife coming first. {Verses} 20 ff. {tell of} Noe's sacrifice. He builds an altar and offers one of each of the pure animals (of which, remember, seven had entered the ark according to the priestly narrative). Verse 21 {is the} first time the Lord is said to be appeased by the odor of sacrifices, and He says "within Himself, I will no more curse the earth for the sake of man." He takes account of the fact that man is prone to evil from his youth and *promises to save the world anyway.* {Verse} 22 {gives} God's promise that the earth will go on in spite of man's wickedness.

Some conclusions about the Deluge narrative:

1. The essential truth that is being told here concerns man's reconciliation with God. The historical "fact" of the deluge and Noe's ark is not the main thing. It is of course absolutely necessary too, but it is not possible for us to understand everything about that fact, told here in popular poetic language. After establishing the broad outlines of the fact, our main purpose should be to find out the truth God is really trying to tell us.

2. Now the spiritual truth of the narrative is first of all contained in the *literal* meaning. {First is} the return of chaos. One man and his family, and all living beings, are enclosed by God in the darkness of the ark and left to the mercy of God. They remain in the ark while all else is destroyed. They emerge at God's command to occupy a "new creation" and "increase and multiply."[93] Noe offers sacrifice, God is appeased, and He promises the earth will continue in spite of the fact that He knows man will once again be wicked. Hence what the narrative says—the true purification from sin—is something God Himself brings about, by His love, mercy and wisdom. This purification destroys much that lives; it is a cleansing, a complete drowning of much that lives and thrives on earth. But all the essence of life remains. It remains by taking refuge in darkness and silence, gathered around Noe, the representative of God in the world—the

---

93. Gen 9:1; cf. Gen 1:28.

Father, the Savior, the Builder, the Provider. Even Noe is in the dark, and does not know what is going on. In order to find things out, he makes use of the birds entrusted to him, sending them forth from the ark, and receiving the timid dove back in his own hands. Noe, the Provider and Protector, has a gentle love for the life entrusted to him. Note: *all life* is entrusted to the care of Noe. When the flood recedes, Noe and the other living beings await the command of God to come forth, and at God's command they become fertile and fill the earth. Noe offers sacrifice and God is appeased.

3. Some very important facts here {include}:

   a) God is appeased both by the deluge and by Noe's sacrifice. The deluge purifies, and is God's work. The sacrifice is a gesture of thanksgiving and recognition, and is Noe's part—besides the building and management of the ark.

   b) It is God Who destroys sin, not Noe. Noe makes provision for himself and for all life, in darkness, in which he allows himself to be enclosed with them by God. Abandonment to the mercy and providence of God is an essential part of our penance, our transformation. God is the One Who must transform all. Our function is to let Him do so, and to rest in the night of faith with "all life," gathered in the mystery of life into which we withdraw, leaving God to work what we do not know. We are content to "be" and God works. {In the} mystery of silence, abandonment, faith, hope, rest, humility, {we are} *waiting* for God. Waiting is of the very essence of penance—patience, remaining enclosed, silent, in hope.

   c) Greater fertility is the result of this, but we must wait God's time, the right day, the day appointed by Him. Then, at His command, we come forth and produce—but not before. Our sacrifice is then offered in the days of fertility, not in the days of darkness, as a recognition that God has done the work.

Noe in the Other Books of the Bible:

A. Old Testament:

Ecclesiasticus 44 (praise of the men of renown): vv. 17–19: Noe was perfect and just; he was a mediator—"in time of wrath a reconciliation." Note: this is the first time in the Bible that we see a man by his actions averting the wrath of God—{this is} very important. Because of him a *remnant* was left—{the} notion of remnant {is} very important too. The Sethites were in a sense a remnant of Abel, but the first "remnant" is the group saved in the ark. We shall see how the Bible uses this idea, especially {the} New Testament. The covenants of the world were made with him—{the} idea of the alliance.

{*The*} *Prophets—Isaias and Ezechiel*: Isaias 54:7-14—As in the days of Noe when Israel was not yet: {this is a} great passage on the mercy of God to the Gentiles, making them His Church. God Himself {is} speaking through the prophet: "For a small moment have I forsaken thee, but with great mercies will I gather thee"—{note the} contrast between the transitory character of His wrath and His everlasting mercy. God recalls His promise to Noe: "so I have sworn not to be angry with thee and not to rebuke thee." My mercy shall not depart from thee . . . the covenant of my peace shall not be moved . . . O poor little one, tossed with tempest, etc.—{this} suggests the remnant adrift in the deluge (he is speaking to Gentiles). He will build His people on a foundation of precious stones (the peace after Noe's sacrifice—the color of the rainbow and the glittering of the sapphires and the jasper). In all this we see Noe as {a} type of Christ. Ezechiel 14:14 ff. seems to contradict the above: God threatens Jerusalem with destruction, and if there were to be in the city Noe, Daniel and Job (Daniel is not the prophet Daniel {but} Danel, {a} Phoenician sage[94]), types of the three just men, they shall not save others, but only themselves. Is there *no remnant*? However, in the end (v. 22) there "shall be some left in it that shall be saved and that shall save sons and daughters." They shall escape from Jerusalem to those in exile, and "comfort them," but *BJ* notes[95] that this comfort will come from the fact that their conduct will be so bad that it will explain the fate of Jerusalem. {The} explanation {is that} Ezechiel always emphasizes *personal responsibility*. This does not contradict the doctrine of the remnant, for the remnant is in fact *among those in Babylon*.

B. New Testament:

Matthew 24:37 {focuses on the} *eschatological import of the deluge*: "As in the days of Noe, so also shall the coming of the son of Man be." READ vv. 36-44,[96] on the importance of vigilance at the last day, "The

---

94. See Auvray, *Ezéchiel*, 58.

95. "Leurs oeuvres mauvaises dont le spectacle justifie la traitement que Dieu fait subir à Jerusalem" (Auvray, *Ezéchiel*, 59).

96. "But of that day and hour no one knoweth, not the angels of heaven, but the Father alone. And as in the days of Noe, so shall also the coming of the Son of man

Day" of the Son of Man (cf. {the} exactitude of the days recorded in {the} Genesis account of the flood: "even till that day in which Noe entered into the ark"—recall {the} solemnity of the description of that entrance). Clearly the deluge is {a} type of {the} Last Judgement—all the rest of the world "knew not until the flood came," but those who obeyed Noe knew. Christ, our Noe, tells us to watch—the time will come for us to enter the ark and be saved, but we do not know when. We must await His signal (read Luke 17:22-37[97]).

{In} 1 Peter 3:18-22, *the Deluge {is} a type of baptism*. Jesus dies for our sins to offer us to God. He dies in the flesh; He rises "Spirit" and "preaches to those spirits who are in prison." This is an allusion to His descent into hell. To whom does He preach in hell? to the fallen spirits, say some. Others say He preaches to those who would not believe in the days of Noe (v. 20 says this clearly, hence {there is} no doubt about it). It is said that these souls, many of whom may have had a certain measure

---

be. For as in the days before the flood, they were eating and drinking, marrying and giving in marriage, even till that day in which Noe entered into the ark, And they knew not till the flood came, and took them all away; so also shall the coming of the Son of man be. Then two shall be in the field: one shall be taken, and one shall be left. Two women shall be grinding at the mill: one shall be taken, and one shall be left. Watch ye therefore, because ye know not what hour your Lord will come. But know this ye, that if the goodman of the house knew at what hour the thief would come, he would certainly watch, and would not suffer his house to be broken open. Wherefore be you also ready, because at what hour you know not the Son of man will come."

97. "And he said to his disciples: The days will come, when you shall desire to see one day of the Son of man; and you shall not see it. And they will say to you: See here, and see there. Go ye not after, nor follow them: For as the lightning that lighteneth from under heaven, shineth unto the parts that are under heaven, so shall the Son of man be in his day. But first he must suffer many things, and be rejected by this generation. And as it came to pass in the days of Noe, so shall it be also in the days of the Son of man. They did eat and drink, they married wives, and were given in marriage, until the day that Noe entered into the ark: and the flood came and destroyed them all. Likewise as it came to pass, in the days of Lot: they did eat and drink, they bought and sold, they planted and built. And in the day that Lot went out of Sodom, it rained fire and brimstone from heaven, and destroyed them all. Even thus shall it be in the day when the Son of man shall be revealed. In that hour, he that shall be on the housetop, and his goods in the house, let him not go down to take them away: and he that shall be in the field, in like manner, let him not return back. Remember Lot's wife. Whosoever shall seek to save his life, shall lose it: and whosoever shall lose it, shall preserve it. I say to you: in that night there shall be two men in one bed; the one shall be taken, and the other shall be left. Two women shall be grinding together: the one shall be taken, and the other shall be left: two men shall be in the field; the one shall be taken, and the other shall be left. They answering, say to him: Where, Lord? Who said to them: Wheresoever the body shall be, thither will the eagles also be gathered together."

of justice, were considered sufficiently punished by the deluge and were ultimately saved—a consoling thought—all the primitive men of prehistoric times who did their best to live according to conscience were not damned, but some were ultimately saved—so too savages and pagans. Verse 20 {says} "a few, that is eight souls were saved by water"—the remnant; verse 21 clearly states that baptism is the antitype. Our life "in Christ" is like the life of the souls gathered around Noe in the ark—our life hidden with Christ in God.[98] At the last judgement Christ will offer His Church to God (cf. Noe's sacrifice, and verse 18 above) and we will enter into the fertility and abundance of the new creation.

{In} 2 Peter 2:4–10, the Deluge is a figure (a) of the trials of the just; (b) of the Last Judgement. Note here as in Luke 17, Noe is associated with Lot {and} the destruction of Sodom and Gomorrha is compared to the deluge—"but spared Noe the eighth person, the preacher of justice."

{In} Hebrews 11:7, Noe's faith is a condemnation of the world; he was made "heir of justice which is by faith."

The Tower of Babel

{For} the sons of Cham see 9:22–25: Cham {is} cursed by Noe; (Gen. 10:6 ff.: from Cham come the Egyptians, Babylonians, Assyrians, Canaanites, etc.) Chus—Nemrod (v. 9) {is} a stout hunter before the Lord—again, a tough guy, self-sufficient, strong in human means, ancestor of the Babylonians and Ninivites: {according to} verse 10, "the beginning of his kingdom was Babylon," that is, he first began to reign in Babylon, considered as the *first city* that ever existed; hence {it} becomes a type of the "city of this world," as Jerusalem is {the} type of the City of God. St. Augustine {in his} *Commentary on Psalm 64*[99] speaks of Jerusalem and Babylon: (1) Babylon (*confusio*[100]) {is the} city of Cain; Jerusalem (*pacis visio*[101]) {is the} city of Abel; (2) in the present life they are so mixed together that we cannot separate them; (3) at the Last Judgement their difference will be made clear, {with} Babylon at the left Hand of the Lord {and} Jerusalem at His right—known by what? *charity*; (4) *Duas istas civitates faciunt duo*

---

98. Col 3:3.
99. Augustine, *In Psalmum LXIV Enarratio* (Migne, *PL* 36, cols. 772–85).
100. "confusion" (n. 2 [Migne, *PL* 36, col. 773]).
101. "vision of peace" (n. 2 [Migne, *PL* 36, col. 773]).

amores: Jerusalem facit amor Dei, Babylon facit amor saeculi[102]—if you test yourself by what you love, then if you find you belong to Babylon, root up cupidity and plant charity; if you find you belong to Jerusalem, bear with your captivity and hope for liberty; (5) the Scriptures are letters from God in which He awakens in us love for our homeland—it is by desire that we tend thither; by hope we are already anchored in heaven, though tossed by the storms of this world. He adds, when we chant in choir our voices can be heard also by the citizens of Babylon, but our hearts can only be heard by God in Sion (*Te decet hymnus Deus in Sion*[103]). Nemrod builds other cities of Mesopotamia—especially Ninive.

{In} chapter 11, the descendents of Nemrod built the Tower of Babel, symbol of man's pride in his own strength. The narrative of the Tower seems inserted as an interpolation, somewhat out of context (the genealogies tend to suggest that man was dispersed everywhere by natural migration—the tower story says it was a punishment).

Verse 1: all the earth was of one tongue—they all used the same words. {We hear of} the nomadic descendants of Noe and their wanderings in the plain of Senaar, and {there they} build a city (here we seem to see another account of the first city—Babel is the first city, Babylon); the "spirit" of the worldly city is the spirit of Babel—pride, domination, arrogant assault on heaven, {the} desire to be equal to God (see Apocalypse c. 17, but especially Isaias 47:7–15).

{Verse} 3 {tells of} the invention of brick; {verse} 4: "Let us build a tower whose top shall reach unto heaven." "Let us make our name famous." One cannot help thinking of New York, etc. in the light of this. There is something very American about the Tower of Babel—an underlying false optimism based on a very fragile unity, an appearance of having one mind and one heart—{but} only an appearance. Men {are} united by pride and self-interest; they hold together as long as there is prosperity. If it fail them . . .?

{Verse} 5: God came down to see the city and the tower (cf. Apocalypse 16:19). Note {the} power of this image. The Old Testament {is} very conscious of the power of God's "look"—cf. St. Benedict:[104] the Presence

---

102. "Two loves make those two cities: the love of God makes Jerusalem; the love of the world makes Babylon" (n. 2 [Migne, *PL* 36, col. 773]).

103. "A hymn, O God, becometh thee in Sion" (Ps 64[65]:2) (n. 3 [Migne, *PL* 36, col. 774]).

104. Discussing the first degree of humility in chapter 7 of the *Rule*, Benedict writes: "*aestimet se homo de caelis a Deo respici omni hora, et facta sua omni loco ab*

of God, the monastic "city" built in the presence of God, and its foundation is humility. The builders of Babel had forgotten God; {they} did not know Him—although the tower may have been a ziggurat or religious pyramid—that is, they did not know Him as He is. They thought of Him as someone only a little more powerful than themselves, someone with whom they could make a deal.

{Verse} 7: "Let us go down and confound their tongues that they may not understand one another's speech." Mankind {is} divided into hostile nations, whose misunderstandings easily develop into bloodthirsty warfare (read ISAIAS 33:19[105]). Contrast Acts 2:1–11 (Pentecost): the formation of the heavenly Jerusalem, {with} the gift of tongues to heal the division caused at Babel and proclaim {the} *wonderful works of God*.

{To} conclude, {look at} Babylon and Jerusalem in {the} Apocalypse: Babylon—c. 18:11–24; Jerusalem—c. 21–22 (cf. Isaias 13:19–22).

ABRAHAM

Abraham is the Father of the People of God, one of the most monumental figures in the Old Testament, {of} tremendous importance. Jesus is the "Son of David, son of Abraham" (Matt. 1:1). With Abraham the history of salvation really begins. {In the story of} Noe and the deluge humanity was saved, in the negative sense that a remnant was spared from complete destruction, but man went on as before—wicked, lost, confused, prone to sin, straying far from God. Now begins the history of God's work to bring man to Himself, God's formation of a Chosen People, to belong to which means to be His son. It will be many centuries before the full meaning of the Chosen People is apparent. The formation of the People of God will not be until after the deliverance from Egypt; the *real* People of God (the Church) will not be manifest until after the descent of the Holy Spirit.

The Importance of Abraham in the New Testament:

---

aspectu Divinitatis videri, et ab angelis omni hora renuntiari" ("let him consider that God is always beholding him from heaven, that his actions are everywhere visible to the eye of the Godhead, and are constantly being reported to God by the angels") (McCann, *Rule*, 38/39). See the discussion of this verse in Merton, *Rule of Saint Benedict*, 176–77.

105. "The shameless people thou shalt not see, the people of profound speech: so that thou canst not understand the eloquence of his tongue, in whom there is no wisdom."

1. The preaching of John (Matt. 3:9): he denounces the Pharisees etc. who believe themselves to be the true sons of Abraham. It is not enough to be a Jew, a physical descendant of Abraham. God can and will miraculously raise up a spiritual descendence for Abraham: "God is able of these stones . . ."

2. Jesus Himself rebukes the Jews, showing that many shall come from the east and west and sit down with Abraham and Isaac and Jacob in the Kingdom of Heaven. This follows the healing of the centurion's servant, and the remark is called forth by the *faith of the centurion* (read Matt. 8:5–13[106]). It is therefore *faith* that makes us sons of Abraham. This makes evident that for the New Testament what is most important about Abraham is not the son and descendence given him by God but the *faith* which God gave him, the faith by which Abraham was able to believe in God's promises and hope against hope.

3. Abraham {was} "justified by faith"[107] rather than by works—a difficult passage which the Protestants misunderstood and twisted to their ruin. Paul is simply saying that justification is not by the Law because Abraham was justified by his belief in God before there was a law, or circumcision or any rites. Hence the promises of God are not for those who are circumcised and ritually "sons of Abraham,"[108] but *for those who have the faith of Abraham* whether they are physically his descendants or not (READ ROM. 4:1–3, 15–25[109]—most im-

---

106. "And when he had entered into Capharnaum, there came to him a centurion, beseeching him, And saying, Lord, my servant lieth at home sick of the palsy, and is grievously tormented. And Jesus saith to him: I will come and heal him. And the centurion making answer, said: Lord, I am not worthy that thou shouldst enter under my roof: but only say the word, and my servant shall be healed. For I also am a man subject to authority, having under me soldiers; and I say to this, Go, and he goeth, and to another, Come, and he cometh, and to my servant, Do this, and he doeth it. And Jesus hearing this, marvelled; and said to them that followed him: Amen I say to you, I have not found so great faith in Israel. And I say to you that many shall come from the east and the west, and shall sit down with Abraham, and Isaac, and Jacob in the kingdom of heaven: But the children of the kingdom shall be cast out into the exterior darkness: there shall be weeping and gnashing of teeth. And Jesus said to the centurion: Go, and as thou hast believed, so be it done to thee. And the servant was healed at the same hour."

107. Rom 5:1.

108. Gal 3:7.

109. "What shall we say then that Abraham hath found, who is our father according to the flesh? For if Abraham were justified by works, he hath whereof to glory,

portant); and Paul (in lines 23–25) points out that for us to have the faith of Abraham and to be sons of Abraham means to believe not just in the promise made to Abraham but *in Christ as the fulfillment of that promise* (24–25). Our justification is in the death of Christ and His Resurrection. We enter "into Christ" by faith and baptism; we remain in Christ by "faith which works through charity"[110]—works {are} absolutely necessary; faith is the first necessary work (cf. John 6) but all the works of charity are essential. Finally, read JOHN 8:31 ff. (to the end)[111]—the great debate of Jesus with the Jews

---

but not before God. For what saith the scripture? Abraham believed God: and it was reputed to him unto justice. . . . For the law worketh wrath. For where there is no law, neither is there transgression. Therefore is it of faith, that according to grace the promise might be firm to all the seed: not to that only which is of the law, but to that also which is of the faith of Abraham, who is the father of us all, (As it is written: I have made thee a father of many nations), before God, whom he believed: who quickeneth the dead and calleth those things that are not, as those that are. Who against hope believed in hope; that he might be made the father of many nations, according to that which was said to him: So shall thy seed be. And he was not weak in faith. Neither did he consider his own body, now dead (whereas he was almost an hundred years old), nor the dead womb of Sara. In the promise also of God he staggered not by distrust: but was strengthened in faith, giving glory to God: Most fully knowing that whatsoever he has promised, he is able also to perform. And therefore it was reputed to him unto justice. Now it is not written only for him. that it was reputed to him unto justice, But also for us, to whom it shall be reputed, if we believe in him that raised up Jesus Christ, our Lord, from the dead, Who was delivered up for our sins and rose again for our justification."

110. Gal 5:6.

111. "Then Jesus said to those Jews, who believed him: If you continue in my word, you shall be my disciples indeed. And you shall know the truth, and the truth shall make you free. They answered him: We are the seed of Abraham, and we have never been slaves to any man: how sayest thou: you shall be free? Jesus answered them: Amen, amen I say unto you: that whosoever committeth sin, is the servant of sin. Now the servant abideth not in the house for ever; but the son abideth for ever. If therefore the son shall make you free, you shall be free indeed. I know that you are the children of Abraham: but you seek to kill me, because my word hath no place in you. I speak that which I have seen with my Father: and you do the things that you have seen with your father. They answered, and said to him: Abraham is our father. Jesus saith to them: If you be the children of Abraham, do the works of Abraham. But now you seek to kill me, a man who have spoken the truth to you, which I have heard of God. This Abraham did not. You do the works of your father. They said therefore to him: We are not born of fornication: we have one Father, even God. Jesus therefore said to them: If God were your Father, you would indeed love me. For from God I proceeded, and came; for I came not of myself, but he sent me: Why do you not know my speech? Because you cannot hear my word. You are of your father the devil, and the desires of your father you will do. He was a murderer from the beginning, and he stood not in

about true sonship of Abraham: the Jews prove they are not sons of Abraham by rejecting Jesus.

The identity of Abraham: chapter 11, v. 10 ff. gives the lineage of Sem, which brings us down to Terah. Terah is the father of Abraham and grandfather of Lot. With his sons and grandsons he moved from Ur to Haran, and there he died (southern Armenia).

The Vocation of Abraham: the sacred writer now starts out to tell the all-important story of the origin of the People of God. This is the result of a free choice on God's part. At a time determined by Him, God calls Abraham to leave his own country and his own people. God will give him a descendence planned by Him.

Chapter 12 (read vv. 1–12[112]):

---

the truth; because truth is not in him. When he speaketh a lie, he speaketh of his own: for he is a liar, and the father thereof. But if I say the truth, you believe me not. Which of you shall convince me of sin? If I say the truth to you, why do you not believe me? He that is of God, heareth the words of God. Therefore you hear them not, because you are not of God. The Jews therefore answered, and said to him: Do not we say well that thou art a Samaritan, and hast a devil? Jesus answered: I have not a devil: but I honour my Father, and you have dishonoured me. But I seek not my own glory: there is one that seeketh and judgeth. Amen, amen I say to you: If any man keep my word, he shall not see death for ever. The Jews therefore said: Now we know that thou hast a devil. Abraham is dead, and the prophets; and thou sayest: If any man keep my word, he shall not taste death for ever. Art thou greater than our father Abraham, who is dead? and the prophets are dead. Whom dost thou make thyself? Jesus answered: If I glorify myself, my glory is nothing. It is my Father that glorifieth me, of whom you say that he is your God. And you have not known him, but I know him. And if I shall say that I know him not, I shall be like to you, a liar. But I do know him, and do keep his word. Abraham your father rejoiced that he might see my day: he saw it, and was glad. The Jews therefore said to him: Thou art not yet fifty years old, and hast thou seen Abraham? Jesus said to them: Amen, amen I say to you, before Abraham was made, I am. They took up stones therefore to cast at him. But Jesus hid himself, and went out of the temple" (vv. 31–59).

112. "And the Lord said to Abram: Go forth out of thy country, and from thy kindred, and out of thy father's house, and come into the land which I shall shew thee. And I will make of thee a great nation, and I will bless thee, and magnify thy name, and thou shalt be blessed. I will bless them that bless thee, and curse them that curse thee, and in thee shall all the kindred of the earth be blessed: So Abram went out as the Lord had commanded him, and Lot went with him: Abram was seventy-five years old when he went forth from Haran. And he took Sarai his wife, and Lot his brother's son, and all the substance which they had gathered, and the souls which they had gotten in Haran: and they went out to go into the land of Chanaan. And when they were come into it, Abram passed through the country into the place of Sichem, as far as the noble vale: now the Chanaanite was at that time in the land. And the Lord appeared to Abram, and said to him: To thy seed will I give this land. And he built there an altar to

1. Yahweh said to Abraham (cf. Acts 7:2 ff.—Stephen says the vocation came to Abraham at Ur, "before he dwelt in Charan"; note in the liturgy [*Ordo Commendationis Animae*]: *Libera Domine animam servi tui sicut liberasti Abraham de Ur chaldaeorum*;[113] in the *Itinerarium*, read the long prayer about Abraham's journeys: "Oh Lord who, having led Abraham out of Ur of the Chaldees didst lead him without harm through all his journeys"[114]). This call of Abraham, the beginning of divinely appointed journeys, is a deep mystery—we shall see it in a minute. Meanwhile, {let us focus on} the vocation: "Leave thy country and thy kindred and thy father's house"—relinquish natural support; for a man to leave his own people and travel alone was hazardous and strange, {and} Ur was the center of the highest civilization at this time (cf. St. Benedict: *a saeculi actibus se facere alienum*[115]). "Go to the country which I will show thee"—{a command} to seek an unknown land, which God alone can find and point out. Note how St. Stephen in the Acts emphasizes the faith and insecurity implied by all this (Acts 7:4-5): "And [God] gave

---

the Lord, who had appeared to him. And passing on from thence to a mountain, that was on the east side of Bethel, he there pitched his tent, having Bethel on the west, and Hai on the east; he built there also an altar to the Lord, and called upon his name. And Abram went forward, going, and proceeding on to the south. And there came a famine in the country; and Abram went down into Egypt, to sojourn there: for the famine was very grievous in the land. And when he was near to enter into Egypt, he said to Sarai his wife: I know that thou art a beautiful woman: And that when the Egyptians shall see thee, they will say: She is his wife: and they will kill me, and keep thee."

113. "O Lord, free the soul of your servant as you freed Abraham from Ur of the Chaldees" (*Rituale Cisterciense*, 196; *Breviarium Cisterciense*, 222*) (from the "Rite for Commending the Soul" [*Rituale Cisterciense*, Bk. 5, c. 5 (192–99); *Breviarium Cisterciense*, 219*–27*]).

114. "*Deus, qui Abraham puerum tuum de Ur Chaldaeorum eductum, per omnes suae peregrinationis vias illaesum custodisti, quaesumus, ut nos famulos tuos custodire digneris: esto nobis, Domine, in procinctu suffragium, in via solatium, in aestu umbraculum, in pluvia et frigore tegumentum, in lassitudine vehiculum, in adversitate praesidium, in lubrico baculus, in naufragio portus; ut te duce quo tendimus, prospere perveniamus, et demum incolumes ad propria redeamus*" ("O God, who led forth and guarded your child Abraham from Ur of the Chaldees unharmed through all the pathways of his pilgrimage, we beg that you deign to guard us your servants: be for us, Lord, support in preparation, comfort on the way, shade in the heat, shelter in rain and cold, uplifting in weariness, protection in adversity, a staff in slippery places, a port in shipwreck, so that with you as the guide where we are heading, we may successfully arrive and safely return at last to our own true home") (from the prayer for those making a journey [*Breviarium Cisterciense*, 228*]).

115. *Rule*, c. 4 (McCann, trans. and ed., *Rule*, 26) ("make ourselves strangers to the ways of the world": Merton's translation in *Rule of Saint Benedict*, 122).

[Abraham] no inheritance in this land—no, not the pace of a foot, but he promised to give it to him in possession and to his seed after him, when as yet he had no child." For at the same time, God has promised childless Abraham, now aged 75, that he will be the father of a great people.

Points {on the} vocation of Abraham:

1. God selects him for a great work, which Abraham does not know or understand. It is in the mind of God. The vocation of Abraham is like a religious vocation. True, we have a clearer idea where we are going and what we are supposed to do—or we think we have a clearer idea than Abraham. Actually, we too are called to do a work we know not. We do not know where our journey will end.

2. This work depends on *Abraham's faith*. Hence that faith is severely tested at various times. The first test is that of the vocation. If Abraham had not responded the consequences might have been disastrous.

3. The whole of Abraham's vocation is contained in the promise, but still he does not see what it is. The promise must be repeated several times, and each time the faith of Abraham will be tested. The severest test will be the sacrifice of Isaac.

4. That Abraham has to go forth from his own people is no accident, nor is it merely a test of his faith. He is not to go just anywhere, but to a promised land. Here we find two things of great importance: (a) the importance of a land especially chosen by God, to be the home of the Kingdom of Promise; (b) the importance of journeys—the mystery of the "journey" in Genesis: man is scattered to the end of the earth, {and} in order to bring man back together, God sends His chosen ones out to travel all over the earth; (c) the journeys have a beginning and an end. The Chosen People will be scattered, but they will return. The Promised Land to which all mankind will return is heaven. The Son of God will journey all over the Promised Land of Palestine. The apostles and their successors will journey all over the world preaching the word of God. In the end mankind will be brought back to unity, to the spiritual homeland, to the Church, to heaven: "*Et demum incolumes ad propria redeamus.*"[116] Every man's life is an apostolic journey. To be called by God is to start on a journey, even though it may not go very far. But we travel through

---

116. See n. 114 above.

time and space, meeting various people, getting involved in certain situations, all of which may seem unimportant, but they all have a bearing on our salvation. The heart of this mystery of travelling is that God Himself is hidden in those He calls and sends; it is He, in them, Who seeks to bring back to unity the scattered family of man; hence the mystery of the stranger, of hospitality, the guest {as} an "angel" or messenger of God.[117] In the materialistic or totalitarian world, this is no longer true: in a business society, the stranger is a customer, another sucker; in a totalitarian society, either you are a policeman, and then the stranger is probably an escapee, {so you need to} look at his papers, or else you are an escapee, and the stranger is probably a policeman. Note how the mystery of iniquity, in the total despiritualization of man, has gone far, apparently, to frustrate God's work. But He works in many different dimensions and areas.

5. Finally, we here see the type and pattern of all vocation. God speaks—God says, "Leave what you know, what you have, what you love. I will lead you to something else—to what you know not, to what you have not, to what you do not yet love." This is the inevitable pattern of vocation: cf. Matt. 10:34–38 (not peace but the sword—he who loves father more than me is not worthy); Luke 14:25 ff. (If anyone comes to me and does not hate his father . . .) (read Matthew 10:34–38;[118] Luke 14:25 ff.[119]); cf. St. John of the Cross: In order to arrive at that which thou knowest not, thou must go by a way that thou knowest not (vol. 1, p. 63[120]).

---

117. See Heb 13:2: "And hospitality do not forget: for by this some, being not aware of it, have entertained angels."

118. "Do not think that I came to send peace upon earth: I came not to send peace, but the sword. For I came to set a man at variance against his father, and the daughter against her mother, and the daughter in law against her mother in law. And a man's enemies shall be they of his own household. He that loveth father or mother more than me, is not worthy of me; and he that loveth son or daughter more than me, is not worthy of me. And he that taketh not up his cross, and followeth me, is not worthy of me."

119. "And there went great multitudes with him. And turning, he said to them: If any man come to me, and hate not his father and mother and wife and children and brethren and sisters, yea and his own life also, he cannot be my disciple. And whosoever doth not carry his cross and come after me cannot be my disciple" (vv. 25–27).

120. Peers, *John of the Cross, Ascent of Mount Carmel*, 1.11; this is part of the series of verse-like maxims, arranged in four stanzas, originally inscribed at the base of the mountain in the sketch that John included preceding the text of the treatise.

6. And as for the promise—is it realized in human terms? Israel never became, humanly speaking, a "great nation"—it was always a small nation. It had a period of prosperity ({cf. the} rather pathetic attempts to exaggerate the power of Solomon in Kings). We who belong to much greater nations, materially, may be tempted to scorn Israel. But the greatness of Israel was that it was the People of God and the custodian of His promises—so too for the Church. The promise to Abraham and the promises of Christ are no indication that the Church will be a great power, humanly speaking, or that when it once seemed to be so that was part of what God promised, a fulfillment. Note the text of the promise (v. 3): "I shall bless those that bless thee . . ." Abraham is the touchstone, the one chosen and favored by God. If we would be in God's favor we must be on good terms with Abraham.

7. "*In thee* shall all the kindred of the earth be blessed" (v. 3). Let us consider this blessing of Abraham:

   a. {For} the idea of a *blessing*, go back to Genesis 9:24–25: Noe curses Cham—this means rejection, disinheritance, degradation; the father rejects the son, despoils him, makes him the servant of his brothers. Noe blesses "the Lord God of Sem": he praises the Lord of Sem, for from Him all true blessings flow. Sem shall be prosperous and mighty because of his union with the true God. Hence to be blessed by one's father is to be in contact with God the Father of all, through the mediation of an earthly father who represents God (cf. St. James, on the Father of Lights etc.: James {1:17}[121]). In blessing Abraham, God is as it were anointing him with a special function to be the father of all the elect, to transmit blessings to all who are his seed, so that in him all the kindred of the earth are blessed. This means that they must all in some way be recognized by Abraham; they must be in the bosom of Abraham. The Jews thought this meant one had to be a visible member of the Chosen People. Actually, to be blessed in Abraham is to become, by the faith like that of Abraham, a member of Christ, in Whom we are really blessed and recognized by the Father.

---

121. Reference omitted in copy text.

b. *Temporal blessings* for Abraham himself and his posterity according to the flesh {follow}: as a reward for faithfully observing God's law, the patriarchs would have riches {and} posterity, and should possess Chanaan (Gen. 15:7; 12:7).

c. *Spiritual blessings* {are} much more important: the children of Abraham will remain in communion with the true God, and not be led away to the worship of false gods that are dead and can do nothing.

d. {There are} *further spiritual blessings*: further than this, the knowledge of the true God was to be communicated to the whole world by the seed of Abraham (read Galatians 3[122]—espe-

---

122. "O senseless Galatians, who hath bewitched you that you should not obey the truth, before whose eyes Jesus Christ hath been set forth, crucified among you? This only would I learn of you: Did you receive the Spirit by the works of the law, or by the hearing of faith? Are you so foolish, that, whereas you began in the Spirit, you would now be made perfect by the flesh? Have you suffered so great things in vain? If it be yet in vain. He therefore who giveth to you the Spirit, and worketh miracles among you; doth he do it by the works of the law, or by the hearing of the faith? As it is written: Abraham believed God, and it was reputed to him unto justice. Know ye therefore, that they who are of faith, the same are the children of Abraham. And the scripture, foreseeing, that God justifieth the Gentiles by faith, told unto Abraham before: In thee shall all nations be blessed. Therefore they that are of faith, shall be blessed with faithful Abraham. For as many as are of the works of the law, are under a curse. For it is written: Cursed is every one, that abideth not in all things, which are written in the book of the law to do them. But that in the law no man is justified with God, it is manifest: because the just man liveth by faith. But the law is not of faith: but, He that doth those things, shall live in them. Christ hath redeemed us from the curse of the law, being made a curse for us: for it is written: Cursed is every one that hangeth on a tree: That the blessing of Abraham might come on the Gentiles through Christ Jesus: that we may receive the promise of the Spirit by faith. Brethren (I speak after the manner of man,) yet a man's testament, if it be confirmed, no man despiseth, nor addeth to it. To Abraham were the promises made and to his seed. He saith not, And to his seeds, as of many: but as of one, And to thy seed, which is Christ. Now this I say, that the testament which was confirmed by God, the law which was made after four hundred and thirty years, doth not disannul, to make the promise of no effect. For if the inheritance be of the law, it is no more of promise. But God gave it to Abraham by promise. Why then was the law? It was set because of transgressions, until the seed should come, to whom he made the promise, being ordained by angels in the hand of a mediator. Now a mediator is not of one: but God is one. Was the law then against the promises of God? God forbid. For if there had been a law given which could give life, verily justice should have been by the law. But the scripture hath concluded all under sin, that the promise, by the faith of Jesus Christ, might be given to them that believe. But before the faith came, we were kept under the law shut up, unto that faith which was to be revealed. Wherefore the law was our pedagogue in Christ, that we might be

cially 5–9, 13–18, 26–29: the blessing of Abraham given to the Gentiles).

Abraham {makes his} *first journey, through Canaan to Egypt* (12:4 ff.): {in} verses 4–5, Abram, seventy-five years old, with his wife Sara, and many children and servants, together with Lot his nephew and all his people, with beasts, etc., {starts}[123] out in a great caravan from Haran. (Abraham had under him 318 men of fighting age—see *CBC*.[124]) {They arrive at} *Sichem*—as far as the noble vale? *BJ* has "the oak of Moré";[125] *CBC* has the "teacher's terebinth"[126] (the same as 35:4—Jacob buries under it the idols of his servants); it is not exactly the Sichem of the Fourth Gospel, but near it (see *CBC* 789[127]). Here the Lord appears, saying, "To thy seed will I give this land," and Abram builds an altar at Sichem "to the Lord Who had appeared to him." {It is} interesting to compare this with the episode in John 4, Jesus and the Samaritan woman at Jacob's well, and Jesus announcing to her first of all that He is the Savior of the world. The *Samaritans* are the first to accept this truth.

{They then proceed to} *Egypt*: see the incident {of} Abram's subterfuge to save his life—Sarai {is} taken into the palace of Pharaoh {and} Abram {is} well-treated, but the Lord scourges Pharaoh. Commentators assert that the "lie" was not a lie, as Sarai was in reality his half-sister,[128] etc., etc., but it is best not to get involved in the moral question—the Patriarchs were on a more primitive ethical level. {The} interest of the mystery here {is that it} foreshadows, in some sense, the sojourn of the chosen people in Egypt, and their deliverance. Was this what the sacred writer intended? What is the purpose of this story?

---

justified by faith. But after the faith is come, we are no longer under a pedagogue. For you are all the children of God by faith, in Christ Jesus. For as many of you as have been baptized in Christ, have put on Christ. There is neither Jew nor Greek: there is neither bond nor free: there is neither male nor female. For you are all one in Christ Jesus. And if you be Christ's, then are you the seed of Abraham, heirs according to the promise."

123. Copy text reads: "start."
124. Sutcliffe, "Genesis," 193 [n. 150b].
125. De Vaux, *Genèse*, 75.
126. Sutcliffe, "Genesis," 193 [n. 150b].
127. Leonard, "St John," 987 [n. 789c].
128. See Sutcliffe, "Genesis," 193 [n. 150c].

Separation of Abram and Lot (c. 13): they return from Egypt, travelling not "to the south"[129] (Douay) but by stages from the south. Again, the immense caravan of Abram and Lot, with their flocks and herdsmen, travels along. There are too many of them for the arid land. The flocks cannot be supported, the herdsmen fight together, {so} Abram and Lot agree to separate. Note the description of the separation (v. 8): Abram says to Lot, let us not quarrel—"behold, the whole land is before thee." Lot, "lifting up his eyes saw all the country about Jordan. . . . It is like the garden of God, like Egypt . . . before God had destroyed Sodom and Gomorrah." Note the real impact of this lies in the fact that Lot picks for himself a land that looks good but which has an evil destiny. Lot lifted up his own eyes—but it was the Lord Himself Who told Abram, lift up thine eyes, and pointed out a better country (READ 14–18[130]); v. 14—"Lift up thine eyes . . . to the north, south, east and west." Lot just looked straight ahead to the Jordan valley and went to dwell there among others. With the saints it is different—they suddenly awake and find that all around them in every direction has been given to them by God. {An} application of the two cases to the spiritual life {can be made}: Lot {has} an ordinary spirituality that gets nowhere, Abram a spirituality guided by God, on an entirely different level. Note that Abram had *given in to Lot* and allowed him to take the first choice, and was left for some time without any special objective of his own (v. 12), until the Lord chose for him. Origen points out[131] the connection with the Beatitudes: "*Blessed are the meek, for they shall possess the land.*"

129. Gen 13:1.

130. "And the Lord said to Abram, after Lot was separated from him: Lift up thy eyes, and look from the place wherein thou now art, to the north and to the south, to the east and to the west. All the land which thou seest, I will give to thee, and to thy seed for ever. And I will make thy seed as the dust of the earth: if any man be able to number the dust of the earth, he shall be able to number thy seed also. Arise and walk through the land in the length, and in the breadth thereof: for I will give it to thee. So Abram removing his tent came and dwelt by the vale of Mambre, which is in Hebron: and he built there an altar to the Lord."

131. This connection, not explicitly stated, is found not in the *Homilies on Genesis* but in Origen's *Notes on Genesis*: "*Etsi Abraham prae mansuetudine eligendi potestatem fecit Lotho; observandum est eum qui elegit, suo delectu non frui, illum autem qui optionem dedit, benedictum habere quod sibi relictum est. . . . Qui virtuti dant operam, eos sequitur a Deo consolatio. Postquam optionem dedit fratri, et ille amoenissimam et uberrimam elegit regionem, apparuit Deus Abrahamo, cujus animam verbis consolatoriis, et bonis promissionibus recreavit, propemodum dicens: Terram hanc minimam et sensibilem contempsisti; ego tibi dabo mansuetorum terram quae est in regione viventium*"

The Expedition of the Four Kings (c. 14): this mysterious story is an insertion, out of context. Its purpose is evidently to show the connection between Abram and Jerusalem. Four kings (none of whom can be identified) come down to make war on five kings in the Palestine area. They defeat the latter; the Kings of Sodom and Gomorrha escape in the bitumen pits {and} the invaders carry off spoils, including Lot and his people. Abram then raises a force of fighting men among his servants and attacks the retiring invaders, delivering Lot. The Kings of Sodom and Gomorrha come forth from hiding and congratulate him, and above all Abram is blessed by MELCHISEDEC (READ 18, to {the} end[132]). {Of} *Melchisedec* (v. 18 ff.) {we learn}: (1) he is King of Salem (Jerusalem—City of Peace) {and} is a Canaanite; (2) he is a priest of the most High God—of the true God—the first reference of any kind to a priest, and to a priest of the True God; there was then someone to whom God had made Himself known besides Abram—perhaps many there were! (3) he offers bread and wine: {the} primary meaning may be that he brings bread and wine to Abraham, perhaps as participation in a sacrifice; at any rate the Church has always seen in this a true sacrifice: Melchisedec sacrificed bread and wine and thus typified the sacrifice of Christ in the New Law; (4) Abram recognizes him as priest of the true God and gives him tithes of all he had gained; (5) Melchisedec meanwhile blesses Abram (v. 19–20). Then Abram in turn refuses to take anything from the King of Sodom, who wishes to reward him for his service. We know {that} in Psalm 109 the Messias is called "a priest forever according to the order of

---

(Migne, *PG* 12, col. 111CD) ("Although Abraham, out of gentleness, gave the power of choice to Lot, it should be noted that the one who chose did not enjoy the result of his selection, but rather he who gave the choice was blessed to have what was left to himself. . . . Consolation from God follows those who are attracted to virtue. After he gave the choice to his kinsman, who selected the most pleasant and fertile area, God appeared to Abraham, whose spirit he renewed with consoling words and good promises, saying in effect: 'You have scorned this lowliest and sensuous land. I shall give you a land of gentleness, which is the region of the living'").

132. "But Melchisedech the king of Salem, bringing forth bread and wine, for he was the priest of the most high God, Blessed him, and said: Blessed be Abram by the most high God, who created heaven and earth. And blessed be the most high God, by whose protection the enemies are in thy hands. And he gave him the tithes of all. And the king of Sodom said to Abram: Give me the persons, and the rest take to thyself. And he answered him: I lift up my hand to the Lord God the most high, the possessor of heaven and earth, That from the very woof thread unto the shoe latchet, I will not take of any things that are thine, lest thou say I have enriched Abram: Except such things as the young men have eaten, and the shares of the men that came with me, Aner, Escol, and Mambre: these shall take their shares" (vv. 18–24).

Melchisedec." READ HEBREWS 7:1–11:[133] St. Paul in Hebrews 7 interprets this. Melchisedec is seen in full mystery—King of justice and King of peace—"without father and without mother, having neither beginning of days nor end of life, etc. . . . but likened unto the son of God"—foreshadowing the Son of God (some of the Fathers thought Jesus Himself had appeared to Abram under the guise of this mysterious figure—perhaps it was here that Abraham saw His day and rejoiced[134]). St. Paul's main point is that Abram paid tithes to Melchisedec, while Levi was not yet born, but Levi paid tithes to Melchisedec "in the loins of Abraham" (v. 10). This shows fully how much mystery is packed into such an incident.

The Renewal of God's Promise—the Ominous Sacrifice (ch. 15): {then comes} a time of trial and discouragement for Abraham. His confidence is not always spontaneous and serene. God has made him wait for the fulfillment of the promise, and his optimism is beginning to vanish. How important it is to be able to *wait*—to suffer deception and reverses, yet believing God will do all. {In} verse 1, the Lord comes to console Abraham: "I am thy protector and thy reward." {In} verses 2–3, Abraham replies with humble reproachfulness—he still has no heir. READ {verses} 4–6:[135] in 4–6, God renews His promise, with emphasis, showing Abraham the

---

133. "For this Melchisedech was king of Salem, priest of the most high God, who met Abraham returning from the slaughter of the kings, and blessed him: To whom also Abraham divided the tithes of all: who first indeed by interpretation, is king of justice: and then also king of Salem, that is, king of peace: Without father, without mother, without genealogy, having neither beginning of days nor end of life, but likened unto the Son of God, continueth a priest for ever. Now consider how great this man is, to whom also Abraham the patriarch gave tithes out of the principal things. And indeed they that are of the sons of Levi, who receive the priesthood, have a commandment to take tithes of the people according to the law, that is to say, of their brethren: though they themselves also came out of the loins of Abraham. But he, whose pedigree is not numbered among them, received tithes of Abraham, and blessed him that had the promises. And without all contradiction, that which is less, is blessed by the better. And here indeed, men that die, receive tithes: but there he hath witness, that he liveth. And (as it may be said) even Levi who received tithes, paid tithes in Abraham: For he was yet in the loins of his father, when Melchisedech met him. If then perfection was by the Levitical priesthood, (for under it the people received the law,) what further need was there that another priest should rise according to the order of Melchisedech, and not be called according to the order of Aaron?"

134. See John 8:56.

135. "And immediately the word of the Lord came to him, saying: He [i.e. Abram's steward Eliezer] shall not be thy heir: but he that shall come out of thy bowels, him shalt thou have for thy heir. And he brought him forth abroad, and said to him: Look up to heaven and number the stars, if thou canst. And he said to him: So shall thy seed be. Abram believed God, and it was reputed to him unto justice."

starry heavens: "so shall thy seed be." The promise was a supreme test for the faith of Abraham, nearly a hundred years old now. (The other promise had been made twenty-five years before!) Abraham {is} *justified by faith*, {by} total abandonment to God {with}: (a) his intelligence, placing God's word before his own reasoning; (b) his will, leaving the execution of the promise to God's own wisdom and will; (c) his whole life, letting everything depend on the execution of this promise in God's own good time; (d) {so that it is} *reputed unto justice*: {he is} justified—he is "adjusted" to the reality of God's will, and this is goodness, sanctity—to fit in, to "click" with God's plan in one's own life. {Then comes} *the sacrifice* (7 ff.): God makes another promise—*Abraham will possess the land of Canaan.* Abraham asks for a sign; in the sign there is a prophetic foreboding of the exile in Egypt. God renews this promise, with a prophecy of what must be gone through before it be accomplished. Read {verses} 9–18:[136] (a) first Abraham sacrifices the animals, the birds descend upon them and he has to drive them away—an evil incident, disturbing; dividing the beasts and walking between them {is} an ancient way of signifying that a contract had been made; the birds of prey signify the enemies of Abraham and his sons; (b) God appears to Abraham in a troubled sleep and explains the incident, referring it to the sojourn in Egypt; (c) 17 ff.: after the sun has set, then God as a column of fire passes through the division of the victims, ratifying His part in the pact.

Agar—The Birth of Ishmael (GEN. c. 16): Sara, according to Mesopotamian law, could legally "have children" through the instrumentality of a serving woman taking her place. This she suggested when she saw she had no children. Abraham was to have a child by Agar, Sara's Egyptian

---

136. "And the Lord answered, and said: Take me a cow of three years old, and a she goat of three years, and a ram of three years, a turtle also, and a pigeon. And he took all these, and divided them in the midst, and laid the two pieces of each one against the other; but the birds he divided not. And the fowls came down upon the carcasses, and Abram drove them away. And when the sun was setting, a deep sleep fell upon Abram, and a great and darksome horror seized upon him. And it was said unto him: Know thou beforehand that thy seed shall be a stranger in a land not their own, and they shall bring them under bondage, and afflict them four hundred years. But I will judge the nation which they shall serve, and after this they shall come out with great substance. And thou shalt go to thy fathers in peace, and be buried in a good old age. But in the fourth generation they shall return hither: for as yet the iniquities of the Amorrhites are not at the full until this present time. And when the sun was set, there arose a dark mist, and there appeared a smoking furnace and a lamp of fire passing between those divisions. That day God made a covenant with Abram, saying: To thy seed will I give this land, from the river of Egypt even to the great river Euphrates."

servant. Note that Abram does not take Agar on his own initiative, but Sara "brings her to him."[137] Agar becomes pregnant, and then exults over Sara, despising her, after the fashion of a primitive and ignorant person, {so} Sara appeals to Abram, saying that it is an injustice for him to allow this to go on. All through this passage we see a totally different, primitive code of morality and justice, utterly unfamiliar to anything we know. Here however Sara may be unreasonable. Abram had presumably continued to live with Agar. When he lifted his protection and sent her back to Sara, then the latter beat her so much that Agar fled into the desert. READ 7–16:[138] Agar sees the "Angel of the Lord" (Mal'ach Yahweh). This is not an angelic spirit that she sees but the visible form which the Lord Himself takes to appear to a creature (*CBC*;[139] see Heinisch: *Theology of {the} Old Testament*:[140] article "Mal'akh Yahweh"—p. 106: sometimes the expression means an angel, sometimes it poses a problem; Heinisch discusses in some detail the "angel of the Lord" in Genesis [p. {104}[141]]: in these passages the mal'akh and the Lord are spoken of interchangeably: "There was no problem for the Jewish mind"[142] as to {the idea that} the Lord might be at the same time Himself and His own messenger; St. Justin thought the Mal'akh Yahweh was the Logos[143]). "Where are you coming

---

137. Gen 16:3.

138. "And the angel of the Lord having found her, by a fountain of water in the wilderness, which is in the way to Sur in the desert, He said to her: Agar, handmaid of Sarai, whence comest thou? and whither goest thou? And she answered: I flee from the face of Sarai, my mistress. And the angel of the Lord said to her: Return to thy mistress, and humble thyself under her hand. And again he said: I will multiply thy seed exceedingly, and it shall not be numbered for multitude. And again: Behold, said he, thou art with child, and thou shalt bring forth a son: and thou shalt call his name Ismael, because the Lord hath heard thy affliction. He shall be a wild man: his hand will be against all men, and all men's hands against him: and he shall pitch his tents over against all his brethren. And she called the name of the Lord that spoke unto her: Thou the God who hast seen me. For she said: Verily here have I seen the hinder parts of him that seeth me. Therefore she called that well, The well of him that liveth and seeth me. The same is between Cades and Barad. And Agar brought forth a son to Abram: who called his name Ismael. Abram was four score and six years old when Agar brought him forth Ismael."

139. Sutcliffe, "Genesis," 195 [n. 151g].

140. Heinisch, *Old Testament*, 104–106.

141. Copy text reads: "107."

142. Heinisch, *Old Testament*, 106, which reads: "The question, how Yahweh could be called *messenger* of Yahweh, did not vex the Jewish mind."

143. Justin, *Dialogue with Trypho*, cc. 56, 59, 60, cited in Heinisch, *Old Testament*, 106.

from, whither are you going"—the Lord speaks to us and immediately brings us face to face with the actual reality of our life, not in a static way, but dynamically, a sudden consciousness of our life in its "becoming," its tending, its development, its meaning, its value. This {is} typical of true religious experience. She says, "I am fleeing"—her existence has become a flight into nowhere. The angel says, "Return and submit." We cannot find our reality, our true self, our place in the world, by merely running away aimlessly from suffering and persecution. However the point here is not merely that it is a good thing to bear suffering with patience but that it is the Lord's will for Agar to go back, suffering or no suffering. It is part of a plan she does not understand. The angel then promises that her son will be *the father of a great race* (note even here the promise for Abraham overflows to his children from others beside Sara, but this is not THE promise). Ishmael means "Yahweh has heard"; he will be a wild man—the fierce Arab tribes living in the desert—he will fight against all. Agar describes her experience: "I have seen Him Who sees me"—in the simplicity of primitive language we have a perfect expression of the deepest experience of God, an expression of the soul's meeting with His infinite Truth in mystery, {with an} emphasis on the concreteness, the personality of God (not just "The Absolute") {but an} emphasis on "presence" which so impressed St. Benedict.[144] The God of Abraham (and

144. Again, see St. Benedict's discussion in chapter 7 of the *Rule* of the first degree of humility: "let him consider that God is always beholding him from heaven, that his actions are everywhere visible to the eye of the Godhead, and are constantly being reported to God by the angels. The prophet teaches us this when he represents God as always present in our thoughts" (McCann, trans. and ed., *Rule*, 39); see also Merton's commentary on this passage: "St. Benedict then gives us the great means for gaining control over all our thoughts and actions: the presence of God. This is the most fundamental thing in our life of prayer and contemplation. Atheists rebel against the thought of a 'god' who can 'intrude' into their inmost self and see what is going on there. But they do not realize that God is in no sense an intruder; rather He is the source and life of our whole being, and if He is absent, our life becomes empty, lifeless, sterile, stupid. Witness the dullness and stupidity of atheist–materialist society and culture: the culture of people with no inner life. The 'presence' of God beings life, light, meaning, to our interior life. *To say that 'God sees' what I do is to say that it has a meaning and a value quite apart from what I may be able to give to it myself*. He Who is infinitely real 'sees' and judges my acts in proportion as they participate in His reality. . . . St. Benedict does not mean that 'God sees' merely in order to punish. We must not take it in this way. God also judges with mercy and sees our good motives and our weakness and the extenuating circumstances, and above all He *sees with love*: He sees our needs also and gives us grace and assistance. The thought that *Love* sees me is a deterrent from sin. Shall I hurt Him Who loves me infinitely? Shall I drive His love and light out of my soul by mortal sin? No one who realizes the meaning of the presence of

Agar) is the *Living God*. Before the great Epiphany of the Father in the Son at the Incarnation there was hardly a more perfect revelation of God than was made to Abraham and Moses. Everywhere we see evidence that God was present to Abraham as He is in Himself, no doubt through an intermediary (the "angel of the Lord"), but in all His infinite mystery and transcendence. Well might Pascal contrast the God of the philosophers with the God of Abraham, Isaac and Jacob.[145] Genesis is one of the great source books for Christian mystical theology.

Agar reacts characteristically: she *names* God—she has {a} Name which fixes and identifies Him in reference to this singular event; she names a *place* to commemorate the event, {and} the place retains its name for future generations. {In} verse 13 {there is a} problem in the text: where Douay has "I have seen the hinder parts of Him that seeth me" ({a} reminiscence of Exodus, where Moses sees God "from behind,"[146] that is to say negatively, by seeing what He is not, rather than face to face), {the} *CBC* suggests: "Have I even seen God and live after my vision?"[147]

{Then follows the} birth of Ishmael: the name means "God hears."[148] Note of course that the name is given by Abram, and it is an expression of his faith. We remark in all this that though Abram sees God frequently and walks with Him in familiar converse, yet the important thing is the birth of a son to carry on his line. It was not enough for Abram to live in the presence of God. He had also to fulfill his mission in the world, to answer the call of God and live out the paradox that God had willed to be his vocation. He is constantly thinking of this, and all his actions are directed toward this: he interprets everything in the light of the great promise. Abraham is entirely centered not on his own happiness and prosperity, not even on his own spiritual peace and contentment with God, but on his vocation to be a Father of a great nation and the instrument for the

---

God will do such a thing" (Merton, *Rule of Saint Benedict*, 176–77).

145. An excerpt from the beginning of Blaise Pascal's "Memorial," his brief account of the divine encounter of November 23, 1654, the "night of fire" that marked Pascal's definitive conversion. For a discussion of this document see the opening chapter of Romano Guardini's *Pascal for Our Time*, 19–44. Merton would later read and praise this book: see his journal entry for January 10, 1967: "Pascal is my kind. The Guardini work on him is fine—one of G.'s best, at least for me. Whole thing so full of ideas they rush in from all sides and I have to stop and walk around" (Merton, *Learning to Love*, 184).

146. See Exod 33:23.
147. Sutcliffe, "Genesis," 195 [n. 151g].
148. Sutcliffe, "Genesis," 195 [n. 151g].

salvation of the world. But he does not think in abstract terms ("salvation of souls") but in concrete terms—the son promised to him—or, as we shall see, that the evil cities be spared.

The Alliance—Circumcision: this is a very important chapter:

1. {There is} a great new development in the "Advent" which is Abraham's preparation for the fulfillment of the promise. Now the promise is made *very clear*.
2. All doubt as to whether the promise is attached to Ishmael or the sons of some other is removed. Only the son of Sara is the child of the promise (21).
3. The exact date of the child's birth is made known ("this time next year").
4. Abram is now ninety-nine—his great year is to be the one when he is a hundred!
5. Abram receives a new name, which confirms his destiny; the promise has begun to take effect in his life. Sara also receives a new name.
6. As a sign of this "conversion" the rite of circumcision is instituted, a sign that the source of life, the means of propagation of the race, is consecrated to God—{a means of} protection against pagan fertility rites.
7. With all this, God renews His promises for the future in the strongest terms.

This is a solemn and important chapter.

Chapter 17:1: Abram is now ninety-nine years old. God appears to him. First, He declares His Name—a new revelation of Himself to Abram, as *El Shaddai*—the Almighty. {Note the} great solemnity of this. {It is a} prelude to giving Abram himself a new name, {which is} further confirmation of all the promises. So too in our own lives, God's plan and His promises are fulfilled by degrees. He subjects us to a long preparation, gradually revealing to us the magnitude of His gift (sanctity—salvation) and the greatness of Him Who gives it to us. The longer and more completely this preparation goes on, the better and holier we will be for it. We should learn seriously to see our own lives in the light of Abraham's life—the child of the promise, Christ, is to be manifested in us. We already possess Him in hope, from the baptismal font, but our life is a gradual growth to the clear vision of Him living in us.

"*Walk in my presence and be perfect*"[149] (again the emphasis {is} on the fact that God is He who sees us). A very weak application of this tremendous injunction would be to say "The practice of the presence of God is very sanctifying"—in the sense of conducive to piety and virtue. Here Yahweh is in fact opening up to Abraham a whole new horizon, a new level of his life. There is the *practice* of the presence of God, and there is the *experience* of that presence, a shift of the center of balance of our lives from *ourselves* to *God*. His reality becomes, as a matter of experience, more important to us than our own. This presence is not known except by love. Love gives us the contact by which we are *aware of His sanctity and power*.

Peculiar characteristics of this awareness {include}:

1. Awareness *that* He is, but not entirely of *What* He is. {It is} the Presence of One we know not, yet curiously, in not knowing Him we seem to know Him better than the beings we know—i.e. more intimately. If we are honest we have to *admit we don't know* Him Whom nevertheless we know.

2. Awareness of His holiness and of His sanctifying power, {giving rise to} awe, adoration, respect.

3. Love—the love of a friend for a friend; peace and tranquility—the sense of *finality* that He is all; in realizing Him to be there, we can relinquish all else, for all else is nothing.

"*I establish my alliance between me and thee*" (note the thou and I theme, borrowed by Bouyer from Buber:[150] read *Meaning of Monastic Life*, page 8[151]). "I will multiply thee exceedingly." The promises of God are not limited within a narrow compass. They are overflowing and immensely rich. Abram will be father not only of the chosen people, through Isaac, but of the Arabs of the desert through Ishmael, and the Arabs of Edom through Esau. Hence in verse 4 he is the "father" of a

---

149. Gen 17:1.

150. Buber, *I and Thou*.

151. "If it is to be *truly* God whom we seek, we have to seek him as a person. Martin Buber . . . has expressed this very adequately: a person is only sought as a person, in dialogue. It is only in the 'I to Thou' relationship that the person remains personal for us. Someone of whom we get into the habit of speaking as 'he' is no longer a person for us. Whether we realize it or not, 'he' is no more than a thing" (Bouyer, *Meaning of Monastic Life*, 8).

multitude of peoples[152]—many nations (Douay). Abram falls flat on his face. The Douay says then God announces "I AM"[153]—it is not in *BJ*,[154] but evidently it is a vivid expression of the presence of the Living God in mystery, uttering His promise. He is infinitely real.

The new name is then given (v. 5). It means "Father of a multitude." A name not only designates the person but determines his being and destiny. God then repeats all the promises: many nations {are} to come from Abraham; they shall possess the land of Canaan; and *the Lord shall be their God*. This last {is} the greatest and most significant mystery—God creating for Himself a people; and *we* are called to be numbered among this people.

Circumcision {is} the sign of fellowship in the people created by God and consecrated to God, as opposed to the pagans with their fertility rites. The "seed" of the people of God belongs to God—but when Christ comes, circumcision is meaningless. A visible sign was necessary, engraved in the very flesh of the people, {but it is} replaced by an invisible and spiritual sign, the seal or character of baptism engraved in our hearts. Note the necessity of spiritual "circumcision" announced by the prophet Jeremias (4:4)—especially spiritual circumcision {as} a faith that clings to the folly of the Cross and lets go of Mosaic ritual (Read Galatians

---

152. Cf. de Vaux, *Genèse*, 87: "père d'une multitude de peuples."

153. "And God said to him: I AM, and my covenant is with thee, and thou shalt be a father of many nations" (Gen 17:4).

154. See de Vaux, *Genèse*, 87.

5, and 6:12–18[155]). Sara's name {is} changed {from}[156] Sarai—both mean the same: princess—but there is emphasis on the fact that she will be the mother of kings (cf. St. Francis—model of spiritual purity).

Abraham's laughter: {note} the mystery of laughter in the promise of Isaac, whose name means laughter. Abraham's laugh is the reaction of a soul completely disconcerted by the greatness and mystery of God and his own littleness. It is just as normal a reaction to the divine as tears, though we have lost the sense that this should be so. It is a very human

---

155. "Stand fast, and be not held again under the yoke of bondage. Behold, I Paul tell you, that if you be circumcised, Christ shall profit you nothing. And I testify again to every man circumcising himself, that he is a debtor to the whole law. You are made void of Christ, you who are justified in the law: you are fallen from grace. For we in spirit, by faith, wait for the hope of justice. For in Christ Jesus neither circumcision availeth any thing, nor uncircumcision: but faith that worketh by charity. You did run well, who hath hindered you, that you should not obey the truth? This persuasion is not from him that calleth you. A little leaven corrupteth the whole lump. I have confidence in you in the Lord: that you will not be of another mind: but he that troubleth you, shall bear the judgment, whosoever he be. And I, brethren, if I yet preach circumcision, why do I yet suffer persecution? Then is the scandal of the cross made void. I would they were even cut off, who trouble you. For you, brethren, have been called unto liberty: only make not liberty an occasion to the flesh, but by charity of the spirit serve one another. For all the law is fulfilled in one word: Thou shalt love thy neighbour as thyself. But if you bite and devour one another; take heed you be not consumed one of another. I say then, walk in the spirit, and you shall not fulfill the lusts of the flesh. For the flesh lusteth against the spirit: and the spirit against the flesh; for these are contrary one to another: so that you do not the things that you would. But if you are led by the spirit, you are not under the law. Now the works of the flesh are manifest, which are fornication, uncleanness, immodesty, luxury, Idolatry, witchcrafts, enmities, contentions, emulations, wraths, quarrels, dissensions, sects, Envies, murders, drunkenness, revellings, and such like. Of the which I foretell you, as I have foretold to you, that they who do such things shall not obtain the kingdom of God. But the fruit of the Spirit is, charity, joy, peace, patience, benignity, goodness, longanimity, Mildness, faith, modesty, continency, chastity. Against such there is no law. And they that are Christ's, have crucified their flesh, with the vices and concupiscences. If we live in the Spirit, let us also walk in the Spirit. Let us not be made desirous of vain glory, provoking one another, envying one another. For as many as desire to please in the flesh, they constrain you to be circumcised, only that they may not suffer the persecution of the cross of Christ. . . . For neither they themselves who are circumcised, keep the law; but they will have you to be circumcised, that they may glory in your flesh. But God forbid that I should glory, save in the cross of our Lord Jesus Christ; by whom the world is crucified to me, and I to the world. For in Christ Jesus neither circumcision availeth any thing, nor uncircumcision, but a new creature. And whosoever shall follow this rule, peace on them, and mercy, and upon the Israel of God. From henceforth let no man be troublesome to me; for I bear the marks of the Lord Jesus in my body. The grace of our Lord Jesus Christ be with your spirit, brethren. Amen."

156. Copy text reads: "to."

reaction to wonder and joy. Sara also will laugh behind the flap of the tent when she hears the promise renewed, but in her laugh there may be some incredulity. In Abraham's laugh we may see also the fact that here this "impossible" promise is repeated once again by the Almighty—hence it *must* happen, yet it still seems impossible. The only way out of the contradiction is laughter—a supreme affirmation of a belief that goes beyond the contrary terms of a dilemma—the laughter of a mystical liberation!

The Destruction of Sodom (chapters 18–19) {is} one of most impressive passages in Genesis, like that of the Tower of Babel. Here we see again the Last Judgement in mystery, with the added note, now, of vicarious reparation and salvation of the wicked by the just, introduced so far just as a possibility that is not in fact realized. Again {note the} contrast between Abraham and Lot (who here appears as the inglorious ancestor of the Moabites and Ammonites). The episode falls into several parts: (1) the vision at Mambre: the renewal of the promise and the visit of the Lord to Abraham; (2) Abraham's intercession for Sodom; (3) the two angels go to Sodom {followed by} the struggle of Lot to save them; (4) the punishment of Sodom and Lot's flight to Segor; (5) Lot and his daughters. What is the main theme of this whole episode? It is a visit of God to the earth, a kind of preliminary to the mystery of the Incarnation. God "comes down"[157] and walks among men. Are there in the "three" who appear to Abraham the Three Divine Persons adumbrated? The Fathers thought so. In any case, we have at least the Lord and the two angels coming to visit Abraham, and to take a look at Sodom. In all this episode we must see Jesus, the "promised seed" of Abraham, adumbrated in His Incarnation. His presence in the world will be a kind of judgement of those who do not receive Him. Note that Isaias called the priests and leaders of Israel "Princes of Sodom" (read Isaias 1:2–10,[158] especially 9 and 10); also Jesus

---

157. Gen 18:21.

158. "Hear, O ye heavens, and give ear, O earth, for the Lord hath spoken. I have brought up children, and exalted them: but they have despised me. The ox knoweth his owner, and the ass his master's crib: but Israel hath not known me, and my people hath not understood. Woe to the sinful nation, a people laden with iniquity, a wicked seed, ungracious children: they have forsaken the Lord, they have blasphemed the Holy One of Israel, they are gone away backwards. For what shall I strike you any more, you that increase transgression? the whole head is sick, and the whole heart is sad. From the sole of the foot unto the top of the head, there is no soundness therein: wounds and bruises and swelling sores: they are not bound up, nor dressed, nor fomented with oil. Your land is desolate, your cities are burnt with fire: your country strangers devour before your face, and it shall be desolate as when wasted by enemies. And the daughter of Sion shall be left as a covert in a vineyard, and as a lodge in a garden of cucumbers,

Himself compares the Jews to the people of Sodom,[159] with the implication that those who rejected Him were worse than the men of Sodom. READ John 3:16–21:[160] God so loved the world ... that those who believe may not perish ... He that doth not believe is already judged ... this is the judgement because the light is come into the world and men loved darkness rather than the light because their works were evil ... He that doth truth cometh to the light. READ John 12:31–36:[161] Now is the judgement of the world ... If I be lifted up ... walk while you have the light, he that walketh in darkness knoweth not where he goeth (cf. Gen. 19:11: the men of Sodom struck with blindness). Jesus then goes away and hides Himself from them. In the episode of the men of Sodom seeking to lay hands upon the angels we see many strange correspondences with the relation of the Pharisees to Jesus in the sense that the Jews, expecting a worldly Messias, tried to corrupt the One sent from God into their own base ways, and because He would not be moved by them, they hated Him. {It is} interesting to read again John 8:44 to the end in this connection.[162]

---

and as a city that is laid waste. Except the Lord of hosts had left us seed, we had been as Sodom, and we should have been like to Gomorrha. Hear the word of the Lord, ye rulers of Sodom, give ear to the law of our God, ye people of Gomorrha."

159. See Matt 10:15, 11:24.

160. "For God so loved the world, as to give his only begotten Son; that whosoever believeth in him, may not perish, but may have life everlasting. For God sent not his Son into the world, to judge the world, but that the world may be saved by him. He that believeth in him is not judged. But he that doth not believe, is already judged: because he believeth not in the name of the only begotten Son of God. And this is the judgment: because the light is come into the world, and men loved darkness rather than the light: for their works were evil. For every one that doth evil hateth the light, and cometh not to the light, that his works may not be reproved. But he that doth truth, cometh to the light, that his works may be made manifest, because they are done in God."

161. "Now is the judgment of the world: now shall the prince of this world be cast out. And I, if I be lifted up from the earth, will draw all things to myself. (Now this he said, signifying what death he should die.) The multitude answered him: We have heard out of the law, that Christ abideth for ever; and how sayest thou: The Son of man must be lifted up? Who is this Son of man? Jesus therefore said to them: Yet a little while, the light is among you. Walk whilst you have the light, that the darkness overtake you not. And he that walketh in darkness, knoweth not whither he goeth. Whilst you have the light, believe in the light, that you may be the children of light. These things Jesus spoke; and he went away, and hid himself from them."

162. "You are of your father the devil, and the desires of your father you will do. He was a murderer from the beginning, and he stood not in the truth; because truth is not in him. When he speaketh a lie, he speaketh of his own: for he is a liar, and the father thereof. But if I say the truth, you believe me not. Which of you shall convince me of sin? If I say the truth to you, why do you not believe me? He that is of God, heareth

The vision at Mambre: {this is} a quiet scene. Abraham has pitched his tent in the valley and is sitting in the tent door at noontime under the big oak tree, famous and held as sacred. The "three men" appear to him, "he lifts up his eyes" and there they are—he does not see them coming up the road. He knows at once that it is the Lord (as opposed {to} *BJ*[163] and other modern commentators). We can follow the Fathers in seeing a special significance in the fact the "*tres vidit et unum adoravit,*"[164] even though it may not perhaps be the strict literal sense of the passage.[165] In any case, Abraham's hospitality, offered in a spirit of faith, is a classic example of supernatural charity which attains directly to God in and through the neighbor. St. Paul refers to this kind of hospitality in Hebrews 13:1–2 (hospitality do not forget for by this some, being not aware of it, have entertained angels—this passage refers rather to Lot than to

---

the words of God. Therefore you hear them not, because you are not of God. The Jews therefore answered, and said to him: Do not we say well that thou art a Samaritan, and hast a devil? Jesus answered: I have not a devil: but I honour my Father, and you have dishonoured me. But I seek not my own glory: there is one that seeketh and judgeth. Amen, amen I say to you: If any man keep my word, he shall not see death for ever. The Jews therefore said: Now we know that thou hast a devil. Abraham is dead, and the prophets; and thou sayest: If any man keep my word, he shall not taste death for ever. Art thou greater than our father Abraham, who is dead? and the prophets are dead. Whom dost thou make thyself? Jesus answered: If I glorify myself, my glory is nothing. It is my Father that glorifieth me, of whom you say that he is your God. And you have not known him, but I know him. And if I shall say that I know him not, I shall be like to you, a liar. But I do know him, and do keep his word. Abraham your father rejoiced that he might see my day: he saw it, and was glad. The Jews therefore said to him: Thou art not yet fifty years old, and hast thou seen Abraham? Jesus said to them: Amen, amen I say to you, before Abraham was made, I am. They took up stones therefore to cast at him. But Jesus hid himself, and went out of the temple" (vv. 44–59).

163. "Abraham ne reconnâit d'abord dans les trois visiteurs que de hôtes humains" ("Abraham initially sees in the three visitors only human guests") (de Vaux, *Genèse*, 90).

164. Ambrose, *De Fide*, 1.13 (Migne, *PL* 16, col. 547B); *De Spiritu Sancto*, 2.Prol. (Migne, *PL* 16, col. 743C); Augustine, *Contra Maximum*, 2.26 (Migne, *PL* 42, col. 809).

165. See de Vaux, *Genèse*, 89–90: "la phrase qu'on cite toujours à ce propos, *tres vidit et unum adoravit*, se rencontre pour la première fois chez saint Hilaire avec ce sens: Abraham vit trois hommes mais il n'en adora qu'un, reconnaissant les deux autres pour des Anges: cette éxegèse lui est commune avec d'autres Pères" ("the phrase that is always cited in this context, 'he saw three and adored one,' is found for the first time in Saint Hillary with this sense: Abraham saw three men but he only adored one, recognizing the two others as angels: this interpretation is common with other Fathers"); the reference is to Hillary of Poitiers, *De Trinitate* 4.27: "*viri tres sedenti assistunt, unum adorat, et Dominum confitetur*" ("Three men are present to the one sitting there; he adores one, and puts his trust in the Lord") (Migne, *PL* 10, col. 117A).

Abraham). Abraham prepares a dinner for the guests and they eat with him—note in preparing the dinner he makes a modest offer of a little bread but in fact puts on a big dinner, killing a calf for them; also he does this with great zeal and application. After they have eaten, the guests say "Where is Sara?"—note again the direct and concrete approach: the promise "I shall return again this time next year and Sara will have a son" (v. 10). The laughter of Sara is tinged with disbelief or at least with a human and natural spirit, in contrast to the earlier laughter of Abraham. Both laughed at the same apparent "impossibility," but Abraham's laugh was that of a spirit overwhelmed by the transcendent paradox of the divine promise; Sara's laugh seems to be centered on the exterior grotesqueness of the promise involving two old and worn-out persons. Her viewpoint is hardly spiritual (v. 12). Commentators absolve her from lack of faith (*BJ*[166]) because she does not yet know Who is speaking, and it is when the Lord says aloud to Abraham "Why did Sara laugh" (when she laughed to herself) and declares that nothing is impossible to the Lord, that she realizes it is a divine promise and is filled with fear and repentance.

Abraham's intercession for Sodom: the meeting of Abraham with the Lord in Mambre and the renewal of the promise is only the prelude to the real business. They all rise up and start out for Sodom, the "Three" and Abraham with them out of politeness, as one accompanies a guest to the door. The lesson in all this is the incomparable solicitude and politeness and piety of Abraham toward the Lord in all this—his love of God needs no higher expression, ordinarily, than the perfect performance of the customary duties practiced among his own people. We should learn something of this sense of *respect coupled with realism* in our relations with Our Lord. St. Benedict would certainly have us do so.[167] But if we have no background of respect for other human beings we would seem

---

166. "Ce rire n'est pas, chez Sara, un manque de 'foi,' puis qu'elle ne connaît pas l'identité de hôte. Cette vieille femme s'amuse seulement de ce qu'elle prenne pour un souhait poli et sans consequence" ("This laugh is not, on Sarah's part, a lack of faith, since she is unaware of the identity of the guest. This old woman is simply amused by what she takes for a polite and inconsequential wish") (de Vaux, *Genèse*, 91).

167. This focus on performing ordinary duties as a way of serving God is found particularly in chapters 31 (the cellarer), 32 (monastery tools), 35 (on service in the kitchen), 36 (care of the sick), 37 (care for the elderly and the young), 38 (the weekly reader), 48 (manual labor), 57 (craftsmen in the monastery) (McCann, trans. and ed., *Rule*, 80, 82/81, 83; 84/85; 86, 88/87, 89; 90/91; 92/93; 92, 94/93, 95; 110, 112/111, 113; 128/129). Merton discusses most of this material in *Rule of Saint Benedict*, 119–42.

to be in a bad position to show respect to God in this particular way. However, constant living in the presence of God is synonymous with a constant attitude of respect and attentive considerateness for God, present as our Lord and as our Father. This sense of respect will greatly improve our consciousness of the reality of His presence—much more than a lot of grandiose and dramatic considerations without foundation in the affections of the heart. At the same time, there are limits and alternations: the Lord is not always present in the same way, and when He is more present to us there should be more respect. Other situations call for less elaborate expressions of this.

Yahweh muses aloud: "Shall I hide from Abraham what I am about to do?" Note the beauty of the narrative and its deep impressiveness. How much more sobering and saddening {are} these words of verse 20: "The cry against Sodom and Gomorrha is multiplied [is getting louder and louder] and their sin is become exceedingly grievous. I will go down and see"—much more saddening than many more dramatic words. Here there is little passion implied, no furious human rage, {but} a deep and calm sorrow, suggesting God's unwillingness to punish, but the fact that He does so when our sins force Him, as He must respect His own truth and reality, for it is indeed reality itself that cries out against Sodom (cf. Romans 1, where homosexuality is linked up with ignorance of God, a perversion of the reality of God by idolatry, leading to a corresponding perversion of the reality of human nature: read Romans 1:18–28[168]).

---

168. "For the wrath of God is revealed from heaven against all ungodliness and injustice of those men that detain the truth of God in injustice: Because that which is known of God is manifest in them. For God hath manifested it unto them. For the invisible things of him, from the creation of the world, are clearly seen, being understood by the things that are made; his eternal power also, and divinity: so that they are inexcusable. Because that, when they knew God, they have not glorified him as God, or given thanks; but became vain in their thoughts, and their foolish heart was darkened. For professing themselves to be wise, they became fools. And they changed the glory of the incorruptible God into the likeness of the image of a corruptible man, and of birds, and of fourfooted beasts, and of creeping things. Wherefore God gave them up to the desires of their heart, unto uncleanness, to dishonour their own bodies among themselves. Who changed the truth of God into a lie; and worshipped and served the creature rather than the Creator, who is blessed for ever. Amen. For this cause God delivered them up to shameful affections. For their women have changed the natural use into that use which is against nature. And, in like manner, the men also, leaving the natural use of the women, have burned in their lusts one towards another, men with men working that which is filthy, and receiving in themselves the recompense which was due to their error. And as they liked not to have God in their knowledge, God delivered them up to a reprobate sense, to do those things which are not convenient."

{In} Abraham's earnest bargaining with God, the tone of confident pleading and reproachfulness mingles with respect. "How can you do such a thing as destroy the just with the wicked?"[169] The Lord listens attentively to Abraham and weighs his words. ({Compare} our own vocation to intercede for sinners.) Note that the ending of chapter 18 is after all inconclusive. The Lord promises to save the city for ten just men, and then departs. Abraham did not press the matter further. It would seem that Abraham assumed that there *would* be ten, that this was a safe number, and that the sacred writer wanted by this to emphasize the wickedness of the cities—there were *not even* ten just men in them. This reminds us of Psalm 13:2 ff.: the Lord looks down from heaven to see if there is anyone who understands and seeks God. They are all become unprofitable; *there is none that doth good, no not one* (read the rest of the psalm[170]); cf. Genesis 18:21: the cry against Sodom and Gomorrha is multiplied—I will go down and see. At the end of the chapter, Abraham, satisfied, returns home and the Lord goes on toward Sodom.

Chapter 19: the angels approach Sodom and are greeted by Lot in the gate. He receives them and fulfills the sacred duties of hospitality. {Note} the quiet scene in Lot's house as he eats with the angels and they prepare to retire, but in this silence there is fear. Lot has already awakened this fear in the reader's heart by the anxiety with which he beseeches the angels not to sleep in the public square; and now, in the darkness, the whole town, from the young to the old, surround Lot's house and demand that the angels be handed over to them to be abused in a frightful manner. Note the presumption, the arrogance of the people of Sodom, as if they claimed their right to do their will with these strangers against all the laws of nature. To the Israelite this crime would represent the climax of evil, not merely because of the perverseness of the vice against nature,

---

169. Gen 18:23.

170. "The Lord hath looked down from heaven upon the children of men, to see if there be any that understand and seek God. They are all gone aside, they are become unprofitable together: there is none that doth good, no not one. Their throat is an open sepulchre: with their tongues they acted deceitfully; the poison of asps is under their lips. Their mouth is full of cursing and bitterness; their feet are swift to shed blood. Destruction and unhappiness in their ways: and the way of peace they have not known: there is no fear of God before their eyes. Shall not all they know that work iniquity, who devour my people as they eat bread? They have not called upon the Lord: there have they trembled for fear, where there was no fear. For the Lord is in the just generation: you have confounded the counsel of the poor man, but the Lord is his hope. Who shall give out of Sion the salvation of Israel? when the Lord shall have turned away the captivity of his people, Jacob shall rejoice and Israel shall be glad."

but because of the violation of the duty of hospitality (the sin is perpetrated against the defenseless stranger), and finally, far beyond all this, there is the element of sacrilege, for these are holy angels, the angels of the Lord Himself. {In} verse 6 ff., Lot goes out and closes the door behind him and stands in the entry with his back up against the door, pleading with the crowd—he will even let them have his daughters, {for} that is a lesser evil. They revile him: "Here is a stranger who *sets himself up as our judge.*"[171] {Here is} the arrogance of sin that refuses to be judged by anyone, that rejects the testimony of truth and seeks only the accomplishment of its own desires. The crowd then presses forward to break down the door. Lot is miraculously saved by the angels who pull him in quickly from behind, while the assailants are struck with blindness. {In verse} 12, the angels then ask Lot, "Have you here any more people of your family . . . all that are yours, bring them out of this city for we will destroy it." Lot summons his future sons-in-law and says, "Come, we must get out of here," and they think he is joking. {Verse} 15: it is dawn; Lot is still waiting. The angels stir him up again: "Get up; get going!" He leaves with his wife and daughters, but he has to be led out by the angels; "such was the pity the Lord had on him." As they lead him out of the town they warn him that he must go forward without looking back. Lot fears to go into the mountains, and asks to be allowed to take refuge in Segor. In their turn the angels promise that the city will be spared on his account. But he must hurry, because they cannot begin until he enters Segor. At sunrise Lot enters Segor and the Lord rains down brimstone on the wicked cities. Lot's wife, looking back, becomes a pillar of salt. {Verse} 27: Abraham is up early and returns to the place where he had pleaded with Yahweh. He looks out silently over the plain and sees smoke going up from it like the smoke of a furnace. {Note the} impressiveness of the silence of Abraham here. But the sacred writer's only comment {is}: God had remembered Abraham and saved Lot. It was not because of Lot's faith that he was saved, but because of Abraham's.

{According to} *the Book of Wisdom* (10:6 ff.), it was Wisdom who delivered Lot when the fire came down upon the five cities. The desolation of that land remains as a testimony of the evil; the trees are without fruit; a pillar of salt stands as a witness to the infidelity of Lot's wife. The people of Sodom were not only ignorant of wisdom but left to future ages a memorial of their folly, so that their sin is made manifest to all generations (cf. {the} *eschatological significance of the passage*—Luke 17:20 ff.:

---

171. Gen 19:9.

here again we are present in mystery at the destruction of the world at the Last Judgement. As it came to pass in the days of Noe . . . as it came to pass in the days of Lot. Jesus Himself explains the typology of this passage: "*Even thus shall it be when the Son of man is revealed*" [17:30]. This brings together two great types of the Last Judgement: the Deluge {and} the destruction of Sodom.) In Wisdom 10 we have the flood referred to also, before the destruction of Sodom (10:4).

{At} Sodom, the sin is more specific; the anger of the Lord is less vehement. Again a just man and his household are saved, but here *because of another* who is a friend of God. Also there is the question of salvation through the merits of a few just men—and the *salvation of sinners*. There is a definite progress over the Deluge narration, a *deepening* of revelation. Hence this passage is tremendously important for us as monks and as Christians. Here precisely is one of the many answers the Scriptures give to us in our quest for God. How do we seek God? How do we find Him? {In Luke} 17:20, the Pharisees have asked, "When will the Kingdom of God come?" and this is Jesus' answer: "It cometh not with observation." It is useless for us to look here and look there in a human way, seeking the Son of Man, Who will come like lightning (v. 24). The great need is not for a special kind of knowledge or wisdom, but for great detachment, a great readiness to leave all and follow God Who comes most unexpectedly, breaking in upon the ordinary routine of life. We must certainly work and live ordinary lives (1 Thessalonians[172]), but in such a way that we are completely detached and ready to let go of what we have at any moment. He that is on the housetop must not turn back to get his goods. REMEMBER LOT'S WIFE (32). Then follow the great Gospel principles of renunciation: "He that shall seek to save his life shall lose it. . . . There shall be two in one bed, and one shall be taken. . . ." "Where, Lord?" "Wheresoever the body shall be, thither will the eagles be gathered together." In other words, no one knows, but the saints will gather where Christ is,

---

172. See 1 Thess 4:10–11: "But we entreat you, brethren, that you abound more: And that you use your endeavour to be quiet, and that you do your own business, and work with your own hands, as we commanded you: and that you walk honestly towards them that are without; and that you want nothing of any man's." However Merton may actually have intended to refer to 2 Thess 3:10–13: "For also when we were with you, this we declared to you: that, if any man will not work, neither let him eat. For we have heard there are some among you who walk disorderly, working not at all, but curiously meddling. Now we charge them that are such, and beseech them by the Lord Jesus Christ, that, working with silence, they would eat their own bread. But you, brethren, be not weary in well doing."

beyond time and space, for life will have taken on an utterly new dimension in the new creation at the second coming. This all brings out clearly the eschatological character of monastic spirituality. Our "contemplative" life is not a matter of sitting in the middle of Sodom thinking about divine things. It is a going forth from this world which passes away to seek and find God we know not where. While we are in this life, we continue to work and to live as other people do—without of course the evil that they do!—but we are living in heaven (*conversatio nostra in coelis*[173]) by hope, and we are ready to leave all things behind at a moment's notice in order to follow Christ wherever He may lead us. It would be well to read here the gospel of the Last Sunday after Pentecost,[174] the closing of the Church year and {the} summary of all the teaching of the liturgy (St. Matthew's parallel to this passage of Luke).

An interlude—chapter 20: *Abimelek marries Sara.* This incident is obviously out of its proper context. Abimelek would not have been

---

173. "our conversation is in heaven" (Col 2:20).

174. Matt 24:15-35: "When therefore you shall see the abomination of desolation, which was spoken of by Daniel the prophet, standing in the holy place: he that readeth let him understand. Then they that are in Judea, let them flee to the mountains: And he that is on the housetop, let him not come down to take any thing out of his house: And he that is in the field, let him not go back to take his coat. And woe to them that are with child, and that give suck in those days. But pray that your flight be not in the winter, or on the sabbath. For there shall be then great tribulation, such as hath not been from the beginning of the world until now, neither shall be. And unless those days had been shortened, no flesh should be saved: but for the sake of the elect those days shall be shortened. Then if any man shall say to you: Lo here is Christ, or there, do not believe him. For there shall arise false Christs and false prophets, and shall shew great signs and wonders, insomuch as to deceive (if possible) even the elect. Behold I have told it to you, beforehand. If therefore they shall say to you: Behold he is in the desert, go ye not out: Behold he is in the closets, believe it not. For as lightning cometh out of the east, and appeareth even into the west: so shall the coming of the Son of man be. Wheresoever the body shall be, there shall the eagles also be gathered together. And immediately after the tribulation of those days, the sun shall be darkened and the moon shall not give her light, and the stars shall fall from heaven, and the powers of heaven shall be moved: And then shall appear the sign of the Son of man in heaven: and then shall all tribes of the earth mourn: and they shall see the Son of man coming in the clouds of heaven with much power and majesty. And he shall send his angels with a trumpet, and a great voice: and they shall gather together his elect from the four winds, from the farthest parts of the heavens to the utmost bounds of them. And from the fig tree learn a parable: When the branch thereof is now tender, and the leaves come forth, you know that summer is nigh. So you also, when you shall see all these things, know ye that it is nigh, even at the doors. Amen I say to you, that this generation shall not pass, till all these things be done. Heaven and earth shall pass, but my words shall not pass" (*Missale Romanum*, 445-46; *Missale Cisterciense*, 317).

especially anxious to marry an old woman of nearly a hundred. It is a "repeat" of the incident in Egypt in another form, by the Elohist writer (says *BJ*[175]). The moral tone is a little higher; the "lie" is explained away satisfactorily (verse 12). Again the purpose {is} to show the beauty of Sara, the protection of Abraham by God, the special place of the marriage of Abraham and Sara in divine providence.

The birth of Isaac (ch. 21): "The Lord visited Sara as He had promised and fulfilled what He had spoken." The narrative is very simple—all the emphasis is on the following facts: (a) the fulfillment of the promise, at the time and in the way promised; (b) Abraham's fulfillment of his part, circumcising the child as he had been commanded; (c) the joy resulting from this miraculous birth. Sara sings a song of triumph and exultation in God, a pure cry of joy in the miracle. She is no longer an old woman; she is a miraculous being beyond age and time, one who lives in a new region, a region of the spirit, in which God alone reigns and acts. Here, in her song, her laughter has reached the mystical quality of the laughter of Abraham. She has caught up with the faith of the Patriarch, and is now on a level with him. (Note: nothing needs to be said about Abraham's reaction—he makes no comment; he is beyond exultation; with great solemnity and perfection he carries out the work of God.) "God hath made a laughter for me":[176] Isaac has become the laughter of Sara and Abraham, or rather the laughter of God in their lives (*BJ* weakens the whole thing by translating: "God has given me something to laugh about"[177]). All who hear and believe will share in the laughter of Abraham and Sara—to be a son of Abraham means to share that laughter. Note how everything here suggests the birth of the Promised Seed of Abraham, of Whom Isaac is only the foreshadowing. The laughter of Sara is the quiet, supernal laughter we feel in our hearts on Christmas night; it is the exultation with which John the Baptist leapt in the womb of Elizabeth at Our Lady's salutation.[178] Mary herself in her Magnificat refers back to the promise to Abraham and develops the primitive and almost inarticulate joy of Sara to a level of high and noble expression.[179] The joy of Sara is reproduced more perfectly in the simple hearts of the shepherds, who "returned

---

175. De Vaux, *Genèse*, 99.

176. Gen 21:6.

177. "Dieu m'a donné de quoi rire" (de Vaux, *Genèse*, 101).

178. See Luke 1:41, 44.

179. Luke 1:46–55, which concludes: "He hath received Israel his servant, being mindful of his mercy: As he spoke to our fathers, to Abraham and to his seed for ever."

glorifying and praising God for all the things they had heard and seen, as it was told to them" (Luke 2:20). And of course the angels, with their *Gloria*, their song of joy, show us the same "laughter," but on a higher and more eminent level. It is the laughter of the created world which wakes up to discover that its God and Creator has become part of it, has taken flesh and lives in the midst of the works of His own hands!

The feast at the weaning of Isaac {is held} (21:8). This text is taken by St. John of the Cross and applied to the dark night: there is greater joy among the angels when the soul begins to be purified and "weaned" from consolations and led into darkness, because now it will begin to be strong and not continue to be carried and babied by others (cf. *Dark Night*, 1:12 [p. 384][180]).

Ishmael cast out (v. 9–20): Sara sees Ishmael (a bigger boy) bullying the child Isaac, and demands that he be "sent away" with his mother. Again, there is jealousy and cruelty in this, although some commentators think she was simply giving Agar her "liberty"—a queer kind of liberty (see 14–16)! Abraham sends Agar off into the desert with the child, with a skin of water which soon runs out. He is sorry to do this but wants to please Sara. He makes up his mind to grant her request when he is reassured by God that the child will be safe. It is necessary, in the providential designs of God, that there be no other beside Isaac, the sole heir. Abraham is not sending them to their death, but is disinheriting Ishmael and repudiating Agar. The deeply touching narrative {focuses on} the sorrow of Agar: she goes away to a different place so as not to see the child die; she weeps, apart, and we see the child lying under a tree, exhausted and weeping helplessly. "And God heard the voice of the boy." An angel calls to Agar; a well is miraculously discovered; the child grows up to be an archer.

Points about this story {include}:

---

180. "This night and purgation of the desire, a happy one for the soul, works in it so many blessings and benefits . . . that, even as Abraham made a great feast when he weaned his son Isaac, even so is there joy in Heaven because God is now taking this soul from its swaddling clothes, setting it down from His arms, making it to walk upon its feet, and likewise taking from it the milk of the breast and the soft and sweet food proper to children, and making it to eat bread with crust, and to begin to enjoy the food of robust persons. This food, in these aridities and this darkness of sense, is now given to the spirit, which is dry and emptied of all the sweetness of sense. And this food is the infused contemplation whereof we have spoken" (Peers, *John of the Cross*, 1:384).

1. St. Paul comments (Romans 9:7 ff.): it is not sufficient to be a son of Abraham according to the flesh in order to be the seed of Abraham. What matters is to be a child of the promise—a child of the miracle which brought forth Isaac, and brought Christ into the world. This "generation" is not by the will of man or by the will of the flesh but by faith.

2. A more important passage {is} Galatians 4:21—a further development of the same theme. Note {that} this new development turns the tables completely on the Jews. Rejoicing in their descendence from Abraham according to the flesh, they were satisfied with the rejection of Ishmael. But now, suddenly, we see that the Jews, descended from Isaac by the flesh, are in reality excluded with Ishmael: Agar is the Old Testament and the earthly Jerusalem; Sara is the heavenly Jerusalem, and we—namely the Christians, gentile as well as Jewish—are Isaac, the sons of the promise. Consequently the curious fact remains that those who are descended from Ishmael according to the flesh can in fact spiritually become children of the promise as well as the sons of Isaac—*eo quod ipsi sumus filii Abrahae*[181]—and St. Paul says the Jews, relying on their carnal descendence from Isaac, are rejected and are *not* sons of Abraham. Hence in the mystery of divine Providence we see what great good was left in store for Ishmael, who would be a "great people" also, not only according to the flesh but also according to the spirit.

3. Another application of this passage {is made} by St. John of the Cross: there can be no compromise in the soul between spiritual and carnal liberty: "The soul that is enamored of a prelacy . . . and longs for liberty of desire is considered and treated in the sight of God not as a son but as a base slave and captive. Such a soul will be unable to attain to true liberty of spirit which is divine union. Slavery can have no part with liberty. Liberty cannot dwell in a heart that is subject to desires" etc. (*Ascent* 1:4 [p. 27][182]).

---

181. "it is from this that we ourselves are children of Abraham"; see Gal 3:7: "*cognoscitis ergo quia qui ex fide sunt hii sunt filii Abrahae*" ("Know ye, therefore, that they who are of faith, the same are the children of Abraham").

182. Text reads: "Wherefore the soul that is enamoured of prelacy, or of any other such office, and longs for liberty of desire, is considered and treated, in the sight of God, not as a son, but as a base slave and captive, since it has not been willing to accept His holy doctrine, wherein He teaches us that he who would be greater must be less, and he who would be less must be greater. And therefore such a soul will be unable

THE SACRIFICE OF ISAAC (ch. 22:1–14): this is the high point of the Book of Genesis, one of the most important passages of the Old Testament and one of the keys to the meaning of Christian revelation. It is absolutely necessary to understand this incident. Without it we cannot truly understand our faith. {See} Wisdom 10:5: "When the nations had conspired together to consent to wickedness [Wisdom] knew the just and preserved him without blame to God, and kept him strong against the compassion for his son." In the background we see again Sodom and Gomorrha, and pagan religion in general. Scripture is here telling us (cf. Romans 1 again) that the gentiles have conspired together to worship false gods and to deny God in the cult of their own passions. This is the ultimate fate of all paganism, even though the select few may rise to high spirituality in it. In contrast, Abraham, "known by" Wisdom, has apprehended the true essence of religion: *obedience to God*, total and unquestioning acceptance of the divine good pleasure, in testimony of His utter holiness and of our creaturehood. Whereas the pagans sank below the level of nature, and sinned against nature itself, Abraham's faith in God raised him above nature and enabled him to obey in a manner that was impossible to nature. Hebrews 11:17–19 brings out fully the supernatural character of Abraham's trial. It would be a *drastic oversimplification* to imagine that Abraham was merely ready to sacrifice Isaac, as if that were all. There is much more involved in this. The test of Abraham's faith is not merely that he is ready to obey God and sacrifice his son. *What is being tested here in a supreme way is Abraham's faith in God's promise.* In other words the trial is twofold:

a) On the more obvious level, Abraham is called to do away with the beloved child in whom all his complacency rests, and all his joy.

b) But on the higher level, Abraham is really called upon to believe that somehow this contradiction will be resolved by God; the promise is not forgotten—this is just the divine and incomprehensible way in which God intends to fulfill the promise. Unlike Lot's wife, Abraham does not look back at all; he simply goes forward in blind obedience to the command of God, believing that this is the way to

---

to attain to that true liberty of spirit which is encompassed in His Divine union. For slavery can have no part with liberty; and liberty cannot dwell in a heart that is subject to desires, for this is the heart of a slave; but it dwells in the free man, because he has the heart of a son. It was for this reason that Sarah bade her husband Abraham cast out the bondwoman and her son, saying that the son of the bondwoman should not be heir with the son of the free woman" (Peers, *John of the Cross*, 1:27).

the fulfillment of the promise, *believing firmly that Isaac will not be lost to him but will somehow be recovered.*

c) We may assume that Abraham knew full well that *God abominated human sacrifice*, since this too was a mark of pagan degeneracy. But Abraham's faith in the voice of God is unquestioning, even in the presence of this contradiction.

d) In Abraham's sacrifice of Isaac we see finally the highest reality, an expression of God the Father's sacrifice of His own divine Son. By the unquestioning faith of his friend Abraham, God the Father manifests Himself in Abraham and in this sacrifice. Hence, as a manifestation of the loving mercy hidden in the bosom of the Father, this passage is scarcely surpassed by any other in the Bible except the great manifestations in the New Testament: the Baptism of Jesus, the Transfiguration, Calvary and the Resurrection.

e) The obedience of Abraham has made him a perfect mirror of the divine mercy. He is momentarily exposed to the light of the divine mystery which shines upon him when he does not realize it, in the moment of his greatest darkness. In the mirror of Abraham's great soul this flash of inaccessible light has been caught and fixed for all ages to behold, if they can but open the eyes of faith to see the mystery.

f) The application of this to us is obvious. Abraham is the pattern of the soul perfectly consecrated to God, the soul that has left its own people, its own friends, its home, its familiar language, {has} gone into a strange country, lived for years on the divine promises, followed God faithfully, walking "before Him"[183] in perfection. Finally comes the greatest trial, when *all that has been acquired* through the grace and mercy of God must also be sacrificed. We must rise above it to God alone—in doing so, however, *we recover all*. In losing all we gain all, and we must have Abraham's faith and courage to do this. Only then can God fully manifest Himself in our lives, in the great darkness like that which came upon Abraham.

{According to} the text of Hebrews (11:17 f.), *by faith* Abraham when he was put to the test offered Isaac. It was a test of his *faith*, manifested by

---

183. See Gen 17:1: "And after he began to be ninety and nine years old, the Lord appeared to him: and said unto him: I am the Almighty God: walk before me, and be perfect."

obedience—not merely obedience, but obedience as a sign of faith: so too with us. *He who had received the promises* reasoned that God has power to raise up even from the dead. Clearly then, it is revealed in the New Testament that Abraham believed that the promises would be fulfilled in spite of everything. *Whence he received him back as a type*: Isaac is a type of Christ—in the sacrifice we see both the death and resurrection of Jesus.

Text of Genesis:

After these things God tempted Abraham[184]—tempted in the sense of tried, tested. After all what things? Everything that God had so far done in the life of Abraham was leading up to this great trial. The promises made to Abraham had been at once a preparation for the trial and a foreshadowing of Abraham's successful negotiation of it. All the graces received by him had given God complete control in Abraham's soul, so that now Abraham was able freely to meet the great test of his faith, and in doing so to be united in an ineffable manner to God in mystery.

Abraham, Abraham—Here I am.[185] Again {there is} the calling of the name, the "awakening" to the special presence of God. Recall: *Adam, ubi es?*[186]—and Adam in hiding. Abraham is not in hiding. He enjoys *parrhesia*, perfect freedom of "communication" with God. He is not afraid, does not have to hide. *Ecce adsum*[187] (the thought occurs—the summoning of the candidates for ordination {as a parallel}[188]). To become fully conscious of one's freedom and responsibility; by no means do we lose ourselves in nonentity when God calls us. He who called us into being by His creative power summons us to fullness of spiritual being by His sanctifying commands. Abraham is ready for absolutely anything, as is proved by the unhesitating promptness with which he will put the divine command into effect.

Take thy only begotten son Isaac whom thou lovest:[189] God reminds Abraham forcibly of the love he has for his son. It is God Himself Who has created this love and placed it in Abraham's heart. It is indeed more

---

184. Gen 22:1.

185. Gen 22:1.

186. Gen 3:9.

187. "Behold, here I am" (Gen 22:1).

188. "*Et vocantur omnes tonsurandi nominatim . . . et quilibet respondet Adsum*" (*Pontificale Romanum*, 12) ("And all to be tonsured are called by name . . . and each answers, 'Here I am'").

189. Gen 22:2.

than a natural tenderness, for in Abraham's love for Isaac is also his love for God, since Isaac is, so to speak, the embodiment of the divine promise and the *pledge of the divine fidelity*.

Go into the land of vision (*in terram visionis*)—"to the land of Moriah"[190] (tradition held that Abraham offered his sacrifice on Mount Moriah, site of the temple of Jerusalem[191])—"upon one of the mountains which I will show thee":[192] everything is regulated by the will of God, down to the last detail.

Abraham rising up in the night (or at break of day), he starts immediately. He saddles the ass, cuts wood for the sacrifice, and "he went his way to the place God had commanded him."[193] It is a three days' journey, during which Abraham is immersed in his thoughts, or in the darkness of deep faith, on a spiritual level higher than our comprehending, yet in the depths of his poverty. Isaac walks beside him with unquestioning trust. One wonders what is more moving—the faith of Abraham or the ingenuous trust of Isaac—both are in a sense the same, for Abraham looks up to God his Father with the same childlike trust with which Isaac looks up to Abraham, and Abraham himself is being led a victim to a spiritual sacrifice greater than physical immolation, for he bears the "burden" of the word he cannot understand but only believes.

On the third day he lifted up his eyes:[194] this is the only indication of the way in which God showed him "the place." He just looked up and he saw it. Then he dismissed the two servants. *We will go yonder . . . after we have worshipped* we will return to you.[195] Here again, Abraham seems in some inexplicable way to understand that he will return with Isaac. One thinks of the two servants, who stood there and passed the time, and when Abraham and Isaac returned they had no idea what had happened. So it is with the great trials and acts of God in the lives of holy men. These things are perhaps never suspected by the bystanders. And {consider} all the bystanders on Calvary—and we also: we too are bystanders in this mystery, long used to it; we take it as a matter of course. But as Abraham suffered in offering his beloved son, so too we

---

190. So the Masoretic Hebrew text (Sutcliffe, "Genesis," 196 [n. 153b]).

191. 2 Par [2 Chr] 3:1 identifies the site with the Temple Mount in Jerusalem (Sutcliffe, "Genesis," 196 [n. 153b]).

192. Gen 22:2.

193. Gen 22:3.

194. Gen 22:4.

195. Gen 22:5.

can surmise what mystery—not of suffering indeed, but of "separation"—took place in the Father when His Beloved Son was given over to be the prey of evil and nothingness. One cannot begin to think what this could have been—I have never seen anything written about it, but if Abraham somehow represents the heavenly Father, and if the Father in the parable of the Prodigal Son felt loss and longing for his son, then we can see in the mystery of Abraham and Isaac the longing of the heavenly Father for sinners, His prodigal sons, and His desire to offer even His only-begotten Son to recover them. Abraham, the father of the Redeemed, gives us then some insight into the unthinkable mystery of what took place in the heart of God our Father, first when He consented to let Adam His son be torn from Him by sin, and then when He recovered him by sending His own Son into the world and letting Him die on the Cross. {Here is} depth beyond depth of mystery.

I and the boy will go yonder:[196] Abraham tells the servants to wait. They would not understand the preparations for sacrifice without an evident victim. Note that he has had three days in which to change his mind, and now too, the last lap, is even more of a chance to change his mind and find some kind of victim, to perform himself the action of substituting a victim for Isaac—a work which belongs to God alone and which he hopes for without hope (for here above all Abraham hopes against hope![197])

He took the wood for the holocaust and laid it upon Isaac his son.[198] In this gesture we see the heavenly Father appear in Abraham—we see the Father lay the Cross upon the shoulders of Jesus with infinite love and pity, and we recognize the fact that just as Abraham suffers more than Isaac in this whole action, so in some inexplicable way the Father is somehow the ultimate recipient of everything that is visited upon Jesus in the passion—not in the sense that He suffers physically or morally, but He is the target of the hatred which wreaks itself upon Jesus, and through Jesus and in Him the Father mystically becomes totally accessible to those who attack Him. The picture {follows} of Abraham and Isaac going on alone, the son with the wood, the father with "fire and a sword."[199] Is it permissible to push this a little far and see in it, at least by application,

---

196. Gen 22:5.
197. See Rom 4:18.
198. Gen 22:6.
199. Gen 22:6.

some suggestion of the Holy Trinity? The fire that consumed the Victim on Calvary was the fire of the Holy Spirit.

Isaac said to his Father—My Father:[200] {there is} constant repetition of the words "Father" and "Son" in every line here; cf. Luke 22:24: "Father, if thou wilt, remove this chalice from me"; Mark 14:36: "Abba, Father, all things are possible for thee, remove this chalice from me: but not as I will, but as thou wilt." (Yet this is more the prayer of Abraham here than of Isaac; Isaac apparently does not doubt—he just asks the innocent question. Abraham is the one who suffers.)

God will provide Himself a victim:[201] Abraham does not fully know what he is saying. Without clearly realizing it, he is prophesying that the ram will be found, and above all prophesying that the Lamb of God Who takes away the sins of the world will be sent by the Father as the antitype of Isaac. "So they went on together." Abraham still has time to provide another victim for himself. He has not committed himself openly yet.

He built an altar . . . and bound Isaac his son:[202] now he has committed himself entirely, and he even lifts the sword. It is the moment of total darkness.

An angel from heaven called to him:[203] in this moment he passes through darkness to light. *By his consent, it is not Isaac who has died, but the last vestige of self has died in Abraham,* and when the angel calls his name it is a new Abraham who answers, and Isaac is recovered to him in a higher and more perfect possession that will not be taken away, for now the promise is confirmed. "Now I know that thou fearest God."[204] The test has been passed, and Abraham is indeed beyond all tests. He fears God not merely potentially, but in all truth. His faith is perfect. He sees the ram, offers it instead of Isaac, and calls the place "The Lord seeth."[205] Modern commentators and translators correct this "name" of the place to mean more accurately: "*On the mountain the Lord provides what He wills.*"[206] This is Abraham's summary of the whole mystery, the inscrutable will of God in which mercy, justice, love, power, etc. are all united

---

200. Gen 22:7.
201. Gen 22:8.
202. Gen 22:9.
203. Gen 22:11.
204. Gen 22:12.
205. Gen 22:14.
206. See Sutcliffe, "Genesis," 196 [n. 152b].

beyond and above all human conceptions. {In} lines 16–18 the promise {is} definitively renewed, in the strongest of terms. Abraham by his action has finally and perfectly left the destiny of the chosen people entirely in the hands of God. He has willed to act in all humility as a perfectly obedient instrument of the divine will, never stopping to question for a moment God's inscrutable wisdom and power. It is with such obedience as this of Abraham that we must meet the problems of obedience in the religious life. Unhesitating obedience, perfect obedience is *not possible* as long as we fall short of the perfection of faith shown by Abraham. This perfection of faith must take us *beyond all human standards of judgement and comparison*. When we receive a hard command, either we believe in God, either we see Him directly present to us, or else we keep Him remote and in the background, and our faith reaches Him only through the veil of many human judgements. Either we accept the command literally as it stands, as coming from God, or we take the obvious and evident desire of the superior and *compare it with some other possible indication of the will of God*. We do not say simply, "God wills this"; we say, "God *might also will* that other thing and still others yet, and maybe in fact He does so will." This is the kind of hesitation in faith which masks as reasonableness and which in fact destroys obedience. We have all the evidence we need to know that this here and now is the will of God for us. But we prefer to evade the issue by calling upon all kinds of abstract arguments which remind us that God *might* will something else. We give these arguments probability by *comparing* what is in fact commanded with what might have been commanded. We take these different commands, and evaluate them as they would be in themselves. Then by our logic we take the one that seems best to us and assert that this must be the will of God, and then prefer this to the will of our superior, saying perhaps, "It is necessary to obey God rather than men."[207] In this way we actually frustrate the will of God entirely; not only that, but we do not scruple to impose our will on Him, dictating to Him what is best, saying in effect, "You cannot will this; there is something more perfect which You are obliged to will." And what is this more perfect thing? It is what appears to me best. Hence, in a word, it is *my will*. We do not see this as long as we are able to hide our disobedience under the cloak of plausible abstract principles, and evade the will of God, in the will of our superiors, by resorting to abstract argument. Our obligation is to embrace the *concrete expression of the will of*

---

207. Acts 5:29.

God for us, here and now—a concrete expression which is apprehended by us through faith (which is of course corroborated by reason—but it is {a} question of a practical judgement, not of a speculative one, and we must not allow speculation to become an evasion from reality). We do not obey with perfect faith if we only obey when we naturally agree with the superior and approve entirely of all that he wants. Note the special interior poverty of one who obeys perfectly. He deprives himself of the luxury of seeing himself think things out and put them into effect as a little god. He is liberated from fixation on his own ideas and ways of doing things. He is taken out of himself and beyond himself in willing the will of another—but he ruins everything if he turns again and contemplates himself obeying. {Thus we see the} special importance of obedience in our time—obedience in the perspectives of the Mystical Body. We cannot see what is ahead, and our destiny *cannot* be regarded as an individual affair. It is almost impossible for the individual to know what is best or not, in the long run. Faith alone will serve, and perfect obedience in view of a result we cannot foresee—obedience as a reparation for the pride of tyrants and impious men who have denied God.

Chapter 23—*The Death and Burial of Sara*: this chapter {is} by the levitical writer, and is therefore especially juridical—a question of legal tradition: who owns what, and where. It remains a very lively chapter, the contract between Abraham and the sons of Heth (Hittites) being recorded in the most human terms—a description of how it actually was made, no doubt a précis of the long, polite, oriental bargaining. The writer no doubt saw in this possession of a burial place the first sign of fulfillment of the divine promise that Abraham's race would possess the land of Canaan (he remains a nomad at this time!).

Chapter 24—*The Servant of Abraham goes to find a Wife for Isaac*: Abraham wants Isaac to marry a girl from his old country, from Ur. But if one cannot be found, it is important that Isaac remain in Canaan, the promised Land; for him to leave and settle elsewhere would be a lack of faith in the promise. They are still living under the regime of faith in the promise of God for everything, including their establishment in Canaan. {In} verse 7, Abraham promises the servant that an angel will guide him and lead him to the place where a wife for Isaac can be found. READ verses 10–33:[208] {note} the beauty and simplicity of the narrative. First

---

208. "And he took ten camels of his master's herd, and departed, carrying something of all his goods with him, and he set forward and went on to Mesopotamia to the city of Nachor. And when he had made the camels lie down without the town near

{notice the} literal sense—the scene with all its charm and reality. Second, {looked at} spiritually, {we find} the *mystery of journeys*, again. The human race {is} divided by sin and selfishness, but everywhere among men God has His chosen ones, and His angels bring them together. The mystery of human love and affection, of human interest in those who are far from us, the desire to seek out kindred souls in a far country—this is a wonderful longing implanted in the heart of man by God, a wonderful nostalgia for unity and peace in Him. It is the natural source of the missionary spirit. It is also connected, again, with the mystery of hospitality.

---

a well of water in the evening, at the time when women are wont to come out to draw water, he said: O Lord the God of my master Abraham, meet me today, I beseech thee, and shew kindness to my master Abraham. Behold I stand nigh the spring of water, and the daughters of the inhabitants of this city will come out to draw water. Now, therefore, the maid to whom I shall say: Let down thy pitcher that I may drink: and she shall answer, Drink, and I will give thy camels drink also: let it be the same whom thou hast provided for thy servant Isaac: and by this I shall understand, that thou hast shewn kindness to my master. He had not yet ended these words within himself, and behold Rebecca came out, the daughter of Bathuel, son of Melcha, wife to Nachor the brother of Abraham, having a pitcher on her shoulder: An exceeding comely maid, and a most beautiful virgin, and not known to man: and she went down to the spring, and filled her pitcher and was coming back. And the servant ran to meet her, and said: Give me a little water to drink of thy pitcher. And she answered: Drink, my lord. And quickly she let down the pitcher upon her arm, and gave him drink. And when he had drunk, she said: I will draw water for thy camels also, till they all drink. And pouring out the pitcher into the troughs, she ran back to the well to draw water: and having drawn she gave to all the camels. But he musing beheld her with silence, desirous to know whether the Lord had made his journey prosperous or not. And after that the camels had drunk, the man took out golden earrings, weighing two sicles: and as many bracelets of ten sicles weight. And he said to her: Whose daughter art thou? tell me: is there any place in thy father's house to lodge? And she answered: I am the daughter of Bathuel, the son of Melcha, whom she bore to Nachor. And she said moreover to him: We have good store of both straw and hay, and a large place to lodge in. The man bowed himself down, and adored the Lord, Saying: Blessed be the Lord God of my master Abraham, who hath not taken away his mercy and truth from my master, and hath brought me the straight way into the house of my master's brother. Then the maid ran, and told in her mother's house, all that she had heard. And Rebecca had a brother named Laban, who went out in haste to the man, to the well. And when he had seen the earrings and bracelets in his sister's hands, and had heard all that she related, saying: Thus and thus the man spoke to me: he came to the man who stood by the camels, and near to the spring of water, And said to him: Come in, thou blessed of the Lord: why standest thou without? I have prepared the house, and a place for the camels. And he brought him in into his lodging: and he unharnessed the camels and gave straw and hay, and water to wash his feet, and the feet of the men that were come with him. And bread was set before him. But he said: I will not eat, till I tell my message. He answered him: Speak."

Note the charm and courtesy of all the talk, the dignity {and} sobriety of all the actions. God manifests Himself and works through these beautiful human qualities. There is a certain courtliness in primitive society which has been lost in so-called civilization. {In} verse 50, after the servant has repeated the whole story, Laban and Bathuel exclaim, "the word hath proceeded from the Lord" (that is to say this happening—the event—is a manifestation of God and of His will). They will certainly do His will; they cannot say either yes or no—it is already decided by God Himself. Read 24:61–67: the meeting of Isaac and Rebecca.[209] Discuss the *spiritual value of the simple literal sense* of this narrative.

REBECCA AND ISAAC IN THE FATHERS: the union of the soul with Jesus, of the Church with the Incarnate Word, {is reflected} through the contemplation of the mysteries revealed in Scripture.

{According to} *Origen*, {in his} Homily 10 on Genesis,[210] as Isaac grew, so grew Abraham's joy not in the things that are seen but in those that are not seen, says Origen. It was in the growth of Isaac, Abraham's joy, that Abraham rejoiced to "see the day of Christ."[211] In Isaac Abraham's hope had a concrete and visible form, but it was still a hope in the invisible—Isaac, as it were, a sacrament of Christ for Abraham. We should have his sacramental view of created things in so far as they are capable of being vehicles and containers of grace (v.g. our monastery, the community, the abbot, the brethren). {In} n. 2, Rebecca came each day to the well to draw water. "This is teaching for our souls, and spiritual doctrine, which forms us and instructs us so that each day we must come to the well of Scripture and to the waters of the Holy Spirit, and ever to draw from these waters and bring home a full vessel as did holy Rebecca, who in no other way could be married to the Patriarch Isaac than by drawing

---

209. "So Rebecca and her maids, being set upon camels, followed the man: who with speed returned to his master. At the same time Isaac was walking along the way to the well which is called Of the living and the seeing: for he dwelt in the south country. And he was gone forth to meditate in the field, the day being now well spent: and when he had lifted up his eyes, he saw camels coming afar off. Rebecca also, when she saw Isaac, lighted off the camel, And said to the servant: Who is that man who cometh towards us along the field? And he said to her: That man is my master. But she quickly took her cloak, and covered herself. And the servant told Isaac all that he had done. Who brought her into the tent of Sara his mother, and took her to wife: and he loved her so much, that it moderated the sorrow which was occasioned by his mother's death."

210. Migne, *PG* 12, cols. 215–20.

211. "*per quod Abrahae visio illa qua videbat Christi diem*" (n. 1 [Migne, PG 12, col. 215B]).

from these waters."[212] "All these things that are written are mysteries—Christ wishes to espouse thee.... Since Christ wishes to espouse thee, He sends to thee His servant. The servant is the prophetic word [of Scripture] and unless you receive him you cannot be united with Christ."[213] Hence Rebecca going to draw water is the soul approaching Scripture each day, not realizing, perhaps, that one day a special messenger from God will be there waiting—a special grace. How {is one} to be disposed to receive that grace?

a) Rebecca is called "patience":[214] one must be patient and humble. (Origen delivers an aside against the arrogant rhetoric of the Greeks—the language in which he treats this question reminds us of the Fathers' commentary on Zacchaeus too—his humility, his neglect of worldly and proud wisdom.) What matters in a word is *simplicity*, not seeking great things in the eyes of men. If one lacks this simplicity, no amount of learning can help one to find Jesus truly in the Scriptures. But with it, learning can be of great help.

b) Just as Jesus sat by the well and asked the Samaritan woman to give Him to drink, so here too the *"propheticus sermo"*[215]—the grace of understanding which will slake the thirst of our souls, at first appears to ask us for a "drink"[216] in asking for our *application—exercitia et vigilantia*.[217] "The soul then that does all things patiently, who is so prompt and supported by such learning, who is used to drawing from the depths of contemplation, such a soul can be joined in marriage with the Word."[218]

---

212. "*Animarum est ista eruditio, et spiritalis doctrina, quae te instituit, et docet quotidie venire ad puteos Scripturarum, ad aquas Spiritus sancti, et haurire semper ac plenum vas domum referre, sicut faciebat et sancta Rebecca, quae non aliter jungi potuisset tanto patriarchae Isaac . . . nisi hauriendo aquas*" (Migne, PG 12, col. 216CD).

213. "*Mysteria sunt cuncta quae scripta sunt: vult te Christus sibi desponsare . . . . Quia ergo vult et te sibi Christus despondere, id est desponsare, praemittit ad te istum puerum. Puer iste sermo propheticus est, quem nisi prius susceperis, nubere Christo non poteris*" (Migne, PG 12, col. 217A).

214. "*Rebecca, quae interpretatur patientia*" (Migne, PG 12, col. 217B).

215. "prophetic word" (Migne, PG 12, col. 217A).

216. "*potum*" (Migne, PG 12, col. 217C).

217. "training and attentiveness" (Migne, PG 12, col. 217C, which reads: "*exercitia et vigilantiam*").

218. "*Ista ergo talis anima, quae agit cuncta patienter, quae tam prompta est et tanta eruditione subnixa, quae de profundis haurire scientiae fluenta consuevit, ipsa potest*

Origen says that the soul must come each day to the *auditorium Verbi*,[219] meaning not only the reading of Scripture but the spoken explanation by a minister of the Church. This expression is very important because St. Bernard used it in his explanations of the Canticle of Canticles.[220] This passage of Origen throws light on the theology of the Cistercian Fathers; so does the next text we shall see, from St. Ambrose.

St. Ambrose: *De Isaac et Anima*[221]—St. Ambrose's treatise on the marriage of Isaac and Rebecca is in reality a brief treatise on mystical theology, on the union of the soul with the Word. St. Ambrose begins by saying that Isaac is of course a type of Christ. His miraculous birth prefigures the virgin birth of the Savior. His very name signifies the joy which Jesus brought us by saving us from the power of death and of the devil. The union of Isaac with Rebecca signifies both the union of Christ with the Church and the union of the Word with the individual soul. Here St. Ambrose begins talking about the mystical ascent, in terms of the Canticle of Canticles. He comments on the first verse, which provides St. Bernard with material for so many sermons: *Osculetur me osculo oris sui*.[222] Here we have the first degree of the mystical life—*primus processus*.[223] St. Ambrose comments: the soul, detached from sin and from material things, longs for the presence of the Word and prays thus to the Father: Hoc est osculum Verbi, Lumen cognitionis sacrae (*PL* 14:506).[224] This kiss

---

copulari nuptiis Christi" (Migne, PG 12, col. 217C).

219. "place of hearing the Word" (n. 3 [Migne, PG 12, col. 217D], which reads: "*auditorio verbi*").

220. "*Quod si sessio significat magisterium; puto illam, qui unus est nobis magister in coelo et in terra, Dei Sapientiam Christum . . . inde tanquam de solemni auditorio docere angelum, docere hominem scientiam*" (*In Cantica*, 19.4 [Migne, PL 183, col. 865A]) ("For if sitting signifies teaching authority, I think that He Who is our one teacher in heaven and on earth, Christ the Wisdom of God . . . as though from that solemn lecture hall, teaches that knowledge to angels and to men"). "*Quid enim tibi aliud de Christi auditorio sonuit, cum paulo ante clamatum est: Qui amat animam suam, perdet eam?* (Ioan. XII, 25.)" (*In Cantica*, 30.11 [Migne, PL 183, col. 939B]) ("For what else did you hear from the lecture hall of Christ, when it was proclaimed a short time before: 'He who loves his life will lose it' (John 12:25)").

221. Migne, *PL* 14, cols. 501A–534B.

222. "Let him kiss me with the kiss of his mouth" (Song 1:1) (Migne, *PL* 14, cols. 505D–506A [c. 3, n. 8]); the first eight of Bernard's Sermons on the Canticle are based on this verse (Migne, *PL* 183, cols. 785A–814D); for a discussion see Merton, *Cistercian Fathers and Their Monastic Theology*, 263–68.

223. C. 3, nn. 8–10 (Migne, *PL* 14, cols. 505D–507C).

224. "For this is the kiss of the Word, indeed the light of sacred understanding"

is explained more in detail: "God the Word kisses us when He *enlightens our heart and the high point of our spirit* with divine knowledge."[225] This is not mere intellectual knowledge, still less speculative knowledge. It is a mystical wisdom, a touch of grace acting on the inmost depths of the spirit by *means of charity* (that is why St. Ambrose says "heart"). "The kiss is that by which lovers are united and cling to one another, and are refreshed with the joy of inner sweetness. By this kiss the soul clings to the Word and receives into its inmost depths the infusion of the Holy Spirit" (506).[226] To explain: there must be a *contact* and an *infusion*. The contact is made above all by the application of loving faith. At least this faith and hope, enlivened by desire and prayer, are our way of opening our soul to the action of the Word. We cannot force Him to give us what we desire; we can only ask Him and leave Him to answer as He wills. But obviously love is the only way to ensure a right answer. If we do not believe in His love, how can we venture to ask for the kiss of His mouth? But, says St. Ambrose, we see this love darkly in the mysteries of Scripture. But He Himself reveals it more clearly in a "kiss" of His Spirit, which "reveals the mysteries of His heart and the interior disciplines of wisdom"[227] (*quid*?). Then the soul is refreshed with the "perfumed ointments"[228] of the Word, that is to say with the *odor gratiae*.[229] This goes back to Origen's doctrine of {the} spiritual senses:[230] charity indeed endows our spirit with special

---

(Migne, *PL* 14, col. 506B [c. 3, n. 8], which reads: "Hoc est enim . . . lumen scilicet . . .").

225. "Osculatur enim nos Deus Verbum, quando cor nostrum, et ipsum principale hominis spiritu divinae cognitionis illuminat" (Migne, *PL* 14, col. 506B [c. 3, n. 8]).

226. "Osculum est enim quo invicem amantes sibi adhaerent, et velut gratiae interioris suavitate potiuntur. Per hoc osculum adhaeret anima Deo Verbo, per quod sibi transfunditur spiritus osculantis" (Migne, *PL* 14, col. 506BC [c. 3, n. 8]).

227. "dogmata sua, et interioris sapientiae disciplinas" (Migne, *PL* 14, col. 506C [c. 3, n. 9]).

228. "odor unguentorum tuorum super omnia aromata" (Song 1:2) (Migne, *PL* 14, col. 506C [c. 3, n. 9]).

229. "the odor of grace" (Migne, *PL* 14, col. 506CD [c. 3, n. 9]).

230. See Merton, *Cassian and the Fathers*, 29: "As we grow in experience, we develop the use of the spiritual senses which give us a kind of experience of ineffable and divine realities, 'sight for contemplating supracorporal objects, hearing, capable of distinguishing voices which do not sound in the air; . . . smell which perceives that which led Paul to speak of the good odor of Christ; touch which St. John possessed when he laid his hands upon the Word of Life' ({*Contra Celsum*, I:48}). The spiritual senses do not develop unless we mortify the carnal senses." See also the extensive discussion of the spiritual senses, particularly in Gregory of Nyssa, developing the teaching of Origen, in Merton, *Introduction to Christian Mysticism*, 82–96.

"senses" by which it perceives as it were directly and experientially certain values which the intelligence alone cannot reach. What St. Ambrose specifically means here is an inner spiritual realization of the goodness and mercy of God our Savior. *He wants us to have that realization*, for has He not said, "Taste and see that the Lord is sweet"?[231] St. Ambrose also points out that Jesus Himself has urged us to seek this spiritual refreshment in Him: "*Venite ad me omnes qui laboratis . . . ego reficiam vos.*"[232] The soul can only pray: "*trahe nos*"[233] and desire to be drawn by the grace of Christ because it has not sufficient strength of its own to follow Him. He sets a fast pace! (507B). So much for the first degree of the mystical life.

Second Degree (*secundus processus*[234]—"going forward"): "*Introduxit me in cubiculum.*"[235] "The {soul} passing beyond all that is understandable [enters into the inner chamber of the Word] and is there nourished and strengthened" (508).[236] St. Ambrose points out that this implies a very great interior solitude. The one who is to enter into the inner chamber of the Word must rely on nothing visible or tangible. Hence it must stand alone, and without the grace of God it will be poor indeed. But because it lives for Him alone Whom it cannot see, it is never less alone than when alone.[237] Such a soul is poor and humble: she is darkened (*fusca sum*[238]); she is criticized by others (*filii matris meae pugnaverunt contra me*[239]); she has been unable to fulfill all of her obligations (*vineam meam non custodivi*[240]). Living still in the body, the soul realizes that it is often tarnished by the onslaughts of indeliberate passion and sin (n. 13,

231. Ps 33[34]:9.

232. "Come to me all you that labor and are burdened, and I will refresh you" (Matt 11:28) (Migne, *PL* 14, col. 507B [c. 3, n. 10]).

233. "Draw us" (Song 1:3) (Migne, *PL* 14, col. 507A [c. 3, n. 10], which reads: "*Attrahe nos*").

234. C. 4, nn. 11–37 (Migne, *PL* 14, cols. 507C–515A).

235. "He hath brought me into his storerooms" (Song 1:3) (Migne, *PL* 14, col. 507D [c. 4, n. 11]).

236. "*ea quae sunt intelligibilia supergressa, in illo confirmatur, atque eo pascitur*" (Migne, *PL* 14, cols. 507D–508A [c. 4, n. 11]); copy text reads: "souls."

237. "*nec minus solum, quam quum solus esset*" (Cicero, *De Officiis*, 3.1, citing Scipio Africanus).

238. "I am black" (Song 1:4) (Migne, *PL* 14, col. 508B [c. 4, n. 13], which reads: "*obfuscata sum*").

239. "the sons of my mother have fought against me" (Song 1:5) (Migne, *PL* 14, col. 508B [c. 4, n. 13], which reads: "*adversum me*").

240. "my vineyard I have not kept" (Song 1:5) (Migne, *PL* 14, col. 508C [c. 4, n. 13]).

p. 508). Complaining of her solitude, she seeks the Word, and the Word replies: "Unless thou knowest thyself..."[241] Unless you grow in sorrow at your own nothingness, and unless you grow in *faith and sincerity*, your complaints will have no meaning. But also, unless you remember the dignity of your nature and the beauty I have placed in thee... etc. (cf. St. Bernard[242]). Know that we are created for union with God, and live up to our calling! Trial and suffering urge us on to this irrevocable choice. {The} second degree is then one in which the soul loses sight of the Word and must seek Him in difficulties, etc.

Third Degree:[243] "*In lectulo meo per noctes*"[244]—in mystical rest and silence. The soul rests, then goes forth and does not find Him, but passing beyond the "guardians of the city"[245] she finds Him inexplicably.

Fourth Degree:[246] "*Ego dormio et cor meum vigilat*."[247] Here the Word Himself comes and wakes the soul from sleep. This is the spiritual marriage, {marked by} perfect union of wills: "*Conformans se ad ejus*

---

241. "*Nisi cognoscas te*" (Song 1:7) (Migne, *PL* 14, col. 509A [c. 4, n. 15]).

242. See Merton's comments on Bernard's discussion of human dignity in chapter 2 of his *De Diligendo Deo*: "Turning inward to our soul we see that He has given us three special gifts among others . . . : *dignitas* (man's supreme dignity is his free will—{his} capacity to love); *scientia* (the light to recognize that he has this dignity and that he does not have it from himself); *virtus* (by which he then devotes himself with all zeal to *seek* God who gave him this dignity, and *clings* to Him with all his strength when he has found Him, attributing all our good to Him alone). Speaking of *scientia*, St. Bernard stresses the importance of self-knowledge, which *knows our dignity*, knows that *it comes from God*, and knows after that *our state as fallen beings*. Without the knowledge of our dignity, our freedom, the rest is nothing. Without true knowledge of our fallen state, our freedom is dangerous. However, our fallen state is essentially ignorance of our true being in God. Two kinds of ignorance are to be fled at all costs—ignorance of our dignity, {our} freedom, {our} capacity to be more than animals; ignorance of the fact that we owe this dignity to God and that it is His image in us, that it makes us capable of being His sons. To know our dignity but not to know its *source* in God leads to pride. Again *scientia* which only knows our dignity, but not its source, turns outward and becomes *curiositas*, and in fact this is ignorance—a mere conformity to outward objects, without realization of our inner spiritual identity" (Merton, *Cistercian Fathers and Their Monastic Theology*, 108–9).

243. C. 5, nn. 38–49 (Migne, *PL* 14, cols. 515A–519B).

244. "In my bed by night" (Song 3:1) (Migne, *PL* 14, col. 515B [c. 5, n. 38], which reads: "*In cubili . . . meo in noctibus*").

245. "*custodes qui in ministerio sunt*" (Song 3:4) (Migne, *PL* 14, col. 515D [c. 5, n. 40]).

246. Cc. 6-8, nn. 50–79 (Migne, *PL* 14, cols. 519C–534B).

247. "I sleep, and my heart watcheth" (Song 5:2) (Migne, *PL* 14, col. 519C [c. 6, n. 50]).

voluntatem ut esse et ipsa conformis imagini Christi"[248] (520). The soul is totally forgetful of itself and of the body; it has put off the "garments of skins"[249] with which God clothed Adam after the Fall (521). Here too the soul *becomes very fruitful*, for in the highest degree of union there is great spiritual fruitfulness for souls (524). The Word praises her for her fruitfulness. Christ is then placed on the soul like a "seal"[250]—He is the Head, the eye, the light, the strength, etc. of the soul (530)—{there has been a} perfect transformation.

Esau and Jacob (READ ch. 25:21–34[251]): {here an} explanation of the hostility between Israelites and Edomites (Arabs) {and} also {of} the contempt of Israel for Edom {is provided} (cf. Numbers 20:14 ff., when the Edomites refuse Israel hospitality as they travel to the promised land). More or less fanciful etymologies {are given} for the names: {in} verse 25, Jacob {is} so called because he held the heel of Esau (*aquob*)—{it is} more likely, says *BJ*,[252] that it came from *Ya'aquob El* (May the Lord protect [me]). {On} the face value of the passage, we tend naturally to sympathize with Esau, because of our folkways and attitude. He represents what we have come to prefer—the rough-and-ready, impulsive, simple, even crude, but basically sincere countryman—outwitted by a city-slicker. Esau is {a} skillful hunter–farmer (or a hunter running over

---

248. "conforming oneself to His will, in order to be conformed to the image of Christ" (Migne, *PL* 14, col. 520D [c. 6, n. 52]).

249. "*tunicam . . . pelliceam*" (Gen 3:21) (Migne, *PL* 14, col. 521A [c. 6, n. 52]).

250. "*sigillum*" (Song 8:6) (Migne, *PL* 14, col. 530B [c. 8, n. 75]).

251. "And Isaac besought the Lord for his wife, because she was barren; and he heard him, and made Rebecca to conceive. But the children struggled in her womb: and she said: If it were to be so with me, what need was there to conceive? And she went to consult the Lord. And he answering said: Two nations are in thy womb, and two peoples shall be divided out of thy womb, and one people shall overcome the other, and the elder shall serve the younger. And when her time was come to be delivered, behold twins were found in her womb. He that came forth first was red, and hairy like a skin: and his name was called Esau. Immediately the other coming forth, held his brother's foot in his hand, and therefore he was called Jacob. Isaac was threescore years old when the children were born unto him. And when they were grown up, Esau became a skillful hunter, and a husbandman, but Jacob a plain man dwelt in tents. Isaac loved Esau, because he ate of his hunting: and Rebecca loved Jacob. And Jacob boiled pottage: to whom Esau, coming faint out of the field, Said: Give me of this red pottage, for I am exceeding faint. For which reason his name was called Edom. And Jacob said to him: Sell me thy first birthright. He answered: Lo I die, what will the first birthright avail me? Jacob said: Swear therefore to me. Esau swore to him, and sold his first birthright. And so taking bread and the pottage of lentils, he ate, and drank, and went his way; making little account of having sold his first birthright."

252. De Vaux, *Genèse*, 120.

the wastelands [*BJ*[253]]), Jacob a quiet man (plain man), staying at home and doing little—thoughtful, etc. But he gains Esau's heritage by a trick; at least he takes advantage of Esau's weariness and passion. Again we must remember {the} oriental viewpoint: to be quiet, helpless, and yet smart at the right time, is a sign of divine predilection. Verse 29 {can be rendered}: "Hey, gimme that red soup." The main point is in 34: "*making little account of having sold his birthright*" (cf. Hebrews 12:16: Esau {is} a "profane person," one who had no notion of the things of God). {Here is a} very important spiritual point: what matters above all is not our skill and our activities, which wear us out and weaken us, sometimes to no purpose whatever, but our birthright—our vocation—God's love for us. St. Louis de Montfort applies this to the reprobate (Esau) and the elect (Jacob) and gives it a Marian slant (Rebecca, the mother, protects and prefers Jacob)[254] (cf. Romans 9:9-16[255]—note especially 11, {which}

---

253. "un habile chasseur, courant la steppe" (de Vaux, *Genèse*, 120).

254. "[W]e must observe that, according to the holy Fathers and the interpreters of Scripture, Jacob is the figure of Jesus Christ and the predestinate, and Esau that of the reprobate. We have but to examine the actions and conduct of each to be convinced of this. Esau, the elder ... took very little pains to please his mother Rebecca, and indeed did nothing for that end. He was such a glutton and loved eating so much, that he sold his birthright for a mess of pottage. He was, like Cain, full of envy against his brother, and persecuted him beyond measure. Now this is the daily conduct of the reprobate. They trust in their own strength and aptitude for temporal affairs.... The reprobate do not love retirement, nor spirituality, nor inward devotion; and they treat as little, or as bigots, or as savages, those who are interior or retired from the world, and who work more within than without. The reprobate care next to nothing for devotion to our Blessed Lady, the Mother of the predestinate.... As to Jacob, the younger son, he was of a feeble constitution, meek and peaceful. He lived for the most part at home, in order to gain the good graces of his mother Rebecca, whom he loved tenderly. If he went abroad, it was not of his own will, or through any confidence in his own skill, but to obey his mother. He loved and honored his mother. It was on this account that he kept at home. He was never so happy as when watching her. He avoided everything which could displease her, and did everything which he thought would please her; and this increased the love which Rebecca already had for him. He was subject in all things to his dear mother. He obeyed her entirely in all matters—promptly, without delaying, and lovingly, without complaining. At the least indication of her will, the little Jacob ran and worked; and he believed, without questioning, everything she said to him.... Such also is the conduct which the predestinate daily observe.... The predestinate tenderly love and truly honor our Blessed Lady as their good Mother and Mistress. They love her not only in word but in truth. They honor her not only outwardly but in the depths of their hearts. They avoid, like Jacob, everything which can displease her; and they practise with fervor whatever they think will make them find favor with her" (Grignion de Montfort, *True Devotion to Mary*, 138-43).

255. "For this is the word of promise: According to this time will I come. And Sara

explains the whole Jacob story to those who are scandalized by the moral angle).

Isaac in Gerara {is a} repetition of the story of Abraham passing off Sara as his sister. {There are} struggles with the Philistines for water: they are jealous of his prosperity {and} fill up the wells, {so} he digs others, {leading to} more rivalry. Finally he ends in Bersabee in relative peace; the Lord appears and renews the promise made to his father Abraham (26:23–25). Isaac builds an altar there. Isaac makes a treaty with Abimelech: another recognition that the Lord is with him {is the} acknowledgement of Abimelech (26:29). Esau marries two Hittite women, who are a cross to Rebecca and Isaac. This is a further sign of his reprobation and of being far from God. He should, like Isaac and Jacob, seek a wife in the "old country."

JACOB (Genesis 27–37)

What we have seen of the birth of Jacob and Esau is the prelude to this whole story. The point is, once more, the Promise. The sons of Jacob are the children of the promise because Jacob is Israel—the man of God, the ancestor of the chosen race in whom the alliance with Abraham is confirmed and definitively established.

Jacob is a shepherd, a fighter, a quiet and thoughtful man, prudent, energetic, patient. In *Bible et Vie Chrétienne* we read:

> His religious experience of personal intimacy with Yahweh profoundly marks the soul of Jacob and gives him a passionate confidence and a deeply felt piety towards the One Who is now no longer the Terror of Isaac but the Strong and Faithful God, the God of Israel. . . . He is a great fighter. His calm and prudent beginnings did not hinder the development of his vigorous maturity. . . . in this fighter a long old age full of sufferings will make him memorable. Jacob fights passionately. Even in his old age he retains a deep subtlety and sensibility. With all his power

---

shall have a son. And not only she. But when Rebecca also had conceived at once, of Isaac our father. For when the children were not yet born, nor had done any good or evil (that the purpose of God according to election might stand): Not of works, but of him that calleth, it was said to her: The elder shall serve the younger. As it is written: Jacob I have loved: but Esau I have hated. What shall we say then? Is there injustice with God? God forbid! For he saith to Moses: I will have mercy on whom I will have mercy. And I will shew mercy to whom I will shew mercy. So then it is not of him that willeth, nor of him that runneth, but of God that sheweth mercy."

> he loves his children, his ancestral traditions, his nomad life. He loves and fears his God completely. His vigor knows how to adapt itself to diplomacy. Jacob is a "smart one," the perfect type of the Bedouin who knows the wastelands, the customs of the desert, etc.... He is ardent, aggressive on occasion, but above all tenacious, and he knows how to hide his anger in order to make his plans succeed (n. 15 [p. 67]).[256]

As for his tricks, they are not something to approve and imitate, but to understand. St. Augustine's explanation that they are not lies but mysteries will not serve.[257] Again he bears witness to the absolute freedom of God's choice.

Chapter 27—The Blessing of Jacob: it is to be read first of all as a story (not as a piece of moral edification). {The} theme {centers on} the deathbed blessing: {the} time of death {is a} time of clearsightedness into the will of God, presumably because then one sees all in a new light and one is no longer disposed to trifle. More obviously, {it is} simply the ancient way of "making a will." The old man wants his favorite dish, some venison brought in by Esau. The Bible respects the primitive appreciation of the values of life—note the calm with which death is viewed. The deception is Rebecca's plan, but Jacob enters into it, at first with a little hesitation but then wholeheartedly and cleverly (cf. v. 20) (N.B. he has a certain right to the blessing as Esau has sold his birthright to him). {Note the} beauty and realism of the story: the cooking, the bread, the clothes, the scent of the fields. The blessing (28–29) {consists} first {of} the temporal goods,

---

256. "Cette expérience religieuse de l'intimité personnelle de Yahweh marque profondément l'âme de Jacob et lui donne une confiance émue et une piété sentie vis-à-vis de la *Terreur d'Isaac*, devenue pour lui le *Dieu fort* et fidèle, le *Dieu-Israël*. Jacob est aussi un grand lutteur: ses débuts calmes et prudents n'ont nui en rien au plein développement de sa vigoureuse maturité. C'est un lutteur qu'une longue vieillesse travaillée par la souffrance rendra digne de mémoire. Ces luttes, Jacob les mène en passionné. Jusque dans sa vieillesse, il garde un finesse et une sensibilité très vives. Il chérit de toutes ses forces ses enfants, ses traditions ancestrales, sa vie de nomade; il aime et craint profondément son Dieu. Mais sa vigueur sait se plier aux lois de la prudence et de la diplomatie. Jacob est un 'malin,' c'est le type parfait du Bédouin qui connaît la steppe, les usages du désert.... Il est ardent, agressif à ses heures, mais surtout tenace, et il sait dissimuler son courroux pour mieux réaliser son plan" (Fransen, "Jacob l'Avisé").

257. "*Iacob autem quod matre fecit auctore, ut patrem fallere videretur, si diligenter et fideliter attendatur, non est mendacium, sed mysterium*" (*Contra Mendacium*, 2.24 [Migne, *PL* 40, col. 533]) ("But that Jacob, with his mother's advice, acted in such a way that he seemed to be deceiving his father, if it is examined diligently and faithfully, is not a lie but a mystery").

then the essential blessing, the domination over the other brethren. This is the transmission of the promised inheritance, through the younger son and not the elder. It had to be explained. Once again the theme {is that} of the *younger son*, the little one, the one who seems to be handicapped, {but who} is preferred by God.

{In its} spiritual application, one thinks immediately of Rebecca as a type of Our Lady. It is Our Lady who takes upon herself the interests of the little ones, the younger and poorer ones who are at a disadvantage, and through her help they come out best. In a way we might almost see in this an allegory for the way Our Lady causes us, the sinners, who have no right to the divine inheritance, to be blessed and accepted by the Father, disguised as His Only Begotten Son. The merits of the Passion of Christ cover us and the Father recognizes in us the sweet fruitful odor of the fields of heaven, His own charity. Thus we inherit in all truth the divine sonship, and are not only "disguised" as Christ or "covered" by His merits but really transformed, sanctified and divinized in Him. Jesus Himself makes this allegory legitimate later on when in John 1:51 He makes Jacob's ladder a symbol of the way in which the mystical Body is sanctified in all its members by grace from the Father (read John 1:47–51).[258] Note also {that} it is at Jacob's well that Jesus talks to the Samaritan,[259] the first one to whom He reveals the fact that He is the Savior of the world; and she is an adulteress and a liar. *Cf. also the parable of the prodigal son*,[260] which is the New Testament version of the same thing—the election of the younger son, the sinner, who has forfeited every right, who has deserved only punishment—and the attitude of the elder son, Esau. Note of course the different attitude of the New Testament: the younger son does not obtain the paternal blessing through trickery but by sincere repentance, but according to the views of the elder brother this is just as much an injustice as Jacob's grabbing the inheritance (read also the parable of

---

258. "Jesus saw Nathanael coming to him: and he saith of him: Behold an Israelite indeed, in whom there is no guile. Nathanael saith to him: Whence knowest thou me? Jesus answered, and said to him: Before that Philip called thee, when thou wast under the fig tree, I saw thee. Nathanael answered him, and said: Rabbi, thou art the Son of God, thou art the King of Israel. Jesus answered, and said to him: Because I said unto thee, I saw thee under the fig tree, thou believest: greater things than these shalt thou see. And he saith to him: Amen, amen I say to you, you shall see the heaven opened, and the angels of God ascending and descending upon the Son of man."

259. John 4:1–42.

260. Luke 15:11–32.

the workers in the vineyard[261]). READ Genesis 27:30 ff.:[262] Esau comes in

261. "The kingdom of heaven is like to an householder, who went out early in the morning to hire labourers into his vineyard. And having agreed with the labourers for a penny a day, he sent them into his vineyard. And going out about the third hour, he saw others standing in the market place idle. And he said to them: Go you also into my vineyard, and I will give you what shall be just. And they went their way. And again he went out about the sixth and the ninth hour, and did in like manner. But about the eleventh hour he went out and found others standing, and he saith to them: Why stand you here all the day idle? They say to him: Because no man hath hired us. He saith to them: Go you also into my vineyard. And when evening was come, the lord of the vineyard saith to his steward: Call the labourers and pay them their hire, beginning from the last even to the first. When therefore they were come, that came about the eleventh hour, they received every man a penny. But when the first also came, they thought that they should receive more: and they also received every man a penny. And receiving it they murmured against the master of the house, Saying: These last have worked but one hour, and thou hast made them equal to us, that have borne the burden of the day and the heats. But he answering said to one of them: Friend, I do thee no wrong: didst thou not agree with me for a penny? Take what is thine, and go thy way: I will also give to this last even as to thee. Or, is it not lawful for me to do what I will? is thy eye evil, because I am good? So shall the last be first, and the first last. For many are called, but few chosen" (Matt 20:1–16).

262. "Isaac had scarce ended his words, when Jacob being now gone out abroad, Esau came, And brought in to his father meats made of what he had taken in hunting, saying: Arise, my father, and eat of thy son's venison; that thy soul may bless me. And Isaac said to him: Why! who art thou? He answered: I am thy firstborn son Esau. Isaac was struck with fear, and astonished exceedingly: and wondering beyond what can be believed, said Who is he then that even now brought me venison that he had taken, and I ate of all before thou camest? and I have blessed him, and he shall be blessed. Esau having heard his father's words, roared out with a great cry: and being in a great consternation, said: Bless me also, my father. And he said: Thy brother came deceitfully and got thy blessing. But he said again: Rightly is his name called Jacob; for he hath supplanted me lo this second time: my first birthright he took away before, and now this second time he hath stolen away my blessing. And again he said to his father: Hast thou not reserved me also a blessing? Isaac answered: I have appointed him thy lord, and have made all his brethren his servants: I have established him with corn and wine, and after this, what shall I do more for thee, my son? And Esau said to him: Hast thou only one blessing, father? I beseech thee bless me also. And when he wept with a loud cry, Isaac being moved, said to him: In the fat of the earth, and in the dew of heaven from above, Shall thy blessing be. Thou shalt live by the sword and shalt serve thy brother; and the time shall come, when thou shalt shake off and loose his yoke from thy neck. Esau therefore always hated Jacob for the blessing wherewith his father had blessed him: and he said in his heart: The days will come of the mourning of my father, and I will kill my brother Jacob. These things were told to Rebecca: and she sent and called Jacob her son, and said to him: Behold Esau thy brother threateneth to kill thee. Now therefore, my son, hear my voice: arise and flee to Laban my brother to Haran: And thou shalt dwell with him a few days, till the wrath of thy brother be assuaged, And his indignation cease, and he forget the things thou hast done to him:

{and} gets his own blessing—{verses} 40 and 41 again explain the relations of Israel and Edom. Rebecca urges Jacob to go to Mesopotamia to get a wife, and Isaac also commands this, renewing the blessing with full consciousness of the facts: READ 28:1-4.[263] Esau, in a clumsy imitation, goes and gets another wife from among his own family, a daughter of Ishmael. He already has a couple of Canaanite wives of whom Rebecca is "sick to death" (27:46).

Jacob's Dream (28:10 ff.—read 28:10-17[264]): {this is the} great revelation of the intimacy of God with man and man with God, (a) literally according to the primitive concept (cf. ziggurats, etc.); (b) spiritually in the Incarnation. God loves man, and the relations between them, once so intimate in Paradise, have been reestablished, not with the same immediacy, but through angels and the workings of Divine Providence. Above all, there are certain holy places on earth where God manifests Himself (N.B. Pseudo-Dionysius: {a} hierarchical universe[265]). {The scene is} Bethel:

---

afterwards I will send, and bring thee from thence hither. Why shall I be deprived of both my sons in one day?" (Gen 27:30-45).

263. "And Isaac called Jacob, and blessed him, and charged him, saying: Take not a wife of the stock of Chanaan: But go, and take a journey to Mesopotamia of Syria, to the house of Bathuel thy mother's father, and take thee a wife thence of the daughters of Laban thy uncle. And God almighty bless thee, and make thee to increase, and multiply thee: that thou mayst be a multitude of people. And give the blessings of Abraham to thee, and to thy seed after thee: that thou mayst possess the land of thy sojournment, which he promised to thy grandfather."

264. "But Jacob being departed from Bersabee, went on to Haran. And when he was come to a certain place, and would rest in it after sunset, he took of the stones that lay there, and putting under his head, slept in the same place. And he saw in his sleep a ladder standing upon the earth, and the top thereof touching heaven: the angels also of God ascending and descending by it; And the Lord leaning upon the ladder, saying to him: I am the Lord God of Abraham thy father, and the God of Isaac; the land, wherein thou sleepest, I will give to thee and to thy seed. And thy seed shall be as the dust of the earth: thou shalt spread abroad to the west, and to the east, and to the north, and to the south: and IN THEE and thy seed all the tribes of the earth shall BE BLESSED. And I will be thy keeper whithersoever thou goest, and will bring thee back into this land: neither will I leave thee, till I shall have accomplished all that I have said. And when Jacob awaked out of sleep, he said: Indeed the Lord is in this place, and I knew it not. And trembling he said: How terrible is this place! this is no other but the house of God, and the gate of heaven."

265. See Merton's comments on the Dionysian view of the universe in *Introduction to Christian Mysticism*: "the cosmos as seen by Dionysius is not simply a fallen world in which individuals are called out by love to salvation and ecstasy. The whole cosmos, or at least the *world of intelligences,* is called to one vast ecstasy. God goes out of Himself ecstatically in creation, and His creatures in turn go out of themselves to return to

here Abraham had already known something of the presence of God (cf. 12:8). In the dream {Jacob sees} the angels, and God on top of the ladder. I am the God of Abraham thy father . . . The land wherein thou sleepest I will give to thee. Thy seed shall be as the dust of the earth—I WILL BE THY KEEPER WHITHERSOEVER THOU GOEST . . . neither will I leave thee. Jacob's reaction {is one of} *interior awe and fear of God*, {marked by} the consecrated stone (cf. {the} Liturgy of {the} dedication of {a} church;[266] cf. {the} use {of this text} also in the Mass for travelers[267]). Verse 16–17 {reads}: "Indeed the Lord is in this place." Philosophy teaches us of the omnipresence of God, but though God is present everywhere by His power, presence and essence, He is present in a different and special way *where He contacts men through His angelic hierarchies*. {This is} a special "religious" presence, in which He makes Himself known and disposes man to receive His messages, and to reply with the offering of his whole being. Our churches are such places. "Places" are therefore necessary for our special religious contact with and worship of God. These places visited by God are "terrible": they are His "house" and the "gate of heaven." They call for special consecration on our part and are the proper place for sacrifice and for the *consecration of ourselves*. The rite with which he pours oil over the stone is a consecration of the stone (not an offering "to the stone" as in Canaanite worship). {Its} meaning {is that} wherever man may go, God is

---

Him and to bring others back to Him. Hence it is a vision of a whole universe of loving intelligences, none of which is concerned with itself, all of which draw one another to the One. 'Ecstatic love forbids each one to belong to himself.' . . . [T]he ecstasy of God reaches down through ordered hierarchies of angels and sacred ministers to attain to those orders that are farthest from Him. . . . The cosmos of Denys is then a vast ecstatic communion of intelligences striving to respond to the call of divine Love summoning them to unity in Christ, each according to his rank and degree of purity. In this cosmos, the love of God flows out in a *thearchy*, a divinely ruled order in which the love of the creature, produced in it by God, leads the creature back to Him. The love of God as *agape* awakens *eros* in the creature. *Eros* is divine *agape* responding to itself in {the} creature. The love of superiors for inferiors in the hierarchy resembles the divine *agape* and serves as {an} instrument of the thearchy. The return of created beings to God by love is not an absorption, a plunging into God and disappearing, but a flowering, a perfection, a *divinization*. Created beings reach their full perfection in their return to God. The generosity of creatures toward one another helps them all to return ecstatically to the One" (139, 141–42).

266. Introit: "*Terribilis est locus iste: hic domus Dei est, et porta coeli: et vocabitur aula Dei*" (Gen 28:17) ("Terrible is this place; here is the house of God and the gate of heaven, and it will be called the hall of God") (*Missale Romanum*, (40); *Missale Cisterciense*, 33*).

267. Epistle: Gen 28:10–22 (*Missale Romanum*, (89); *Missale Cisterciense*, 68*).

capable of opening to him the door to heaven, and God looks down from heaven upon man. When this contact is established, the place is forever hallowed, and the incident will definitely repeat itself there. Note the importance of this sense of the special presence of God, looking down from heaven. It is true that our awareness of God constantly dwelling in our hearts by grace is itself more perfect, but we must be careful that it does not degenerate by such steps as the following: (a) confusion with the presence of God as Creator everywhere and in all things; (b) which then becomes a vague, impersonal sort of presence; (c) and finally ends in foggy pantheism, {an} identification of the being of God with my own being—and this in the end is *no presence at all*. We have to realize that our heart, consecrated by baptism and "anointed" with the oil of sanctifying grace, is a special consecrated place, a House of God and a gate of heaven, a special sanctuary which can be defiled, from which God can be absent. In other words, our sense of the presence of God must be kept *religious* and *holy*—not a mere matter of course; and then also we must remember that though God is intimately present in our hearts, He also infinitely transcends them and the "ladder" of angelic ministers is necessary if we are to be in true religious contact with Him. These angels are by no means superfluous! (In later times Bethel became the rival sanctuary, set up by Israel in the division of the Kingdoms.)

Read 28:18-22:[268] *Jacob's vow*—a prayer in the form of a vow (cf. Cassian[269]). Jacob repeats what the Lord has already promised, and adds his own promise. He deals with God in true character, as a perfect Bedouin: "The Lord will be my God" (inserted perhaps by a later writer to make sure nobody takes this to be stone-worship). The God of the Psalms is the "God of Jacob"—we are the generation that is blessed because we "seek the face of the God of Jacob" (Ps. 23:1-6); Ps. 80: The God of Jacob

---

268. "And Jacob, arising in the morning, took the stone, which he had laid under his head, and set it up for a title, pouring oil upon the top of it. And he called the name of the city Bethel, which before was called Luza. And he made a vow, saying: If God shall be with me, and shall keep me in the way by which I walk, and shall give me bread to eat, and raiment to put on, And I shall return prosperously to my father's house: the Lord shall be my God: And this stone, which I have set up for a title, shall be called the house of God: and of all things that thou shalt give to me, I will offer tithes to thee."

269. See Merton, *Cassian and the Fathers*, 239: "*Prayers (orationes)*: Are especially those in which we offer, promise or vow something to God. Here the direction of the heart is to resolve something good and promise its accomplishment while praying for grace to carry it out, and desiring that God may be pleased with the offering" (see John Cassian, *Collationes*, 10.12 [Migne, *PL* 49, col. 784]).

and Joseph, the God of the Exodus, is our God, and we have only to listen to Him and receive the same blessings in evidence of His power.

JACOB AND HIS WIVES AND SONS: chapters 29, 30 and 31 tell the story of the births of the Fathers of the (eleven) tribes of Israel (Benjamin {is} in c. 35), and Jacob's struggle with the miserly Laban. The theme {is} how God protects the interests of Jacob against the power and craft of his father-in-law, and brings him out richer than ever, with a large and prosperous family. *CBC*[270] piously regards Jacob's sufferings and toil with Laban as a punishment for his trickery in getting the blessing from Esau. Jacob turns up without any gifts to offer for the bride and in place of them is left at the mercy of his uncle and has to slave and toil for his wives. To appreciate this story we must clearly understand the characters and the actions, and not miss the oriental allusions in every line.

But first, a general outline {of} the wives and children of Jacob {is in order}: Jacob arrives in Abraham's home country, finds flocks gathered at a well, meets Rachel his cousin and falls in love with her. He proposes to marry her, {but} Laban substitutes the less attractive Lia in her place after Jacob has served seven years. Rachel is his after the wedding week but she turns out to be barren. He serves a second seven years. Lia is fruitful but never gains the heart of Jacob. The devices of the wives to capture his esteem and affection and to have children "by proxy" through their maidservants when all else fails {are described}. Hence {there are} the sons of Jacob by various mothers: sons by Lia—Ruben (29:32), Simeon (*id.* 33), Levi (*id.* 34), Juda (*id.* 35); by Bala (Rachel's maid)—Dan (30:6), Nephtali (*id.* 8); by Zelpha (Lia's maid)—Gad (*id.* 11), Aser (*id.* 13); by Lia (as a result of the bargain with the mandrakes)—Issachar (*id.* 18), Zabulon (*id.* 20), (Dina: *id.* 21); by Rachel, finally—Joseph (*id.* 24) (at last Rachel dies giving birth to Benjamin: 35:18). These facts have to be remembered in order fully to understand the story of Joseph, the enmity of Joseph's brethren, and Joseph's special love for Benjamin—also Jacob's special love for those two.

{Now we may turn to} the text in detail. {In} chapter 29, where does he go? somewhere northeast of Palestine. Laban {is a} nomad shepherd. Jacob comes to a well used by several owners of flocks—he will meet his bride by the well. The other flocks have got there first; they will have the right to drink first, but they all wait until all are there before rolling away the stone—{the} water supply is limited. But Jacob, hearing {that} Rachel

---

270. Sutcliffe, "Genesis," 197 [n. 153q].

will come, tried to get rid of the shepherds so as to be alone with her, but they do not go (read 29:9–15[271]). Our first insight into the character of Laban is in the fact that Rachel is in charge of his flock—he saves the wages of a shepherd by giving her the job. Jacob, like a true oriental, after rolling away the stone single-handed (not to impress Rachel but to show his usefulness as a laborer for Laban), embraces her and bursts into tears, {a typical} oriental expression of emotion. Afterwards {he} tells her who he is. Laban takes him on with eagerness and seems to promise good treatment. He is already planning to exploit him. Jacob himself proposes the seven years of work.

Lia and Rachel (read 29:16–21,[272] 29:20): Lia {is} blear-eyed; Rachel {is} beautiful. Jacob felt that seven years were short. The eagerness of his love takes a different form from what we would expect: {there is} a profound sense of the value of his love, rather than an eagerness to enjoy its possession—a homage to the reality and goodness seen in Rachel. {This is an} important note in the psychology of mature love!—a real expression of the homage and respect which characterize *amor amicitiae*.[273] Laban, the pragmatist, senses this and takes advantage of it, perhaps with the "practical man's" contempt for idealism. {For} the marriage, Laban gathers everyone together, has a big feast, leads Lia in veiled to the bride-chamber, and Jacob only discovers the substitution the next morning. By that time it is too late, but he is very indignant, and there is always a chance that he will reject her. Laban says, "Wait out the seven days of the

---

271. "They were yet speaking, and behold Rachel came with her father's sheep: for she fed the flock. And when Jacob saw her, and knew her to be his cousin-german, and that they were the sheep of Laban, his uncle: he removed the stone wherewith the well was closed. And having watered the flock, he kissed her: and lifting up his voice, wept. And he told her that he was her father's brother, and the son of Rebecca: but she went in haste and told her father. Who, when he heard that Jacob his sister's son was come, ran forth to meet him; and embracing him, and heartily kissing him, brought him into his house. And when he had heard the causes of his journey, He answered: Thou art my bone and my flesh. And after the days of one month were expired, He said to him: Because thou art my brother, shalt thou serve me without wages? Tell me what wages thou wilt have."

272. "Now he had two daughters, the name of the elder was Lia: and the younger was called Rachel. But Lia was blear eyed: Rachel was well favoured, and of a beautiful countenance. And Jacob being in love with her, said: I will serve thee seven years for Rachel thy younger daughter. Laban answered: It is better that I give her to thee than to another man; stay with me. So Jacob served seven years for Rachel: and they seemed but a few days, because of the greatness of his love. And he said to Laban: Give me my wife; for now the time is fulfilled, that I may go in unto her."

273. "the love of friendship."

marriage feast—don't make a scene; in the end you will have Rachel also." Laban was probably banking on the fact that Jacob would be too timid to assert his rights and would simply take {Lia} and serve another seven years for {Rachel}.²⁷⁴ This seems to have been one of the main purposes of the trick.

The Children of Jacob: note the rivalry at the two wives, the joys and sorrows, the anxieties and satisfactions of the struggle, the tricks resorted to: see for instance the passion of 30:1–2, or the incident of the mandrakes (14 ff.) by which Lia again recovers her marriage rights. Finally, at the birth of Joseph, Jacob decides to leave Laban. Then follows the great struggle to get away.

{In the episode of the} *contract regarding the flocks*, Jacob makes a proposal in order to provide himself with flocks: he will take all the white sheep and black goats and tend them, and will ask for his services only the offspring that are variegated or brown. Laban agrees gladly, separates all the variegated and brown sheep and goats {and} takes them three days' journey away (read 30:31–42²⁷⁵). How did Jacob outwit Laban, in caus-

---

274. Copy text reads: "... take Rachel ... for Lia."

275. "And Laban said: What shall I give thee? But he said: I require nothing: but if thou wilt do what I demand, I will feed, and keep thy sheep again. Go round through all thy flocks, and separate all the sheep of divers colours, and speckled: and all that is brown and spotted, and of divers colours, as well among the sheep, as among the goats, shall be my wages. And my justice shall answer for me tomorrow before thee when the time of the bargain shall come: and all that is not of divers colours, and spotted, and brown, as well among the sheep as among the goats, shall accuse me of theft. And Laban said: I like well what thou demandest. And he separated the same day the she goats, and the sheep, and the he goats, and the rams of divers colours, and spotted: and all the flock of one colour, that is, of white and black fleece, he delivered into the hands of his sons. And he set the space of three days' journey betwixt himself and his son in law, who fed the rest of his flock. And Jacob took green rods of poplar, and of almond, and of plane trees, and pilled them in part: so when the bark was taken off, in the parts that were pilled, there appeared whiteness: but the parts that were whole remained green: and by this means the colour was divers. And he put them in the troughs, where the water was poured out: that when the flocks should come to drink, they might have the rods before their eyes, and in the sight of them might conceive. And it came to pass that in the very heat of coition, the sheep beheld the rods, and brought forth spotted, and of divers colours, and speckled. And Jacob separated the flock, and put the rods in the troughs before the eyes of the rams: and all the white and the black were Laban's: and the rest were Jacob's, when the flocks were separated one from the other. So when the ewes went first to ram, Jacob put the rods in the troughs of water before the eyes of the rams, and of the ewes, that they might conceive while they were looking upon them: But when the latter coming was, and the last conceiving, he did not put them. And those that were lateward, became Laban's: and they of the first time, Jacob's. And

ing variegated sheep to be born from white? {by} putting the half-peeled branches of almond, poplar and sycamore in the troughs to be before the eyes of the sheep when they conceived. St. Jerome says[276] this was practiced in Spain by horse breeders. Anyway, it worked for Jacob. But he did this only with the sheep of {the} best quality; the weaker ones he left for Laban (the ones that arrived last: v. 42–43). Jacob thus becomes very rich.

{In} chapter 31, Laban is now angry with him. Jacob calls Rachel and Lia and discusses his departure and his rights (v. 8 {has} a wrong reading, following {the} Septuagint: {it} should be speckled and *striped*, not *white*[277]). He explains his success by the vision of an angel in the night, a sequel to the dream at Bethel (12–14). Rachel and Lia support Jacob, saying he is indeed right and has been unjustly treated by their avaricious father, and has done well to get compensation. Read 31:16–27:[278] they leave without telling Laban while he is away shearing his sheep. He runs after them, catches up, reproaches him for "stealing away" his daughters {and} also reproaches him with stealing "his gods"—Rachel has them, unknown to Jacob. His rash promise (v. 32) puts her life in danger, but she outwits Laban by a ruse (v. 34) (the idols—teraphim—{are} household

---

the man was enriched exceedingly, and he had many flocks, maid servants and men servants, camels and asses."

276. Jerome, *Liber Hebraicarum Questionum in Genesim* (Migne, PL 23, col. 1035B); see Sutcliffe, "Genesis," 198 [n. 154l].

277. See Sutcliffe, "Genesis," 198 [n. 154m].

278. "But God hath taken our father's riches, and delivered them to us, and to our children: wherefore do all that God hath commanded thee. Then Jacob rose up, and having set his children and wives upon camels, went his way. And he took all his substance, and flocks, and whatsoever he had gotten in Mesopotamia, and went forward to Isaac his father to the land of Chanaan. At that time Laban was gone to shear his sheep, and Rachel stole away her father's idols. And Jacob would not confess to his father in law that he was flying away. And when he was gone, together with all that belonged to him, and having passed the river, was going on towards mount Galaad, It was told Laban on the third day that Jacob fled. And he took his brethren with him, and pursued after him seven days; and overtook him in the mount of Galaad. And he saw in a dream God saying to him: Take heed thou speak not any thing harshly against Jacob. Now Jacob had pitched his tent in the mountain: and when he with his brethren had overtaken him, he pitched his tent in the same mount of Galaad. And he said to Jacob: Why hast thou done thus, to carry away, without my knowledge, my daughters, as captives taken with the sword. Why wouldst thou run away privately and not acquaint me, that I might have brought thee on the way with joy, and with songs, and with timbrels, and with harps?"

gods[279]). Jacob's complaints against Laban {follow} (36–42); Laban agrees and they make a treaty.

{In} chapter 32, *Jacob sends {a} messenger to Esau*, who comes out with 400 men. Jacob {is} very much afraid {and} sends ahead more messengers and presents of sheep and goats and camels. READ 32:22–32:[280] *Jacob wrestles with the angel*. The caravan has just crossed the Jabbok (a mountain torrent running into the Jordan). Jacob, alone by the river bank, is approached by "someone" who grabs him, and they fight in the dark until dawn. Commentators say {that} this story of a "fight with God" in the dark, without arms and without recognizing Who is the assailant, means the story is of great antiquity: (a) Jacob fights with superhuman strength and stubbornness; (b) the stranger miraculously sprains his thigh and asks to be let go—Jacob demands a blessing (a sign of peace); (c) the stranger gives *Jacob his new name*—he has been strong against God and he will be strong with men; (d) Jacob, now surprised greatly, asks His name and gets no answer—he realizes that he has fought with God (31) {and} he is astonished to find he is still alive. The whole thing, leaving him crippled and with a new name, is a renewed promise of victory and a pledge of God's favor (cf. *Dark Night of the Soul*[281]).

Chapter 33: *the Meeting of Jacob and Esau*. Jacob sees Esau coming with 400 men, and is very much afraid of him. The main interest of the chapter is to show the immense crowd of camels, sheep, children, servants, wives, etc. of Jacob, the bewilderment of Esau, the tact and care

---

279. See Sutcliffe, "Genesis," 198 [n. 154m].

280. "And rising early he took his two wives, and his two handmaids, with his eleven sons, and passed over the ford of Jaboc. And when all things were brought over that belonged to him, He remained alone: and behold a man wrestled with him till morning. And when he saw that he could not overcome him, he touched the sinew of his thigh, and forthwith it shrank. And he said to him: Let me go, for it is break of day. He answered: I will not let thee go except thou bless me. And he said: What is thy name? He answered: Jacob. But he said: Thy name shall not be called Jacob, but Israel: for if thou hast been strong against God, how much more shalt thou prevail against men? Jacob asked him, Tell me by what name art thou called? He answered: Why dost thou ask my name? And he blessed him in the same place. And Jacob called the name of the place Phanuel, saying: I have seen God face to face, and my soul has been saved. And immediately the sun rose upon him, after he was past Phanuel; but he halted on his foot. Therefore the children of Israel, unto this day, eat not the sinew, that shrank in Jacob's thigh: because he touched the sinew of his thigh and it shrank."

281. While John refers to the dream of Jacob at Bethel in *Dark Night* (II.18.4 [Peers, *John of the Cross*, 1:462]), there is no reference to the wrestling with the angel there or elsewhere.

of Jacob to protect himself in case Esau has some hidden hostile plan, and finally Jacob's settling at Socoth and offering sacrifice at Salem to the "mighty God of Israel." It is a first sight of the great people of God promised to Abraham. READ chapter 33:1–3:[282] Jacob puts his wives and children in order, so that Rachel, the favorite, comes last. Verses 4–7 {show} the genuine wonderment of Esau; he is glad to be with Jacob {and} admires Jacob's achievement. This sympathetic presentation shows that the tradition is *genuine* ({the} natural tendency would be to show Esau in an unsympathetic light). {Verses} 8–11 {relate} the oriental courtesy of the offering, first refused, then accepted. {In verses} 12–15, Jacob {is} maneuvering so that Esau will not accompany him. As CBC says,[283] he prefers to "see Esau's back" (v. 13 {contains} an application of St. Benedict[284]). {At the} end of {the} chapter, Jacob settles at "Soccoth" ({he} makes huts of branches); it {is a} section near the Jordan. He will live here for ten years or so, for in the next {verses} his sons are grown up. *Jacob* {later lives} *at Sichem* (not Salem[285]): he buys land from the natives and sets up an altar. Here he himself will be buried, and here is his well (John 4:11).

Dina (ch. 34): Dina {is} ravished by Sichem the son of Hemor, the chief of the Sichemites; her brothers, by a trick, get the young man to persuade all the males of the town to be circumcised, so that a marriage can be lawfully contracted, then when they are incapacitated, Simeon and Levi go into the town and kill them all; the other brothers follow and plunder the place and take all the women and the stock, but Jacob is very displeased, because he is afraid this will turn the natives against him.

{In} chapter 35, Jacob gets rid of all the idols from among his followers, buries them under the (sacred) turpentine tree at Sichem, and moves to Bethel, where God had first appeared to him. Verse 9 ff. {relates} a new vision of God and a renewal of the promise; Jacob's new name is

---

282. "And Jacob lifting up his eyes, saw Esau coming, and with him four hundred men: and he divided the children of Lia, and of Rachel, and of the two handmaids: And he put both the handmaids and their children foremost: and Lia and her children in the second place: and Rachel and Joseph last. And he went forward and bowed down with his face to the ground seven times until his brother came near."

283. Sutcliffe, "Genesis," 199 [n. 155c].

284. In chapter 64 of the *Rule*, Benedict quotes part of this verse in referring to the abbot: "Let him be prudent and considerate in all his commands; and whether the work which he enjoins concern God or the world, let him always be discreet and moderate, bearing in mind the discretion of holy Jacob, who said: *If I cause my flocks to be overdriven, they will all perish in one day*" (McCann, trans. and ed., *Rule*, 147).

285. As in the Vulgate and Douay-Rheims translation of Genesis 33:18.

Israel (repeated). READ 35:16 ff.[286]—the birth of Benjamin, in Ephrata, near Bethlehem. {The} end of the chapter {tells of the} death of Isaac at the age of 180. {In} chapter 36 Esau separates from Jacob and dwells in Edom; a list of his descendants {is given}. {This is the} end of the Jacob story—Joseph now begins (c. 37).

Background for {the} Story of Joseph and the Exodus: EGYPT. Let us study the ancient civilization of the Nile Valley, most important for our understanding of the next chapters of Genesis, and for Exodus. Egypt extended from the Nile Delta to the first cataract of Assuan,[287] {a} stretch of five to six hundred miles of very fertile land. Deposits of potassium and alluvial mud give the valley the name "the black country."[288] The flood of the Nile (fed by summer rains of {the} mountains of Abyssinia) begins in June; at first the waters are green, full of vegetable matter carried away from upland forests; then red at {the} end of July, when the tropical rains feed the sources and upper reaches of the river. {The} flood lasts all summer, reaches its height in September, and dies down in October. During this time the flood waters must be managed and controlled, for irrigation purposes. It has been known for the flood to fail several years in succession.[289] It is also a land rich in quarries and minerals, exploited from ancient times. But metals had to be brought from Nubia and other places, wood from Syria, etc. Geographically, Egypt is protected and isolated by the sea, the desert and mountains to the south. {With regard to} productivity—especially cereals—it was the granary of the ancient world, also {producing} all kinds of fruits, vegetables, fish. {With regard to} ethnography: (1) {for the} prehistoric {period there is a} dispute whether or

---

286. "And going forth from thence, he came in the springtime to the land which leadeth to Ephrata: wherein when Rachel was in travail, By reason of her hard labour she began to be in danger, and the midwife said to her: Fear not, for thou shalt have this son also. And when her soul was departing for pain, and death was now at hand, she called the name of her son Benoni, that is, The son of my pain: but his father called him Benjamin, that is, The son of the right hand. So Rachel died, and was buried in the highway that leadeth to Ephrata, this is Bethlehem. And Jacob erected a pillar over her sepulchre: this is the pillar of Rachel's monument, to this day" (vv. 16–20).

287. See Hyvernat, "Egypt," 329.

288. See Trevor, *Ancient Egypt*, 13: "Ham signifies *dark*; and, as applied to the country, may have referred to the black alluvial mud which covered the fields . . . . it seems probable that it was originally known as the Black Country." While Merton almost certainly did not draw on Trevor's book directly for his overview of Egypt, the similarity in phrasing here suggests that whatever source he did use may have been dependent on this work for some of the information it provided.

289. See Hyvernat, "Egypt," 332.

not there were originally two races in Egypt, one in the south, one in the north. Egypt {was} inhabited from at least 13,000 B.C. ({the period of the} Ice Age in Europe); (2) {in the} historic {period the} earliest evidence shows a mixed race, with notable Semitic and Mediterranean elements, without Negro elements—probably from Asia. The Semitic elements increase with time. Joseph was in Egypt in the Hyksos period, when Egypt was ruled by Semites.

In the beginning, Egypt was divided into two kingdoms—Upper Egypt {and} Lower Egypt—then {became} united; Memphis, long the principal city of Lower Egypt, was the capital of the Old Kingdom (first dynasties). Thebes, principal city of Upper Egypt, became capital of the Middle Kingdom. Heliopolis (Lower Egypt) was for long the great religious center. It is probable that dynastic civilization, religion, hieroglyphic writing, etc. began first in the delta region, perhaps under Asiatic influence (Thoth, the god of writing, is a delta god—{identified with the} ibis). Calendars, also a product of Lower Egypt, calculated the beginning of the year from the rising of Sirius at the latitude of Memphis. {The} growth of art and building belongs also to {the} delta area, under Asiatic influence. Note: the Egyptian calendar furnishes serious problems in chronology—calculating the beginning of the year from the rising of Sirius, there was a yearly lag which meant that in 1460 years, one year was lost. This period was called the "sothic period," and we cannot calculate exactly the "sothic periods": there are two schools of opinion—those for the long chronology and those for the short chronology. Note that during the second millennium B.C.—around 2600—upheavals in Mesopotamia had repercussions in Egypt: migrations of Asiatics entered Egypt, probably during {the} ninth and tenth dynasties; and the Hyksos invaded Egypt too between the fourteenth and seventeenth dynasties—and Joseph came to Egypt during this period. Note {that} the chronology of the reigns of the pharaohs, as recorded, is always misleading, because the figures given are allegorical and have to do with religious symbolism rather than with historical fact.

Outline of Egyptian history—covering about *5000 years*: {the} *prehistoric* period {was} followed by an *archaic* or transition period, in which the upper and lower kingdoms are already united, with {the} capital at Thinis. {The} *archaic* period is that of the first–second dynasties (4241 B.C. {according to the} calendar, {which} adopted {the} correct date[290]).

---

290. See Hyvernat, "Egypt," 336.

{The} *Old Kingdom*, {with its} capital {at} Memphis, {includes} dynasties three {to} ten (beginning about 4000 B.C.); {the} empire extends to Nubia {and} Sinai; {this period saw the} construction of {the} great pyramids (Cheops—fourth dynasty). Heliopolis {was the} religious center ({with the} worship of Ra). {The} seventh {through the} tenth dynasties {were an} era of anarchy and revolution. {The} *Middle Kingdom* (eleventh–seventeenth {dynasties}), {which saw a} restoration of order and power, begins about 3000 B.C. Thebes {is now} the capital. {The} thirteenth {through the} seventeenth dynasties {were an} era of division; during this time {occurred the} Asiatic invasions—*the Hyksos* (Hittites? Canaanites?) came by infiltration. {During this} era of decadence, Memphis {was the} capital; {the rulers} introduce horses. {The} Hyksos {were} finally driven out by feudal lords.[291] {The} *New Kingdom* begins with {the} eighteenth dynasty ({it has a} *certain date: 1580 B.C.*). {The} capital is at Thebes. Expansion into Asia {takes place with the} conquest of Syria (Rameses II beat {the} Hittites; Tuthmes III {was the} conqueror at Megiddo {in} 1479 {and at} Karkhemish {in} 1476, {and} receives tribute from Assyria, Babylonia, etc.). Joseph was with Putiphar probably between 1580 and 1450 B.C. The Jews came in to the corner of the delta country (Goshen) and were there until the Exodus (between 1400 and 1320). This was, then, a little before the reign of Tutankhamen. {The} nineteenth dynasty {was marked by a} struggle with {the} Hittites; {the} twentieth dynasty {saw the} loss of Syria, followed by interior division; {during the} twenty-second dynasty Libyan invaders {arrived, while in the} twenty-fourth {and} twenty-fifth {there were} Ethiopian invaders (foreign elements {continued to appear} to {the} thirtieth dynasty). It is with the twenty-second dynasty onward that we have to do in the Old Testament historical accounts of Egyptian wars and politics in Asia Minor: Assyria, Babylonia, Persia conquer Egypt. Finally Alexander conquers Egypt after beating Darius at Issus (332).

Egyptian society {included} at the bottom, *slaves* (captured in war); then *serfs* (cf. sharecroppers) and *laborers*; *administrators*—of the laboring masses; *proprietors* of great estates—the ruling class (feudal lords); *the clergy, the courtiers, and Pharaoh*. Between the sixth and tenth dynasties, at the end of the Old Kingdom, there was a period of revolution, after which there was less oppression; the town dweller was more free and also more able to rise in the social scale; the peasant was also more

---

291. See Hyvernat, "Egypt," 339.

independent (this in particular under the New Kingdom). Nevertheless, the eighteenth to {the} twentieth dynasties, {at the} beginning of the New Kingdom, were the time of {the} greatest royal power and autocracy. After the twenty-first dynasty, power broke up and wealth was divided among several ruling families, {and} also dissipated by foreign invasions.

The Middle Kingdom was a time of transition from feudalism. Labor troubles were frequent—struggles between serfs and labor on one hand, with the administrators who refused them pay and food. Strikes occurred: for instance workers who had not received wages for eighteen days barricaded themselves in the Temple of Ramses II at Thebes, and the army was called out against them. They were paid, but the trouble soon broke out again ({the} record {is found} in {a} papyrus of Turin). {The} source of these troubles {was} the avarice of the bosses, who cheated on the payroll. The slaves lived in forced labor camps.

Agriculture {was} the occupation of the majority of the laborers. N.B. papyrus, {a} reed, made boats, shoes, ropes, clothes, baskets, PAPER—now extinct ({due to a high} tax).[292] Harvests {consisted} of wheat, grapes, oranges, lemons, dates; note—figs were sometimes harvested with the aid of trained monkeys. {There were} rich gardens and orchards {as well as} stock-raising. *One tenth of everything went to Pharaoh. Hunting and fishing* {were} another source of income. Antelopes, wild bulls, elephants, rhinoceros, hippopotamus, ostrich, etc. {were hunted}; later, hunting became the great sport of the rich, {who} hunted with dogs and trained hyenas. The great ones went hunting in Nubia (principally for lions—Amenophis III caught 102 lions). *Industry* of all kinds {existed}; *trade* {was} mostly by water, up and down the Nile and along the Mediterranean coasts. *Recreation* {included} singing, dancing, {music with} harps, lyres, guitars, flutes, trumpets, trombones, drums, bells, castanets; games like checkers and chess, dice, and something analogous to pinball games, {along with} wrestling, boxing {and} sham naval battles with jousting boats.

The Rulers: the pharaohs were held to be divine, and to have lived among the gods before birth, and to return there after death. They were worshipped during life as gods and had temples dedicated to them. At the same time, the pharaoh is the supreme head of the state religion ({centered on} worship of his own ancestors) and the head of the priesthood. However, in the twenty-first dynasty, the powerful priestly class

---

292. See Hyvernat, "Egypt," 331 for this and the following details on produce.

took over royal power. There was then a further division; the power was shared with other priests. This led to the disintegration of Egyptian royalty, which was then taken over by the Libyans. The king was surrounded by functionaries, especially a *vizir*, after the eighteenth dynasty. The vizir would generally be a son of the king, in complete charge of either upper or lower Egypt. His functions {were} to represent the king in everything—as judge, administrator, overseer, etc.; under him were other judges, treasurers, princes, ministers, etc., etc. {As for} *the clergy*, generally speaking the priests were also civil servants. It was a theocratic bureaucracy, under the king. {The priests} became even more numerous and more important under the New Kingdom, {accompanied by} great material prosperity of the temples. They replaced the feudal nobility in the New Kingdom. Note {the} struggles of king vs. clergy under the New Kingdom, in {a} time of royal decadence. Amenophis IV ({at the} end of {the} eighteenth dynasty) tried to break {the} power of {the} priests of Amon; {he} abolished {the} cult of Amon, broke idols, closed temples, tried to make all change over to {the} cult of another God—Aton (with different priests, a group more under his own control). Later the Amon cult revived and the priests of Amon eventually took over the country after Ramses IX ({the} cult of Amon {was} centered at Thebes). After Ramses {IX},[293] the priest of Amon was always the vizir. Priestly charges were hereditary.

Religion {was} mostly exterior, {a} matter of cult, {with} liturgical and ritual perfection stressed. The priests were the educated class, the students, the scientists, the doctors. *Religion* {began} basically {as} a cult of *local divinities*, originally gods (totems) of the clan, with a temple in the center of the "nome" or district of the clan. The god was at first a totem animal; then the animal's head remained on a human body. Later there grew up the cult of *cosmic divinities*: Ra—the sun, worshipped at Heliopolis—the greatest of the Egyptian gods; also *Amon* (the same god, but worshipped under a different name at Thebes); *Horus* (the falcon)—another version of Ra; *Osiris*, god of death and of vegetation, governor of the world, enemy of *Seth*, husband of *Isis*. Seth kills Osiris and usurps {the} government of the world, but in turn is killed by Horus, son of Isis and Osiris—Isis collects fragments of dismembered Osiris and revives him, and he becomes king of the dead.[294] Egyptian religion is *polytheistic*, {with an} enormous number of gods. {It is also} *animistic*: natural

---

293. Copy text reads: "II."
294. See Hyvernat, "Egypt," 344.

phenomena {are} attributed to {the} presence of a god living within the thing. {It also includes} *fetishism*; {it was a} religion of nature and cosmic forces, especially of the stars. Characteristic of Egyptian religion is the *parallel cult of the gods and of the souls of the departed*: in either case {there is} an elaborate ceremonial. In the beginning, cult was offered only to the deceased kings, who were "gods"; later, deceased nobles, then all the dead received a cult. {The} "theology" behind the cult of the dead, {as found in the} "Book of the Dead," {consisted in the} belief that the souls of the departed went to the land of the dead and of the gods (in the west). This {was} preceded by a judgement, in the presence of forty-two gods, which, if favorable, permitted the soul to be admitted into the Kingdom of Osiris; otherwise {it was} cast out with Seth. But the soul might have to travel a long journey in order to arrive at the Kingdom of Osiris, and might have to fight evil spirits on the way. {The} Book of {the} Dead gives instructions. The rites of the dead were to help the soul continue in its travels beyond the grave. Bodies were embalmed because it was felt {that} the fate of the soul depended on the continued existence of the body. Sacrifice was offered in the funeral rites. Meanwhile, a statue of the deceased is seated at a table, food is brought, rites are carried out on every member to indicate the *revival* of all the members of the body; only after this was the mummy entombed. {With regard to} *pyramids* and other tombs, the dwelling of the dead had to be eternal. {There were} secret treasure chambers ({due to} the problem of tomb robbers): how they were kept secret {was through} the killing of the slave-builders. Pyramid texts {included the} Book of Funerals {and the} Book of the Dead (cf. {the} Book of the Lower Hemisphere, {concerning} the journey of the sun from west to east during the night).[295] {As for} *morality*, {there was} great respect for certain virtues: justice, religion ("Piety to the gods is the highest virtue"[296]), hospitality, truthfulness, not speaking evil of others (note: Proverbs 22:17—24:22 seems to be inspired to some extent by an Egyptian collection, the *Wisdom of Amenemope*:[297]): "Keep this in mind whenever thou has to make a decision—even as the most aged die, thou also shalt lie down among them."[298]

295. See Hyvernat, "Egypt," 348.

296. From the advice given by Ani, a scribe of the nineteenth dynasty, to his son, Khons-Hotep, quoted in Hyvernat, "Egypt," 349.

297. See Dyson, "Poetical and Wisdom Literature," 415 [n. 316ef]; Dyson, "Proverbs," 484–85 [n. 372a].

298. From the advice of Ani to Khons-Hotep, quoted in Hyvernat, "Egypt," 349.

The Story of Joseph

One of the most important and detailed sections of Genesis.

Outline: Joseph, especially gifted by God, as witnessed by his prophetic dreams, and loved above others by Jacob, is hated by his brothers. As a boy of sixteen he is sold to traders and goes with a caravan into Egypt, where he is sold to Putiphar (ch. 37). Chapter 38, an interlude, {is} the story of Juda, Onan and Thamar. Joseph in Egypt is falsely accused by Putiphar's wife and thrown into prison (ch. 39), and there he gains a reputation as an interpreter of dreams, and this comes to the ears of Pharaoh (ch. 40). After interpreting Pharaoh's dreams Joseph is elevated to the highest position in the kingdom. During the predicted famine Jacob sends his sons into Egypt to buy grain. Joseph's game with them {ensues} (ch. 42). They return {and} Joseph continues his game with them and finally makes himself known (ch. 43–45). Finally Jacob and all his family go down into Egypt, and Pharaoh gives them the land of Goshen. Jacob, blind, blesses Ephraim and Manasses, sons of Joseph born in Egypt—that is, he adopts them (ch. 48). Finally Jacob, dying, blesses all his sons (ch. 49). In the end, Jacob is buried and all mourn him. Joseph prophesies the return to the promised land (50).

{With respect to its} *teaching*, this very important phase in the early history of Israel has a great lesson to teach. Joseph tells us in Genesis 50:19–20: "*Fear not; can we resist the will of God? You thought evil against me, but God turned it into good that He might exalt me, as at present you see, and might save many people*"; and in 45:5 {he says}: "*Pro {salute} enim vestra misit me Deus ante vos in Aegyptum*"[299] (cf. {the} interesting parallel with John 11:51–52: the prophecy of Caiphas). The teaching of the dogma of *Divine Providence* {is given}, in which the inscrutable wisdom and love of God triumphs over all apparent obstacles (in reality there are no obstacles), and the *problem of evil* is also luminously solved here, for even evil enters into God's plan for the greater good of His elect: "All things work together for the good of those who love God."[300] As St. Augustine says, "God preferred to draw good out of evil rather than to

---

299. "for God sent me before you into Egypt for your preservation" (copy text reads: "*salutem*").

300. Rom 8:28.

prevent the existence of evil"³⁰¹ (cf. *Breviary*: Good Friday³⁰²). {Note the} difference from previous narratives: (1) {there are} no direct revelations of Yahweh—theophanies {are} replaced by dreams, which show His will, and by His action in hearts; (2) {there is} greater psychological realism and detail, closer to the style of the novel. Hence we are naturally reminded of the obvious fact that Joseph is a *type of the suffering Redeemer*: (a) sold by His brethren; (b) for the salvation of the gentiles; (c) and for the ultimate salvation of the Jews themselves (cf. Acts 4:27–28: "For of a truth there assembled together in this city against Thy holy child Jesus, whom Thou hast anointed, Herod and Pontius Pilate and the Gentiles and the People of Israel, TO DO WHAT THY HAND AND THY COUNSEL DECREED TO BE DONE"; cf. also Romans 11:15: IF THE LOSS OF THEM [THE JEWS] BE THE RECONCILIATION OF THE WORLD WHAT SHALL THE RECEIVING OF THEM BE BUT LIFE FROM THE DEAD?—read {in} context³⁰³). The whole

301. "*Melius enim judicavit de malis bene facere, quam mala nulla esse permittere*" (Augustine, *Enchiridion*, c. 27 [Migne, *PL* 40, col. 245]).

302. Second nocturne, *lectio* 4 (Augustine, *In Ps.* 63, v. 3): "*Protexisti me Deus a conventu malignantium, a multitudine operantium iniquitatem. Jam ipsum caput nostrum intueamur. Multi Martyres talia passi sunt, sed nihil sic elucet, quomodo caput Martyrum; ibi melius intueamur, quod illi experti sunt. Protectus est a multitudine malignantium, protegente se Deo, protegente carnem suam ipso Filio, et homine, quem gerebat: quia Filius hominis est, et Filius Dei est. Filius Dei, propter formam Dei: Filius hominis, propter formam servi, habens in potestate ponere animam suam, et recipere eam. Quid ei potuerunt facere inimici? Occiderunt corpus, animam non occiderunt. Intendite. Parum ergo erat, Domino hortari Martyres verbo, nisi firmaret exemplo*" ("You have protected me, O God, from the assembly of the malicious, from the crowd of the evildoers. Now let us look upon our Head himself. Many martyrs have suffered such things, but nothing shines forth as does the Head of the martyrs; there we better recognize what they have experienced. He was protected from the assembly of the malicious, protected by God himself, the Son himself, also a man, protecting his own flesh which he bore: for he is the Son of Man, and the Son of God—the Son of God, because he is in the form of God—the Son of Man, because he is in the form of a servant, having it in his power to lay down his life and to pick it up. What were his enemies able to do to him? They killed his body; they did not kill his soul. Pay attention. For it was too little for the Lord to encourage the martyrs by word, if he did not confirm it by example") (*Breviarium Cisterciense, Vernalis*, 289).

303. "I say then: Hath God cast away his people? God forbid! For I also am an Israelite of the seed of Abraham, of the tribe of Benjamin. God hath not cast away his people which he foreknew. Know you not what the scripture saith of Elias, how he calleth on God against Israel? Lord, they have slain thy prophets, they have dug down thy altars. And I am left alone: and they seek my life. But what saith the divine answer to him? I have left me seven thousand men that have not bowed their knees to Baal. Even so then, at this present time also, there is a remnant saved according to the election of grace. And if by grace, it is not now by works: otherwise grace is no more grace. What

mystery of evil in the history of the world and of the Church is revealed here in figure. Of all the evil that God has permitted, greater good shall come forth and in the end His promises will be fulfilled to the wonder of all His elect in a most marvelous and complete fashion, so that the glory of His grace may be made manifest in the Church, in which all things are recapitulated in Christ and restored to God the Father.

Joseph sold by his brethren (c. 37): {in} chapter 37:2–4, *Joseph* {is} *introduced* as a boy of *seventeen* (not sixteen),[304] who keeps the flocks of sheep with his brothers (the little ones). He is in the habit of reporting to Jacob the evil that is told about the boys (not a special crime as {the} Vulgate might seem to indicate[305]). Jacob loves Joseph in a special way, the "son of his old age" (and also of Rachel) and he makes him a *long-sleeved tunic* (a special formal costume for dressing up, evidently, not just something to work in). Hence the brothers are jealous, and "become incapable of speaking a civil word to him." This gives us an immediate insight into the psychological finesse of the story. *His dreams* {are related}

---

then? That which Israel sought, he hath not obtained: but the election hath obtained it. And the rest have been blinded. As it is written: God hath given them the spirit of insensibility; eyes that they should not see and ears that they should not hear, until this present day. And David saith: Let their table be made a snare and a trap and a stumbling block and a recompense unto them. Let their eyes be darkened, that they may not see: and bow down their back always. I say then: Have they so stumbled, that they should fall? God forbid! But by their offence salvation is come to the Gentiles, that they may be emulous of them. Now if the offence of them be the riches of the world and the diminution of them the riches of the Gentiles: how much more the fulness of them? For I say to you, Gentiles: As long indeed as I am the apostle of the Gentiles, I will honour my ministry, If, by any means, I may provoke to emulation them who are my flesh and may save some of them. For if the loss of them be the reconciliation of the world, what shall the receiving of them be, but life from the dead? For if the firstfruit be holy, so is the lump also: and if the root be holy, so are the branches. And if some of the branches be broken and thou, being a wild olive, art ingrafted in them and art made partaker of the root and of the fatness of the olive tree: Boast not against the branches. But if thou boast, thou bearest not the root: but the root thee. Thou wilt say then: The branches were broken off that I might be grafted in. Well: because of unbelief they were broken off. But thou standest by faith. Be not highminded, but fear. For if God hath not spared the natural branches, fear lest perhaps also he spare not thee. See then the goodness and the severity of God: towards them indeed that are fallen, the severity; but towards thee, the goodness of God, if thou abide in goodness. Otherwise thou also shalt be cut off " (Rom 11:1–22).

304. See Sutcliffe, "Genesis," 200 [n. 156h].

305. "*accusavitque fratres suos apud patrem crimine pessimo*" ("and he accused his brethren to his father of a most wicked crime") (Gen 37:2).

(READ 5–11[306]): {note the} ingenuousness with which he tells the brothers his dream, {and} the ease with which they interpret it, as if everyone in those days was familiar with dream interpretation—it was not yet an unknown language. {After} the second dream he is scolded by his father; the jealousy of the brothers grows beyond measure, but the father nevertheless takes the dream seriously—he stores the fact away in his memory; his scolding was not a final judgement. *Joseph* {is} *sold* (READ 12–36[307]):

306. "Now it fell out also that he told his brethren a dream, that he had dreamed: which occasioned them to hate him the more. And he said to them: Hear my dream which I dreamed. I thought we were binding sheaves in the field: and my sheaf arose as it were, and stood, and your sheaves standing about, bowed down before my sheaf. His brethren answered: Shalt thou be our king? or shall we be subject to thy dominion? Therefore this matter of his dreams and words ministered nourishment to their envy and hatred. He dreamed also another dream, which he told his brethren, saying: I saw in a dream, as it were the sun, and the moon, and eleven stars worshipping me. And when he had told this to his father and brethren, his father rebuked him, and said: What meaneth this dream that thou hast dreamed? shall I and thy mother, and thy brethren worship thee upon the earth? His brethren therefore envied him: but his father considered the thing with himself."

307. "And when his brethren abode in Sichem feeding their father's flocks, Israel said to him: Thy brethren feed the sheep in Sichem: come, I will send thee to them. And when he answered: I am ready: he said to him: Go, and see if all things be well with thy brethren, and the cattle: and bring me word again what is doing. So being sent from the vale of Hebron, he came to Sichem: And a man found him there wandering in the field, and asked what he sought. But he answered: I seek my brethren; tell me where they feed the flocks. And the man said to him: They are departed from this place: for I heard them say: Let us go to Dothain. And Joseph went forward after his brethren, and found them in Dothain. And when they saw him afar off, before he came nigh them, they thought to kill him. And said one to another: Behold the dreamer cometh. Come, let us kill him, and cast him into some old pit: and we will say: Some evil beast hath devoured him: and then it shall appear what his dreams avail him: And Ruben hearing this, endeavoured to deliver him out of their hands, and said: Do not take away his life, nor shed his blood: but cast him into this pit, that is in the wilderness, and keep your hands harmless: now he said this, being desirous to deliver him out of their hands and to restore him to his father. And as soon as he came to his brethren, they forthwith stript him of his outside coat, that was of divers colours: And cast him into an old pit, where there was no water. And sitting down to eat bread, they saw some Ismaelites on their way coming from Galaad, with their camels, carrying spices, and balm, and myrrh to Egypt. And Juda said to his brethren: What will it profit us to kill our brother, and conceal his blood? It is better that he be sold to the Ismaelites, and that our hands be not defiled: for he is our brother and our flesh. His brethren agreed to his words. And when the Madianite merchants passed by, they drew him out of the pit, and sold him to the Ismaelites, for twenty pieces of silver: and they led him into Egypt. And Ruben, returning to the pit, found not the boy: And rending his garments he went to his brethren, and said: The boy doth not appear and whither shall I go? And they took his coat, and dipped it in the blood of a kid, which they had killed: Sending some to

(a) 12–17: the brothers have gone to Sichem, over fifty miles away,[308] with the flocks. Jacob sends Joseph after them to get news. Therefore, when they see him coming, they will be angry for many reasons: he is the "dreamer," the little favorite; he is also the tale-bearer, and he has come to spy on them, and he is wearing his long-sleeved tunic, which is for one who does no work, etc.; Joseph arrives at Sichem {but} his brothers have gone on to Dothan; (b) the brothers see Joseph coming (18–20) {and} they plot to kill him while he is coming toward them over the open country; (c) Ruben saves "the child": he pretends to propose a different kind of death which will be "less guilty"—no blood will be shed—{but} in reality he hopes to rescue him from the dried-up well later; {in verse} 23, "They strip off his tunic"—{a} striking foreshadowing of the stripping of Jesus in the Passion; also like the Passion, after they have thrown him in the cistern they sit down to eat—cf. the callousness of the Pharisees who sit down to watch Jesus die on the cross; (d) the caravan comes (Ishmaelites, Madianites? Is this a discrepancy; does it indicate double authorship? CBC says no[309]); here Juda is the one who intervenes for Joseph (26–27); Ruben returns and finds the boy gone (he has not been present at the sale); Joseph has been sold for twenty pieces of silver (cf. the price paid to Judas[310]—close enough); (e) {in verses} 31–36, note the idea of substitution here—the blood of the goat; {there are} curious similarities with the sacrifice of Isaac; Jacob is deceived and mourns; note that Jacob himself, the deceiver of Isaac, is now deceived by his sons. Again, as a result of the deception, the chosen one of God goes away to prepare the further history of the chosen people; {in verse} 35 {note} the simultaneity of the pictures: Jacob weeping, Joseph sold to Putiphar.

Juda and Thamar etc.: Juda separates from his brothers in the region of Sichem {and} marries a Canaanite woman, Shua. One of his sons by her

---

carry it to their father, and to say: This we have found: see whether it be thy son's coat, or not. And the father acknowledging it, said: It is my son's coat, an evil wild beast hath eaten him, a beast hath devoured Joseph. And tearing his garments, he put on sackcloth, mourning for his son a long time. And all his children being gathered together to comfort their father in his sorrow, he would not receive comfort, but said: I will go down to my son into hell, mourning. And whilst he continued weeping, The Madianites sold Joseph in Egypt to Putiphar, an eunuch of Pharao, captain of the soldiers."

308. Sutcliffe, "Genesis," 200 [n. 156i].

309. "This is not a discrepancy or proof of diversity of sources. The names were used indifferently as may be seen in Jg 8:22, 24, 26. The two tribes were closely related, 25:2, 12, and intermingled" (Sutcliffe, "Genesis," 200 [n. 155i]).

310. I.e., thirty pieces of silver (Matt 26:15).

is Onan, {who} refuses to beget children by Thamar, the wife of the other deceased son of Juda. The fact that displeases Yahweh the most is not just the "onanism" of Onan but also the fact that he refuses to be the father of a family that will be "his brother's" line. Onan is struck down by God. Hence {there are} no more sons of Juda to beget sons by Thamar—except a younger one, Shela. Juda tells her to wait until Shela grows up, but she deceives him, disguised, is united with him, and has a child. When he learns she is pregnant he condemns her to be burned alive, until he learns that he himself is the father. In {verse} 26 Juda recognizes that she was "right," for he had gone back on his promise to give her Shela, and she was justified in wanting a child from her husband's blood. She brings forth twins—Zara being the one mentioned in the genealogy of Jesus. This was the one who put his hand out first and had a red thread tied to his wrist, but was born second (cf. Matthew 1:3—the "younger" supplants the elder as {the} ancestor of {the} Messias[311]).

Joseph in the House of Putiphar: on arrival in Egypt, Joseph is bought as {a} slave by Putiphar (this name exists in Egyptian inscriptions), a high officer in the court. The Lord is "with Joseph"[312] and everything he does succeeds. Because of Joseph, the blessing of God descends upon the house of Putiphar, and Putiphar puts him in charge of everything "but the bread which he ate"—{a} picturesque way of saying the only work left for Putiphar was to convey food from the plate to his own mouth. Note {that} Putiphar "knew very well that the Lord was with Joseph."[313] Joseph is handsome and elegant. {The} emphasis on Joseph's success means that Yahweh is the true God and rules as He pleases, even amid the many gods of the Egyptians; they are all false gods. After all this good fortune, Putiphar's wife begins to take notice of Joseph and falls in love with him. She tries to seduce him, though he refuses to commit an injustice against his master. (Note the emphasis is on justice and loyalty first of all, on not betraying a trust. This is important. Justice is a higher virtue than temperance. It is objective. We in our day seem to retain a preference for the subjective virtues. {It is} good to have a greater appreciation of *justice*, of the reality of obligations, and the homage we offer to God by living up to them. This has many subjective advantages. Among others, we are saved from the error of making everything stand or fall by our

---

311. Merton is in error here: both children are mentioned in the genealogy of Matthew, but it is Perez rather than Zara (Zerah) who is in the ancestral line of Jesus.

312. Gen 39:2.

313. Gen 39:3.

own subjective feelings. To keep an objective obligation is a great thing, even if it does not make us feel anything special.) The narrative of the attempted seduction of Joseph is told with color and drama, {with} much living psychological detail, {especially} her revenge for wounded feelings after his refusal. She accuses him falsely—a vivid study of passion. Joseph is thrown into prison. How often carnal love turns into hatred! (cf. the story of Susanna—Saturday after {the} third Sunday of Lent[314]).

Joseph in Prison (READ 39:19-23[315]): here again the "Lord is with Joseph" and he finds favor in the eyes of the warden. Once again "everything is in his charge"; he practically runs the prison.

The Dreams of the Baker and Butler (READ c. 40 *in toto*[316]): {in verses} 7-8, the court officials are sad when Joseph comes in brightly one

---

314. Dan 13:1-62 (*Missale Romanum*, 107-108; *Missale Cisterciense*, 96-98).

315. "His master hearing these things, and giving too much credit to his wife's words, was very angry. And cast Joseph into the prison, where the king's prisoners were kept, and he was there shut up. But the Lord was with Joseph and having mercy upon him gave him favour in the sight of the chief keeper of the prison: Who delivered into his hand all the prisoners that were kept in custody: and whatsoever was done was under him. Neither did he himself know any thing, having committed all things to him: for the Lord was with him, and made all that he did to prosper."

316. "After this, it came to pass, that two eunuchs, the butler and the baker of the king of Egypt, offended their lord. And Pharao being angry with them (now the one was chief butler, the other chief baker) He sent them to the prison of the commander of the soldiers, in which Joseph also was prisoner, But the keeper of the prison delivered them to Joseph, and he served them. Some little time passed, and they were kept in custody. And they both dreamed a dream the same night, according to the interpretation agreeing to themselves: And when Joseph was come in to them in the morning, and saw them sad, He asked them, saying: Why is your countenance sadder today than usual? They answered: We have dreamed a dream, and there is nobody to interpret it to us. And Joseph said to them: Doth not interpretation belong to God? Tell me what you have dreamed. The chief butler first told his dream: I saw before me a vine, On which were three branches, which by little and little sent out buds, and after the blossoms brought forth ripe grapes: And the cup of Pharao was in my hand: and I took the grapes, and pressed them into the cup which I held, and I gave the cup to Pharao. Joseph answered: This is the interpretation of the dream: The three branches are yet three days: After which Pharao will remember thy service, and will restore thee to thy former place: and thou shalt present him the cup according to thy office, as before thou wast wont to do. Only remember me, when it shall be well with thee, and do me this kindness: to put Pharao in mind to take me out of this prison: For I was stolen away out of the land of the Hebrews, and here without any fault was cast into the dungeon. The chief baker seeing that he had wisely interpreted the dream, said: I also dreamed a dream, That I had three baskets of meal upon my head: And that in one basket which was uppermost, I carried all meats that are made by the art of baking, and that the birds ate out of it. Joseph answered: This is the interpretation of

morning. They have had dreams, and these are important things, but alas they cannot get to consult a dream-interpreter. Joseph reproves them for depending on human means: God is the only one who can really interpret dreams. {First comes} the butler's dream; a butler is a *bouteiller*, the one in charge of the bottles; he is in charge of the wine supply of Pharaoh (today the butler is simply the head servant). He dreams a prosperous and happy dream. He will return to his office. The baker's dream reflects insecurity and fear in every way. It is a weird and wonderful picture, with three baskets on his head and in the top basket cakes, loaves, buns, etc. which the birds are eating. {This is an} ill omen: he will die and hang on a gibbet, and the birds will eat his flesh, the worst thing that could happen to an Egyptian, since happiness in {the} afterlife seemed to them to depend on preservation of the body. Note the beauty and vividness of the narrative, ending with the forgetfulness of the chief butler. Elements in the beauty of the narrative {include} *balance*, contrast, movement, leading to a result and a final surprise—a perfect part of a greater whole, a moment of excitement and hope for Joseph, ending in a disappointment which prolongs the suspense. It would make {a} wonderful scene set to modern music!—perhaps a ballet!

Joseph at the Court of Pharaoh (read c. 41:1–16[317]): Pharaoh's dreams {are followed by} the repentance of the butler, who confesses his

---

the dream: The three baskets are yet three days: After which Pharao will take thy head from thee, and hang thee on a cross, and the birds shall tear thy flesh. The third day after this was the birthday of Pharao: and he made a great feast for his servants, and at the banquet remembered the chief butler, and the chief baker. And he restored the one to his place to present him the cup: The other he hanged on a gibbet, that the truth of the interpreter might be shewn. But the chief butler, when things prospered with him, forgot his interpreter."

317. "After two years Pharao had a dream. He thought he stood by the river, Out of which came up seven kine, very beautiful and fat: and they fed in marshy places. Other seven also came up out of the river, ill favoured, and leanfleshed: and they fed on the very bank of the river, in green places: And they devoured them, whose bodies were very beautiful and well conditioned. So Pharao awoke. He slept again, and dreamed another dream: Seven ears of corn came up upon one stalk full and fair: Then seven other ears sprung up thin and blasted, And devoured all the beauty of the former. Pharao awaked after his rest: And when morning was come, being struck with fear, he sent to all the interpreters of Egypt, and to all the wise men: and they being called for, he told them his dream, and there was not any one that could interpret it. Then at length the chief butler remembering, said: I confess my sin: The king being angry with his servants, commanded me and the chief baker to be cast into the prison of the captain of the soldiers: Where in one night both of us dreamed a dream foreboding things to come. There was there a young man a Hebrew, servant to the same captain

ingratitude to Joseph. Joseph is summoned by Pharaoh. Note: Joseph has been left for two more years in prison. Divine Providence gets him out not when it is convenient for Joseph himself, but when it is for the good of all. This is an important lesson: God does not merely consider our own interests, in answering our prayers. Our desires, however good, inspired by Him, always fit in with the needs and interests of someone else, and, in fact, of the whole. Their fulfillment must also fit in with the whole plan of God. Our happiness is subordinated to His whole plan—or rather, more accurately, is incorporated in that plan. We have no real hope of fulfillment and happiness merely in the line of our own personal and individual perspectives. Joseph's answer when the King asks him to interpret the dream {is}: "Without me God shall give Pharaoh a prosperous answer" (v. 16). {This is} not merely humility for show, but a deep realization of his own dependence on God for everything, but especially for supernatural gifts. The interpretation of the dreams {follows}; they are really one dream (v. 25)—to dream the same thing twice is a sign that it will certainly come true soon (v. 32). "God hath shown to Pharaoh what He is about to do." There will be seven good years, followed by seven years of famine: Joseph proposes a plan: (a) appoint a "special commissioner" to supervise a project for storing up food; (b) gather in supplies of food by a tax, one-fifth of all the produce in the good years {and} use it (in fact sell it) during the lean years. Pharaoh is pleased and gives Joseph this job (READ 41:37–46[318]). Joseph gets a new name, but this time it is not a new

---

of the soldiers: to whom we told our dreams, And we heard what afterwards the event of the thing proved to be so. For I was restored to my office: and he was hanged upon a gibbet. Forthwith at the king's command, Joseph was brought out of the prison, and they shaved him, and changing his apparel, brought him in to him. And he said to him: I have dreamed dreams, and there is no one that can expound them: Now I have heard that thou art very wise at interpreting them. Joseph answered: Without me, God shall give Pharao a prosperous answer."

318. "The counsel pleased Pharao and all his servants. And he said to them: Can we find such another man, that is full of the spirit of God? He said therefore to Joseph: Seeing God hath shewn thee all that thou hast said, can I find one wiser and one like unto thee? Thou shalt be over my house, and at the commandment of thy mouth all the people shall obey: only in the kingly throne will I be above thee. And again Pharao said to Joseph: Behold, I have appointed thee over the whole land of Egypt. And he took his ring from his own hand, and gave it into his hand: and he put upon him a robe of silk, and put a chain of gold about his neck. And he made him go up into his second chariot, the crier proclaiming that all should bow their knee before him, and that they should know he was made governor over the whole land of Egypt. And the king said to Joseph: I am Pharao; without thy commandment no man shall move hand or foot in all the land of Egypt. And he turned his name, and called him in the Egyptian tongue, The

name from God, but only one in Egyptian, from an earthly king, but the Scripture gives no hint of blame: it is for the People of God, eventually. What is this new name? Douay calls him "Saviour of the World";[319] *CBC* thinks it meant "something like feeder of the land"[320]—probably an expression of his wisdom, something to do with his plan. {He is} married to {the} daughter of the high priest of Ra at Heliopolis; he is now a member of the highest nobility in the land (again, the name Putiphar, {which is} common, means "Gift of Ra"). By this Egyptian wife, Aseneth, Joseph has two sons, Manasses and Ephraim—the names signify his contentment in Egypt, his happiness in exile. (Chapter 48 will be an important one, for there Jacob will adopt Ephraim and Manasses as his own, to enable them to become heads of tribes. Note—Jacob in his old age will not be tricked into giving a mistaken blessing like Isaac.)

READ 41:53–57:[321] the coming of the famine. The whole world suffers famine. The people of Egypt {are} crying for food. We do not realize the terror of famine, especially for millions of poor who live at the bare level of subsistence and for whom there is no support at all if there is a bad harvest. Now there are seven bad years. Such famines lead to immense unrest and universal trouble, {to} movement of populations seeking food. All this must be "seen" in these few vivid lines. Then we get the full effect of the statement about Joseph "opening the barns." The people cried to Pharaoh and he said, "Go to Joseph." (See the application of this to St. Joseph {in the} responsories of the first nocturn of his feast.[322] St. Joseph {is presented as} the good provider *of the poor*. As he was the provider for the Holy Family, so too he is provider and protector for Holy

---

saviour of the world. And he gave him to wife Aseneth the daughter of Putiphare priest of Heliopolis. Then Joseph went out to the land of Egypt: (Now he was thirty years old when he stood before king Pharao) and he went round all the countries of Egypt."

319. "*Salvatorem mundi*" (Vulgate).

320. Sutcliffe, "Genesis," 201 [n. 157d].

321. "Now when the seven years of the plenty that had been in Egypt were past: The seven years of scarcity, which Joseph had foretold, began to come: and the famine prevailed in the whole world, but there was bread in all the land of Egypt. And when there also they began to be famished, the people cried to Pharao for food. And he said to them: Go to Joseph: and do all that he shall say to you. And the famine increased daily in all the land: and Joseph opened all the barns, and sold to the Egyptians: for the famine had oppressed them also. And all provinces came into Egypt, to buy food, and to seek some relief of their want."

322. *Lectio* 2, responsory: "*Ite ad Joseph, et quidquid vobis dixerit, facite*" ("Go to Joseph and do whatever he tells you") (*Breviarium Cisterciense, Vernalis,* 432).

Church—but not just a money-raiser for parish and convent projects: no, he is an instrument of divine providence to help those who have no other help but God.)

Joseph's Brethren Come to Egypt (READ C. 42[323]): one of the most impressive things about this story is the way Joseph takes his revenge on his brethren: by heaping coals of fire upon their heads[324] with goodness—and merely playing with them. This sublimation of violence is dwelt on at great length by the author—he goes into every detail. In every other line of the story one sees allusions to this fact: v.g. 42:4: Jacob keeps the youngest, Benjamin, with him, "lest he take any harm" (obviously remembering Joseph); 6: the brethren bow down before Joseph—in fulfillment of his dream; 9: "and remembering the dreams" and everything that followed: this makes clear that his motive is to "get even" in a spiritual and innocent way; 21: they talk it over in the presence of Joseph, not knowing he understands, and they admit their guilt, and Ruben chides them for not listening to him; Joseph understands and weeps (24).

Joseph's Game with His Brethren: the mainspring of the plot is a matter of dramatic irony—the question of Joseph's unknown identity. This is by far the most developed and sophisticated story yet told in the Bible, and perhaps the most marked by these qualities in the Old Testament. READ 42:8–25:[325] Joseph treats his brethren roughly, accuses them of be-

---

323. "And Jacob hearing that food was sold in Egypt, said to his sons: Why are ye careless? I have heard that wheat is sold in Egypt: go ye down, and buy us necessaries, that we may live, and not be consumed with want. So the ten brethren of Joseph went down, to buy corn in Egypt: Whilst Benjamin was kept at home by Jacob, who said to his brethren: Lest perhaps he take any harm in the journey. And they entered into the land of Egypt with others that went to buy. For the famine was in the land of Chanaan. And Joseph was governor in the land of Egypt, and corn was sold by his direction to the people. And when his brethren had bowed down to him, And he knew them, he spoke as it were to strangers somewhat roughly, asking them: Whence came you? They answered: From the land of Chanaan, to buy necessaries of life" (vv.1–7).

324. See Rom 12:20.

325. And though he knew his brethren, he was not known by them. And remembering the dreams, which formerly he had dreamed, he said to them: You are spies. You are come to view the weaker parts of the land. But they said: It is not so, my lord, but thy servants are come to buy food. We are all the sons of one man: we are come as peaceable men, neither do thy servants go about any evil. And he answered them: It is otherwise: you are come to consider the unfenced parts of this land. But they said: We thy servants are twelve brethren, the sons of one man in the land of Chanaan: the youngest is with our father, the other is not living. He saith: This is it that I said: You are spies. I shall now presently try what you are: by the health of Pharao you shall not depart hence, until your youngest brother come. Send one of you to fetch him: and you

ing spies, tells them their story is a lie, throws them in jail for three days, tells them to prove their story by bringing Benjamin back with them, binds Simeon and keeps him as a hostage—but then secretly puts their purchase money back in the sacks of wheat which they have bought. They find the money in their sacks and are struck with fear: "What has God done to us?" Note in this their recognition of God's action, and the fact that this action is the "punishment" of their sin against Joseph. Remember that we are all the while dealing spiritually with a "type" of the death of Christ at the hands of the Jews.

READ 42:35–38:[326] Jacob, hearing their story, refuses to let Benjamin go. Ruben passionately promises to guarantee his safety, but Jacob still refuses. Note the intensity of the passions and the feelings involved, and the heightened tension of the plot. Again the effectiveness of the irony {is evident}—it continues in chapter 43.

READ 43:3–15:[327] note the desperateness of Jacob, his willingness at all costs to placate the Egyptian governor. He is now no longer merely

---

shall be in prison, till what you have said be proved, whether it be true or false: or else by the health of Pharao you are spies. So he put them in prison three days. And the third day he brought them out of prison, and said: Do as I have said, and you shall live: for I fear God. If you be peaceable men, let one of your brethren be bound in prison: and go ye your ways and carry the corn that you have bought, unto your houses. And bring your youngest brother to me, that I may find your words to be true, and you may not die. They did as he had said. And they talked one to another: We deserve to suffer these things, because we have sinned against our brother, seeing the anguish of his soul, when he besought us, and we would not hear: therefore is this affliction come upon us. And Ruben one of them, said: Did not I say to you: Do not sin against the boy: and you would not hear me? Behold his blood is required. And they knew not that Joseph understood, because he spoke to them by an interpreter. And he turned himself away a little while, and wept: and returning he spoke to them. And taking Simeon, and binding him in their presence, he commanded his servants to fill their sacks with wheat, and to put every man's money again in their sacks, and to give them besides provisions for the way: and they did so."

326. "When they had told this, they poured out their corn and every man found his money tied in the mouth of his sack: and all being astonished together, Their father Jacob said: You have made me to be without children: Joseph is not living, Simeon is kept in bonds, and Benjamin you will take away: all these evils are fallen upon me. And Ruben answered him: Kill my two sons if I bring him not again to thee: deliver him into my hand, and I will restore him to thee. But he said: My son shall not go down with you: his brother is dead, and he is left alone: if any mischief befall him in the land to which you go, you will bring down my gray hairs with sorrow to hell."

327. "Juda answered: The man declared unto us with the attestation of an oath, saying: You shall not see my face, unless you bring your youngest brother with you. If therefore thou wilt send him with us, we will set out together, and will buy necessaries

shrewd and aggressive, but in his love for his sons is willing to let himself be "taken" in any way, provided they are safe. Again Jacob's sons go down to Egypt, taking Benjamin. {In verses} 16 ff., Joseph prepares a feast, and they suspect another trap. They return all the money and protest their honesty. They are afraid he will take them and make them all slaves. Again, they bow down and offer him gifts—{a} reference to the dream. Joseph's emotions on seeing Benjamin {are shown}; they are so strong that he has to get out of sight to conceal his tears. He washes his face and returns. {At} the feast (31–34), Benjamin gets five times as big a portion as the rest. (*CBC* says, "Beef and goose were the favourite dishes."[328]) {In verse} 33, Joseph has seated them all in rank according to their age and birthright, hence showing that he has a secret inside knowledge of the whole family. Still they do not catch on, and are more afraid, wondering what will come next.

The Plot—Benjamin "Framed" (c. 44): again they are sent away, this time with the money in their sacks as usual. But if they go now they will never come back, {but} Joseph's plan is to get Jacob and all the remaining family back to Egypt. He put his silver cup in Benjamin's sack, then sends his servants to catch up with them and accuse them of theft—of the cup with which he "does his divining"—note how fully he enters into his part. READ 44:4–13,[329] {a} perfect narrative. {In verses} 15 ff. they

---

for thee. But if thou wilt not, we will not go: for the man, as we have often said, declared unto us, saying: You shall not see my face without your youngest brother. Israel said to them: You have done this for my misery in that you told him you had also another brother. But they answered: The man asked us in order concerning our kindred: if our father lived: if we had a brother: and we answered him regularly, according to what he demanded: could we know that he would say: Bring hither your brother with you? And Juda said to his father: Send the boy with me, that we may set forward, and may live: lest both we and our children perish. I take the boy upon me, require him at my hand: unless I bring him again, and restore him to thee, I will be guilty of sin against thee for ever. If delay had not been made, we had been here again the second time. Then Israel said to them: If it must needs be so, do what you will: take of the best fruits of the land in your vessels, and carry down presents to the man, a little balm, and honey, and storax, myrrh, turpentine, and almonds. And take with you double money, and carry back what you found in your sacks, lest perhaps it was done by mistake. And take also your brother, and go to the man. And may my almighty God make him favourable to you; and send back with you your brother, whom he keepeth, and this Benjamin: and as for me I shall be desolate without children. So the men took the presents, and double money, and Benjamin: and went down into Egypt, and stood before Joseph."

328. Sutcliffe, "Genesis," 201 [n. 157j].

329. "And when they were now departed out of the city, and had gone forward a

return. Joseph claims he has found out all this by his "divining." Joseph's "solution" {is that} he will keep Benjamin as a slave and let the others go. This throws them all into consternation. Juda now has to work hard to keep his promise. (Juda and Ruben both made promises to save Benjamin, just as Juda and Ruben both tried to save Joseph.) Juda's desperate pleading {now follows}: he offers himself in Benjamin's place so as not to cause the death of his father.

Chapter 45: finally Joseph can stand it no longer. He throws everybody out except his brethren, and makes himself known—not with the laconic sangfroid of an Englishman or the casualness of an American: he lifts up his voice in a wail that is heard all through the palace (v. 2). READ {verses} 2–9:[330] Joseph's theological explanation {of} the mystery of divine Providence. "God sent me before .... Not by your counsel was I sent here but by the will of God." The tremendous truth {expressed is} that nothing happens but for the good of those loved by God; even sins

---

little way; Joseph sending for the steward of his house, said: Arise, and pursue after the men: and when thou hast overtaken them, say to them: Why have you returned evil for good? The cup which you have stolen is that in which my lord drinketh, and in which he is wont to divine: you have done a very evil thing. He did as he had commanded him. And having overtaken them, he spoke to them the same words. And they answered: Why doth our lord speak so, as though thy servants had committed so heinous a fact? The money, that we found in the top of our sacks, we brought back to thee from the land of Chanaan: how then should it be that we should steal out of thy lord's house, gold or silver? With whomsoever of thy servants shall be found that which thou seekest, let him die, and we will be the bondmen of my lord. And he said to them: Let it be according to your sentence: with whomsoever it shall be found, let him be my servant, and you shall be blameless. Then they speedily took down their sacks to the ground, and every man opened his sack. Which when he had searched, beginning at the eldest and ending at the youngest, he found the cup in Benjamin's sack. Then they rent their garments, and loading their asses again, returned into the town."

330. "And he lifted up his voice with weeping, which the Egyptians and all the house of Pharao heard. And he said to his brethren: I am Joseph: is my father yet living? His brethren could not answer him, being struck with exceeding great fear. And he said mildly to them: Come nearer to me. And when they were come near him, he said: I am Joseph, your brother, whom you sold into Egypt. Be not afraid, and let it not seem to you a hard case that you sold me into these countries: for God sent me before you into Egypt for your preservation. For it is two years since the famine began to be upon the land, and five years more remain, wherein there can be neither ploughing nor reaping. And God sent me before, that you may be preserved upon the earth, and may have food to live. Not by your counsel was I sent hither, but by the will of God: who hath made me as it were a father to Pharao, and lord of his whole house, and governor in all the land of Egypt. Make haste, and go ye up to my father, and say to him: Thus saith thy son Joseph: God hath made me lord of the whole land of Egypt: come down to me, linger not."

fit in to the providential plan for the good of all. Again, remembering the typical sense, we have in this passage a foreshadowing of the Last Judgement: compare St. Matthew 25:31 ff.—the Last Judgement. The essential thing {is} the recognition of Jesus in His glory, Who was once known in poverty and humility and weakness, and the recognition that what was done to others was done to Him. Note that the Joseph story indicates a special mildness, an unexpected solution that is kept hidden in the Gospel story. For as Joseph is not harsh to his brethren but receives them to himself with tears, so Jesus will receive to Himself all who have not made it absolutely impossible for Him to do so. He will go out of his way to circumvent their wickedness with His love and mercy, so that as far as possible no one shall be able to escape from His forgiveness—yet escape will always be possible because freedom will always remain freedom. But only the most deliberate malice and hardness of heart will be able to refuse Him: this no doubt {is} the "sin against the Holy Ghost."[331] {Note} the wonderful line (v. 12): "Behold your eyes and the eyes of my brother Benjamin see that it is my mouth that speaketh to you. You shall tell your father of my glory" (cfr. Matthew 28:8–10, John 20:11–18—apparitions of Jesus after the Resurrection). {In verses} 14 ff. {in} his display of affection for his brethren he "kissed all his brethren and wept upon every one of them"—{evidence of} his perfect forgiveness. {In verse} 16, everybody hears that Joseph's family has come, and all, including Pharaoh, are delighted. Pharaoh lends wagons and says they must all move down into Egypt. Further gifts {are given} by Joseph. {In} the wonderful ending of the chapter, Jacob receives the news as one waking out of a deep sleep; {he} sees the wagons {and} decides to go to see Joseph and then die (READ 25–28[332]).

    N.B. *Blessed Guerric's First Sermon for Easter*[333] {was presented} as a commentary on Genesis 45:26–28: on Jacob's reaction to the news that

---

    331. Cf. Mark 3:29.

    332. "And they went up out of Egypt, and came into the land of Chanaan to their father Jacob. And they told him, saying: Joseph thy son is living: and he is ruler in all the land of Egypt. Which when Jacob heard, he awaked as it were out of a deep sleep, yet did not believe them. They, on the other side, told the whole order of the thing. And when he saw the wagons and all that he had sent his spirit revived, And he said: It is enough for me, if Joseph my son be yet living: I will go and see him before I die."

    333. Guerric of Igny, *De Resurrectione Domini, Sermo* 1 (Migne, *PL* 185, cols. 141B–144D). Merton returns to this sermon in a pair of conferences from April 6 and 7, 1963 (Gethsemani tapes 51.2 and 48.4; the first was issued commercially as "Life and Celebration"); for a transcription see Merton, *Cistercian Fathers and Forefathers,*

Joseph is alive. Guerric starts out by anticipating objections to this as a text for an Easter sermon: What has this got to do with Easter? This is a Lenten text, and Lent is over. "Our heart is burning for Jesus; we desire Jesus.... we are hungry for Jesus, not Joseph; we want the Savior, not the dreamer, the Lord of heaven, not the viceroy of Egypt, not the one who fed stomachs but Him who feeds souls."[334] Guerric's reply is a vindication of the "spiritual interpretation" of the Old Testament, in which, as we know, Joseph is a type of Christ. He says: "I have placed an egg or a nut before you, brethren: break the shell and you will find nourishment inside. We may indeed be speaking of Joseph but in doing so we shall find Jesus the Paschal Lamb" (*PL* 185:141[335]). {He considers} in what ways Joseph is a type of Christ—not only that but one of the clearest types in the Old Testament (*id.* 142): He was more beautiful than all his brethren[336] (Christ {is} the most beautiful of the sons of men[337]); He was innocent, prudent, betrayed by his own brethren, and having been betrayed by them, saved their lives; He was humbled and placed in prison, but afterwards exalted to the throne, and received the name of Savior of the world (Gen. 41:45). But now Guerric proceeds to his application of the text about Joseph—this indeed is {an} application, not true spiritual interpretation.[338] Jacob is to be taken as the College of the Apostles, who believed slowly, "as though waking from a deep sleep."[339] *Revixit spiritus ejus:*[340] when he gets to this point, Guerric begins to display the depths of his thought on the subject: the Apostles came to know the risen Jesus by the fact that He gave them

---

186–215; a condensed and rearranged transcription was published in Merton, "Guerric of Igny's Easter Sermons."

334. "*Ardens est cor nostrum in nobis de Jesu, Jesum desideramus . . . . Jesus, non Joseph, esurimus; Salvatorem, non somniatorem; dominatorem coeli, non Aegypti; non qui pavit ventres, sed qui pascit mentes*" (Migne, *PL* 185, col. 141BC [n. 1]).

335. "*Ovum sive nucem apposui vobis, fratres; frangite testam, et invenietis escam. Joseph discutiatur, et Jesus invenietur agnus paschalis*" (Migne, *PL* 185, col. 141D [n. 2]).

336. "*prae caeteris fratribus pulchra facie et decorus aspectu*" (Gen 39:6: "of a beautiful countenance, and comely to behold") (Migne, *PL* 185, col. 142B [n. 2]).

337. "*decore pulchrior es filiis hominum*" ("Thou art beautiful above the sons of men") (Ps 44[45]:3).

338. For this distinction, see Pius XII, *Divino Afflante Spiritu*, 16 [n. 27]; and Merton, *Monastic Introduction*, xxxi, 117.

339. "*quasi de gravi somno evigilans*" (Gen 45:26) (Migne, *PL* 185, col. 142D [n. 3]).

340. "his spirit revived" (Gen 45:27) (Migne, *PL* 185, col. 443A [n. 3]).

the Holy Spirit—they knew Him, in other words, by the effects of the Resurrection in their own souls, that *is, in their own spiritual resurrection.* This applies to all of us: it is the Holy Spirit within us Who testifies to the truth of the resurrection, and without Him we cannot know the Risen Christ. The grace of Easter is then the gift of the Holy Spirit, in an inchoate way leading up to the fullness of His coming at Pentecost. Hence the Paschal season is a season of new life in the Spirit of the Risen Jesus. It is interesting to note the concrete way in which the Fathers are able to bring home these truths to us by their use of the Scriptures. "It is the Spirit Who bears witness in the hearts of the saints and on their lips that Christ is the truth, is true resurrection and life. . . . After the Apostles had tasted the life-giving Spirit they bore witness to the resurrection with great power" (143).[341] Guerric then goes on to point out that this interior and mystical knowledge of Jesus is greater and more perfect than actually seeing or hearing Him with our outward senses: "It is a greater thing to know Jesus in one's own heart than to see Him with the eyes, or to hear Him with the ears: so much more powerful is the action of the Holy Spirit on the interior man than the action of bodily things on the exterior senses" (143).[342] This interior witness of the Holy Spirit gives *supreme certitude,* since in fact He Who bears witness (the Spirit) and He concerning Whom the witness is given, are one in the divine nature. In other words, when the Spirit "tells us" that Christ lives, by that very fact we experience the life of Christ Himself, the Word of God, in our own souls, and this experience is much more direct and intimate than anything that could be experienced through the outward senses. Note that when Guerric here speaks of the action of the Holy Spirit on the "interior senses," he does not mean simply the imagination, memory, common sense, etc., which are what scholastic philosophy would refer to by that name; he is certainly talking about the "mystical senses" of spiritual sight, touch, taste and so forth which were accepted by the Fathers from Origen on down.[343] The soul that has been "awakened" to a new life by the presence of the Holy Spirit within itself then rises up to go and see Jesus—not to die but to live with Him forever

---

341. "*Spiritus enim est qui testificatur apud sanctorum corda et per eorum ora, quoniam Christus est veritas, vera resurrectio et vita. . . . post gustum spiritus vivificantis, virtute magna reddebant testimonium resurrectionis*" (Migne, *PL* 185, col. 143B [n. 4]).

342. "*Adeo plus est corde Jesum concipere, quam oculis videre, vel auribus de ipso audire; tantoque potentior est operatio Spiritus apud sensus hominis interioris, quam corporalium apud sensus exterioris*" (Migne, *PL* 185, col. 143BC [n.4]).

343. See above, n. 230.

in heaven. Guerric then turns to his own monks and tells them that they too are "Jacob," and in the Church, on this day, "so many witnesses of the resurrection cry out"[344] to them that they awake and exclaim: "MY JESUS LIVES"—*Jesus Deus meus vivit*.[345] In this, we are like those souls whom Jesus has drawn back to the light of day from the darkness of hell. But the sure sign of the presence of the life-giving Spirit in us is, he says, our love which makes us content that Jesus is risen, so that we seek no joy in anything else: this is our greatest joy. "*Sufficit mihi si Jesus vivit*" (144).[346] If we say this with sincerity, then it is an indication that His life is our life and we need no other. That is to say, since our love has entirely gone out to Him, we truly live in Him and no longer need to live in and for ourselves. This is the true consummation of the monastic life, the real summit of Cistercian prayer and spirituality.

> If He lives, I live, since my soul depends entirely on Him; indeed He Himself is my life and my all. What can be lacking to me, if Jesus lives? Indeed, let all other things be taken away, I no longer care if only Jesus be alive. Let Jesus Himself be lacking to me, if He so pleases: it is sufficient for me that He lives in Himself and for Himself. When the love of Christ has so taken possession of a man that he forgets himself and neglects himself and feels only those things which concern Jesus Christ, then at last in my opinion he has reached perfect charity. Such a one is not burdened by poverty, does not feel insults, smiles at rejection, contemns all loss, considers death a gain since he seeks only to pass from death to life. (144)[347]

This is traditional Cistercian doctrine, true to the spirit of St. Bernard, for whom *amor castus*[348] is the perfection of love that takes us out of our-

---

344. "*tam crebro . . . personant et consonant nuntii Resurrectionis*" (Migne, *PL* 185, col. 143D [n. 5]).

345. "Jesus my God lives" (Migne, *PL* 185, col. 143D [n. 5]).

346. "It is enough for me if Jesus lives" (Migne, *PL* 185, col. 144A [n. 5]).

347. "*Si vivit, vivo, cum de ipso pendeat anima mea, imo ipse sit vita mea, ipse sufficentia mea. Quid enim mihi deesse poterit, si Jesus vivit? Imo desint omnia alia, nihil interest mea, dummodo Jesus vivat. Ipse ergo, si placet ei, desit mihi; sufficit mihi, dummodo vivat ipse vel sibi. Cum sic amor Christi totum absorbuerunt affectum hominis, ut, negligens et immemor sui nonnisi Jesum Christum et ea quae sunt Jesu Christi sentiat, tunc demum, ut arbitror, perfecta est in eo charitas. Huic utique qui sic affectus est, non est onerosa paupertas: iste non sentit injurias, ridet opprobria, contemnit damna, mortem lucrum deputat; imo nec mori se putat, cum magis de morte ad vitam transire se sciat*" (Migne, *PL* 185, col. 144AB [n. 5]).

348. "pure love": see Gilson's discussion of Bernard's doctrine of pure love (*Mystical*

selves and unites us to the Word, the Spouse of our souls. But what of the average monk, who has not reached this purity of love? (Note: the first Cistercians are practical as well as idealistic, and one who simply aspires to the heights without taking the steps to reach them will never truly love Christ.) Even though we realize our imperfections, let us nevertheless go forward and seek Jesus with what love we can. This is the important lesson of hope and courage in spite of our deficiencies, also typically Cistercian. Let us not complain that we have no way of reaching Jesus. As ample wagons were sent to "poor old Jacob,"[349] we have something much more: we have the very Body of Christ, which will bring us to union with God. He Himself is the "chariot of Israel and the horseman thereof";[350] and where we go is not Egypt but heaven.

JACOB IN EGYPT: chapter 46 {relates} Jacob's journey into Egypt {and includes} the list of all those who went with him. {In verses} 1–7, Jacob stops to sacrifice at Bersabee, where Isaac had built an altar and dug a well. Here he is reassured by God in a dream which confirms all the promises. This was necessary because he was after all *leaving the land* which God had promised to Abraham and he might have been deeply troubled over this possible defection. But he is reassured. The journey

---

Theology of Saint Bernard, 140–49), an analysis particularly of Sermon 83 on the Song of Songs. In his April 1963 conference on this sermon of Guerric, Merton says of this passage: "That's again St. Bernard: that's Sermon 83 on the Canticle of Canticles. St. Bernard defines pure love: it's pure when there are no other affections left in the soul but love. What does he mean by that? He means that love has swallowed up fear. This is standard Cistercian. There's no more distinction between fear and love: that now you fear, now you love. There's no distinction. You just love. There's no longer any desire for gain. Christ Himself is my gain: *'mihi vivere Christus est.'* Death is gain, he says: 'For me to live is Christ and death is gain.' There is no sadness. There is no grief. There is no special joy outside of love. Love has absorbed all the affections. This is a standard Cistercian approach. He says finally, 'The soul is completely neglectful of itself, forgetful of itself, thinks only of Jesus and seeks only those things that are pleasing to Him, and therefore I will say that in such a soul charity has become perfect.'" (Merton, *Cistercian Fathers and Forefathers*, 206, quoting Phil 1:21 and providing a somewhat different translation of part of the passage from Guerric cited immediately above). See also St. Bernard, *De Diligendo Deo*, c. 9 (Migne, *PL* 182, col. 990A), a discussion of the third of Bernard's four degrees of love, the love of God for His own sake, as being *"castus," "justus,"* and *"gratus"* ("pure," "just," and "freely given") (see Merton, *Cistercian Fathers and Their Monastic Theology*, 123–24).

349. *"missa sunt pauperi seni sumptus et vehicula"* (Migne, *PL* 185, col. 144BC [n. 6]).

350. *"ipse currus Israel et auriga ejus"* (4Kgs [2Kgs] 2:12) (Migne, *PL* 185, col. 144C [n. 6]).

into Egypt is part of God's plan, just as later on the exile and captivity in Babylon is part of His plan. *CBC* says: "This promise is the culmination of the introductory character of Genesis and prepares the reader for the subsequent history narrated in Exodus."[351] {Verses} 7 ff. {provide} the list of Jacob's family. *Read 28–34:*[352] Joseph meets Jacob, and after their affectionate greeting, he briefs the family {about} what they are to tell Pharaoh. The story is slightly obscure here, and the commentaries are not fully satisfactory. The main facts are clear, the reasons obscure. *Joseph wants them to dwell in Goshen*—because it is particularly good land (see 47:6)? because it is border land, and they can leave quickly, and also he will not be accused of introducing a large block of aliens into the heart of the land??? In order that they may get the permission to dwell there, they must declare that they are shepherds, and Pharaoh will give the permission "because the Egyptians have all shepherds in abomination"—{according to} *CBC*, because shepherds do not live up to "the high standards of personal cleanliness, etc.";[353] {according to} Pirot,[354] because *nomads* are regarded as barbarians. The most likely reason would be (whatever might have been the attitude of Egyptians toward shepherds) that the Israelites might be *left alone* and not absorbed into the Egyptian nation, but might retain their own independence and character, on the border, ready to move out when God's will is signified. *The passage must be interpreted in the light of the Divine Promise.*

Chapter 47 {describes} Pharaoh's reception of Jacob and Joseph's brethren. {In verses} 6–7, Pharaoh consents to their petition, gives them Gessen, "the best land," and offers some of them jobs taking care of his

---

351. Sutcliffe, "Genesis," 202 [n. 158a].

352. "And he sent Juda before him to Joseph, to tell him; and that he should meet him in Gessen. And when he was come thither, Joseph made ready his chariot, and went up to meet his father, in the same place: and seeing him, he fell upon his neck, and embracing him wept. And the father said to Joseph: Now shall I die with joy, because I have seen thy face, and leave thee alive. And Joseph said to his brethren, and to all his father's house: I will go up, and will tell Pharao, and will say to him: My brethren and my father's house, that were in the land of Chanaan, are come to me: And the men are shepherds, and their occupation is to feed cattle: their flocks and herds, and all they have, they have brought with them. And when he shall call you, and shall say: What is your occupation? You shall answer: We thy servants are shepherds, from our infancy until now, both we and our fathers. And this you shall say, that you may dwell in the land of Gessen, because the Egyptians have all shepherds in abomination."

353. Sutcliffe, "Genesis," 202 [n. 158c], which reads: "... that high standard of personal cleanliness cultivated in Egyptian society."

354. Pirot and Clamer, eds., *Sainte Bible*, 1:471.

own herds. (Here another reason for Joseph's action transpires: he wanted them to be accepted as shepherds so that they could be well placed *without arousing jealousy* on the part of the Egyptians.) *Read 7–10:*[355] the meeting between Jacob and Pharaoh is a moving little document. Jacob's character shines out (9)—his greatness and simplicity—a surprising reminiscence of the last chapter of St. Benedict:[356] one of the signs of nobility in an old man, one of the signs of true magnanimity, is this acceptance of the fact that his achievements and works have been small indeed. This does not exclude a certain disillusionment in the attitude taken. All is part of a natural whole, proper to one who, at the end of his life, sees that he has been a useless servant, and turns spontaneously to prepare himself for the truly great event in which he will go back to the great God Who made him and Who alone is great. A wonderful sense of proportion and of the meaning of life is evident here. {From verses} 11 forward Joseph's administration during the famine {is described}. He gets all the cattle and all the land of the Egyptians and turns it all over to Pharaoh, so that by the time he is finished, Egypt is a nation of sharecroppers in complete dependence on the King. (This coincides with the real historical transition from the ancient feudalism to the new state of affairs in the New Kingdom.) {In verses} 27 ff., Israel is about to die. He gets Joseph to promise to bury him in his own land.

Chapter 48 {relates} *the adoption of Ephraim and Manasses*: dying Jacob sits up in bed and with a rambling sort of solemnity recalls the promise that he shall become a great nation, to justify his action in "including" Manasses and Ephraim. The narrative is confused because of the intertwining of the three traditions, Yahwist, Elohist and Sacerdotal. Its purpose {is} to explain the powerful position of the tribes of Ephraim and Manasses at the time when the book was written. Jacob's eagerness

---

355. "After this Joseph brought in his father to the king, and presented him before him: and he blessed him. And being asked by him: How many are the days of the years of thy life? He answered: The days of my pilgrimage are a hundred and thirty years, few, and evil, and they are not come up to the days of the pilgrimage of my fathers. And blessing the king, he went out."

356. "Then the Conferences of Cassian and his Institutes, and the Lives of the Fathers, as also the Rule of our holy father Basil: what else are they but tools of virtue for good-living and obedient monks? But we slothful, ill-living, and negligent people must blush for shame. Whoever, therefore, thou art that hastenest to thy heavenly country, fulfil first of all by the help of Christ this little Rule for beginners. And then at length, under God's protection, shalt thou attain those aforesaid loftier heights of wisdom and virtue" (McCann, trans. and ed., *Rule*, 161, 163).

to adopt and endow these two boys comes from the fact that they belong to the line descended from his beloved Rachel. The whole story of the blessing is beautiful and profoundly moving, again because of the stature of old Jacob. In his rambling and solemn declarations, he first proposes to bless the two boys. He then reminisces about the death of Rachel (v. 7), then {declares} his joy at "seeing" the sons of Joseph (dimly, because he is half-blind). Joseph carefully places them so that they will be properly blessed—the older with the right hand, the younger with the left. Jacob changes hands and blesses them in moving terms (15–16). Joseph, intensely put out by the whole affair, tries to move his father's hands by force, but Jacob resists and explains, evidently under the impulsion of divine prophecy.

Chapter 49: *Jacob's Blessings of the Twelve Patriarchs*: to be more accurate, Jacob is prophesying the *future of the twelve tribes* and their place in the promised land. In the case of Ruben, Simeon and Levi, we cannot say that Jacob "blessed" them. The term "blessing" is used however in the special Old Testament and patriarchal sense—and here more than ever.

a) The blessing of the patriarch is the sign of God's "summing up" in the case of each son—and in the case of his descendants—{indicating} in what way each tribe will participate in the divine promises. It is as an instrument of God, as a prophet and as a Father with divinely given power that Jacob speaks. Hence {it is} at the same time a *judgement* on the past, a handing down of the *promises* (in some sense as rewards, according to merit) for the future, and also *prophesying* the future. The most important item in the whole prophecy is of course the mention of the Messias and of the time of His coming. This passage is then the culmination of Genesis; {it} is supremely important as well as beautiful, {and} was for the Jews the fulfillment of all that had been narrated and the foundation of all that followed.

b) In the light of this, one cannot help but be disappointed at the minimizing approach taken by the *CBC*. The "blessings" are "elaborate and poetic," and "it is agreed that they *cannot* have been pronounced by the dying and aged Jacob in their present form. They must have been recast and embellished at a later time. . . . such an inspired poet may well have also been responsible for certain additions to the substance. God could, of course, have revealed the future to Jacob in all its details, but it is *not in accord with God's ordinary providence* to reveal in advance the geographical location of the territory to be allotted to a tribe . . . etc."³⁵⁷ Comment: it is quite possible that the "blessings" were recast and embellished—no argument. But this is a minimizing approach in the sense that it assumes gratuitously that we have here a case where God would work according to His "ordinary providence" and indeed would in some sense be bound to do so and not reveal details, and that it would somehow be out of place for God to inspire an "old man" with beautiful prophetic words etc. This is a dim, pedestrian, modernistic view, certainly not that of the authors or of the early readers of Genesis—or of contemporary Moslem readers, who still retain some religious sense. It is necessary to be on our guard against these pedestrian tendencies, these trends towards the dilution and the de-spiritualization of Scripture. Modern scientific study has indeed added much, and should be followed wherever it can, and it is by no means in itself contrary to a spiritual and religious understanding of the Word of God. Nevertheless, this tendency to water everything down and to seek as far as possible to find a prosaic common-sense and "reasonable" explanation for everything may in many cases completely empty a real mystery of all its content, and explain nothing in the process. If followed too far, these modern commentators would inevitably succeed in leading us to the extremes of the ancient school of Antioch with its literalism and its Nestorianism and its fear of things spiritual.³⁵⁸ Sound scien-

357. Sutcliffe, "Genesis," 203 [n. 159b], which reads: ". . . aged and dying . . . at some later . . . . of course, reveal . . ."

358. On this issue, see Merton, *Bread in the Wilderness*, 32–33: "Origen and the exegetical School of Alexandria developed the spiritual interpretation of Scripture to a high degree of perfection and the influence of Origen was to extend down through the Christian Middle Ages in spite of the reaction of the School of Antioch. This school was somewhat suspicious of the freedom with which the 'mystical' interpretation handled the Scriptures, and it returned to a more cautious emphasis on the 'letter.' . . . At the same time, the Antiochian suspicion of the 'spiritual sense' finally brought upon itself an open condemnation of extreme literalism in the interpretation of Scripture. Theodore of Mopsuestia, who had commented on the Psalms and reduced the number of messianic 'types' in the Psalter to an absolute minimum, was condemned by the second Council of Constantinople. . . . The real reason for his condemnation was his Nestorianism, of which this exegetical error was only a result and an expression." Nestorianism was the heresy condemned at the Council of Ephesus (431), named after Nestorius, Patriarch of Constantinople, whose rejection of the Marian title *theotokos* ("God-bearer" or Mother of God) was interpreted as separating the human Jesus and the divine Word into two distinct persons, a position Nestorius himself vehemently denied holding. Theodore, the leading scriptural commentator of the Antiochene school, was an older contemporary and perhaps relative of Nestorius and had actually

tific exegesis should always be taken into account, but everything that "sounds scientific" should not be swallowed uncritically. We must be on our guard against a pseudo-scientific and rationalistic attitude which always, *a priori*, leans toward an interpretation that is pedestrian and common-sense and so ultra-safe that it ends by saying nothing at all. Let us be willing to take a few risks in order to believe in the *inspired Word of God*, the Word of a God Who is not bound to limit Himself to the categories and perspectives of literal-minded scientists who were never gifted with an ounce of imagination, poetry, or even, in some cases, of religious sense. Once this is admitted, we can of course also agree that it is highly likely that the text was reshaped and improved and that *as it stands* it was not uttered word for word by Jacob. But surely the substance is of Jacob, and with all due respect to Lagrange,[359] one sees no earthly

---

died in 428, three years before the council. Modern scholarship rejects the attribution of a Nestorian Christology to Theodore: see Kelly, *Early Christian Doctrines*, 303–309 for a discussion of Theodore's position; see also 310–17 for an analysis of Nestorius himself, who was strongly influenced by Theodore, and who according to Kelly "was not a Nestorian in the classic sense of the word" (316) but was the victim of his own faulty and at times intemperate use of terminology and of the hostility of his rival Cyril of Alexandria, who engineered his condemnation at the council. See also Kelly, 75–78, for an overview of the Antiochene exegetical tradition, developed especially by Theodore.

359. See Lagrange, "Prophétie de Jacob," 525–40, especially "Critique Littéraire et Caractère du Récit" (538–40): "Quel est l'auteur du poème? Il est incontestable que le texte les attribue à Jacob, mais les historiens n'ont jamais hésité, sans encourir le moindre reproche d'erreur ou de fausseté, à placer dans la bouche de certains personnages des harangues composées à loisir. Il suffit pour la vérité historique qu'elles soient en situation. Le cas se résout par les vraisemblances, par les indications fournies par l'auteur lui-même. Or il n'est pas vraisemblable qu'un vieillard mourant compose un poésie aussi soignée, et l'auteur lui-même met sur la voie au v. 7; Jacob pouvait-il dire en personne: Je les répartirai dans Jacob, je les dispersai dans Israel? Il est étonnant qu'un ancêtre emploie son proper nom comme celui du people qui doit descendre de lui, et dans un sens qui ne peut être que postérieur. L'auteur insinue ici que Jacob, à supposer qu'il ait prophétisé tout cela, n'a pas du moins composé le poème. On a pu recueillir l'écho de ses paroles et lui donner sa forme actuelle" ("Who is the author of the poem? It is unquestionable that the text attributes it to Jacob, but historians have never hesitated, without incurring the least reproach of error or falsity, to place in the mouth of certain figures speeches composed in their own time. It is sufficient for historical accuracy that they be properly situated. The matter is taken care of by being compatible with the truth, by indications provided by the author himself. But it is not likely that a dying old man composed so well-organized a poem, and the author himself puts us on the right track in verse 7; could Jacob say in his own person: 'I will divide them in Jacob, and will scatter them in Israel'? It is unbelievable that an ancestor

reason why the substance of the *poetry*, and of the *prophecy*, should not be attributed to Jacob himself.

{Verses} 3–4 {focus on} *Ruben*: "Thou art my strength and the beginning of my vigor [CBC³⁶⁰], preeminent in majesty and preeminent in power, uncontrollable like flowing water thou shalt not have preeminence." Ruben is blamed and rejected for his incest (with Bala [Gen. 35:22]). He is {a} violent man, like a raging torrent. Because he cannot control himself, he has lost his inheritance—another instance of the rejection of the firstborn, proud of his own strength and attached to his own will. Ruben is like a mountain torrent, a *wadi*, rushing madly to the sea after heavy rains ({the} Zodiac theory assigns to Ruben the sign of Aquarius³⁶¹). For the lands given to Ruben, see Numbers 32:33 ff. and Josue 13:23. Ruben, beyond the Jordan, gradually declined, owing to attacks of hostile neighbors.

{Verses} 5–7 {consider} *Simeon and Levi*: "in their fury they slew a man and in their willfulness they lamed an ox" (i.e. they killed men and mutilated cattle in revenge for the rape of Dina [Gen. 34:25]). Simeon (Jos. 19:1–9) received lands in the midst of the very large inheritance of Juda; thus absorbed in Juda he diminishes and disappears.³⁶² Levi receives many cities, in all parts of Israel, as a result of their fidelity in the incident of the Golden Calf, which cancelled out Jacob's curse (Exod. 32:26–29 and Jos. 21).³⁶³ The fact that Levi is still condemned here is taken as proof of the *antiquity* of the poem. They are called brothers—some interpreters prefer "hyenas" or "owls." Here, read the blessing of Ephraim and Manasses,³⁶⁴ who were chosen in place of Ruben and Simeon (48:16). Ja-

---

would use his own name as that of the people who are to descend from him, and in a sense that can only be that of a later period. The author implies here that Jacob, even supposing that he had prophesied all this, has not composed the poem at all. He has been able to catch the echo of his words and give them an updated form" [538–39]).

360. Sutcliffe, "Genesis," 203–4 [n. 159e].
361. See Sutcliffe, "Genesis," 203 [n. 159d], 204 [n. 159e].
362. Sutcliffe, "Genesis," 204 [n. 159f].
363. Sutcliffe, "Genesis," 204 [n. 159f].
364. "And he said: I will cause thee to increase and multiply, and I will make of thee a multitude of people: and I will give this land to thee, and to thy seed after thee for an everlasting possession. So thy two sons who were born to thee in the land of Egypt before I came hither to thee, shall be mine: Ephraim and Manasses shall be reputed to me as Ruben and Simeon. But the rest whom thou shalt have after them, shall be thine, and shall be called by the name of their brethren in their possessions. For, when I came out of Mesopotamia, Rachel died from me in the land of Chanaan in the very

cob blesses them, invoking the protection of "the angel that delivereth me from all evils," and calling down the protection of his own name and of the names of Isaac and {Abraham}[365]—note the parallelism: the "name" and the "angel." {It is the} same with Yahweh: we are protected now by His "Name," now by His "angel." The Name of Jesus, {when} invoked, brings us His Holy Spirit, {for it} cannot be invoked except by His Spirit.[366]

{Verses} 8–12 {turn to} JUDA: the first three sons being passed over, Juda receives the "lion's share" in more ways than one. He shall be powerful, victorious, prosperous, and from him shall come the Messias, the king over all the nations. All shall bow before him. He will be like a lion cub. "The sceptre shall not be taken from him nor the staff from between his feet." The Hebrew is not clear on the coming of "the one who is to be sent"—{there are} diverse readings.[367] Whatever the difficulties, it means the coming of a King and Judge, and is the *first strict and personal messianic prophecy*. Juda {is described as} resting like a lion in his strength. In

---

journey, and it was springtime: and I was going to Ephrata, and I buried her near the way of Ephrata, which by another name is called Bethlehem. Then seeing his sons, he said to him: Who are these? He answered: They are my sons, whom God hath given me in this place. And he said: Bring them to me that I may bless them. For Israel's eyes were dim by reason of his great age, and he could not see clearly. And when they were brought to him, he kissed and embraced them. And said to his son: I am not deprived of seeing thee: moreover God hath shewed me thy seed. And when Joseph had taken them from his father's lap, he bowed down with his face to the ground. And he set Ephraim on his right hand, that is, towards the left hand of Israel; but Manasses on his left hand, to wit, towards his father's right hand, and brought them near to him. But he stretching forth his right hand, put it upon the head of Ephraim the younger brother; and the left upon the head of Manasses who was the elder, changing his hands. And Jacob blessed the sons of Joseph, and said: God, in whose sight my fathers Abraham and Isaac walked, God that feedeth me from my youth until this day; The angel that delivereth me from all evils, bless these boys: and let my name be called upon them, and the names of my fathers Abraham, and Isaac, and may they grow into a multitude upon the earth. And Joseph seeing that his father had put his right hand upon the head of Ephraim, was much displeased: and taking his father's hand he tried to lift it from Ephraim's head, and to remove it to the head of Manasses. And he said to his father: It should not be so, my father: for this is the firstborn, put thy right hand upon his head. But he refusing, said: I know, my son, I know: and this also shall become peoples, and shall be multiplied: but this younger brother shall be greater than he: and his seed shall grow into nations. And he blessed them at that time, saying: In thee shall Israel be blessed, and it shall be said: God do to thee as to Ephraim, and as to Manasses. And he set Ephraim before Manasses" (48:4–20).

365. Copy text reads: "Jacob."
366. See 1 Cor 12:3.
367. See Sutcliffe, "Genesis," 204 [n. 157g].

this we have an allusion to the strength of the Messias Himself, the main object of this blessing: He is the strong man armed Who overcomes the devil. The *vineyards* of Jacob {symbolize} his great prosperity, but also the prosperity of Messianic times (cf. Amos 9:13–14; Joel 3:16–21—cf. verse 18:[368] the *"vidi aquam"*;[369] Isaias 25:6; Acts 2:15—Pentecost). "His eyes shall *sparkle with* wine"[370] (not *"pulchriores vino"*[371])—again {a} reference to this abundance of joy of Messianic times, {the} joy of the Spirit (read St. Paul: *Gaudete, iterum dico gaudete*[372] [Phil. 4:4–7]; *Modestia vestra:*[373] recollection, joy, sanctity—cf. Fra Angelico's picture of St. Dominic[374]).

{In verse} 13, *Zabulon* lives near Sidon and by the seacoast, and shall live by fishing—{they are} GALILEANS; {they} did not have an important role in Jewish history (cf. Zabulon in {the} New Testament[375]). {In verse} 14, *Issachar* {is described as} a farmer and laborer in the fertile plains of Esdraelon[376]—{also} GALILEANS; {he is} a "strong-built ass" (cf. Hector in

---

368. "And it shall come to pass in that day, that the mountains shall drop down sweetness, and the hills shall flow with milk: and waters shall flow through all the rivers of Juda: and a fountain shall come forth of the house of the Lord, and shall water the torrent of thorns."

369. I.e. the antiphon for the *asperges* (sprinkling with holy water) at the beginning of Mass during paschal time (based on the vision in Ezekiel 47): "*Vidi aquam egredientem de templo, a latere dextro, alleluia: et omnes ad quos pervenit aqua ista, salvi facti sunt, et dicent: alleluia, alleluia*" ("I saw water flowing from the temple on the right side, alleluia: and all those to whom this water came were saved, and they shall say: alleluia, alleluia" [Hoever, ed., *Saint Joseph Daily Missal*, 640]).

370. Gen 49:12.

371. The Vulgate reading ("more beautiful than wine" [Douay]).

372. "Rejoice [in the Lord always]: again, I say, rejoice" (Phil 4:4).

373. "[Let] your modesty [be known to all men]" (Phil 4:5).

374. A Dominican himself, Fra Angelico painted numerous portraits of the order's founder, so it is not certain which one Merton may be referring to here; but a particularly well-known image, taken from a 1441 fresco of the Mocking of Christ in the convent of St. Marco in Florence, depicts Dominic seated in a reflective state with an open book on his lap and corresponds quite closely to Merton's description of his "recollection, joy, sanctity" here. This and other images may be found online at https://www.google.com/search?q=fra+angelico+st+dominic/.

375. "And leaving the city Nazareth, he came and dwelt in Capharnaum on the sea coast, in the borders of Zabulon and of Nephthalim; That it might be fulfilled which was said by Isaias the prophet: Land of Zabulon and land of Nephthalim, the way of the sea beyond the Jordan, Galilee of the Gentiles: The people that sat in darkness, hath seen great light: and to them that sat in the region of the shadow of death, light is sprung up" (Matt 4:13–16; cf. Is 8:23–9:1).

376. Sutcliffe, "Genesis," 204 [n. 160b].

Iliad 11:557 ff.;³⁷⁷ cf. Judges 5:15—the fight against Sisara); {he is situated} between the shelters—i.e. {has} many sheepfolds. {In verse} 16, *Dan* {is presented as} weak in numbers, struggling for survival with the cleverness of a serpent. He is not blamed—craft is the defense of the weak. Highwaymen were numerous in the tribe of Dan. Samson, a member of the tribe of Dan, played injurious tricks on the Philistines. ({Verse} 18—{is this} an interpolation?³⁷⁸) {With regard to verse} 19, *Gad* lives in Galaad (across {the} Jordan) and fights the Ammonites and Arab tribes;³⁷⁹ {they are} highwaymen and strong soldiers—{they} furnished David with some of his best men (1 Par. 12:8–15). {In verse} 20, *Aser* (also GALILEANS) {are presented as} rich farmers, {and in verse} 21 *Nephthali*, {likewise} GALILEANS, {are described as} "a hart let loose, a spreading terebinth" (*CBC*—{this} can refer to branches of a tree or to antlers of a stag; {it} depends on various theories and texts³⁸⁰); {he} lived by {the} Lake of Genesareth. {Verse} 22 {focuses on} JOSEPH: the blessings of Ephraim and Manasses {are} intended here—Joseph becomes a "double tribe." {What are the} difficulties in {the} readings? Joseph {is} a fertile branch: his branches grow along the wall. {Is he described as being} attacked by archers? He shall receive {a} special blessing: to him that hath it shall be given.³⁸¹ {These tribes} dominated all others in {the} time of {the} Judges—from Sichem ({occupied by the} Samaritans in Our Lord's time). {With respect to verse} 25, note how Osee reversed this blessing (*Osee 9–14*); note the desire of the eternal hills—i.e. the blessing of the ancient mountains. {In verse} 26, Benjamin {is called a} *lupus rapax*³⁸² (cf. Judges 3:15–30, Judges 5:14). {Verses} 29–33 {describe} Jacob's death {with} a last characteristic life-like image; "he drew up his feet in his bed and died."

{In} *chapter 50*, Joseph has Jacob embalmed in the Egyptian manner, so as to bury him in Israel. {There is a} great funeral procession from Egypt to Canaan (v. 11), {with} the Canaanites looking on from afar and saying: "There is a great mourning among the Egyptians"!—an impressive detail. {Verses} 15–21 {present} the moving and definitive reconciliation

---

377. The epithet is applied by Homer to Ajax rather than to Hector (see Sutcliffe, "Genesis," 204 [n. 160b]).

378. See Sutcliffe, "Genesis," 204 [n. 160b]: "18, which makes a half-line only, may be a gloss."

379. See Sutcliffe, "Genesis," 204 [n. 160d].

380. See Sutcliffe, "Genesis," 204 [n. 160f].

381. Cf. Matt 13:12, 25:29; Mark 4:25.

382. "a ravenous wolf."

of Joseph with his brethren, {marked by} Joseph's charity and his sense of the divine plan, and {his} neglect of trivial and base personal feelings. {In verses} 24–25 Joseph dies prophesying that they will return to their land, and making them promise to take his body there (cf. Hebrews 11:22: praising the faith of Joseph).

Conclusion: it is very fitting that we close this study of Genesis by reading and explaining the blessings of the patriarchs on the very *Feast of Pentecost*. There is a deep relationship between these blessings and the mystery of Pentecost. Both are eschatological:

1. Jacob's blessing of his sons—the Twelve Patriarchs of the People of God—*foreshadows the Church, the true Kingdom of God*. In these blessings we can see Jacob as a *type of Christ* sending forth His Twelve Apostles, dividing as it were the whole world between them ({cf.} Mark 16:15–18, {the} gospel of Ascension Day:[383] He sends the Apostles forth with special characteristic gifts; this mandate does not take effect until *the Spirit Himself* comes, bringing with Himself every gift *secundum mensuram donationis Christi*[384]—the Holy Spirit is the inheritance of the sons of the true Jacob).

2. The City of God {is the} New Jerusalem, {the} Promised Land (*Apocalypse* 21:10–14). The twelve gates and the twelve foundation stones {are the} Patriarchs and Apostles ({see the} epistle {for the} Dedication of the Church[385]). The "twelve tribes" dwell mystically in our monastic church; they are very close to us. {In} *Apocalypse* 7:2–12, the tribes enter into their reward: "12,000 signed." Note {that} this is the epistle of All Saints[386] which practically closes and sums up the post-Pentecostal season and is closely related to Pentecost, as the fruit to the flower. *Note {that} in this list* Ruben, Simeon and Levi *are included*; Joseph (Ephraim) is included as John's own tribe, but Dan is excluded as the tribe of Antichrist.

3. {All this pertains to} *the monastic vocation*: {cf.} Matthew 19:27–29—Mass of a Holy Abbot:[387] "You that have followed me ... shall sit on twelve thrones judging the twelve tribes of Israel"—that is, they

---

383. *Missale Romanum*, 369; *Missale Cisterciense*, 257.

384. "according to the measure of the giving of Christ" (Eph 4:7).

385. Apoc [Rev] 21:2–5 (*Missale Romanum*, (40); *Missale Cisterciense*, 33*).

386. Apoc [Rev] 7:2–12 (*Missale Romanum*, 778–79; *Missale Cisterciense*, 550–51).

387. *Missale Romanum*, (28); *Missale Cisterciense*, 23*.

will govern the whole new creation with Christ. This {is intended} for *priests* (and abbots) and the others who have renounced all {and who} will have life everlasting. *In closing*, read 1 Paralipomenon 12:23–40:[388] the men of the twelve tribes who flee to join David (Christ) and defend him against Saul.

Feast of Pentecost, 1957

---

388. "And this is the number of the chiefs of the army who came to David, when he was in Hebron, to transfer to him the kingdom of Saul, according to the word of the Lord. The sons of Juda bearing shield and spear, six thousand eight hundred well appointed to war. Of the sons of Simeon valiant men for war, seven thousand one hundred. Of the sons of Levi, four thousand six hundred. And Joiada prince of the race of Aaron, and with him three thousand seven hundred. Sadoc also a young man of excellent disposition, and the house of his father, twenty-two principal men. And of the sons of Benjamin the brethren of Saul, three thousand: for hitherto a great part of them followed the house of Saul. And of the sons of Ephraim twenty thousand eight hundred, men of great valour renowned in their kindreds. And of the half tribe of Manasses, eighteen thousand, every one by their names, came to make David king. Also of the sons of Issachar men of understanding, that knew all times to order what Israel should do, two hundred principal men: and all the rest of the tribe followed their counsel. And of Zabulon such as went forth to battle, and stood in array well appointed with armour for war, there came fifty thousand to his aid, with no double heart. And of Nephtali, a thousand leaders: and with them seven and thirty thousand, furnished with shield and spear. Of Dan also twenty-eight thousand six hundred prepared for battle. And of Aser forty thousand going forth to fight, and challenging in battle. And on the other side of the Jordan of the sons of Ruben, and of Gad, and of the half of the tribe of Manasses a hundred and twenty thousand, furnished with arms for war. All these men of war well appointed to fight, came with a perfect heart to Hebron, to make David king over all Israel: and all the rest also of Israel, were of one heart to make David king. And they were there with David three days eating and drinking: for their brethren had prepared for them. Moreover they that were near them even as far as Issachar, and Zabulon, and Nephtali, brought loaves on asses, and on camels, and on mules, and on oxen, to eat: meal, figs, raisins, wine, oil, and oxen, and sheep in abundance, for there was joy in Israel."

NOTES ON EXODUS

(incomplete) f m Louis Novitiate 1957–'58.

SCRIPTURE SEMINAR—Program:
    1—GENESIS
1. The Creation and Fall of Man (Genesis 1–3)
2. Cain—and the Deluge (4–11)
3. Abraham—the Promise and the Alliance (12–25)
4. Isaac and Jacob (25–36)
5. Joseph (37–50)
    2—EXODUS
1. The Deliverance from Egypt (Exodus 1–14)
2. The Journey through the Desert (15–18)
3. The Alliance of Sinai (15–31)
4. The Apostasy of Israel (32–34)
5. The Construction of the Tabernacle (35–40)
    3—LEVITICUS
1. The Sacrifices and Priesthood of the Old Law (*passim*)
2. Other Laws (*passim*)
    4—NUMBERS
1. The Journey through the Desert—continued (9–14, 20–26)
2. The War against Madian (31–36)
    5—DEUTERONOMY
1. The Infidelity of Israel—Reproaches of Moses (Deut. 1–11)
2. The Vocation of Israel Resumed by Moses—His Death (26–33)
    6—JOSUE
1. Conquest of the Promised Land (Jos. 1–12)
2. The Division of the Land (14–24)
    7—JUDGES
1. The First Judges—Gedeon (1–12)
2. Samson (13–16)
    8—RUTH

Exodus: Preamble from Origen—{the} search for God (Moses): "Let Moses be big and strong in us—that is, let there be in our understanding of Exodus nothing small and petty, but let all be greatness, sublimity and beauty. In spiritual things there is nothing but what is great, for all must proceed from a lofty understanding. We must ask Jesus to show us all that is sublime and great in Moses"[1]—maturity, loftiness (sublimity), prayer.

Exodus—Preamble: this {is} the *great work of God*, the great sign of His fidelity and mercy. {See} Osee 10:1 (Out of Egypt have I called my son); cf. Osee 13:4–5, 2:14—here we learn *how God saves* (Israel—Jesus—ourselves); Jeremias 2:1–10; Psalm 135:10 ff., 77:12–3. {The} lesson {is to} trust in God and obey Him, in order to come out of this world to the Father. {Among the} New Testament texts on {the} importance of Exodus {see} 1 Corinthians 10:2–4.

I. The Deliverance from Egypt ({chapters} 1–14)—this alone is really the "exodus":

1. Israel {is} in Egypt for 430 years[2]—{a period of the} silence of God {and of} prosperity: the two {are} correlative, yet {it is} also a time of preparation. *Read Exodus 1:1–7*:[3] {then comes the} beginning of persecution (8–22), hard labor, killing the firstborn. N.B. {the} "demoniacal" character of tyranny (cf. Nazism). {Note the} internal contradictions—Pharaoh wants to destroy them and yet he needs them. N.B. {as to the} date of {the} exodus {there are} *two theories*: (1) {the} fifteenth century B.C. (Eighteenth Dynasty); (2) {the} thirteenth century B.C. (Nineteenth Dynasty)—under Ramses II—*probabilius*:[4] (1) {there was} construction in {the Nile} delta area at that time;[5] (2) Canaan {was} no longer under Hittite or Egyptian control and Jews could get in.[6]

---

1. "*Grandem et validum habeamus Moysen, nihil de eo parvum, nihil humile sentiamus; sed magnificum totum, totum egregium, totum elegans. Totum enim magnum est, quidquid spiritale, quidquid sublimis intelligentiae est. Et oremus Dominum Jesum Christum ut ipse nobis revelet et ostendat quomodo magnus est Moyses, et quomodo sublimis est*" (Origen, *Homily 2 on Exodus* [Migne, *PG* 12, cols. 309D–310A]).

2. See Exod 12:40.

3. "These are the names of the children of Israel, that went into Egypt with Jacob: they went in, every man with his household: Ruben, Simeon, Levi, Juda, Issachar, Zabulon, and Benjamin, Dan, and Nephtali, Gad and Aser. And all the souls that came out of Jacob's thigh, were seventy: but Joseph was in Egypt. After he was dead, and all his brethren, and all that generation, The children of Israel increased, and sprung up into multitudes, and growing exceedingly strong they filled the land."

4. "more likely."

5. See Power, "Exodus," 207 [n. 163ad].

6. See Power, "History of Israel to 130 B.C.," 88 [n. 63a].

2. *God reveals Himself to Moses*—{the} *first step* {in} the preparation of a great prophet, a man of God. Moses {is shown} as a contemplative, the great man of the Old Testament: (a) Moses comes as the answer to the prayer of the persecuted people; (b) the birth of Moses: {note the} significance of the fact that he is adopted by Pharaoh's daughter; (c) his character {is shown}: he kills the Egyptian (read 2:11–15[7]), {which is} *his attempt to take matters in hand and* {shows} *his failure*—the anger of man does not work the justice of God; (d) read 2:15–25:[8] *Moses in Madian*—he defends Jethro's daughters {and later} marries one; {he undergoes} *forty years of preparation* in solitude; {then} the prayer of Israel is heard—God "looks upon them and knows them."[9] Read chapter 3[10]—*The Burning Bush* (c. 3), {including} (a) *the theophany* (1–7);

---

7. "In those days after Moses was grown up, he went out to his brethren: and saw their affliction, and an Egyptian striking one of the Hebrews his brethren. And when he had looked about this way and that way, and saw no one there, he slew the Egyptian and hid him in the sand. And going out the next day, he saw two Hebrews quarrelling: and he said to him that did the wrong: Why strikest thou thy neighbour? But he answered: Who hath appointed thee prince and judge over us? Wilt thou kill me, as thou didst yesterday kill the Egyptian? Moses feared, and said: How is this come to be known? And Pharao heard of this word and sought to kill Moses: but he fled from his sight, and abode in the land of Madian, and he sat down by a well."

8. "And the priest of Madian had seven daughters, who came to draw water: and when the troughs were filled, desired to water their father's flocks. And the shepherds came and drove them away: and Moses arose, and defending the maids, watered their sheep. And when they returned to Raguel their father, he said to them: Why are ye come sooner than usual? They answered: A man of Egypt delivered us from the hands of the shepherds: and he drew water also with us, and gave the sheep to drink. But he said: Where is he? why have you let the man go? call him that he may eat bread. And Moses swore that he would dwell with him. And he took Sephora his daughter to wife: And she bore him a son, whom he called Gersam, saying: I have been a stranger in a foreign country. And she bore another, whom he called Eliezer, saying: For the God of my father, my helper hath delivered me out of the hand of Pharao. Now after a long time the king of Egypt died: and the children of Israel groaning, cried out because of the works: and their cry went up unto God from the works. And he heard their groaning, and remembered the covenant which he made with Abraham, Isaac, and Jacob. And the Lord looked upon the children of Israel, and he knew them."

9. Exod 2:25.

10. "Now Moses fed the sheep of Jethro his father in law, the priest of Madian: and he drove the flock to the inner parts of the desert, and came to the mountain of God, Horeb. And the Lord appeared to him in a flame of fire out of the midst of a bush: and he saw that the bush was on fire and was not burnt. And Moses said: I will go and see this great sight, why the bush is not burnt. And when the Lord saw that he went forward to see, he called to him out of the midst of the bush, and said: Moses, Moses. And he answered: Here I am. And he said: Come not nigh hither, put off the shoes from thy feet: for the place whereon thou standest is holy ground. And he said: I am the God of

(b) *the Name of God* (13–15; cf. 6:3 ff.). {The} importance of Exodus as {the} revelation of God, {of} His plan and His will {is evident}—and {it is a} revelation to His People (before, {revelation was made} only to individuals). {The} *vocation* of Israel {is revealed}. {The} correlative importance of Israel's inability to accept the revelation and the need for false gods {is shown}. This too is part of the divine revelation!

a) {The} *Theophany—the Burning Bush* at Horeb/Sinai (note on Sinai: where {is it}? etc.) *The Angel of Yahweh* {is present}—*quid*?[11] {The}

---

thy father, the God of Abraham, the God of Isaac, and the God of Jacob. Moses hid his face: for he durst not look at God. And the Lord said to him: I have seen the affliction of my people in Egypt, and I have heard their cry because of the rigour of them that are over the works: And knowing their sorrow, I am come down to deliver them out of the hands of the Egyptians, and to bring them out of that land into a good and spacious land, into a land that floweth with milk and honey, to the places of the Chanaanite, and Hethite, and Amorrhite, and Pherezite, and Hevite, and Jebusite. For the cry of the children of Israel is come unto me: and I have seen their affliction, wherewith they are oppressed by the Egyptians. But come, and I will send thee to Pharao, that thou mayst bring forth my people, the children of Israel out of Egypt. And Moses said to God: Who am I that I should go to Pharao, and should bring forth the children of Israel out of Egypt? And he said to him: I will be with thee: and this thou shalt have for a sign, that I have sent thee: When thou shalt have brought my people out of Egypt, thou shalt offer sacrifice to God upon this mountain. Moses said to God: Lo, I shall go to the children of Israel, and say to them: The God of your fathers hath sent me to you. If they should say to me: What is his name? what shall I say to them? God said to Moses: I AM WHO AM. He said: Thus shalt thou say to the children of Israel: HE WHO IS, hath sent me to you. And God said again to Moses: Thus shalt thou say to the children of Israel: The Lord God of your fathers, the God of Abraham, the God of Isaac, and the God of Jacob, hath sent me to you: This is my name for ever, and this is my memorial unto all generations. Go, gather together the ancients of Israel, and thou shalt say to them: The Lord God of your fathers, the God of Abraham, the God of Isaac, and the God of Jacob, hath appeared to me, saying: Visiting I have visited you: and I have seen all that hath befallen you in Egypt. And I have said the word to bring you forth out of the affliction of Egypt, into the land of the Chanaanite, the Hethite, and the Amorrhite, and Pherezite, and Hevite, and Jebusite, to a land that floweth with milk and honey. And they shall hear thy voice: and thou shalt go in, thou and the ancients of Israel, to the king of Egypt, and thou shalt say to him: The Lord God of the Hebrews hath called us: we will go three days' journey into the wilderness, to sacrifice unto the Lord our God. But I know that the king of Egypt will not let you go, but by a mighty hand. For I will stretch forth my hand and will strike Egypt with all my wonders which I will do in the midst of them: after these he will let you go. And I will give favour to this people, in the sight of the Egyptians: and when you go forth, you shall not depart empty: But every woman shall ask of her neighbour, and of her that is in her house, vessels of silver and of gold, and raiment: and you shall put them on your sons and daughters, and shall spoil Egypt."

11. "what [does this mean]?"—see above, page 50 and below, page 160.

significance of {the} Burning Bush {is found in its manifestation of} divine transcendency—in creation, incarnation, Mary: multiple signs {of} one reality. {In} conclusion, {it} points to the new creation, all transfigured in Christ ({see} 1 Peter 3:1–14).

Exodus 3 {in the} *Fathers—St. Gregory of Nyssa:*[12]

1. Moses proved himself a lover of justice by defending the daughters of Jethro.[13]

2. He was also a lover of solitude, having retired to the innermost desert.[14]

3. The vision: "He saw a bush from which light came forth in a flame, yet the branches of the bush remained fresh in the flame as if they were covered with dew."[15] As he approached, "The miracle of the bush affected not only his eyes, but more surprising still the rays of light shone also in his sense of hearing. The beauty of the light played upon both these senses, enlightening the eyes by the play of the rays and instructing the ears with pure and incorruptible teachings. The voice of the light forbade Moses to approach the mountain wearing dead shoes. When he had cast aside his shoes he could step on the earth that was within the field of light."[16]

4. Explanation: (a) The burning bush is the *Epiphany of the Word*, divinity manifested in human flesh. It is the light of divine truth, the light of God Himself that is seen in the burning bush. This light does not appear among other lights, but in a bush burning and

---

12. Gregory of Nyssa, *De Vita Moysis* (*Life of Moses*) (Migne, *PG* 44, cols. 297A–430D); Merton uses the French translation of Jean Daniélou, SJ in Grégoire de Nysse, *Vie de Moïse*.

13. See Grégoire de Nysse, *Vie de Moïse*, 9 (1.19); Migne, *PG* 44, col. 306AB.

14. See Grégoire de Nysse, *Vie de Moïse*, 9 (1.19); Migne, *PG* 34, col. 306C.

15. "vit un buisson d'où la lumière jaillissait comme une flame. Les branches du buisson restaient fraîches dans la flame comme sous une rosée" (Grégoire de Nysse, *Vie de Moïse*, 10 [1.20]; Migne, *PG* 34, col. 306C).

16. "le miracle du buisson n'affecta plus seulement ses yeux, mais, ce qui est le plus étonnant, les rayons de la lumière se mirent à briller aussi à ses oreilles. En effect la beauté de la lumière se distribuait à l'un et l'autre sens, illuminant les yeux par le miroitement des rayons et éclairant les oreilles par de enseignements incorruptibles. La voix de la lumière empêcha Moïse de s'approcher de la montagne, alourdi par des chaussures mortes. Mais, quand il eut défait ses pieds des chaussures, il put toucher la terre qui était dans le champ de la lumière" (Grégoire de Nysse, *Vie de Moïse*, 10 [1.20]; Migne, *PG* 34, col. 306CD).

unconsumed, to show us that it is a divine light. "Coming forth from a simple bush of the earth it nevertheless surpasses with its rays all the heavenly bodies"[17] {and is} "a figure of that flesh which was radiant for us and which is true light and truth."[18] (b) {It represents} also the virgin birth[19]—Gregory {of} Nyssa is perhaps the first to have made this application.

5. Lessons: (a) to see the divine light we must put off the garments of skins with which we were clothed after original sin;[20] (b) when we have put off worldly knowledge, truth becomes clear of itself; then we see the difference between reality—what really *is*—and what merely *appears to be*;[21] (c) Moses understood that God alone really is and all things have existence only from and in Him: "That which is immutable, which is subject neither to growth nor to diminution, which is opposed to all change either for better or for worse—perfectly sufficient to Itself and alone desirable, in which all else participates, and which is not diminished by their participation, *here truly is He who really is*, and *to apprehend Him is to know truth*";[22] (d) one who has seen God, the ultimate truth, is able to help others save their souls because he has a sure knowledge of what really is, and not just a book-knowledge of words and theories[23]—{this is the} *traditional doctrine on action and contemplation.*

St. Bonaventure {writes}: *In qualibet enim creatura est refulgentia divini exemplaris, sed cum tenebra permixta; unde est sicut quaedam*

---

17. "sortant d'un simple buisson de la terre, elle surpasse cependant par ses rayons les astres du ciel" (Grégoire de Nysse, *Vie de Moïse*, 37 [2.20]; Migne, *PG* 34, col. 331D).

18. "figure de la chair, qui a brillé pour nous et qui est . . . la vraie Lumière et la Verité" (Grégoire de Nysse, *Vie de Moïse*, 39 [2.26]; Migne, *PG* 34, col. 334C).

19. See Grégoire de Nysse, *Vie de Moïse*, 37 (2.21); Migne, *PG* 34, col. 331D.

20. See Grégoire de Nysse, *Vie de Moïse*, 37–38 (2.22); Migne, *PG* 34, cols. 331D, 334A.

21. See See Grégoire de Nysse, *Vie de Moïse*, 38 (2.23); Migne, *PG* 34, col. 334B.

22. "Mais ce qui est immuable, qui n'est sujet ni à la croissance ni à la diminution, qui est également réfractaire à tout changement, soit en mieux, soit en pire . . . qui se suffit parfaitement à lui-même, qui est seul desirable, dont tout le reste participe et qui ne subit pas de diminution du fait de cette participation, voilà vraiment Celui qui est réellement et son appréhension est la connaissance de la vérité" (Grégoire de Nysse, *Vie de Moïse*, 39 [2.25]; Migne, *PG* 34, col. 334B).

23. See Grégoire de Nysse, *Vie de Moïse*, 39 (2.26); Migne, *PG* 34, col. 334C.

*opacitas admixta lumini.*²⁴ *Deus interior intimo meo et superior summo meo.*²⁵

{The} *Name of God*—thoughts from St. Thomas:²⁶

1. Can God be given a name? A name can be given by us to God, in so far as we know Him from creatures. This name does not express the divine essence as it is in itself. His essence remains beyond and above that which our name for Him signifies. The perfections we assign to God are known to us only in creatures: (a) some are *abstract* (like our names for formal perfections of creatures)—to signify His simplicity (mercy, goodness) (ad {2}); (b) others are *concrete*—to signify His subsistence (Lord; living God). *Both* kinds of name fall infinitely short of the real truth.²⁷

2. Positive names given to God—living, good, etc.—refer to His substance but do not adequately represent it. They represent Him imperfectly, as do creatures.²⁸

3. These names, in so far as they represent the substance of God, are *properly* applied to Him (not metaphor), but in their mode of signification they are not properly applied to Him.²⁹

4. Perfections {are} predicated *analogically* of God and creatures.³⁰

5. The Name *Deus* (θεος) is given to God by reason of a divine operation—His Providence by which He sees and governs all³¹ (cf. Abraham in Genesis—Read from Guardini: "God sees"³²).

---

24. "For in every creature there is a shining forth of the divine Exemplar, but mixed with darkness; from this it is as though a certain opaqueness has been mixed with light" (Bonaventure, *Collationes in Hexaemeron*, 12.14 [Bonaventure, *Opera Omnia*, 5:386]).

25. St. Augustine, *Confessions*, 3.6.11 (Migne, *PL* 38, col. 688) ("God, more deeply within than my inmost self and far beyond my highest reach"); Bonaventure refers to this passage in *Soliloquia*, 1.5 (Bonaventure, *Opera Omnia*, 8.31).

26. St. Thomas, *Summa Theologiae* [*ST*], *Pars Prima*, quaestio 13: "*De Nominibus Dei*" (Thomas Aquinas, *Opera Omnia*, 1.47–58).

27. *ST* Ia, q. 13, a. 1 (Thomas Aquinas, *Opera Omnia*, 1.47–48) (copy text reads: "ad 1").

28. *ST* Ia, q. 13, a. 2 (Thomas Aquinas, *Opera Omnia*, 1.48–49).

29. *ST* Ia, q. 13, a. 3 (Thomas Aquinas, *Opera Omnia*, 1.4–50).

30. *ST* Ia, q. 13, a. 5 (Thomas Aquinas, *Opera Omnia*, 1.51–52).

31. *ST* Ia, q. 13, a. 8 (Thomas Aquinas, *Opera Omnia*, 1.54–55).

32. "The twenty-second chapter of the book of Genesis contains the story of the most difficult hour in Abraham's life, when God tested him and required of him the

6. (article 11[33]) The name *"qui est"*[34] *is most proper to God*—it is His real Name (a) because God *is* His Being—the name is not of a *form by which* He is—and He alone is His Being, without any other form; (b) It is the most universal name of God, least determined to a particular *aspect* of God: *"Pelagus substantiae infinitum et indeterminatum"*;[35] (c) *Significat esse in praesenti*[36]—actual existence; ad 1: yet in a sense *Deus* is a more proper name—in what sense???;[37] {the} *Tetragrammaton* {is} even more appropriate, {as it} signifies the incommunicability of {the} divine nature.

Names of God in the Old Testament—The Tetragrammaton: before Exodus, the name of God was *El*, used by all Semitic peoples to designate any "god" true or false—{its} derivation {was} probably from {a} very ancient word meaning "strong." {Other terms used were} Elohim (plural of El??); El Elyon—the Most High God;[38] El Shaddai—God Almighty;[39] Adonai—the Lord. {In} Exodus 6:2–3, God explains to Moses that He appeared to the Patriarchs but did not reveal His name. Yahweh—this is the "ineffable" word used to express God's revelation of Himself to Moses: "I am who am." {There are} *peculiarities*—from time immemorial the Jews refused to *pronounce* the Name Yahweh ({it was} *written* {in} consonants only: יהוה—JHVH): (a) they used circumlocutions: "the Name above all

---

sacrifice of the only son he had waited for so long. Abraham obeyed, in an obedience of faith and trust which sealed him forever in God's promise. But in the bitterest moment the angel of God called him and released him from the awful test. 'And Abraham called the place: God sees.' When the darkness of the ordeal surrounded him he must have felt he was engulfed in blind darkness, alone in his hopeless affliction. But now the dark walls fell and he realized that he had not been forsaken but had been standing in the sight of God. God is He who sees. The mystery of the seeing of the Living God!" (Guardini, *Living God*, 28–29).

33. Thomas Aquinas, *Opera Omnia*, 1.56–57.

34. "He Who is" (Thomas Aquinas, *Opera Omnia*, 1.56).

35. "an ocean of substance, infinite and unlimited" (citing St. John Damascene, *De Fide Orthodoxa*, 1.9 [Migne, *PG* 94, col. 836]) (Thomas Aquinas, *Opera Omnia*, 1.57).

36. "it signifies being in the present" (Thomas Aquinas, *Opera Omnia*, 1.57, which reads: "*Significat enim esse . . .*").

37. After stating that *"qui est"* is more appropriate than *"Deus"* because it signifies existence, in an unrestricted way, in the present tense, he then points out that in another way *"Deus"* is more appropriate in that its meaning signifies the divine nature, and that the Tetragrammaton is even more appropriate because it signifies the incommunicable and in a sense the individual divine substance (Thomas Aquinas, *Opera Omnia*, 1.57).

38. See Gen 14:18–22.

39. See Gen 17:1.

Names"; "the glorious Name"; "the unspeakable Name" etc.; Josephus[40] would not write it in transcribing the revelation of Sinai; (b) the high priest said it in a low voice or a whisper when he entered the holy of holies; Adonai was substituted in the synagogue services; (c) *hence the true pronunciation has been forgotten*; *Jehovah* {is} a false pronunciation, going back to {the} middle ages—{the} confusion {is} due to {the} fact that {the} Massoretes[41] put {the} vowels of Adonai with {the} consonants of {the} Tetragrammaton to warn {the} reader to say "Adonai" instead (in synagogue readings). {As for} *Yahweh*, this pronunciation goes back to {the} Samaritan tradition, via Theodoret[42] (Samaritans {were} not scrupulous); *Yah* (ιαω)—a short form—{was} used widely (also by {the} Cabala[43]). God has revealed His Name in Jesus—{let us} say this Name in the depths of our heart!

The Deliverance of Israel ({chapters} 4–18): God reveals Himself in this act of deliverance, in a duel with the gods of Egypt, in which He proves Himself the true God. He confounds the demoniacal mimicry of His power. Pharaoh {is} the incarnation of demoniacal resistance. The plagues of Egypt {are the} eschatological anticipation of the Last Judgement. {The} deliverance of Israel {is a} type of baptism and of {the} general resurrection. *Pascha Christi*: the "passing" of the Most High in the Night of Judgement, will be commemorated in the Feast of the Pasch (READ Exodus 12:1–28,[44]

---

40. Jewish historian (37–c. 100), author of *The Antiquities of the Jews*, as well as a history of the Jewish war with Rome, in which he had served as a general of the Jewish forces until he was captured.

41. I.e., the early medieval Jewish textual scholars who were the first to insert marks indicating vowels into the Hebrew text.

42. Migne, *PG* 80, col. 244; Migne, *PG* 83, col. 460.

43. Medieval Sephardic Jewish mystical movement (usually spelled "Kabbalah" today) centered in southern France and Spain, represented particularly by the *Zohar* ("Book of Splendor"), traditionally attributed to the second-century rabbi Shimon bar Yohai but actually written by the Spanish rabbi Moses de León (d. 1305), which is based on the pattern of the ten sefirot, or manifestations of the divine attributes, through which divine life is communicated to creation in a series of emanations, and by which created being returns in mystical ascent to the One.

44. "And the Lord said to Moses and Aaron in the land of Egypt: This month shall be to you the beginning of months: it shall be the first in the months of the year. Speak ye to the whole assembly of the children of Israel, and say to them: On the tenth day of this month let every man take a lamb by their families and houses. But if the number be less than may suffice to eat the lamb, he shall take unto him his neighbour that joineth to his house, according to the number of souls which may be enough to eat the lamb. And it shall be a lamb without blemish, a male, of one year: according to which rite also you shall take a kid. And you shall keep it until the fourteenth day of this month: and the whole multitude of the children of Israel shall sacrifice it in the

13:1–16;[45] cf. 1 Peter 2:11). N.B. {the} Canticle of Moses (Exodus 15)

evening. And they shall take of the blood thereof, and put it upon both the side posts, and on the upper door posts of the houses, wherein they shall eat it. And they shall eat the flesh that night roasted at the fire, and unleavened bread with wild lettuce. You shall not eat thereof any thing raw, nor boiled in water, but only roasted at the fire: you shall eat the head with the feet and entrails thereof. Neither shall there remain any thing of it until morning. If there be any thing left, you shall burn it with fire. And thus you shall eat it: you shall gird your reins, and you shall have shoes on your feet, holding staves in your hands, and you shall eat in haste: for it is the Phase (that is the Passage) of the Lord. And I will pass through the land of Egypt that night, and will kill every firstborn in the land of Egypt both man and beast: and against all the gods of Egypt I will execute judgments: I am the Lord. And the blood shall be unto you for a sign in the houses where you shall be: and I shall see the blood, and shall pass over you: and the plague shall not be upon you to destroy you, when I shall strike the land of Egypt. And this day shall be for a memorial to you: and you shall keep it a feast to the Lord in your generations with an everlasting observance. Seven days shall you eat unleavened bread: in the first day there shall be no leaven in your houses: whosoever shall eat any thing leavened, from the first day until the seventh day, that soul shall perish out of Israel. The first day shall be holy and solemn, and the seventh day shall be kept with the like solemnity: you shall do no work in them, except those things that belong to eating. And you shall observe the feast of the unleavened bread: for in this same day I will bring forth your army out of the land of Egypt, and you shall keep this day in your generations by a perpetual observance. The first month, the fourteenth day of the month in the evening, you shall eat unleavened bread, until the one and twentieth day of the same month in the evening. Seven days there shall not be found any leaven in your houses: he that shall eat leavened bread, his soul shall perish out of the assembly of Israel, whether he be a stranger or born in the land. You shall not eat any thing leavened: in all your habitations you shall eat unleavened bread. And Moses called all the ancients of the children of Israel, and said to them: Go take a lamb by your families, and sacrifice the Phase. And dip a bunch of hyssop in the blood that is at the door, and sprinkle the transom of the door therewith, and both the door cheeks: let none of you go out of the door of his house till morning. For the Lord will pass through striking the Egyptians: and when he shall see the blood on the transom, and on both the posts, he will pass over the door of the house, and not suffer the destroyer to come into your houses and to hurt you. Thou shalt keep this thing as a law for thee and thy children for ever. And when you have entered into the land which the Lord will give you as he hath promised, you shall observe these ceremonies. And when your children shall say to you: What is the meaning of this service? You shall say to them: It is the victim of the passage of the Lord, when he passed over the houses of the children of Israel in Egypt, striking the Egyptians, and saving our houses. And the people bowing themselves, adored. And the children of Israel going forth did as the Lord had commanded Moses and Aaron."

45. "And the Lord spoke to Moses, saying: Sanctify unto me every firstborn that openeth the womb among the children of Israel, as well of men as of beasts: for they are all mine. And Moses said to the people: Remember this day in which you came forth out of Egypt, and out of the house of bondage, for with a strong hand hath the Lord brought you forth out of this place: that you eat no leavened bread. This day you go forth in the month of new corn. And when the Lord shall have brought thee into the

which echoes in the liturgy of heaven (Apoc. 15:3). *Jesus {is} the true Paschal Lamb* (John 1:29; 1 Cor. 5:7; 1 Peter 1:17–21)—{He} fulfills the figures of Exodus, as we shall see.

{There is a} struggle between grace and the heart of Pharaoh, who "will not *see*"—will not realize (cf. {the} fool in {the} sapiential books;⁴⁶ cf. Israel {in} Psalm 77—n.b. implications): Pharaoh won't let {the} people go to sacrifice because HE "is god." It is also a "business deal" in which Moses twists Pharaoh's arm and gets more and more out of him (although he does not give!).

"The Hardening of Pharaoh's heart"—*God's will—Providence—and man's freedom.*

a. Avoid {the} Thomist–Molinist dispute,⁴⁷ which is a blind alley— because both treat God's will as if it were a human (created) and limited will.

---

land of the Chanaanite, and the Hethite, and the Amorrhite, and the Hevite, and the Jebusite, which he swore to thy fathers that he would give thee, a land that floweth with milk and honey, thou shalt celebrate this manner of sacred rites in this month. Seven days shalt thou eat unleavened bread: and on the seventh day shall be the solemnity of the Lord. Unleavened bread shall you eat seven days: there shall not be seen any thing leavened with thee, nor in all thy coasts. And thou shalt tell thy son in that day, saying: This is what the Lord did to me when I came forth out of Egypt. And it shall be as a sign in thy hand, and as a memorial before thy eyes: and that the law of the Lord be always in thy mouth, for with a strong hand the Lord hath brought thee out of the land of Egypt. Thou shalt keep this observance at the set time from days to days. And when the Lord shall have brought thee into the land of the Chanaanite, as he swore to thee and thy fathers, and shall give it thee: Thou shalt set apart all that openeth the womb for the Lord, and all that is first brought forth of thy cattle: whatsoever thou shalt have of the male sex, thou shalt consecrate to the Lord. The firstborn of an ass thou shalt change for a sheep: and if thou do not redeem it, thou shalt kill it. And every firstborn of men thou shalt redeem with a price. And when thy son shall ask thee tomorrow, saying: What is this? thou shalt answer him: With a strong hand did the Lord bring us forth out of the land of Egypt, out of the house of bondage. For when Pharao was hardened, and would not let us go, the Lord slew every firstborn in the land of Egypt, from the firstborn of man to the firstborn of beasts: therefore I sacrifice to the Lord all that openeth the womb of the male sex, and all the firstborn of my sons I redeem. And it shall be as a sign in thy hand, and as a thing hung between thy eyes, for a remembrance: because the Lord hath brought us forth out of Egypt by a strong hand."

46. See Pss 13[14]:1–3, 52[53]:1–3; Prov 9:13–18, 14:1–35, 18:1–24, 19:1–29; Eccli [Sir] 18:15–18, 19:11–12, 22–25, 20:6–7, 13–22, 21:11–28, 31:5–7, 33:1–6; throughout these texts there is an emphasis on the willful refusal of the fool to see reality as it is and an obstinate clinging to illusion of one sort or another.

47. A controversy about the relationship between grace and free will in sixteenth-century Spain, in which the Jesuit Luis de Molina (1535–1600), basing his position on Saint Thomas, emphasized free will while the Dominican Domingo Bañez (1528–1604) and others, likewise claiming the authority of Aquinas, stressed the doctrine of

b. {According to} *St. Thomas*:

(1) God directly moves every created will—*exteriorly*, as the universal good which is the object of the will; *interiorly*, inclining it to choose the good—Himself (I, q. 105, a. 4, ad 1: *Deus movendo voluntatem non cogit ipsam* quia dat ei ejus propriam inclinationem[48]—i.e. He creates in us the very interior principle of liberty by which it moves itself). "Omnis inclinatio alicujus rei vel naturalis vel voluntaria *nihil est aliud quam quaedam impressio a primo movente*"[49] ({note the} consequences for contemplative life even in action!). "*Omnia quae agunt . . . quasi propria sponte perveniunt in id ad quod divinitus ordinantur.*"[50]

(2) God indirectly acts on every created will exteriorly *through secondary causes*. Deus in omnibus [gentibus] intime operetur;[51] hence scripture attributes the actions of created agents to God Himself.

(3) God also acts *without* secondary causes or *against* them, and this is no disorder.

(4) In governing all things, God is the governor, but He can leave the *execution* of *His designs to secondary causes, thus giving them the privilege of sharing His government and His causality* (I, q. 103, a. 6): "*si solus Deus gubernaret subtraheretur perfectio causalis a rebus*"[52] (ad 2);

(5) I, q. 103, a. 7: God governs all things—nothing can resist His divine order, in general; how about *evil*?—Malum semper fundatur in bono {. . . .} *Res aliqua dicitur mala per hoc quod* exit ab ordine alicujus particularis boni.[53]

---

efficacious grace; the discord became very bitter and continued between Jesuits and Dominicans long after the death of the two main antagonists.

48. "In moving the will God does not compel it, because He gives to it its own proper tendency" (Thomas Aquinas, *Opera Omnia*, 1:405).

49. "Every inclination of anything, whether natural or voluntary, is nothing other than a certain impression from the Prime Mover" (Ia, q. 103, a. 8 [Thomas Aquinas, *Opera Omnia*, 1:399]).

50. "Everything that acts . . . arrives as though by its own will at that to which divinity directs" (Ia, q. 103, a. 8 [Thomas Aquinas, *Opera Omnia*, 1:399]).

51. "God works in all from within" (Ia, q. 105, a. 5 [Thomas Aquinas, *Opera Omnia*, 1:405]).

52. "If God alone were to govern all things, causal perfection would be taken away from things" (Thomas Aquinas, *Opera Omnia*, 1:398).

53. "Evil is always based on a good . . . . something is called evil due to the fact

God's order *in a particular case* can be resisted, but even this resistance contributes to the general good; the sinners *contranituntur cuidam determinato bono quod est eis conveniens secundum suam naturam aut statum.*[54] I, q. 19, a. 6: "*Quod recedere videtur a Divina voluntate secundum unum ordinem, relabitur in ipsam secundum alium.*"[55] *God's will*: (1) in God, is His very being itself (I, q. 19, a. 1).[56] *The concept of will*: when we speak of our will, we think primarily of the faculty which *controls* and *orders* our passions and exterior reality, so that we attain our end. We impose this idea on God, and His will appears to us as the executive faculty which imposes His *power* on others. But the will is the faculty of LOVE, the faculty which *desires good*. By God's will, *He communicates His good to all beings—He communicates and gives Himself*. His will is not just a faculty which struggles with His creation to keep it from getting away from Him. By his will *He gives Himself to all*, totally and perfectly, to be ALL IN ALL. By His will, in a sense He *becomes all* (while remaining inviolably Himself). In God, love is not a passion or an emotion. It is an act of willing the good, *an act identical with His being*. (2) By it He wills Himself and all other things (a. 2)[57]—communicating to them His goodness: *Alia a se vult volendo bonitatem suam*[58]—hence {there is} no passion in God; (3) *Voluntas Dei est causa rerum*;[59] (4) in God's will, {it is necessary to} distinguish what He wills *antecedenter*—the good of all, that all should be saved; {and} *consequenter*[60]—that the *particular good* of some be taken away in so far as they have refused to do His will for themselves (I, q. 19, a. 6, ad 1: *Quidquid Deus simpliciter vult, fit, licet illud quod antecedenter vult non fiat*[61]). God permits sin out *of love for human liberty*. He loves the

---

that it departs from the order of some particular good" (Ia, q. 103, a. 7, ad 1 [Thomas Aquinas, *Opera Omnia*, 1:398]).

54. "They are in conflict with some specific good that is suited to them in their own nature or state of life" (I, q. 103, a. 8, ad 1 [Thoms Aquinas, *Opera Omnia*, 1:399]).

55. "What seems to depart from the divine will according to one perspective returns to it according to another" (Thomas Aquinas, *Opera Omnia*, 1:83).

56. Thomas Aquinas, *Opera Omnia*, 1:83–84.

57. Thomas Aquinas, *Opera Omnia*, 1:84–85.

58. "He wills things other than himself in willing his own goodness" (Ia, q. 19, a. 2, ad 2 [Thomas Aquinas, *Opera Omnia*, 1:85]).

59. "The will of God is the cause of things" (Ia, q. 19, a. 11 [Thomas Aquinas, *Opera Omnia*, 1:91]).

60. Thomas Aquinas, *Opera Omnia*, 1:88.

61. "Whatever God simply wills, happens, albeit that what he antecedently wills may not" (Thomas Aquinas, *Opera Omnia*, 1:88).

dignity of freedom (i.e. He loves to communicate His freedom to man) more than He hates the offense of sin!

Contingency—God wills that some effects be produced *necessarily*, others contingently. Contingency is not merely the result, a defect in the secondary cause. In God's order, contingent effects have just as much place as necessary effects, and are equally willed by Him—*consequenter—voluntas beneplaciti*.[62] Evil (I, q. 19, a. 9): *Non volente Deo fit homo deterior*.[63] *Deus non vult mala*:[64] (1) *no one* seeks an evil as such, but always a good with which it is accompanied; (2) God in no way wills {the} evil of sin, but wills {the} evil of punishment, not as evil, but for {the} sake of {the} good that goes with it—healing souls.

Points on Providence from Thomas Philippe:[65]

62. "will of good pleasure" (Ia, q. 19, a. 11 [Thomas Aquinas, *Opera Omnia*, 1:91).

63. "A person does not become worse by God willing it" (Thomas Aquinas, *Opera Omnia*, 1:90, which reads: "*Non ergo volente* . . .").

64. "God does not will evil" (Thomas Aquinas, *Opera Omnia*, 1:90).

65. Thomas Philippe (1905–1993) was a French Dominican who became the spiritual director of Jean Vanier and was the original inspiration behind the L'Arche movement founded by Vanier. In 1953 Robert Lax wrote to Merton: "I send you a letter from Jean Vanier (who is the son of the Canadian Ambassador to France & who runs a house for lay contemplatives & students, where I live a lot of the time.) He wonders if you would read a book by his spiritual director Pere Thomas Phillipe [*sic*], OP (who was cofounder with Jacques Maritain of this house.) The essays are all on the Blessed Virgin Mary and the Contemplative Life, and those Ive read Ive certainly found good" (Merton/Lax, *When Prophecy*, 119). In a second letter he writes: "Here it is five months later. . . . Here too is the letter from Vanier. I have met and talked a couple of times with Pere Thomas Philippe and he is wonderful (a living flame) and marvel of sweetness (his qualities are totally communicable). Think hell be writing and translating for Rices magazine. . . . Cant for the moment find Vaniers letter describing Eau Vive & Pere Thomas but will send it soon" (Merton/Lax, *When Prophecy* 120–21). There is no Vanier letter in the Merton archives at Bellarmine University, and no further information on the book that is mentioned in the first letter; various mimeographed sets of his conferences in French had been produced, some of which Merton was familiar with. In his December 1967 retreat for contemplative prioresses at Gethsemani, he refers to material by Thomas Philippe as "marvelous stuff" circulating in "mimeographed conferences" (Merton, *Solitude and Togetherness*); in the published transcription of the retreat this material is erroneously attributed to "Paul Philippe, formerly secretary of the congregation for religious" (Merton, *Springs*, 49–50), whereas what Merton actually said was that Thomas Philippe was "no relation to Paul Philippe, who used to be the secretary of the congregation." It is possible that the material cited here, otherwise unidentified and no longer extant at the Abbey of Gethsemani, was drawn from this mimeographed material referred to by Merton. Philippe is now known to have been a serial sexual abuser of adult women under his direction, a fact largely concealed during his lifetime; shortly after the death of Jean Vanier it became known that he too had

1. Creation: {the} whole universe and its order and all in it depend entirely on a free act of God's love, His *good pleasure*: He did not have to create me; He does not have to keep me in being—or anything else. True, His love is guided by His wisdom—{it is} nothing arbitrary—{He} respects natures as He has made them. N.B. all other causes act on something preexisting. God in creation acts on *what He Himself has called out of nothingness*—His glory above all is this—not in the qualities of the creature as much as in the mode of creation.

2. Government: *God governs what He has created*, moving things according to the demands of their natures. Providence {is the} work of *all-embracing wisdom and love* (read {the} Book {of} *Wisdom*, 11:16 {to the} end;[66] cf. also 7:16 ff. and 8:1). {He} moves all things *not only exteriorly* but *from within*.

3. *God governs bodily and spiritual beings differently*: *bodies* have no end but the end of the whole, of which they are nothing but parts; {the} end of bodies {is to} contribute to the harmony of the whole, in which God's wisdom is manifest—{the} universe has its end in God—to realize His designs for it. God's love reaches bodies *only in and through the whole*—i.e. indirectly. He moves bodies *through secondary causes, from the exterior*. God's "love" for bodies {is} only

---

abusive relationships with women, evidently under the influence of Philippe's bizarre, esoteric sexual theories.

66. "But for the foolish devices of their iniquity, because some being deceived worshipped dumb serpents and worthless beasts, thou didst send upon them a multitude of dumb beasts for vengeance. That they might know that by what things a man sinneth, by the same also he is tormented. For thy almighty hand, which made the world of matter without form, was not unable to send upon them a multitude of bears, or fierce lions, Or unknown beasts of a new kind, full of rage: either breathing out a fiery vapour, or sending forth a stinking smoke, or shooting horrible sparks out of their eyes: Whereof not only the hurt might be able to destroy them, but also the very sight might kill them through fear. Yea and without these, they might have been slain with one blast, persecuted by their own deeds, and scattered by the breath of thy power: but thou hast ordered all things in measure, and number, and weight. For great power always belonged to thee alone: and who shall resist the strength of thy arm? For the whole world before thee is as the least grain of the balance, and as a drop of the morning dew, that falleth down upon the earth: But thou hast mercy upon all, because thou canst do all things, and overlookest the sins of men for the sake of repentance. For thou lovest all things that are, and hatest none of the things which thou hast made: for thou didst not appoint, or make any thing hating it. And how could any thing endure, if thou wouldst not? or be preserved, if not called by thee. But thou sparest all: because they are thine, O Lord, who lovest souls" (vv. 16–27).

in what happens to them. He cannot communicate His love fully to bodies. {As for} *spirits*, especially man: (a) every spirit is a whole in itself, a universe, not just part of the universe—i.e. each can direct itself, as the universe runs itself; (b) each *spirit shares in God's government* of itself—thus {it} is *more loved*; (c) man can attain to God *directly* in his own *immanent, spiritual operations*—without going through exterior things. Man can attain his last end directly within himself by his intelligence and will. Man is not obliged, like {an} animal, to take the *nearest* good—he can transcend, select, choose. {For} example, to show how man attains God *interiorly* and material beings *exteriorly*, suppose the universe is suddenly destroyed. All material beings are destroyed with it—{share a} common fate. But souls can transcend that common fate and attain to God, no matter what happens to all the rest. My soul {is} greater than {the} universe—one free act {is} greater than {the} universe. *Man* has finality not only as part of a whole, in which he freely determines his own place, but also he has God as {his} immediate last end. *God* guides man providentially to both these ends. As *Father* He directly guides and governs souls—these do not depend on secondary causes. N.B. God's first causality *takes away nothing* from my causality. They are moved directly by Him—i.e. they are the efficient causes of their own actions. {This is the} creative dignity of free will (our nature demands creativity—not just servile compliance; if we are not creative, the talent of liberty goes to waste). *Every fully free act has something of the divine in it.* As Father, *God presides over the education of our freedom*: (a) causing *from within* our autonomy and our free act; (b) giving grace *from within* to perfect our freedom spiritually and supernaturally; (c) in both these *ways giving us a full share in His causality*—causing us to be *causes* (cf. {the} difference from {a} human chief—e.g. Napoleon—who could only form *subordinates*). {We must} not treat God as a human chief whose subordinates we are—we are SONS: *Servire Deo regnare est.*[67] The more we are independent of secondary causes, the more our activity is immanent and autonomous, the more we are like God—*the more we are moved by Him.* {See the} New Testament emphasis on being moved by {the} Holy Spirit. {This is the true} meaning of asceticism. God treats each

---

67. "to serve God is to reign"; cf. *Sermo* 64 (attributed to St. Augustine): "*jugum enim ejus obedientiae merito est suave, cui servire est regnare*" (Migne, *PL* 39, col. 1867) ("rightly pleasant is the yoke of obedience to him, to serve whom is to reign").

one not as a part but as a *whole* in itself. *Note {the} implications for human love*—respect for the other *person's freedom* and *uniqueness* ({we are to} help him deliver himself from subjection). *He who has received most is in {the} most intimate relation with God, the source.* Because He is all-powerful, God can move *with extreme sweetness—more sweetly than nature itself,* by {the} mode of *love* not of nature, especially in mystical graces. *Conclusion*: abandonment does not and cannot mean simply resignation to God, acting on us through exterior things. Above all, {let us} recognize His will and His grace within—*living by love*. But we are nothing and have nothing—{there is a} *total dependence on grace* to supply us from within. Here is where heroism comes in.

Deliverance of Israel: {in} chapter 4, Moses' struggle and diffidence {are depicted}. God gives him miraculous powers and he still hesitates (*interpret especially* {verses} 10–18). {Verse} 21 {is the first mention of the} hardening of Pharaoh's heart. Moses goes down into Egypt: interpret especially {verses} 22—"Israel is my son"—{and} 24–26: the circumcision of Moses' son (hitherto neglected). Moses {is} threatened, to teach him fidelity; {this is} also {an} anticipation of the Pasch (cf. Abraham's "gloomy vision"[68]). Chapter 5 {focuses on} the pride of Pharaoh {and} the intensification of {his} tyranny over Israel. {See} especially {verse} 2: Who is the Lord that I should hear His voice? {verse} 3: his resistance to the *call* of God to go into {the} wilderness and sacrifice; {verse} 19: the resistance of the People of Israel. {In} chapter 6:3, God reveals His name again and renews the promises; {in verses} 12 {and} 30, Moses still hesitates (comment on {the} phrase "uncircumcised eyes"). {In} 7:3, comment {on}: "*I shall harden his heart*" (cf. 4:21, 8:15, 32, 9:34)—God hardens Pharaoh's heart as {the} primary cause; Pharaoh hardens his own heart as {the} secondary cause—moderns emphasize this last element.

PLAGUES OF EGYPT: {chapters} 7 ff.: the Plagues (*read* 1–7[69]—comment especially {on verse} 4: "very great judgements"); {in} 7:10–13 {the}

---

68. See Genesis 15: and above, page 48–49.

69. "And the Lord said to Moses: Behold I have appointed thee the God of Pharao: and Aaron thy brother shall be thy prophet. Thou shalt speak to him all that I command thee; and he shall speak to Pharao, that he let the children of Israel go out of his land. But I shall harden his heart, and shall multiply my signs and wonders in the land of Egypt, And he will not hear you: and I will lay my hand upon Egypt, and will bring forth my army and my people the children of Israel out of the land of Egypt, by very great judgments. And the Egyptians shall know that I am the Lord, who have stretched

rod {is turned} into {the} serpent, {which is} not so much a "plague" as a prodigy and a threat. {In} 15 ff. water {is turned} into blood: "{The} Egyptians do likewise." {Does this mean they} changed blood back into water?? and got other sources of water? 8:1 ff. {is about} the frogs: n.b. here Aaron does it; {in verse} 8 Pharaoh begins to soften up: "Pray the Lord . . ." but then turns back—l. 15 {says he} "hardened his own heart"; 16 ff. {describes} the sciniphs—quid? mosquitoes; {according to verse} 19, digitus Dei est hic,[70] but "Pharaoh's heart hardened" (BJ[71]). 8:20 ff. {refers to} "all kinds of flies"; {here there is a} division—{the} Jews {are} not affected, Egyptians—yes. Pharaoh begins to give in: {in verse} 28 {he} permits sacrifice {and} even says: "pray for me"; 32: but his heart is hardened afterwards (s'entêta [BJ][72]). 9:1 ff. {describes the} cattle plague—again, {the} beasts of {the} Jews {are} not affected, and {it takes place} at a special appointed time, {making the point} yet more clear. {In verse} 7, Pharaoh goes out to see; {in verse} 8, "boils and blains" {appear}, from ashes scattered by Moses. {According to verse} 12, {the} Lord hardened Pharaoh's heart; {verse} 14 {gives the reason for the plagues}: "That thou mayest know that there is none like me"; {in verses} 15–16 {the Lord says}: "Therefore have I raised thee that I may show my power in thee." {In verses} 18 ff. {the} hail {comes—the} Lord Himself gives warning: take in your cattle; {verses} 23–27 {provide a} description of the hail and the "fire running along the ground"; {in} 27 Pharaoh {says}: "I have sinned" {but in verse} 30 {Moses responds}: "I know that thou dost not fear the Lord"; {in verses} 34–35, Pharaoh "increased his sin"—{his} heart {is} made "exceeding hard." The more one resists God's light, the more one is rooted in stubbornness; hence the mere sending of a "sign" which will be resisted is a "hardening" of the heart (cf. {the} explanation: 10:1–2). 10:4 ff. {describes the} locusts; {note verses} 7–11: this time Pharaoh bargains before the plague, urged by his people, but will not let everyone go; again Pharaoh says: I have sinned. {In verses} 10:21 ff. {comes the} darkness, {which is} SYMBOLIC; {the} outcome ({vv.} 24–29) {is that} this time Moses wants to take the flocks also (HERE read Ps. 77:43 ff.;[73]

---

forth my hand upon Egypt, and have brought forth the children of Israel out of the midst of them. And Moses and Aaron did as the Lord had commanded: so did they. And Moses was eighty years old, and Aaron eighty-three, when they spoke to Pharao."

70. "This is the finger of God."
71. "Le coeur de Pharaon s'endurcit" (Sainte Bible, 68).
72. Sainte Bible, 69.
73. "How he wrought his signs in Egypt, and his wonders in the field of Tanis. And

Apocalypse 16[74]—{it is} obvious that {the} plagues of Egypt are types of {the} final tribulation before {the} Last Day). {Chapter} 11 {describes the}

---

he turned their rivers into blood, and their showers that they might, not drink. He sent amongst them divers sorts of flies, which devoured them: and frogs which destroyed them. And he gave up their fruits to the blast, and their labours to the locust. And he destroyed their vineyards with hail, and their mulberry trees with hoarfrost. And he gave up their cattle to the hail, and their stock to the fire. And he sent upon them the wrath of his indignation: indignation and wrath and trouble, which he sent by evil angels. He made a way for a path to his anger: he spared not their souls from death, and their cattle he shut up in death. And he killed all the firstborn in the land of Egypt: the firstfruits of all their labour in the tabernacles of Cham. And he took away his own people as sheep: and guided them in the wilderness like a flock" (vv. 43–52).

74. "And I heard a great voice out of the temple, saying to the seven angels: Go, and pour out the seven vials of the wrath of God upon the earth. And the first went, and poured out his vial upon the earth, and there fell a sore and grievous wound upon men, who had the character of the beast; and upon them that adored the image thereof. And the second angel poured out his vial upon the sea, and there came blood as it were of a dead man; and every living soul died in the sea. And the third poured out his vial upon the rivers and the fountains of waters; and there was made blood. And I heard the angel of the waters saying: Thou art just, O Lord, who art, and who wast, the Holy One, because thou hast judged these things: For they have shed the blood of saints and prophets, and thou hast given them blood to drink; for they are worthy. And I heard another, from the altar, saying: Yea, O Lord God Almighty, true and just are thy judgments. And the fourth angel poured out his vial upon the sun, and it was given unto him to afflict men with heat and fire: And men were scorched with great heat, and they blasphemed the name of God, who hath power over these plagues, neither did they penance to give him glory. And the fifth angel poured out his vial upon the seat of the beast; and his kingdom became dark, and they gnawed their tongues for pain: And they blasphemed the God of heaven, because of their pains and wounds, and did not penance for their works. And the sixth angel poured out his vial upon that great river Euphrates; and dried up the water thereof, that a way might be prepared for the kings from the rising of the sun. And I saw from the mouth of the dragon, and from the mouth of the beast, and from the mouth of the false prophet, three unclean spirits like frogs. For they are the spirits of devils working signs, and they go forth unto the kings of the whole earth, to gather them to battle against the great day of the Almighty God. Behold, I come as a thief. Blessed is he that watcheth, and keepeth his garments, lest he walk naked, and they see his shame. And he shall gather them together into a place, which in Hebrew is called Armagedon. And the seventh angel poured out his vial upon the air, and there came a great voice out of the temple from the throne, saying: It is done. And there were lightnings, and voices, and thunders, and there was a great earthquake, such an one as never had been since men were upon the earth, such an earthquake, so great. And the great city was divided into three parts; and the cities of the Gentiles fell. And great Babylon came in remembrance before God, to give her the cup of the wine of the indignation of his wrath. And every island fled away, and the mountains were not found. And great hail, like a talent, came down from heaven upon men: and men blasphemed God for the plague of the hail: because it was exceeding great."

preparation for the final plague: borrowing the vessels; {the} death of {the} firstborn {is} threatened.

Then {comes} THE PASCH. All that has been said about the plagues is merely a preparation for the Pasch. When Yahweh said He wanted to use Pharaoh to show His great power, we must see this in the light of the Pasch—in its typical sense—in its plenary sense: "Christ our Pasch is slain."[75] Pharaoh {is a figure of} the devil—God has permitted the devil to do evil in order to show His own mercy all the more clearly. *The Pasch* {represents} not only {the} deliverance of {the} Jews but {the} institution of the great Paschal sacrifice. Before this {the} year began in September; now it begins in Nisan (12:1).

1. {In} chapter 11, note the complete difference of the tenth plague from all the others: 11:1, 8: now Egypt will even ask them to leave; 11:4: Yahweh Himself will pass through Egypt in *deep darkness*; 11:6: N.B. Israel will be in darkness and silence {in contrast to the} great clamor of {the} Egyptians.

2. {In} chapter 12, *the Paschal Lamb* {is described with its} prescriptions: (a) {this is} a family feast; (b) {the} purity of the victim {is stressed}; (c) {it is} a community sacrifice (12:6); (d) {as well as} a sacrifice of reconciliation ({the} angel passes over doors anointed with {the} Blood of {the} Lamb): READ 12:1-11[76]—{it is} *literally Good Friday* (cf. {the} context—Ps. 139, then the Passion); (e) 9-10:

---

75. 1 Cor 5:7.

76. "And the Lord said to Moses and Aaron in the land of Egypt: This month shall be to you the beginning of months: it shall be the first in the months of the year. Speak ye to the whole assembly of the children of Israel, and say to them: On the tenth day of this month let every man take a lamb by their families and houses. But if the number be less than may suffice to eat the lamb, he shall take unto him his neighbour that joineth to his house, according to the number of souls which may be enough to eat the lamb. And it shall be a lamb without blemish, a male, of one year: according to which rite also you shall take a kid. And you shall keep it until the fourteenth day of this month: and the whole multitude of the children of Israel shall sacrifice it in the evening. And they shall take of the blood thereof, and put it upon both the side posts, and on the upper door posts of the houses, wherein they shall eat it. And they shall eat the flesh that night roasted at the fire, and unleavened bread with wild lettuce. You shall not eat thereof any thing raw, nor boiled in water, but only roasted at the fire: you shall eat the head with the feet and entrails thereof. Neither shall there remain any thing of it until morning. If there be any thing left, you shall burn it with fire. And thus you shall eat it: you shall gird your reins, and you shall have shoes on your feet, holding staves in your hands, and you shall eat in haste: for it is the Phase (that is the Passage) of the Lord."

why {is the lamb} roasted? Why {is} nothing to be left? {For the} *meaning* {see} 12:12-14, 12:25-28 (READ[77]). *Azymes* {is the} seven-day feast of unleavened bread (READ 12:11-23[78]): (a) {note the} strictness of the prescription; (b) {there is to be} no labor—a seven-day Sabbath; (c) {the} meaning {involves} exile—{a} readiness to go

---

77. "And I will pass through the land of Egypt that night, and will kill every firstborn in the land of Egypt both man and beast: and against all the gods of Egypt I will execute judgments: I am the Lord. And the blood shall be unto you for a sign in the houses where you shall be: and I shall see the blood, and shall pass over you: and the plague shall not be upon you to destroy you, when I shall strike the land of Egypt. And this day shall be for a memorial to you: and you shall keep it a feast to the Lord in your generations with an everlasting observance. . . . And when you have entered into the land which the Lord will give you as he hath promised, you shall observe these ceremonies. And when your children shall say to you: What is the meaning of this service? You shall say to them: It is the victim of the passage of the Lord, when he passed over the houses of the children of Israel in Egypt, striking the Egyptians, and saving our houses. And the people bowing themselves, adored. And the children of Israel going forth did as the Lord had commanded Moses and Aaron."

78. "And thus you shall eat it: you shall gird your reins, and you shall have shoes on your feet, holding staves in your hands, and you shall eat in haste: for it is the Phase (that is the Passage) of the Lord. And I will pass through the land of Egypt that night, and will kill every firstborn in the land of Egypt both man and beast: and against all the gods of Egypt I will execute judgments: I am the Lord. And the blood shall be unto you for a sign in the houses where you shall be: and I shall see the blood, and shall pass over you: and the plague shall not be upon you to destroy you, when I shall strike the land of Egypt. And this day shall be for a memorial to you: and you shall keep it a feast to the Lord in your generations with an everlasting observance. Seven days shall you eat unleavened bread: in the first day there shall be no leaven in your houses: whosoever shall eat any thing leavened, from the first day until the seventh day, that soul shall perish out of Israel. The first day shall be holy and solemn, and the seventh day shall be kept with the like solemnity: you shall do no work in them, except those things that belong to eating. And you shall observe the feast of the unleavened bread: for in this same day I will bring forth your army out of the land of Egypt, and you shall keep this day in your generations by a perpetual observance. The first month, the fourteenth day of the month in the evening, you shall eat unleavened bread, until the one and twentieth day of the same month in the evening. Seven days there shall not be found any leaven in your houses: he that shall eat leavened bread, his soul shall perish out of the assembly of Israel, whether he be a stranger or born in the land. You shall not eat any thing leavened: in all your habitations you shall eat unleavened bread. And Moses called all the ancients of the children of Israel, and said to them: Go take a lamb by your families, and sacrifice the Phase. And dip a bunch of hyssop in the blood that is at the door, and sprinkle the transom of the door therewith, and both the door cheeks: let none of you go out of the door of his house till morning. For the Lord will pass through striking the Egyptians: and when he shall see the blood on the transom, and on both the posts, he will pass over the door of the house, and not suffer the destroyer to come into your houses and to hurt you."

to {the} promised land in HASTE—see especially 12:39 ({the} Jews did not see {the} meaning: 13:8–10).

The slaying of the firstborn {is now described} (READ 12:29–39[79]—no explanation {is given}). *For special comment* {see} Exodus 12:6: *Immolabitque eum universa multitudo filiorum Israel*[80] (cf. narration of the Passion;[81] cf. *Cat. Rom.*;[82] {cf. the} liturgy {of} Corpus Christi[83]); {see also} 12:12: *transibo per terram Aegypti in nocte illa*[84] (cf. the *Exultet*[85]). READ

---

79. "And it came to pass at midnight, the Lord slew every firstborn in the land of Egypt, from the firstborn of Pharao, who sat on his throne, unto the firstborn of the captive woman that was in the prison, and all the firstborn of cattle. And Pharao arose in the night, and all his servants, and all Egypt: for there was not a house wherein there lay not one dead. And Pharao calling Moses and Aaron, in the night, said: Arise and go forth from among my people, you and the children of Israel: go, sacrifice to the Lord as you say. Your sheep and herds take along with you, as you demanded, and departing, bless me. And the Egyptians pressed the people to go forth out of the land speedily, saying: We shall all die. The people therefore took dough before it was leavened: and tying it in their cloaks, put it on their shoulders. And the children of Israel did as Moses had commanded: and they asked of the Egyptians vessels of silver and gold, and very much raiment. And the Lord gave favour to the people in the sight of the Egyptians, so that they lent unto them: and they stripped the Egyptians. And the children of Israel set forward from Ramesse to Socoth, being about six hundred thousand men on foot, beside children. And a mixed multitude without number went up also with them, sheep and herds and beasts of divers kinds, exceeding many. And they baked the meal, which a little before they had brought out of Egypt, in dough: and they made earth cakes unleavened: for it could not be leavened, the Egyptians pressing them to depart, and not suffering them to make any stay: neither did they think of preparing any meat."

80. "and the whole multitude of the children of Israel shall sacrifice it."

81. See John 19:36, which quotes Exodus 12:46, specifying that no bone of the paschal lamb is to be broken; also John 19:14, which notes that Jesus is condemned at noon on the preparation day for Passover (the hour when the priests in the Temple began to slaughter the lambs to be consumed at the paschal meal).

82. "First of all, Abel, who fell a victim of the envy of his brother, Isaac who was commanded to be offered in sacrifice, the lamb immolated by the Jews on their departure from Egypt, and also the brazen serpent lifted up by Moses in the desert, were all figures of the Passion and death of Christ the Lord" (*Catechism of Council of Trent*, 52–53).

83. See the third last stanza of the sequence for the Feast of Corpus Christi: "*In figuris praesignatur, / Cum Isaac immolatur, / Agnus Paschae deputatur, / Datur manna patribus*" ("It is foreshadowed in signs / When Isaac is sacrificed, / The Lamb of the Pasch is slain, / Manna is given to the fathers") (*Missale Romanum*, 398).

84. "And I will pass through the land of Egypt that night."

85. "*Haec nox est, in qua primum patres nostros, filios Israel eductos de Aegypto, Mare Rubrum sicco vestigio transire fecisti. Hæc igitur nox est, quae peccatorum tenebras*

12:29-39 (the departure)—this scene colors {the} whole spirituality of {the} Jews—and OURS also (comment: the Last Judgement); then read 12:42,⁸⁶ and then the *Exultet*.⁸⁷ {For} *Jesus the Lamb of God*, {see} John 1:35-39—*Ecce agnus Dei*;⁸⁸ Matthew 26:26-32—I will strike the SHEP-HERD!!! (not Pharaoh!); Mark 14:22-29—This is my Body . . . my Blood; Luke 22:14-20—With desire have I desired etc.; John 19:31-36—the "great Sabbath" must not be defiled! A bone of Him shall not be broken (Jesus {is} slain at {the} time when {the} paschal lamb was sacrificed); *Christ our Pasch is slain* (1 Cor. 5:6-8)—{a} new feast (cf. 1 Peter 1:17-21). Summing up, {see} Hebrews 10:8-25—comment in light of Exodus 12; {the} completion of Jesus' victory {is} compared with {the} temporary character of {the} Old Testament victory—{it is} the *only true liberation* (Bouyer 60⁸⁹).

---

columnae illuminatione purgavit. Haec nox est, quae hodie per universum mundum in Christo credentes, a vitiis saeculi et caligine peccatorum segregatos, reddit gratiae, sociat sanctitati. Haec nox est, in qua, destructis vinculis mortis, Christus ab inferis victor ascendit" (*Missale Romanum*, 93-94; *Missale Cisterciense*, 166) ("This is the night on which you first made our fathers, the sons of Israel brought forth from Egypt, cross the Red Sea with dry feet. This is indeed the night which purified the darkness of sins by the light of the column. This is the night which today, throughout the whole world, restores to grace believers in Christ, set apart from the vices of the world and from the gloom of sins, and joins them to holiness. This is the night on which Christ destroyed the chains of death and arose victorious from the depths").

86. "This is the observable night of the Lord, when he brought them forth out of the land of Egypt: this night all the children of Israel must observe in their generations."

87. "*Haec sunt enim festa paschalia, in quibus verus ille Agnus occiditur, cuius sanguine postes fidelium consecrantur*" (*Missale Romanum*, 93; *Missale Cisterciense*, 166) ("This is the paschal festival, in which that true Lamb is slain, with Whose blood the doorposts of the faithful are consecrated").

88. "Behold the Lamb of God."

89. See Bouyer, *Meaning of the Monastic Life*, 60: "But to die to the present world by faith in Christ, in Christ dead and risen again, is no longer simply to die. It is to overcome the very power of death which dominated the whole life of the present world and made it a perpetual slavery. It is to find again, through the great act of reparation through faith and love, the divine sonship which we had lost. By dying to a human life which had become disfigured into the image of the devil by the very fact of becoming mortal, we are born again to angelic life, to the life which brings to life in us again the imprint of the Son of God, the unfolding Image of the Logos of light and life." Merton explicitly refers to this book twice in his conferences on monastic observances, which he was presenting concurrently with the Exodus conferences (see Merton, *Monastic Observances*, 39, 58).

Exodus 13—READ the "sanctification" of the firstborn (1–15):[90] (1) {the} meaning of the rite; (2) the mystery of the purification ({cf.} Luke 2:23 ff.—comment: Jesus, the true Lamb of God, is NOT redeemed by doves; here again {note} the necessity of a special fulfillment of {the} Old Testament) (cf. verse 9—used in {the} Feast of {the} Miraculous Medal[91]). The departure {ties up} a few loose ends: (a) they head for the desert, not for land of {the} Philistines (v. 17) (cf. *Cat. Rom.*[92]); (b) v. 19—Moses takes Joseph's bones.

90. "And the Lord spoke to Moses, saying: Sanctify unto me every firstborn that openeth the womb among the children of Israel, as well of men as of beasts: for they are all mine. And Moses said to the people: Remember this day in which you came forth out of Egypt, and out of the house of bondage, for with a strong hand hath the Lord brought you forth out of this place: that you eat no leavened bread. This day you go forth in the month of new corn. And when the Lord shall have brought thee into the land of the Chanaanite, and the Hethite, and the Amorrhite, and the Hevite, and the Jebusite, which he swore to thy fathers that he would give thee, a land that floweth with milk and honey, thou shalt celebrate this manner of sacred rites in this month. Seven days shalt thou eat unleavened bread: and on the seventh day shall be the solemnity of the Lord. Unleavened bread shall you eat seven days: there shall not be seen any thing leavened with thee, nor in all thy coasts. And thou shalt tell thy son in that day, saying: This is what the Lord did to me when I came forth out of Egypt. And it shall be as a sign in thy hand, and as a memorial before thy eyes: and that the law of the Lord be always in thy mouth, for with a strong hand the Lord hath brought thee out of the land of Egypt. Thou shalt keep this observance at the set time from days to days. And when the Lord shall have brought thee into the land of the Chanaanite, as he swore to thee and thy fathers, and shall give it thee: Thou shalt set apart all that openeth the womb for the Lord, and all that is first brought forth of thy cattle: whatsoever thou shalt have of the male sex, thou shalt consecrate to the Lord. The firstborn of an ass thou shalt change for a sheep: and if thou do not redeem it, thou shalt kill it. And every firstborn of men thou shalt redeem with a price. And when thy son shall ask thee tomorrow, saying: What is this? thou shalt answer him: With a strong hand did the Lord bring us forth out of the land of Egypt, out of the house of bondage. For when Pharao was hardened, and would not let us go, the Lord slew every firstborn in the land of Egypt, from the firstborn of man to the firstborn of beasts: therefore I sacrifice to the Lord all that openeth the womb of the male sex, and all the firstborn of my sons I redeem."

91. Introit (*Missale Romanum*, (202); not in *Missale Cisterciense*).

92. "Finally, the time and place, in which the people of Israel received this Law from God should be noted. They received it after they had been delivered from Egypt and had come into the wilderness; in order that, impressed by the memory of a recent benefit and awed by the dreariness of the place in which they journeyed, they might be the better disposed to receive the Law. For man becomes closely attached to those whose bounty he has experienced, and when he has lost all hope of assistance from his fellow-man, he then seeks refuge in the protection of God" (*Catechism of the Council of Trent*, 365).

Exodus 14—crossing the Red Sea—READ 14:5–14:[93] Pharaoh starts our after them; the fear of the Jews {leads them to say} "better to stay and serve Pharaoh." Apply {this} to {the} spiritual life—to conversion and vocation (is this {a} mere application?—cf. {the} *Confessions* of St. Augustine; St. John of the Cross?) Verse 14—"*Dominus pergerabit pro vobis et vos tacebitis*"—{presents} an important Old Testament theme (READ Isaias 30:12–18:[94] *In silentio et spe erit fortitudo vestra* [15][95]). READ 15–

---

93. "And it was told the king of the Egyptians that the people was fled: and the heart of Pharao and of his servants was changed with regard to the people, and they said: What meant we to do, that we let Israel go from serving us? So he made ready his chariot, and took all his people with him. And he took six hundred chosen chariots, and all the chariots that were in Egypt: and the captains of the whole army. And the Lord hardened the heart of Pharao king of Egypt, and he pursued the children of Israel: but they were gone forth in a mighty hand. And when the Egyptians followed the steps of them who were gone before, they found them encamped at the sea side: all Pharao's horse and chariots, and the whole army were in Phihahiroth before Beelsephon. And when Pharao drew near, the children of Israel, lifting up their eyes, saw the Egyptians behind them: and they feared exceedingly, and cried to the Lord. And they said to Moses: Perhaps there were no graves in Egypt, therefore thou hast brought us to die in the wilderness: why wouldst thou do this, to lead us out of Egypt? Is not this the word that we spoke to thee in Egypt, saying: Depart from us that we may serve the Egyptians? for it was much better to serve them, than to die in the wilderness. And Moses said to the people: Fear not: stand and see the great wonders of the Lord, which he will do this day: for the Egyptians, whom you see now, you shall see no more for ever. The Lord will fight for you, and you shall hold your peace."

94. "Therefore thus saith the Holy One of Israel: Because you have rejected this word, and have trusted in oppression and tumult, and have leaned upon it: Therefore shall this iniquity be to you as a breach that falleth, and is found wanting in a high wall, for the destruction thereof shall come on a sudden, when it is not looked for. And it shall be broken small, as the potter's vessel is broken all to pieces with mighty breaking, and there shall not a sherd be found of the pieces thereof, wherein a little fire may be carried from the hearth, or a little water be drawn out of the pit. For thus saith the Lord God the Holy One of Israel: If you return and be quiet, you shall be saved: in silence and in hope shall your strength be. And you would not: But have said: No, but we will flee to horses: therefore shall you flee. And we will mount upon swift ones: therefore shall they be swifter that shall pursue after you. A thousand men shall flee for fear of one: and for fear of five shall you flee, till you be left as the mast of a ship on the top of a mountain, and as an ensign upon a hill. Therefore the Lord waiteth that he may have mercy on you: and therefore shall he be exalted sparing you: because the Lord is the God of judgment: blessed are all they that wait for him."

95. "in silence and in hope shall your strength be."

23:⁹⁶ n.b. verse 19 etc. {are read for the} Feast of {the} Guardian Angels⁹⁷ (explain); 20: *Erat nubes tenebrosa, et illuminans noctem*⁹⁸ (cf. St. John {of the} Cross {on} FAITH: *Ascent {of} Mount Carmel*, 1:72⁹⁹). READ 24–31:¹⁰⁰

96. "And the Lord said to Moses: Why criest thou to me? Speak to the children of Israel to go forward. But lift thou up thy rod, and stretch forth thy hand over the sea, and divide it: that the children of Israel may go through the midst of the sea on dry ground. And I will harden the heart of the Egyptians to pursue you: and I will be glorified in Pharao, and in all his host, and in his chariots, and in his horsemen. And the Egyptians shall know that I am the Lord, when I shall be glorified in Pharao, and in his chariots and in his horsemen. And the angel of God, who went before the camp of Israel, removing, went behind them: and together with him the pillar of the cloud, leaving the forepart, Stood behind, between the Egyptians' camp and the camp of Israel: and it was a dark cloud, and enlightening the night, so that they could not come at one another all the night. And when Moses had stretched forth his hand over the sea, the Lord took it away by a strong and burning wind blowing all the night, and turned it into dry ground: and the water was divided. And the children of Israel went in through the midst of the sea dried up: for the water was as a wall on their right hand and on their left. And the Egyptians pursuing went in after them, and all Pharao's horses, his chariots and horsemen through the midst of the sea."

97. Exodus 14:19 ("*Tollens se Angelus Domini, qui praecedebat castra Israel, abiit post eos*" ["And the angel of God, who went before the camp of Israel, removing, went behind them"]) is used as an antiphon for the first nocturn of this feast (*Breviarium Cisterciense, Autumnalis*, 381). The office for the feast also makes extensive use of the passage on the angel in Exodus 23:20–23: capitulum for vespers (vv. 21–22 [379]); first reading for the first nocturn (vv. 20–23 [382]); capitula for lauds (vv. 20–21 [389]), for terce (vv. 20–21 [390]), for sext (v. 21 [390]), and for none (vv. 22–23 [390]).

98. "it was a dark cloud, and enlightening the night."

99. See *Ascent of Mount Carmel*, 2.3: "*How faith is dark night to the soul. This is proved with arguments and quotations and figures from Scripture*" (Peers, ed., *John of the Cross*, 1:70–73), in which Exodus 14:20 is quoted.

100. "And now the morning watch was come, and behold the Lord looking upon the Egyptian army through the pillar of fire and of the cloud, slew their host. And overthrew the wheels of the chariots, and they were carried into the deep. And the Egyptians said: Let us flee from Israel: for the Lord fighteth for them against us. And the Lord said to Moses: Stretch forth thy hand over the sea, that the waters may come again upon the Egyptians, upon their chariots and horsemen. And when Moses had stretched forth his hand towards the sea, it returned at the first break of day to the former place: and as the Egyptians were fleeing away, the waters came upon them, and the Lord shut them up in the middle of the waves. And the waters returned, and covered the chariots and the horsemen of all the army of Pharao, who had come into the sea after them, neither did there so much as one of them remain. But the children of Israel marched through the midst of the sea upon dry land, and the waters were to them as a wall on the right hand and on the left: And the Lord delivered Israel on that day out of the hands of the Egyptians. And they saw the Egyptians dead upon the sea shore, and the mighty hand that the Lord had used against them: and the people feared the Lord, and they believed the Lord, and Moses his servant."

comment {on this passage} for {its} *literary quality*—{a} grandiose and terrible scene, the destruction of the Egyptians. *The conclusion*—they believed. This {is} the grand finale to the whole plague sequence.

Exodus 15 {includes the} *Canticle of Moses*. READ especially 1–13[101] (cf. Apoc. 15:1–8); n.b. {verses} 20–21: Mary the sister of Moses (cf. *Popule meus*[102]—Michaeas 6:1–5). READ 22–27[103]—*the waters of Mara*—{and} apply {this passage} to {the} spiritual life: the Cross of Christ must "sweeten" our trials. How? {see the} comments of Origen[104] etc.

---

101. "Then Moses and the children of Israel sung this canticle to the Lord: and said: Let us sing to the Lord: for he is gloriously magnified, the horse and the rider he hath thrown into the sea. The Lord is my strength and my praise, and he is become salvation to me: he is my God and I will glorify him: the God of my father, and I will exalt him. The Lord is as a man of war, Almighty is his name. Pharao's chariots and his army he hath cast into the sea: his chosen captains are drowned in the Red Sea. The depths have covered them, they are sunk to the bottom like a stone. Thy right hand, O Lord, is magnified in strength: thy right hand, O Lord, hath slain the enemy. And in the multitude of thy glory thou hast put down thy adversaries: thou hast sent thy wrath, which hath devoured them like stubble. And with the blast of thy anger the waters were gathered together: the flowing water stood, the depth were gathered together in the midst of the sea. The enemy said: I will pursue and overtake, I will divide the spoils, my soul shall have its fill: I will draw my sword, my hand shall slay them. Thy wind blew and the sea covered them: they sunk as lead in the mighty waters. Who is like to thee, among the strong, O Lord? who is like to thee, glorious in holiness, terrible and praiseworthy, doing wonders? Thou stretchedst forth thy hand, and the earth swallowed them. In thy mercy thou hast been a leader to the people which thou hast redeemed: and in thy strength thou hast carried them to thy holy habitation."

102. "O my people, [what have I done to thee . . . ? For I brought thee up out of the land of Egypt, and delivered thee out of the house of slaves: and I sent before thy face Moses, and Aaron, and Mary]" (Mic 6:3–4).

103. "And Moses brought Israel from the Red Sea, and they went forth into the wilderness of Sur: and they marched three days through the wilderness, and found no water. And they came into Mara, and they could not drink the waters of Mara, because they were bitter: whereupon he gave a name also agreeable to the place, calling it Mara, that is, bitterness. And the people murmured against Moses, saying: What shall we drink? But he cried to the Lord, and he shewed him a tree, which when he had cast into the waters, they were turned into sweetness. There he appointed him ordinances, and judgments, and there he proved him, Saying: If thou wilt hear the voice of the Lord thy God, and do what is right before him, and obey his commandments, and keep all his precepts, none of the evils that I laid upon Egypt, will I bring upon thee: for I am the Lord thy healer. And the children of Israel came into Elim, where there were twelve fountains of water, and seventy palm trees: and they encamped by the waters."

104. In his *Homily 7 on Exodus*, nn. 1–2 (Migne, *PG* 12, cols. 341A–343B), Origen associates the bitterness of the waters of Mara with the Law and the letter of scripture, and the wood that sweetens it with the tree of life which is Christ and with the mystery of the cross.

[HERE {include the} map and general outline (cf. Numbers 33)]

The Journey of Israel through the Desert: outline (NUMBERS 33 gives {this} outline {of the stages of the journey}). {In} *Exodus* {there is} a long series of murmurings and further miracles. As Yahweh struggled with Pharaoh, now He struggles with His own people—their hardness of heart.

1. 15:22 ff: at the *waters of Mara*—{the} water {is} made sweet by "the Cross";

2. {chapter} 16: the manna and the quails (Desert of Sin); institution of {the} Sabbath;

3. 17:1-7: {the} Desert of Raphidim—water from the rock; verses 8-16: the fight against Amelec;

4. chapter 18: {the} meeting with Jethro {followed by} sacrifice; the "deans" (judges);

5. chapter 19: in {the} Desert of Sinai—three months out of Egypt—THE COVENANT: (a) 19:3-15: preparation to ascend {the} mountain; (b) 16-24: the first ascent; (c) 20: the Ten Commandments and {the} first ritual prescriptions (other laws {in} chapters 21-23); promises (23:20 ff.); sacrifices to ratify the covenant; (d) 24:9-11: the second ascent—Moses, Aaron and the seventy; (e) {the} third ascent—Moses {stays} forty days on {the} mountain (chapters 25-31 {contain} further ritual prescriptions); (f) {chapter} 32: the *golden calf*; the anger of God; Moses pleads on the mountain; the anger of Moses and the slaughter of the guilty; {chapter} 33 (with the tabernacle): God's love for Moses {and} Moses' desire to see God; (g) {chapter} 34: the fourth ascent—{the} vision on the mountain ({along with} further laws, about relations with gentiles); (h) {chapters} 35-40: making the Tabernacle; 40:32 to {the} end—the Shekinah descends on the Tabernacle. *Numbers* 1: (i) the census; (j) {the} Pasch in the desert and departure; 9:15 ff., 33-36: the journey with the Tabernacle; {chapter} 11: Tabeera (qibrot hattaavah[105])—part of the camp {is} struck by fire for murmuring; Moses argues with Yahweh for the people. {In chapters} 11-12, Miryam {is} struck with leprosy etc. {Chapter} 13 {recounts the} reconnoitering in Chanaan {and} further revolt. {Chapters} 16-17 {tell of the} revolt of Core, Dathan and Abiron. {Chapter} 20 {presents the} desert of Sin {and the}

---

105. Place name taken to mean "the graves of lust" (Num 11:34).

NOTES ON EXODUS 163

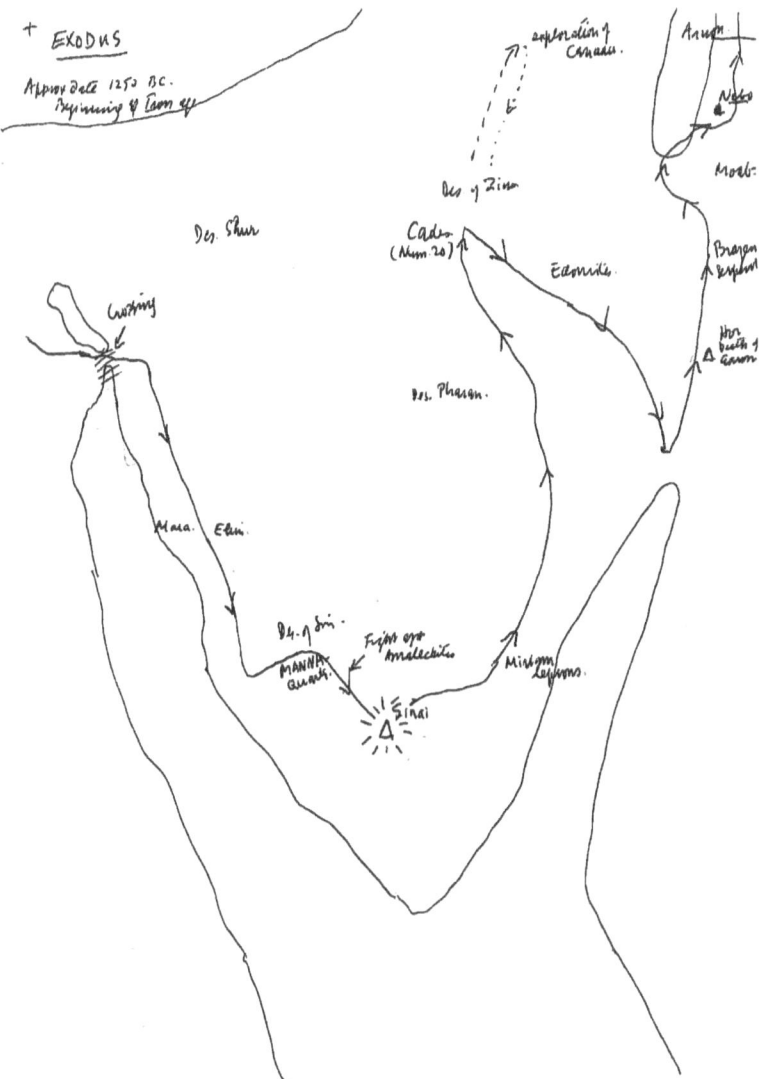

death of Miryam; {at} MERIBA, water {comes} from the rock {and the} punishment of Moses and Aaron {is} foretold, {followed by the} dispute with {the} Edomites {and the} death of Aaron. {Chapter} 21 {includes the} Brazen serpents; Numbers 21 {also features the} Desert of Moab {and} war with the Amhorites (Sehon); Og King of Bashan {is also} overcome. {Chapters} 22–23 {tell of the} Moabites {and} Balaam. {In chapter} 25 {the} Israelites revel with Moabite women at Peor—Phineas {responds}. {In} 27:12 ff. Moses prepares for death outside {the} Promised Land (because of Meriba); Josue {is appointed} to succeed Moses. *Deuteronomy* 31–34 {recounts the} death of Moses.

Exodus—*Israel in the Desert*: chapter 16 to the end—details: 15:22 to {the} end—Mara (*vide super*[106]). *Chapter* 16 {reveals the} significance of the trial in the desert: READ first of all *Deuteronomy* 8:1–6[107]—Yahweh wanted to see the depths of Israel's heart; {He provided} manna because man does not live by bread alone. Exodus = temptation (cf. Mt. 4:4—this brings out {the} striking parallel—Jesus {was} also tempted in {the} desert—but not by Yahweh). *The daily exodus: then* {see} *Psalm 94 and Hebrews 3:13*; cf. Amos 8:11–12, {which speaks of} hunger for the word of God—light {is} thrown on this passage; {note the} importance of "hunger" in {the} spiritual life—*hunger and thirst for justice*;[108] cf. John 6 (later); *Read* 16:1–5:[109] {the} murmuring of the people, {especially verse} 4: "that I may prove them." St. Benedict on murmuring[110] {is} to be seen

---

106. "See above."

107. "All the commandments, that I command thee this day, take great care to observe: that you may live, and be multiplied, and going in may possess the land, for which the Lord swore to your fathers. And thou shalt remember all the way through which the Lord thy God hath brought thee for forty years through the desert, to afflict thee and to prove thee, and that the things that were in thy heart might be made known, whether thou wouldst keep his commandments or no. He afflicted thee with want, and gave thee manna for thy food, which neither thou nor thy fathers knew: to shew that not in bread alone doth man live, but in every word that proceedeth from the mouth of God. Thy raiment, with which thou wast covered, hath not decayed for age, and thy foot is not worn, lo this is the fortieth year, That thou mayst consider in thy heart, that as a man traineth up his son, so the Lord thy God hath trained thee up. That thou shouldst keep the commandments of the Lord thy God, and walk in his ways, and fear him."

108. Matt 5:6.

109. "And they set forward from Elim, and all the multitude of the children of Israel came into the desert of Sin, which is between Elim and Sinai: the fifteenth day of the second month, after they came out of the land of Egypt. And all the congregation of the children of Israel murmured against Moses and Aaron in the wilderness. And the children of Israel said to them: Would to God we had died by the hand of the Lord in the land of Egypt, when we sat over the flesh pots, and ate bread to the full. Why have you brought us into this desert, that you might destroy all the multitude with famine? And the Lord said to Moses: Behold I will rain bread from heaven for you: let the people go forth, and gather what is sufficient for every day: that I may prove them whether they will walk in my law, or not. But the sixth day let them provide for to bring in: and let it be double to that they were wont to gather every day."

110. *Rule*, cc. 4, 5, 23, 34, 35, 40, 41, 53 (McCann, trans. and ed., *Rule*, 28, 34, 72, 86, 88, 96, 98, 120); see Merton, *Rule of Saint Benedict*, 112–14, 150–51.

against this background; words of obedience = words of God by which man *lives*; verse 5 {relates the} institution of {the} Sabbath; {for verses} 7–8, cf. *qui vos audit me audit*.[111] Read 16:6–18:[112] {verses} 6–7 {are used in the} liturgy {of} Christmas Eve[113]—{what is the} *connection*? {Note} the "*Gloria Domini*": problem of verse 10—{is it} a gloss, looking forward to {the} shekinah over {the} Tabernacle???; {in verse} 13 {are found} the quails {and a} description of manna; {according to verses} 16–18, *each one gets what he needs* (cf. Acts: *Dividebatur unicuique sunt opus sui*;[114] {also} St. Benedict {on the} common life;[115] q.v. contemplation—apply {this} to {the} life of prayer).

111. "He that heareth you, heareth me" (Luke 10:16).

112. "And Moses and Aaron said to the children of Israel: In the evening you shall know that the Lord hath brought you forth out of the land of Egypt: And in the morning you shall see the glory of the Lord: for he hath heard your murmuring against the Lord: but as for us, what are we, that you mutter against us? And Moses said: In the evening the Lord will give you flesh to eat, and in the morning bread to the full: for he hath heard your murmurings, with which you have murmured against him, for what are we? your murmuring is not against us, but against the Lord. Moses also said to Aaron: Say to the whole congregation of the children of Israel: Come before the Lord: for he hath heard your murmuring. And when Aaron spoke to all the assembly of the children of Israel, they looked towards the wilderness: and behold the glory of the Lord appeared in a cloud. And the Lord spoke to Moses, saying: I have heard the murmuring of the children of Israel: say to them: In the evening you shall eat flesh, and in the morning you shall have your fill of bread: and you shall know that I am the Lord your God. So it came to pass in the evening, that quails coming up, covered the camp: and in the morning, a dew lay round about the camp. And when it had covered the face of the earth, it appeared in the wilderness small, and as it were beaten with a pestle, like unto the hoar frost on the ground. And when the children of Israel saw it, they said one to another: Manhu! which signifieth: What is this! for they knew not what it was. And Moses said to them: This is the bread, which the Lord hath given you to eat. This is the word, that the Lord hath commanded: Let every one gather of it as much as is enough to eat: a gomor for every man, according to the number of your souls that dwell in a tent, so shall you take of it. And the children of Israel did so: and they gathered, one more, another less. And they measured by the measure of a gomor: neither had he more that had gathered more: nor did he find less that had provided less: but every one had gathered, according to what they were able to eat."

113. Introit, gradual (*Missale Romanum*, 14; *Missale Cisterciense*, 13, 14).

114. "And distribution was made to every one, according as he had need" (Acts 4:35, which reads: "*Dividebatur autem singulis prout cuique opus erat*").

115. See *Rule*, c. 34, "*Se Omnes Aequaliter Debeant Necessaria Accipere*" ("Whether All Should Receive Necessaries in Like Measure"), which begins by quoting Acts 4:35 and goes on to point out that those who through some weakness have greater needs should be treated accordingly, and that those with lesser needs should be grateful to God while those with greater needs should be humbled, and thus all will be at peace

Israel in the Desert: Exodus 16—*in the Desert of Sin*. Read 1–12:[116] the rebellion of Israel against Moses—*the* MANNA; n.b. verse 6—*vespere scietis* etc.—{finds an} application in {the} liturgy of Christmas Eve (*discuss*); verse 10 {describes} the *Shekinah*: *Ecce Gloria Domini apparerit in nube*.[117] Read 13–36:[118] the manna, the miraculous food given by God's

---

(McCann, trans. and ed., *Rule* 86/87); on this chapter see Merton, *Rule of Saint Benedict*, 148–51.

116. "And they set forward from Elim, and all the multitude of the children of Israel came into the desert of Sin, which is between Elim and Sinai: the fifteenth day of the second month, after they came out of the land of Egypt. And all the congregation of the children of Israel murmured against Moses and Aaron in the wilderness. And the children of Israel said to them: Would to God we had died by the hand of the Lord in the land of Egypt, when we sat over the flesh pots, and ate bread to the full. Why have you brought us into this desert, that you might destroy all the multitude with famine? And the Lord said to Moses: Behold I will rain bread from heaven for you: let the people go forth, and gather what is sufficient for every day: that I may prove them whether they will walk in my law, or not. But the sixth day let them provide for to bring in: and let it be double to that they were wont to gather every day. And Moses and Aaron said to the children of Israel: In the evening you shall know that the Lord hath brought you forth out of the land of Egypt: And in the morning you shall see the glory of the Lord: for he hath heard your murmuring against the Lord: but as for us, what are we, that you mutter against us? And Moses said: In the evening the Lord will give you flesh to eat, and in the morning bread to the full: for he hath heard your murmurings, with which you have murmured against him, for what are we? your murmuring is not against us, but against the Lord. Moses also said to Aaron: Say to the whole congregation of the children of Israel: Come before the Lord: for he hath heard your murmuring. And when Aaron spoke to all the assembly of the children of Israel, they looked towards the wilderness: and behold the glory of the Lord appeared in a cloud. And the Lord spoke to Moses, saying: I have heard the murmuring of the children of Israel: say to them: In the evening you shall eat flesh, and in the morning you shall have your fill of bread: and you shall know that I am the Lord your God."

117. "Behold the glory of the Lord appeared in a cloud."

118. "So it came to pass in the evening, that quails coming up, covered the camp: and in the morning, a dew lay round about the camp. And when it had covered the face of the earth, it appeared in the wilderness small, and as it were beaten with a pestle, like unto the hoar frost on the ground. And when the children of Israel saw it, they said one to another: Manhu! which signifieth: What is this! for they knew not what it was. And Moses said to them: This is the bread, which the Lord hath given you to eat. This is the word, that the Lord hath commanded: Let every one gather of it as much as is enough to eat: a gomor for every man, according to the number of your souls that dwell in a tent, so shall you take of it. And the children of Israel did so: and they gathered, one more, another less. And they measured by the measure of a gomor: neither had he more that had gathered more: nor did he find less that had provided less: but every one had gathered, according to what they were able to eat. And Moses said to them: Let no man leave thereof till the morning. And they hearkened not to him, but some of them left until the morning, and it began to be full of worms, and it putrified, and Moses was

special love: verse 4 {presents} *the test—obedience—*to take only what God gives and trust Him (*cf.* {*the*} *Sermon on* {*the*} *Mount*[119])—lack of trust foreshadowed future idolatry; {in} verses 7-8, obedience to Moses and Aaron {is} also at issue here; {in} verse 13, it is a sign that Yahweh is the true God; verse 17 {describes the} first disobedience: those who seek to have more do not have it—*all have enough*; {in} verse 19 f., those who keep manna for the morrow lose it—it rots, except on the Sabbath. {In verse} 27, those who went to gather {it} on {the} Sabbath found none. Summary—manna {was} put in the tabernacle; Israel fed on manna for forty years. {In its} *spiritual* {application}: (1) manna {is a} type of {the} Blessed Sacrament: READ cf. *John* 6: (a) {in verses} 25-35,[120] Jesus {is} the

---

angry with them. Now every one of them gathered in the morning, as much as might suffice to eat: and after the sun grew hot, it melted. But on the sixth day they gathered twice as much, that is, two gomors every man: and all the rulers of the multitude came, and told Moses. And he said to them: This is what the Lord hath spoken: Tomorrow is the rest of the sabbath sanctified to the Lord. Whatsoever work is to be done, do it: and the meats that are to be dressed, dress them: and whatsoever shall remain, lay it up until the morning. And they did so as Moses had commanded, and it did not putrify, neither was there worm found in it. And Moses said: Eat it today, because it is the sabbath of the Lord: today it shall not be found in the field. Gather it six days: but on the seventh day is the sabbath of the Lord, therefore it shall not be found. And the seventh day came: and some of the people going forth to gather, found none. And the Lord said to Moses: How long will you refuse to keep my commandments, and my law? See that the Lord hath given you the sabbath, and for this reason on the sixth day he giveth you a double provision: let each man stay at home, and let none go forth out of his place the seventh day. And the people kept the sabbath on the seventh day. And the house of Israel called the name thereof Manna: and it was like coriander seed white, and the taste thereof like to flour with honey. And Moses said: This is the word, which the Lord hath commanded: Fill a gomor of it, and let it be kept unto generations to come hereafter, that they may know the bread, wherewith I fed you in the wilderness, when you were brought forth out of the land of Egypt. And Moses said to Aaron: Take a vessel, and put manna into it, as much as a gomor can hold: and lay it up before the Lord to keep unto your generations, As the Lord commanded Moses. And Aaron put it in the tabernacle to be kept. And the children of Israel ate manna forty years, till they came to a habitable land: with this meat were they fed, until they reached the borders of the land of Chanaan. Now a gomor is the tenth part of an ephi."

119. See Matt 6:25-34.

120. "And when they had found him on the other side of the sea, they said to him: Rabbi, when camest thou hither? Jesus answered them, and said: Amen, amen I say to you, you seek me, not because you have seen miracles, but because you did eat of the loaves, and were filled. Labour not for the meat which perisheth, but for that which endureth unto life everlasting, which the Son of man will give you. For him hath God, the Father, sealed. They said therefore unto him: What shall we do, that we may work the works of God? Jesus answered, and said to them: This is the work of God, that you believe in him whom he hath sent. They said therefore to him: What sign therefore

true Bread of Life—manna {is} only a figure (N.B. here as yet communion {is} not yet in question—*faith in {the} Person of Jesus* is nourishment); (b) {in verses} 47–59,[121] the Living Bread here, explicitly, {is} the Eucharist, which gives *eternal life*; (2) translate and discuss *Ecce Panis angelorum*[122] (*Laudes vesp.* p. 6[123]); cf. in *Panis Angelicus*: "*Dat panis caelicus figuris terminum.*"[124] *Vide* {the} Corpus Christi liturgy;[125] (3) manna {can be} applied to interior prayer.

---

dost thou shew, that we may see, and may believe thee? What dost thou work? Our fathers did eat manna in the desert, as it is written: He gave them bread from heaven to eat. Then Jesus said to them: Amen, amen I say to you; Moses gave you not bread from heaven, but my Father giveth you the true bread from heaven. For the bread of God is that which cometh down from heaven, and giveth life to the world. They said therefore unto him: Lord, give us always this bread. And Jesus said to them: I am the bread of life: he that cometh to me shall not hunger: and he that believeth in me shall never thirst."

121. "Amen, amen I say unto you: He that believeth in me, hath everlasting life. I am the bread of life. Your fathers did eat manna in the desert, and are dead. This is the bread which cometh down from heaven; that if any man eat of it, he may not die. I am the living bread which came down from heaven. If any man eat of this bread, he shall live for ever; and the bread that I will give, is my flesh, for the life of the world. The Jews therefore strove among themselves, saying: How can this man give us his flesh to eat? Then Jesus said to them: Amen, amen I say unto you: Except you eat the flesh of the Son of man, and drink his blood, you shall not have life in you. He that eateth my flesh, and drinketh my blood, hath everlasting life: and I will raise him up in the last day. For my flesh is meat indeed: and my blood is drink indeed. He that eateth my flesh, and drinketh my blood, abideth in me, and I in him. As the living Father hath sent me, and I live by the Father; so he that eateth me, the same also shall live by me. This is the bread that came down from heaven. Not as your fathers did eat manna, and are dead. He that eateth this bread, shall live for ever. These things he said, teaching in the synagogue, in Capharnaum."

122. "*Ecce Panis Angelorum, / Factus cibus viatorum, / Vere panis filiorum, / Non mittendus canibus. // In figuris praesignatur, / Cum Isaac immolatur, / Agnus Paschae deputatur, / Datur manna patribus. // Bone pastor, panis vere, / Jesu, nostri miserere: / Tu nos pasce, nos tuere, / Tu nos bona fac videre / In terra viventium. // Tu qui cuncta scis et vales, / Qui nos pascis hic mortales: / Tuos ibi commensales, / Coheredes et sodales / Fac sanctorum civium*" ("Behold the Bread of Angels, / Made the food of travelers / Truly the bread of children, / Not to be given to dogs. // It is foreshadowed in signs / When Isaac is sacrificed, / The Lamb of the Pasch is slain, / Manna is given to the fathers. // Good Pastor, true bread, / Jesus, have mercy on us: / Feed us, guard us, / Make us see good things / In the land of the living. // You who know and will all, / Who feed us mortals here, / There make us fellow partakers / Coheirs and companions / Of the holy citizens").

123. I.e. hymns for Benediction of the Blessed Sacrament: see *Laudes Vespertinae*.

124. "The heavenly Bread brings an end to foreshadowings" (ll. 3–4).

125. The "*Ecce Panis Angelorum*" is comprised of the final four stanzas of "*Lauda, Sion*," the Corpus Christi Sequence (*Missale Romanum*, 398).

The Shekinah (article by Bouyer in BVC #20[126]—based on Lev Gillet: *Communion in the Messiah*) Shekinah (from shakan—to dwell in a tent[127]) {is the} special presence of God in His People, localized in the Tabernacle and in the Temple. Prelude—{in} the episode of the Burning Bush (Exodus 3) in the Desert of Sinai, Moses gets {his} first indication of God's presence in *fire* (*not* in idols, etc.); God {is} a consuming fire (Heb. 12:29); but He comes to save, and He reveals His Name—{He is} present in His Name.[128]

1. {In} *Exodus* 13:21–22; 14:19–20, 24, the "glory of God"—{the} Angel of God[129]—{is encountered} in the passage of the Red Sea.

2. {At} *Sinai* (READ Exodus 24:15–18;[130] {in} 24:9–11,[131] the elders also see {the} glory of God; {in} 34:29,[132] Moses is shining after seeing the glory of God[133]).

3. *The Tabernacle*[134]—here God will habitually descend and show Himself in the luminous cloud. Why? because of the presence in

---

126. Bouyer, "Schékinah: Dieu avec Nous."
127. See Bouyer, "Schékinah," 7.
128. See Bouyer, "Schékinah," 8.
129. See Bouyer, "Schékinah," 8: "*L'Ange de Yahweh* ici mentionné mériterait une étude à part pour lui-même. Ici comme ailleurs il est lié à la manifestation localisée de Dieu. Il est *envoyé* par Dieu (c'est le sens propre du mot *ange*). Mais Dieu est si bien avec lui qu'Il se fait reconnaître et adorer, et finalement qu'Il parle en personne et se révèle" ("The Angel of Yahweh mentioned here would merit a separate study of its own. Here as elsewhere it is connected to the localized manifestation of God. It is sent by God (this is the proper sense of the word 'angel'). But God is so much with it that he makes himself recognized and adored, and finally speaks and reveals himself in person").
130. "And when Moses was gone up, a cloud covered the mount. And the glory of the Lord dwelt upon Sinai, covering it with a cloud six days: and the seventh day he called him out of the midst of the cloud. And the sight of the glory of the Lord was like a burning fire upon the top of the mount, in the eyes of the children of Israel. And Moses, entering into the midst of the cloud, went up into the mountain: and he was there forty days, and forty nights."
131. "Then Moses and Aaron, Nadab and Abiu, and seventy of the ancients of Israel went up: And they saw the God of Israel: and under his feet as it were a work of sapphire stone, and as the heaven, when clear. Neither did he lay his hand upon those of the children of Israel, that retired afar off, and they saw God, and they did eat and drink."
132. "And when Moses came down from the mount Sinai, he held the two tables of the testimony, and he knew not that his face was horned from the conversation of the Lord."
133. See Bouyer, "Schékinah," 10.
134. See Bouyer, "Schékinah," 10–12.

it of the ark. *The Shekinah tells them when to move and when to stop*: (1) READ Exodus 25:22[135] (the ark); Numbers 7:89;[136] Leviticus 16:2;[137] (2) READ Exodus 40:32–36;[138] (3) READ 1 Kings 8[139]—{the} *exact place* of manifestation {is} in the midst of the cherubim ("*qui sedes super cherubim*":[140] Hab. 3:2, Dan. 3:55 [Greek], Ps. 98:1); (4) Isaias 6: {the} inaugural vision; (5) Hebrews 9:6–14 ({the} final development = {the} sanctuary of Heaven).

135. "Thence will I give orders, and will speak to thee over the propitiatory, and from the midst of the two cherubims, which shall be upon the ark of the testimony, all things which I will command the children of Israel by thee."

136. "And when Moses entered into the tabernacle of the covenant, to consult the oracle, he heard the voice of one speaking to him from the propitiatory, that was over the ark between the two cherubims, and from this place he spoke to him."

137. "And he commanded him, saying, Speak to Aaron thy brother, that he enter not at all into the sanctuary, which is within the veil before the propitiatory, with which the ark is covered, lest he die, (for I will appear in a cloud over the oracle)."

138. "The cloud covered the tabernacle of the testimony, and the glory of the Lord filled it. Neither could Moses go into the tabernacle of the covenant, the cloud covering all things and the majesty of the Lord shining, for the cloud had covered all. If at any time the cloud removed from the tabernacle, the children of Israel went forward by their troops: If it hung over, they remained in the same place. For the cloud of the Lord hung over the tabernacle by day, and a fire by night, in the sight of all the children of Israel throughout all their mansions."

139. "Then all the ancients of Israel with the princes of the tribes, and the heads of the families of the children of Israel were assembled to king Solomon in Jerusalem: that they might carry the ark of the covenant of the Lord out of the city of David, that is, out of Sion. And all Israel assembled themselves to king Solomon on the festival day in the month of Ethanim, the same is the seventh month. And all the ancients of Israel came, and the priests took up the ark, And carried the ark of the Lord, and the tabernacle of the covenant, and all the vessels of the sanctuary, that were in the tabernacle: and the priests and the Levites carried them. And king Solomon, and all the multitude of Israel, that were assembled unto him went with him before the ark, and they sacrificed sheep and oxen that could not be counted or numbered. And the priests brought in the ark of the covenant of the Lord into its place, into the oracle of the temple, into the holy of holies under the wings of the cherubims. For the cherubims spread forth their wings over the place of the ark, and covered the ark, and the staves thereof above. And whereas the staves stood out, the ends of them were seen without in the sanctuary before the oracle, but were not seen farther out, and there they have been unto this day. Now in the ark there was nothing else but the two tables of stone, which Moses put there at Horeb, when the Lord made a covenant with the children of Israel, when they came out of the land of Egypt. And it came to pass, when the priests were come out of the sanctuary, that a cloud filled the house of the Lord" (3 Kgs 8:1–10).

140. "who sittest upon the cherubims" (also Isa 37:16, Ps 79[80]:2; not Hab 3:2).

4. *The Temple*¹⁴¹ (see Solomon {and the} dedication of {the} Temple: READ 1 K 8—{the} danger {is that} Israel becomes "UN PEOPLE INSTALLÉ"¹⁴²—God {is} "at its disposition." *But* Israel profanes the Temple by introducing idols. Ezechiel sees {the} departure of the Shekinah for Babylon. The Temple is destroyed. {The} lesson {is that the} Temple {is} not an "idol." READ Ezech 10:1–{22}:¹⁴³ {the} *Sheki-*

141. See Bouyer, "Schékinah," 12–14.
142. "a settled people" (Bouyer, "Schékinah," 13).
143. "And I saw and behold in the firmament that was over the heads of the cherubims, there appeared over them as it were the sapphire stone, as the appearance of the likeness of a throne. And he spoke to the man, that was clothed with linen, and said: Go in between the wheels that are under the cherubims and fill thy hand with the coals of fire that are between the cherubims, and pour them out upon the city. And he went in, in my sight: And the cherubims stood on the right side of the house, when the man went in, and a cloud filled the inner court. And the glory of the Lord was lifted up from above the cherub to the threshold of the house: and the house was filled with the cloud, and the court was filled with the brightness of the glory of the Lord. And the sound of the wings of the cherubims was heard even to the outward court as the voice of God Almighty speaking. And when he had commanded the man that was clothed with linen, saying: Take fire from the midst of the wheels that are between the cherubims: he went in and stood beside the wheel. And one cherub stretched out his arm from the midst of the cherubims to the fire that was between the cherubims: and he took, and put it into the hands of him that was clothed with linen: who took it and went forth. And there appeared in the cherubims the likeness of a man's hand under their wings. And I saw, and behold there were four wheels by the cherubims: one wheel by one cherub, and another wheel by another cherub: and the appearance of the wheels was to the sight like the chrysolite stone: And as to their appearance, all four were alike: as if a wheel were in the midst of a wheel. And when they went, they went by four ways: and they turned not when they went: but to the place whither they first turned, the rest also followed, and did not turn back. And their whole body, and their necks, and their hands, and their wings, and the circles were full of eyes, round about the four wheels. And these wheels he called voluble, in my hearing. And every one had four faces: one face was the face of a cherub, and the second face, the face of a man: and in the third was the face of a lion: and in the fourth the face of an eagle. And the cherubims were lifted up: this is the living creature that I had seen by the river Chobar. And when the cherubims went, the wheels also went by them: and when the cherubims lifted up their wings, to mount up from the earth, the wheels stayed not behind, but were by them. When they stood, these stood: and when they were lifted up, these were lifted up: for the spirit of life was in them. And the glory of the Lord went forth from the threshold of the temple: and stood over the cherubims. And the cherubims lifting up their wings, were raised from the earth before me: and as they went out, the wheels also followed: and it stood in the entry of the east gate of the house of the Lord: and the glory of the God of Israel was over them. This is the living creature, which I saw under the God of Israel by the river Chobar: and I understood that they were cherubims. Each one had four faces, and each one had four wings: and the likeness of a man's hand was under their wings. And as to the likeness of their faces, they were the same faces which I had

nah appears with the faithful remnant in exile (Ezech. 1; cf. Ezech. 11:16).

5. *Wisdom* in the hearts of faithful Israelites is the Shekinah:[144] READ Eccli 24:3–15[145]—cf. {the} Blessed Mother.

{The} *Sapiential Tradition and Jewish Mysticism*:[146] "Where two are seated together with the Torah, there am I in the midst of them."[147] {This is} a purifying and holy presence—the shekinah of Ezechiel and Isaias! When a pious man is sick, the shekinah hovers over his bed. The prayers of the pious Jew give God hospitality and rest on earth—cf. Abraham in Genesis (Read Genesis[148]) and in turn, the pious Jew takes his delight

---

seen by the river Chobar, and their looks, and the impulse of every one to go straight forward" (copy text reads: "1–24").

144. See Bouyer, "Schékinah," 14.

145. "And in the midst of her own people she shall be exalted, and shall be admired in the holy assembly. And in the multitude of the elect she shall have praise, and among the blessed she shall be blessed, saying: I came out of the mouth of the most High, the firstborn before all creatures: I made that in the heavens there should rise light that never faileth, and as a cloud I covered all the earth: I dwelt in the highest places, and my throne is in a pillar of a cloud. I alone have compassed the circuit of heaven, and have penetrated into the bottom of the deep, and have walked in the waves of the sea, And have stood in all the earth: and in every people, And in every nation I have had the chief rule: And by my power I have trodden under my feet the hearts of all the high and low: and in all these I sought rest, and I shall abide in the inheritance of the Lord. Then the creator of all things commanded, and said to me: and he that made me, rested in my tabernacle, And he said to me: Let thy dwelling be in Jacob, and thy inheritance in Israel, and take root in my elect. From the beginning, and before the world, was I created, and unto the world to come I shall not cease to be, and in the holy dwelling place I have ministered before him. And so was I established in Sion, and in the holy city likewise I rested, and my power was in Jerusalem."

146. See Bouyer, "Schékinah," 14–17.

147. "Là où deux sont assis ensemble avec la Torah entre eux, la schékinah est au milieu d'eux" (Bouyer, "Schékinah," 15, quoting *Pirke Aboth*, 3.2b, a saying attributed to Rabbi Chamina ben Teradion).

148. "And the Lord appeared to him in the vale of Mambre as he was sitting at the door of his tent, in the very heat of the day. And when he had lifted up his eyes, there appeared to him three men standing near him: and as soon as he saw them he ran to meet them from the door of his tent, and adored down to the ground. And he said: Lord, if I have found favour in thy sight, pass not away from thy servant: But I will fetch a little water, and wash ye your feet, and rest ye under the tree. And I will set a morsel of bread, and strengthen ye your heart, afterwards you shall pass on: for therefore are you come aside to your servant. And they said: Do as thou hast spoken. Abraham made haste into the tent to Sara, and said to her: Make haste, temper together three measures of flour, and make cakes upon the hearth. And he himself ran to

in the Holy Presence in all these things. {The} *principle* {is}: "*From the first day on which God created the universe, He willed to dwell here below with His creatures*"¹⁴⁹ (from a Jewish commentary on Numbers). N.B. medieval Jewish theology strives to define {the} ontological status of the shekinah, in terms similar to {the} Christian theology of grace (cf. Orthodox theologians on the "uncreated light"¹⁵⁰).

{In the} *New Testament*,¹⁵¹ Jesus is the Shekinah (John 1:14: *The Word was made flesh and* εσκένοσεν—*pitched His tent—among us*); {cf. the} *Transfiguration* (Matt. 17:1-8; 2 Peter 1:17-18). *The Church is God's Temple* (Col. 2:9: {the} plenitude of divinity in Christ; 2 Cor. 6:16: we are His Temple; cf. Apoc. 21:3; 3:18: we are transformed from glory to glory); {this takes place} BY CHARITY (cf. St. John 14:23 etc. etc.; Apoc. 3:20—behold I stand at the door and knock). But the Blessed Sacrament—{the} sacrament of charity, by which we are built into "one Christ," is our shekinah, Whom we adore in order to receive Him into our souls. In the New Testament, *the glorified Body of the Word Incarnate*, destroyed by lovers

---

the herd, and took from thence a calf very tender and very good, and gave it to a young man: who made haste and boiled it. He took also butter and milk, and the calf which he had boiled, and set before them: but he stood by them under the tree" (Gen 18:1-8).

149. "Depuis le premier jour où Dieu a créé l'univers, il a voulu demeurer ici-bas avec ses créatures" (Bouyer, "Schékinah," 16, quoting the treatise Rabba, on Numbers 13:6).

150. See Merton, "Mount Athos" (in *Disputed Questions*, 78): "St. Gregory Palamas . . . defended the thesis that the 'divine light'—the same light that was seen by the three Apostles who saw the vision of the Transfigured Savior on Mount Thabor—could be experienced directly in this present life. He held that this light was not a mere symbol of the divinity, but an experience of the 'divine energies'—though not of the divine essence. . . . Gregory Palamas taught that the 'uncreated energies' of God could communicate themselves directly to men even in the present life (he rejected the idea of created grace)." See also Merton, "Russian Mystics" (in *Mystics and Zen Masters*, 182): "Seraphim of Sarov is . . . the most perfect example of that mysticism of light which is characteristic of the Orthodox Church: completely positive and yet compatible with, indeed based on, the apophatic (negative) theology of Pseudo-Dionysius and St. Maximus the Confessor. It is perhaps this which distinguishes Russian mysticism in its pure state. Not an intellectualist and negative ascent to the invisible above all that is visible, but more paradoxically an apprehension of the invisible as visible insofar as all creation is suddenly experienced as transfigured in a light for which there is no accounting in terms of any philosophy, a light which is given directly by God, proceeds from God, and in a sense *is* the Divine Light. Yet this experience is not a substantial vision of God, because in Oriental theology the light experienced by the mystic is a divine 'energy,' distinct from God's nature but which can be apprehended in contact with the *Person* of the Holy Spirit, by mystical love and grace."

151. See Bouyer, "Schékinah," 17-22.

of the Temple of stone, {is} built again in three days by the power of God and {has} become life-giving spirit. {It} is the true and eternal temple of God (Apoc. 21:22).

The Law (chapter in Guardini, *The Lord*[152]): Jesus was crucified because He was thought to be an overthrower of the Law. "We will never understand the destiny of the Lord until we have clarified the Biblical meaning of this word."[153] Before the Law {there was} *sin* {but} Abraham, the faithful one, {was} living with God in freedom. This was the original pattern for the People of God (cf. Isaac, Jacob). {In} Egypt, the Jews *lost* {the} love of God and of liberty. "The possibility of serving God in free faith is gradually lost."[154] God *completely revises* His manner of leading them to salvation—now {there is} a LAW! Promises {are} renewed—under the Law. Law grew until it entered everything and became the *whole life* of the nation. All the different observances reflected deep wisdom and insight into human nature, but it was all a tremendous burden and got heavier all the time. Socially, ethically, the whole thing becomes incomprehensible. It was a *religious system*. It was *meant* to be a heavy yoke—to be FELT to keep the Jews from {the} seduction of idolatry and nature cults. The people was meant *to feel what sin is*, so that they would *long for salvation*, and *to feel failure*. Cf. here St. Paul—St. Paul saw that the real function of the Law was to *convince man utterly of his failure* and thus strip him of all his illusions and make him turn to God.[155] {There was a} *perversion of the Law* by {the} scribes and Pharisees, who *make the Law an instrument of their own will* and *use it against God* ({this tendency was} constantly opposed by {the} prophets, spokesmen of God and of freedom). They succeed in reducing God and His will to a guarantor of the glory of human law. "The covenant, founded on loyalty and grace, became a documented charter of rights and demands."[156]

---

152. Guardini, *Lord*, 164–71.
153. Guardini, *Lord*, 165, which reads: "... Lord before we have clarified ..."
154. Guardini, *Lord*, 166.
155. See Rom 3:19–20, 7:7–25; Gal 3:15–29.
156. Guardini, *Lord*, 169, which reads: "Thus the covenant founded on faith and grace, that wonderful exchange of loyalty for loyalty, of trust for divine aid, became a documented charter of rights and demands."

Exodus—The Ten Commandments:

1. *Are there really Ten Commandments?*—read *Exodus* 34:27–35[157]—renewal of the covenant. God writes the *Ten* Commandments on the tablets of stone (v. 28) (explain "horned"[158]).

2. *Exodus* 20—*what are the Ten Commandments?* There are two divisions—both Jewish in origin: one (Deuteronomy) {is} taken over by the *Greeks* and followed by Calvinists; {the} other (Exodus) {is} taken over by {the} *Latins* and followed by Lutherans.[159]

Latins—and Lutherans	Greeks (at least Origen et al.)—and Calvinists
1. Adoration of one God—no images	1. Deut. {5}:6–7—I am the Lord thy God (adoration of the one God)
	2. Deut. 8—No graven images
2. Name of God	3. Deut. 11—Name of God
3. Sabbath	4. Deut 12—The Sabbath
4. Parents	5. Deut. 16—Honor of parents
5. No murder	6. Deut. 17—Thou shalt not kill
6. No adultery	7. Deut. 18—Thou shalt not commit adultery
7. No theft	8. Deut. 19—Thou shalt not steal

157. "And the Lord said to Moses: Write these words by which I have made a covenant both with thee and with Israel. And he was there with the Lord forty days and forty nights: he neither ate bread nor drank water, and he wrote upon the tables the ten words of the covenant. And when Moses came down from the mount Sinai, he held the two tables of the testimony, and he knew not that his face was horned from the conversation of the Lord. And Aaron and the children of Israel seeing the face of Moses horned, were afraid to come near. And being called by him, they returned, both Aaron and the rulers of the congregation. And after that he spoke to them. And all the children of Israel came to him: and he gave them in commandment all that he had heard of the Lord in mount Sinai. And having done speaking, he put a veil upon his face. But when he went in to the Lord, and spoke with him, he took it away until he came forth, and then he spoke to the children of Israel all things that had been commanded him. And they saw that the face of Moses when he came out was horned, but he covered his face again, if at any time he spoke to them."

158. See Power, "Exodus," 228 [n. 181j]: "Horns are lightning flashes which accompany a theophany (Hab 3:4) and similarly here indicate not excrescences but rays of light. St Paul explains the phenomenon as meaning that the brightness of the face of Moses, produced by his intimate and prolonged intercourse with Yahweh, was unsupportable to the Israelites and had to be concealed by a veil which he only removed when he spoke with God (2 Cor 3:7)."

159. See Power, "Exodus," 218 [n. 172f-h].

8. No lying
9. No evil desires of {the} flesh
10. No evil desires for material goods

9. Deut. 20—No false witness
10. Deut. 21—No evil desires.

EXODUS 19-24—the Alliance and the Law; 32-34—the apostasy and the renewal. *Chapter 19*—READ 3-8:[160] {the} promise of {the} alliance: one can look at "exodus" as applicable to religious life: leaving Egypt = leaving the world; from Egypt to Sinai = novitiate ({the} Canticle of Moses at {the} Red Sea {is comparable to the} consolations of {the} beginning); Mara—the bitter waters—{are} sweetened by the Cross; Elim {can represent a} love of {the} Scriptures etc.; manna {can symbolize} learning to live supported directly by God. {Chapter} 17 {includes the episodes of} Massa and Meriba; 17:8 ff. {presents the} battle with Amaleck, {exemplifying the} power of prayer; the institution of judges {is an instance of} learning to share responsibility.

{According to verse} 5, *if* they obey His Law, they will be peculiarly loved as His people, *a kingdom of priests, a consecrated nation,* His own property, sacred and set apart for Him alone (*read* Deut. 7:1-24[161]—no consorting with gentiles, {being under the} special protection of Yahweh; *read* Jeremias 2:1-3[162]—this is compared to an ESPOUSAL; *read* Osee

---

160. "And Moses went up to God: and the Lord called unto him from the mountain, and said: Thus shalt thou say to the house of Jacob, and tell the children of Israel: You have seen what I have done to the Egyptians, how I have carried you upon the wings of eagles, and have taken you to myself. If therefore you will hear my voice, and keep my covenant, you shall be my peculiar possession above all people: for all the earth is mine. And you shall be to me a priestly kingdom, and a holy nation. Those are the words thou shalt speak to the children of Israel. Moses came, and calling together the elders of the people, he declared all the words which the Lord had commanded. And all the people answered together: All that the Lord hath spoken, we will do."

161. See notes 168-70 below.

162. "And the word of the Lord came to me, saying: Go, and cry in the ears of Jerusalem, saying: Thus saith the Lord: I have remembered thee, pitying thy soul, pitying thy youth, and the love of thy espousals, when thou followedst me in the desert, in a land that is not sown. Israel is holy to the Lord, the first fruits of his increase: all they that devour him offend: evils shall come upon them, saith the Lord."

11:1–9[163]—Israel {is} the unfaithful spouse, Yahweh {the} faithful {one}; 2:8–22[164]—Israel {is} the unfaithful spouse {but} *Israel will return*).

Full realization of the Alliance {is found} in the Church—in {the} New Testament the members of the Church are called saints because they belong to God (cf. {the} opening of 1 Corinthians: 1:1–3); read 1

---

163. "As the morning passeth, so hath the king of Israel passed away. Because Israel was a child, and I loved him: and I called my son out of Egypt. As they called them, they went away from before their face: they offered victims to Baalim, and sacrificed to idols. And I was like a foster father to Ephraim, I carried them in my arms: and they knew not that I healed them. I will draw them with the cords of Adam, with the bands of love: and I will be to them as one that taketh off the yoke on their jaws: and I put his meat to him that he might eat. He shall not return into the land of Egypt, but the Assyrian shall be his king: because they would not be converted. The sword hath begun in his cities, and it shall consume his chosen men, and shall devour their heads. And my people shall long for my return: but a yoke shall be put upon them together, which shall not be taken off. How shall I deal with thee, O Ephraim, shall I protect thee, O Israel? how shall I make thee as Adama, shall I set thee as Seboim? my heart is turned within me, my repentance is stirred up. I will not execute the fierceness of my wrath: I will not return to destroy Ephraim: because I am God, and not man: the holy one in the midst of thee, and I will not enter into the city."

164. "And she did not know that I gave her corn and wine, and oil, and multiplied her silver, and gold, which they have used in the service of Baal. Therefore will I return, and take away my corn in its season, and my wine in its season, and I will set at liberty my wool, and my flax, which covered her disgrace. And now I will lay open her folly in the eyes of her lovers: and no man shall deliver her out of my hand: And I will cause all her mirth to cease, her solemnities, her new moons, her sabbaths, and all her festival times. And I will destroy her vines, and her fig trees, of which she said: These are my rewards, which my lovers have given me: and I will make her as a forest, and the beasts of the field shall devour her. And I will visit upon her the days of Baalim, to whom she burnt incense, and decked herself out with her earrings, and with her jewels, and went after her lovers, and forgot me, saith the Lord. Therefore, behold I will allure her, and will lead her into the wilderness: and I will speak to her heart. And I will give her vinedressers out of the same place, and the valley of Achor for an opening of hope: and she shall sing there according to the days of her youth, and according to the days of her coming up out of the land of Egypt. And it shall be in that day, saith the Lord, That she shall call me: My husband, and she shall call me no more Baali. And I will take away the names of Baalim out of her mouth, and she shall no more remember their name. And in that day I will make a covenant with them, with the beasts of the field, and with the fowls of the air, and with the creeping things of the earth: and I will destroy the bow, and the sword, and war out of the land: and I will make them sleep secure. And I will espouse thee to me for ever: and I will espouse thee to me in justice, and judgment, and in mercy, and in commiserations. And I will espouse thee to me in faith: and thou shalt know that I am the Lord. And it shall come to pass in that day: I will hear, saith the Lord, I will hear the heavens, and they shall hear the earth. And the earth shall hear the corn, and the wine, and the oil, and these shall hear Jezrahel."

Peter 2:5–9:[165] the new People of God, built on Christ; read Apocalypse 21:1–4:[166] the Tabernacle of God with men.

Chapter 19:9–14 {presents} the necessary preparation of the people: (1) no one may touch the mountain, on pain of death; (2) all must wash their clothes and be physically clean; (3) all must abstain from contact of a sexual nature (cf. Deut. 23:10–15). The Theophany (19:16–22: read[167]).

---

165. "Be you also as living stones built up, a spiritual house, a holy priesthood, to offer up spiritual sacrifices, acceptable to God by Jesus Christ. Wherefore it is said in the scripture: Behold, I lay in Sion a chief corner stone, elect, precious. And he that shall believe in him, shall not be confounded. To you therefore that believe, he is honour: but to them that believe not, the stone which the builders rejected, the same is made the head of the corner: And a stone of stumbling, and a rock of scandal, to them who stumble at the word, neither do believe, whereunto also they are set. But you are a chosen generation, a kingly priesthood, a holy nation, a purchased people: that you may declare his virtues, who hath called you out of darkness into his marvellous light."

166. "And I saw a new heaven and a new earth. For the first heaven and the first earth was gone, and the sea is now no more. And I John saw the holy city, the new Jerusalem, coming down out of heaven from God, prepared as a bride adorned for her husband. And I heard a great voice from the throne, saying: Behold the tabernacle of God with men, and he will dwell with them. And they shall be his people; and God himself with them shall be their God. And God shall wipe away all tears from their eyes: and death shall be no more, nor mourning, nor crying, nor sorrow shall be any more, for the former things are passed away."

167. "And you shall be to me a priestly kingdom, and a holy nation. Those are the words thou shalt speak to the children of Israel. Moses came, and calling together the elders of the people, he declared all the words which the Lord had commanded. And all the people answered together: All that the Lord hath spoken, we will do. And when Moses had related the people's words to the Lord, The Lord said to him: Lo, now will I come to thee in the darkness of a cloud, that the people may hear me speaking to thee, and may believe thee for ever. And Moses told the words of the people to the Lord. And he said to him: Go to the people, and sanctify them today, and tomorrow, and let them wash their garments. And let them be ready against the third day: for on the third day the Lord will come down in the sight of all the people upon mount Sinai. And thou shalt appoint certain limits to the people round about, and thou shalt say to them: Take heed you go not up into the mount, and that ye touch not the borders thereof: every one that toucheth the mount dying he shall die. No hands shall touch him, but he shall be stoned to death, or shall be shot through with arrows: whether it be beast, or man, he shall not live. When the trumpet shall begin to sound, then let them go up into the mount. And Moses came down from the mount to the people, and sanctified them. And when they had washed their garments, He said to them: Be ready against the third day, and come not near your wives. And now the third day was come, and the morning appeared: and behold thunders began to be heard, and lightning to flash, and a very thick cloud to cover the mount, and the noise of the trumpet sounded exceeding loud, and the people that was in the camp, feared. And when Moses had brought them forth to meet God from the place of the camp, they stood at the bottom of the mount. And all mount Sinai was on a smoke: because the Lord was come down

The Law {is found in} *two* versions: Exodus 20:1-17 {and} Deuteronomy 5:6-21. {The} problem of our Scripture studies {is that} everything remains external and verbal only; {as for the} question of *realizing*, {of} understanding, this {is} not just a matter of a few catchwords—Law and alliance (what is the connection? {the} idea of marriage: see {the} texts above); {the} problem of idolatry—a problem of interior surrender or spiritual fornication. Today, {there is a link between} idolatry and neurosis, religion and magic thinking driven into {the} subconscious—{with} pathological rituals etc.—guilt complexes, scruples. Idolatry and the magic mentality {are connected}: was the idol the god, or did it *contain* him, and give power over him? {Was there an} "exchange"—{a} possession BY the idol? {The} *idol* {was a} meeting place with {the} devil (1 Cor. 10, especially 13-22; cf. Exodus 32).

The Ten Commandments—Group A {focuses on} duties to God. The first three commandments imply loving God with our whole heart, tending to Him as our last end; the next seven {are concerned with} loving {one's} neighbor as {one's} self.

1. {This commands} faith in the One God, adoration of Him alone. God alone is to be worshipped, because He alone is the true and living God—{it is directed} against {the} temptation to *idolatry*. N.B. the gravity of the temptation!! {For an} *explanation*, READ DEUTERONOMY 7:1-6[168]

---

upon it in fire, and the smoke arose from it as out of a furnace: and all the mount was terrible. And the sound of the trumpet grew by degrees louder and louder, and was drawn out to a greater length: Moses spoke, and God answered him. And the Lord came down upon mount Sinai, in the very top of the mount, and he called Moses unto the top thereof. And when he was gone up thither, He said unto him: Go down, and charge the people: lest they should have a mind to pass the limits to see the Lord, and a very great multitude of them should perish. The priests also that come to the Lord, let them be sanctified, lest he strike them."

168. "When the Lord thy God shall have brought thee into the land, which thou art going in to possess, and shall have destroyed many nations before thee, the Hethite, and the Gergezite, and the Amorrhite, and the Chanaanite, and the Pherezite, and the Hevite, and the Jebusite, seven nations much more numerous than thou art, and stronger than thou: And the Lord thy God shall have delivered them to thee, thou shalt utterly destroy them. Thou shalt make no league with them, nor shew mercy to them: Neither shalt thou make marriages with them. Thou shalt not give thy daughter to his son, nor take his daughter for thy son: For she will turn away thy son from following me, that he may rather serve strange gods, and the wrath of the Lord will be kindled, and will quickly destroy thee. But thus rather shall you deal with them: Destroy their altars, and break their statues, and cut down their groves, and burn their graven things. Because thou art a holy people to the Lord thy God. The Lord thy God hath chosen thee, to be his peculiar people of all peoples that are upon the earth."

(separation from gentiles); 7–15[169] (chosen because of Yahweh's fidelity and mercy); 17–26[170] (especially 25–26): hence {there is need for} trust and courage:

(a) Thou shalt have no other God but me—"before me" implies {the} *immediate presence of God* in His people—{there is} no need of intermediaries;

169. "Not because you surpass all nations in number, is the Lord joined unto you, and hath chosen you, for you are the fewest of any people: But because the Lord hath loved you, and hath kept his oath, which he swore to your fathers: and hath brought you out with a strong hand, and redeemed you from the house of bondage, out of the hand of Pharao the king of Egypt. And thou shalt know that the Lord thy God, he is a strong and faithful God, keeping his covenant and mercy to them that love him, and to them that keep his commandments, unto a thousand generations: And repaying forthwith them that hate him, so as to destroy them, without further delay immediately rendering to them what they deserve. Keep therefore the precepts and ceremonies and judgments, which I command thee this day to do. If after thou hast heard these judgments, thou keep and do them, the Lord thy God will also keep his covenant to thee, and the mercy which he swore to thy fathers: And he will love thee and multiply thee, and will bless the fruit of thy womb, and the fruit of thy land, thy corn, and thy vintage, thy oil, and thy herds, and the flocks of thy sheep upon the land, for which he swore to thy fathers that he would give it thee. Blessed shalt thou be among all people. No one shall be barren among you of either sex, neither of men nor cattle. The Lord will take away from thee all sickness: and the grievous infirmities of Egypt, which thou knowest, he will not bring upon thee, but upon thy enemies."

170. "If thou say in thy heart: These nations are more than I, how shall I be able to destroy them? Fear not, but remember what the Lord thy God did to Pharao and to all the Egyptians, The exceeding great plagues, which thy eyes saw, and the signs and wonders, and the strong hand, and the stretched out arm, with which the Lord thy God brought thee out: so will he do to all the people, whom thou fearest. Moreover the Lord thy God will send also hornets among them, until he destroy and consume all that have escaped thee, and could hide themselves. Thou shalt not fear them, because the Lord thy God is in the midst of thee, a God mighty and terrible: He will consume these nations in thy sight by little and little and by degrees. Thou wilt not be able to destroy them altogether: lest perhaps the beasts of the earth should increase upon thee. But the Lord thy God shall deliver them in thy sight: and shall slay them until they be utterly destroyed. And he shall deliver their kings into thy hands, and thou shalt destroy their names from under Heaven: no man shall be able to resist thee, until thou destroy them. Their graven things thou shalt burn with fire: thou shalt not covet the silver and gold of which they are made, neither shalt thou take to thee any thing thereof, lest thou offend, because it is an abomination to the Lord thy God. Neither shalt thou bring any thing of the idol into thy house, lest thou become an anathema, like it. Thou shalt detest it as dung, and shalt utterly abhor it as uncleanness and filth, because it is an anathema."

(b) {this entails the} exclusion of (1) *idolatry*—were *all* images forbidden? no[171] (cf. Exodus 25:18 ff.;[172] cf. Ezechiel 1 [{the} cherubim]; cf. *Numbers* 21 [{the} brazen serpent]; and 4 Kings 18:1–4[173]). Only images of false gods and worship of images {were banned}; {note the} *proscription of the massebah*—Canaanite phallic columns (read Exodus 23:23–26:[174] destroy the massebah); cf. {also the} *Ashera*—other fertility symbols, connected with Astarte (Exodus 34:12–17); {it is} clear how {the} first commandment is especially slanted toward dwelling in {the} Promised Land and resisting temptation to join in fertility cults *which kept man {a} prisoner of nature*. READ Deuteronomy 7:1–6—a very clear text: Israel {is} chosen and consecrated to Yahweh, {and therefore} must avoid all taint of paganism; Deuteronomy 12:2–7:[175] the *place* of worship is important—not just any place. BUT cf. in {the} New Law: Acts 7:47–53—Stephen's speech; John 4: Jesus to the Samaritan {woman}. *Teraphim* {were} household gods, also {referred to} in {the} above passages (cf. Gen. 31:34 etc.—Rachel stole Laban's "idols"). (2) necromancy—magic—divination ({cf. the} *Witch of Endor*: 1 Kings 28:7–20); (3) superstition and vain observance. {Note the oracles of the} prophets about idols: Baruch 6 ({the} Letter of Jeremiah); Isaias 44:9 ff. (see especially 25—false prophets and idols); 1 Kings 15:9 ff.—Saul's

---

171. See Power, "Exodus," 218 [n. 172i].

172. These verses relate the directive to make the two cherubim for the sanctuary.

173. Here Ezechias (Hezekiah) destroys the brazen serpent because it is being worshipped by the people.

174. "And my angel shall go before thee, and shall bring thee in unto the Amorrhite, and the Hethite, and the Pherezite, and the Chanaanite, and the Hevite, and the Jebusite, whom I will destroy. Thou shalt not adore their gods, nor serve them. Thou shalt not do their works, but shalt destroy them, and break their statues. And you shall serve the Lord your God, that I may bless your bread and your waters, and may take away sickness from the midst of thee. There shall not be one fruitless nor barren in thy land: I will fill the number of thy days."

175. "Destroy all the places in which the nations, that you shall possess, worshipped their gods upon high mountains, and hills, and under every shady tree: Overthrow their altars, and break down their statues, burn their groves with fire, and break their idols in pieces: destroy their names out of those places. You shall not do so to the Lord your God: But you shall come to the place, which the Lord your God shall choose out of all your tribes, to put his name there, and to dwell in it: And you shall offer in that place your holocausts and victims, the tithes and firstfruits of your hands and your vows and gifts, the firstborn of your herds and your sheep. And you shall eat there in the sight of the Lord your God: and you shall rejoice in all things, whereunto you shall put your hand, you and your houses wherein the Lord your God hath blessed you."

unacceptable sacrifice (especially 22–23); his mentality {is such that} *he serves Yahweh as one would serve an idol*—as one god among many; Saul does not understand that obedience is sacrifice because it testifies to {the} divine supremacy of Yahweh. *How about images in the New Law?*

(c) {there is a} duty to believe in God's word and trust in Him alone—His FIDELITY {is the} supreme reason for abandoning false gods that can do nothing; {they are called} to trust in God's mercy {and} *above all* {*in His*} *love*: READ Deuteronomy 6:4–13;[176] READ Deuteronomy 10:12—11:1;[177] n.b. 6:13 {is} quoted by Jesus in {His} time in {the}

---

176. "Hear, O Israel, the Lord our God is one Lord. Thou shalt love the Lord thy God with thy whole heart, and with thy whole soul, and with thy whole strength. And these words which I command thee this day, shall be in thy heart: And thou shalt tell them to thy children, and thou shalt meditate upon them sitting in thy house, and walking on thy journey, sleeping and rising. And thou shalt bind them as a sign on thy hand, and they shall be and shall move between thy eyes. And thou shalt write them in the entry, and on the doors of thy house. And when the Lord thy God shall have brought thee into the land, for which he swore to thy fathers Abraham, Isaac, and Jacob: and shall have given thee great and goodly cities, which thou didst not build, Houses full of riches, which thou didst not set up, cisterns which thou didst not dig, vineyards and oliveyards, which thou didst not plant, And thou shalt have eaten and be full: Take heed diligently lest thou forget the Lord, who brought thee out of the land of Egypt, out of the house of bondage. Thou shalt fear the Lord thy God, and shalt serve him only, and thou shalt swear by his name."

177. "And now, Israel, what doth the Lord thy God require of thee, but that thou fear the Lord thy God, and walk in his ways, and love him, and serve the Lord thy God, with all thy heart, and with all thy soul: And keep the commandments of the Lord, and his ceremonies, which I command thee this day, that it may be well with thee? Behold heaven is the Lord's thy God, and the heaven of heaven, the earth and all things that are therein. And yet the Lord hath been closely joined to thy fathers, and loved them and chose their seed after them, that is to say, you, out of all nations, as this day it is proved. Circumcise therefore the foreskin of your heart, and stiffen your neck no more. Because the Lord your God he is the God of gods, and the Lord of lords, a great God and mighty and terrible, who accepteth no person nor taketh bribes. He doth judgment to the fatherless and the widow, loveth the stranger, and giveth him food and raiment. And do you therefore love strangers, because you also were strangers in the land of Egypt. Thou shalt fear the Lord thy God, and serve him only: to him thou shalt adhere, and shalt swear by his name. He is thy praise, and thy God, that hath done for thee these great and terrible things, which thy eyes have seen. In seventy souls thy fathers went down into Egypt: and behold now the Lord thy God hath multiplied thee as the stars of heaven. Therefore love the Lord thy God and observe his precepts and ceremonies, his judgments and commandments at all times."

desert; {in relation to} 10:20, read Matt 4:8–11[178]—the world as {an} "idol"—{worship of} POWER.

(d) {for the} sins of Israel against {the} first commandment, cf. Amos 5:25 etc.; Exodus 32 (above).

{The} Second Commandment—read Exodus 20:7:[179] Thou shalt not take the Name of the Lord thy God in vain ("Tu ne prononceras pas le nom de Yahvé ton Dieu *à faux*" [*BJ*][180]); cf. Deuteronomy 5:11; Leviticus 19:12: "Thou shalt not swear falsely by my Name, nor profane the Name of thy God. I am the Lord"; Deuteronomy 6:13 and 10:20: "Thou shalt fear the Lord . . . and *swear by His Name*." {Note the} *paradox*—the inadequacy of any Name for God, but the fact that His Name really represents His Nature, His true identity. {The} Bible stresses the fact that *words are not to be treated as meaningless* (n.b. semantics); {there is a} mystique of the "word"—God's word denotes His will (*Dixit et facta sunt*[181]). Our words for things try to grasp and identify His will as expressed in that thing: "That is a tree"—God speaks the tree; we bear witness to the tree existing—our witness is a reflection of God's creative act. N.B. {the} Indians {recognize the} *power* of words[182]—to know {the} name of a thing {as} more than its "essence"—{there is an} existential confrontation, {a} "dialogue" with creatures: cf. the snake ({the} resonance of legends;[183]

---

178. "Again the devil took him up into a very high mountain, and shewed him all the kingdoms of the world, and the glory of them, And said to him: All these will I give thee, if falling down thou wilt adore me. Then Jesus saith to him: Begone, Satan: for it is written, The Lord thy God shalt thou adore, and him only shalt thou serve. Then the devil left him; and behold angels came and ministered to him."

179. "Thou shalt not take the name of the Lord thy God in vain: for the Lord will not hold him guiltless that shall take the name of the Lord his God in vain."

180. *Sainte Bible*, 82.

181. "For he spoke and they were made" (Ps 32[33]:9).

182. See "Power of the Word" in Astrov, ed., *Winged Serpent*, 19–52.

183. "The snake in North American mythology is usually associated not only with sky and water, rainbow, stars, and lightning, but also with the powers of the underworld, with night, destruction, and renewal. The serpent is conceived as a power that rules life as well as death. The origin myth of the southern Diegueño, for instance, tells how song came into being. After Tcikumat, the creator, had died, Wild Cat took charge of the cremation ceremonies. He ordered an enclosure to be built of wood, then he sent for Mattiawit, the mythical snake. He came. And he coiled his length around the pyre upon which the remains of the god were to be burned. Then fire was set to the structure. The serpent, amid the leaping flames, burst asunder—'part flew back to the place he had come from, the rest burst into fragments. Each piece that flew off to the people was a song. Each gens received a song. . . .' The serpent had come from the

{the} *power of silence*—read[184]). {There is a} mystique of the Name—the mystery of our own identity, in itself inexpressible but expressed to some extent by our "name" (cf. {the} Sacred Heart). God's Name makes Him present in a special way. How? {when it is} invoked, we confront Him and He us—{He is} *present as* {a} *witness of our act*. {The} Name of God and {a} sense of {the} presence of God {are connected}. Compare St. Benedict's first degree of humility[185] and the constant "absence" of God in the words of the blasphemer, which make Him present without thinking of Him—{the intrinsic} relation of God's Name to the respect for truth itself. To invoke God falsely {is} *to make oneself* {*the*} *ultimate criterion of truth and falsity in His place*. READ Matt. 5:33 ff.[186] {Its} *basic meaning* {is the} understanding of and respect for the presence of God. This excludes magic incantation {by which the} power of God {is} debased {and} becomes our means; {it also excludes} blasphemy {and} thoughtless and silly oaths ({note the} difference {between} blasphemy and cursing). READ Deuteronomy 12:1-14,[187] especially {verse} 3: destroy the

---

underworld, the realm of death, and, dying, he created song for man" ("Power of the Word" in Astrov, ed., *Winged Serpent*, 50-51).

184. "Wherever the word is revered as a tool around which still vibrates the magic halo of primeval creation, there silence, too, is esteemed a reservoir of spiritual strength. Wherever the value of the word deteriorated, turning into a cheap weapon and an easy coin, the intrinsic meaning of silence was also lost. We, indeed, live in a period of an alarming inflation of the word, and nothing is more symptomatic of it, than our aversion to silence and quietude that amounts to phobia. A mother of our civilization is deeply worried when her child prefers the ways of solitude and reticent seclusion. The attitude of the Indian toward the various forms of solitude and silence is altogether different, and the education in quietude and reticence are crucial parts of the child's training" ("Power of the Word" in Astrov, ed., *Winged Serpent*, 39).

185. "*Aestimet se homo de caelis a Deo respici omni hora, et facta sua omni loco ab aspectu Divinitatis videri*" / "Let him consider that God is always beholding him from heaven, that his actions are everywhere visible to the eye of the Godhead" (McCann, trans. and ed., *Rule* 38/39); see Merton's commentary on this line in Merton, *Rule of St. Benedict*, 176-77.

186. "Again you have heard that it was said to them of old, Thou shalt not forswear thyself: but thou shalt perform thy oaths to the Lord. But I say to you not to swear at all, neither by heaven, for it is the throne of God: Nor by the earth, for it is his footstool: nor by Jerusalem, for it is the city of the great king: Neither shalt thou swear by thy head, because thou canst not make one hair white or black. But let your speech be yea, yea: no, no: and that which is over and above these, is of evil" (vv. 33-37).

187. "These are the precepts and judgments, that you must do in the land, which the Lord the God of thy fathers will give thee, to possess it all the days that thou shalt walk upon the earth. Destroy all the places in which the nations, that you shall possess, worshipped their gods upon high mountains, and hills, and under every shady tree:

"names" of the idols; {and verses} 5, 11: the Name of the Lord dwells in special places and there sacrifice will be offered ({cf.} Jeremias 7:3–15: though the Name of God dwells in the Temple, it is useless to confide in the Temple if one's works do not correspond to a fear of God's name). {The} *Name of Yahweh* signifies separate attributes: v.g. justice (*Nomen Dei venit de longinquo* [Isa. 30:27][188]), might and mercy (Prov. 18:10; Ps. 19:2). N.B. {the} first positive obligation {is} to *praise the Name of God* by confessing Him before men, especially by confessing Christ our Savior, {and} by loving His word and meditating on it and seeking to do His will, {by} thanking Him in all things; {by reciting the} divine praises in choir ({as} reparation for infidelity and blasphemy).

{The} Third Commandment: *the Sabbath*: (1) work {is} not an end—{we should} never lose ourselves in work—we are not created for this world but for God; (2) God has a full and complete right to *all* our time (Paradise); (3) ETERNITY. READ Exodus 20:8–11;[189] Deuteronomy

---

Overthrow their altars, and break down their statues, burn their groves with fire, and break their idols in pieces: destroy their names out of those places. You shall not do so to the Lord your God: But you shall come to the place, which the Lord your God shall choose out of all your tribes, to put his name there, and to dwell in it: And you shall offer in that place your holocausts and victims, the tithes and firstfruits of your hands and your vows and gifts, the firstborn of your herds and your sheep. And you shall eat there in the sight of the Lord your God: and you shall rejoice in all things, whereunto you shall put your hand, you and your houses wherein the Lord your God hath blessed you. You shall not do there the things we do here this day, every man that which seemeth good to himself. For until this present time you are not come to rest, and to the possession, which the Lord your God will give you. You shall pass over the Jordan, and shall dwell in the land which the Lord your God will give you, that you may have rest from all enemies round about: and may dwell without any fear, In the place, which the Lord your God shall choose, that his name may be therein. Thither shall you bring all the things that I command you, holocausts, and victims, and tithes, and the firstfruits of your hands: and whatsoever is the choicest in the gifts which you shall vow to the Lord. There shall you feast before the Lord your God, you and your sons and your daughters, your menservants and maidservants, and the Levite that dwelleth in your cities. For he hath no other part and possession among you. Beware lest thou offer thy holocausts in every place that thou shalt see: But in the place which the Lord shall choose in one of thy tribes shalt thou offer sacrifices. and shalt do all that I command thee."

188. "The name of the Lord cometh from afar."

189. "Remember that thou keep holy the sabbath day. Six days shalt thou labour, and shalt do all thy works. But on the seventh day is the sabbath of the Lord thy God: thou shalt do no work on it, thou nor thy son, nor thy daughter, nor thy manservant, nor thy maidservant, nor thy beast, nor the stranger that is within thy gates. For in six days the Lord made heaven and earth, and the sea, and all things that are in them, and rested on the seventh day: therefore the Lord blessed the seventh day, and sanctified it."

5:12–15:[190] (1) The Sabbath is a day "for God" and not for our own works. (2) It is a day of rest for all, man and beast. Rest here really means *repose and leisure*—relaxation—*liberty* from pressing obligations and not a fresh and heavier obligation—people do not always know how to rest—{it is} *positive* not *negative*—a very lofty ideal that reaches into {the} inmost essence of man's vocation. (3) Exodus gives {the} reason {in relation to} creation—God's rest on {the} seventh day; Deuteronomy gives {the} reason {in relation to} the liberation from Egypt:[191] Pharaoh {was} a hard master; God {is} a liberator ({there is a} Pharaoh within us—{we must} not fall back into his power). (4) Hence this day is blessed by God and consecrated.

Developments of {the} Law of {the} Sabbath: READ Exodus 23:9–12[192]—{the} *Sabbath of years*; Leviticus 23:1–22[193] (especially 15–16)—

---

190. "Observe the day of the sabbath, to sanctify it, as the Lord thy God hath commanded thee. Six days shalt thou labour, and shalt do all thy works. The seventh is the day of the sabbath, that is, the rest of the Lord thy God. Thou shalt not do any work therein, thou nor thy son nor thy daughter, nor thy manservant nor thy maidservant, nor thy ox, nor thy ass, nor any of thy beasts, nor the stranger that is within thy gates: that thy manservant and thy maidservant may rest, even as thyself. Remember that thou also didst serve in Egypt, and the Lord thy God brought thee out from thence with a strong hand, and a stretched out arm. Therefore hath he commanded thee that thou shouldst observe the sabbath day."

191. See Power, "Exodus," 219 [n. 172b].

192. "Thou shalt not molest a stranger, for you know the hearts of strangers: for you also were strangers in the land of Egypt. Six years thou shalt sow thy ground, and shalt gather the corn thereof. But the seventh year thou shalt let it alone, and suffer it to rest, that the poor of thy people may eat, and whatsoever shall be left, let the beasts of the field eat it: so shalt thou do with thy vineyard and thy oliveyard. Six days thou shalt work: the seventh day thou shalt cease, that thy ox and thy ass may rest: and the son of thy handmaid and the stranger may be refreshed."

193. "And the Lord spoke to Moses, saying: Speak to the children of Israel, and thou shalt say to them: These are the feasts of the Lord, which you shall call holy. Six days shall ye do work: the seventh day, because it is the rest of the sabbath, shall be called holy. You shall do no work on that day: it is the sabbath of the Lord in all your habitations. These also are the holy days of the Lord, which you must celebrate in their seasons. The first month, the fourteenth day of the month at evening, is the phase of the Lord: And the fifteenth day of the same month is the solemnity of the unleavened bread of the Lord. Seven days shall you eat unleavened bread. The first day shall be most solemn unto you, and holy: you shall do no servile work therein: But you shall offer sacrifice in fire to the Lord seven days. And the seventh day shall be more solemn, and more holy: and you shall do no servile work therein. And the Lord spoke to Moses, saying: Speak to the children of Israel, and thou shalt say to them: When you shall have entered into the land which I will give you, and shall reap your corn, you shall bring sheaves of ears, the firstfruits of your harvest to the priest: Who shall lift up the

Pentecost—the sacred fifty days ({the} *sabbath of weeks*); {the} feast of unleavened bread {comes} at {the} beginning of {the} barley harvest; {the} feast of Pentecost at {the} end of {the} wheat harvest. {The} *Sabbath* {foreshadows the} messianic reign of peace (cf. Ezech 39:9 etc.—burn weapons {every} seven years; Isaias 60:15-22, 65:16-25). N.B. {the} care of {the} poor—*tithe every third year* for {the} poor (Deut. 14:28–29). The *Poor* and the *Sabbath* {contains a} deep mystery—{the} Sabbath {is} connected with {the} idea of freedom, economic independence, mercy and charity. Read Deut 15:1–18:[194] (a) *Deuteronomy 15* {presents} the year of

---

sheaf before the Lord, the next day after the sabbath, that it may be acceptable for you, and shall sanctify it. And on the same day that the sheaf is consecrated, a lamb without blemish of the first year shall be killed for a holocaust of the Lord. And the libations shall be offered with it, two tenths of flour tempered with oil for a burnt offering of the Lord, and a most sweet odour: libations also of wine, the fourth part of a hin. You shall not eat either bread, or parched corn, or frumenty of the harvest, until the day that you shall offer thereof to your God. It is a precept for ever throughout your generations, and all your dwellings. You shall count therefore from the morrow after the sabbath, wherein you offered the sheaf of the firstfruits, seven full weeks. Even unto the morrow after the seventh week be expired, that is to say, fifty days, and so you shall offer a new sacrifice to the Lord. Out of all your dwellings, two leaves of the firstfruits, of two tenths of flour leavened, which you shall bake for the firstfruits of the Lord. And you shall offer with the leaves seven lambs without blemish of the first year, and one calf from the herd, and two rams, and they shall be for a holocaust with their libations for a most sweet odour to the Lord. You shall offer also a buck goat for sin, and two lambs of the first year for sacrifices of peace offerings. And when the priest hath lifted them up with the leaves of the firstfruits before the Lord, they shall fall to his use. And you shall call this day most solemn, and most holy. You shall do no servile work therein. It shall be an everlasting ordinance in all your dwellings and generations. And when you reap the corn of your land, you shall not cut it to the very ground: neither shall you gather the ears that remain; but you shall leave them for the poor and for the strangers. I am the Lord your God."

194. "In the seventh year thou shalt make a remission, Which shall be celebrated in this order. He to whom any thing is owing from his friend or neighbour or brother, cannot demand it again, because it is the year of remission of the Lord, Of the foreigner or stranger thou mayst exact it: of thy countryman and neighbour thou shalt not have power to demand it again. And there shall be no poor nor beggar among you: that the Lord thy God may bless thee in the land which he will give thee in possession. Yet so if thou hear the voice of the Lord thy God, and keep all things that he hath ordained, and which I command thee this day, he will bless thee, as he hath promised. Thou shalt lend to many nations, and thou shalt borrow of no man. Thou shalt have dominion over very many nations, and no one shall have dominion over thee. If one of thy brethren that dwelleth within the gates of thy city in the land which the Lord thy God will give thee, come to poverty: thou shalt not harden thy heart, nor close thy hand, But shalt open it to the poor man, thou shalt lend him, that which thou perceivest he hath need of. Beware lest perhaps a wicked thought steal in upon thee,

remission ({every} seventh year); {for the} *reason* see verse 4: "There shall be no poor among you"—i.e. no permanent poor class, no underprivileged; {see} *verse 11: there will always be those temporarily in need*. (b) *Leviticus* 25 {describes} (1) {the} sabbatical year of rest for the *land* (vv. 1-7); (2) the fiftieth year—{the} Jubilee (vv. 8 ff.); (3) *the land shall not be sold*—part of this mystery (v. 23-43). N.B. care of the poor {is shown by the} tithe every third year for {the} poor (Deut. 14:2-29).

{The} *Sabbath in* {the} *New Testament* {is likewise important}. {With regard to the} exodus {see} 1 Corinthians {10} ({the} epistle {for the} Ninth Sunday after Pentecost[195]): {verse} 2: all our fathers were *baptized* in the cloud and in the sea—ergo {it is a} figure of baptism; {verse} 6: all these things happened for *a figure to us*, that we should not covet evil things as they did. What follows is a résumé of the prevarications of Israel in the desert: (1) *evil desire*—tempting God (see Psalm 105:14; Exodus 17:1-7); (2) {verse} 7, {on} *idolatry*, refers expressly to *Exodus* 32—READ to v. 28[196] (cf. 1 Cor. 10, v. 8); n.b. {verse} 25—{it is} not that they were

---

and thou say in thy heart: The seventh year of remission draweth nigh; and thou turn away thy eyes from thy poor brother, denying to lend him that which he asketh: lest he cry against thee to the Lord, and it become a sin unto thee. But thou shalt give to him: neither shalt thou do any thing craftily in relieving his necessities: that the Lord thy God may bless thee at all times, and in all things to which thou shalt put thy hand. There will not be wanting poor in the land of thy habitation: therefore I command thee to open thy hand to thy needy and poor brother, that liveth in the land. When thy brother a Hebrew man, or Hebrew woman is sold to thee, and hath served thee six years, in the seventh year thou shalt let him go free: And when thou sendest him out free, thou shalt not let him go away empty: But shalt give him for his way out of thy flocks, and out of thy barnfloor, and thy winepress, wherewith the Lord thy God shall bless thee. Remember that thou also wast a bondservant in the land of Egypt, and the Lord thy God made thee free, and therefore I now command thee this. But if he say: I will not depart: because he loveth thee, and thy house, and findeth that he is well with thee: Thou shalt take an awl, and bore through his ear in the door of thy house, and he shall serve thee for ever: thou shalt do in like manner to thy womanservant also. Turn not away thy eyes from them when thou makest them free: because he hath served thee six years according to the wages of a hireling: that the Lord thy God may bless thee in all the works that thou dost."

195. 1 Cor 10:6-13 (*Missale Romanum*, 412-13; *Missale Cisterciense*, 290) (copy text reads: "1 Corinthians 6").

196. "And the Lord spoke to Moses, saying: Go, get thee down: thy people, which thou hast brought out of the land of Egypt, hath sinned. They have quickly strayed from the way which thou didst shew them: and they have made to themselves a molten calf, and have adored it, and sacrificing victims to it, have said: These are thy gods, O Israel, that have brought thee out of the land of Egypt. And again the Lord said to Moses: See that this people is stiffnecked: Let me alone, that my wrath may be kindled

naked—they had "broken loose" into idolatry (however, see verse 8 {and} 1 Cor. 2); {verse} 8 {speaks of} fornication (cf. also Numbers 25:1-9; cf. Psalm 105:28-30); (3) *neque tentemus Christum*[197] ({see} Numbers 21:9: murmuring; the fiery serpents; the Destroyer: Numbers 14:1-24, 36-45)—cf. {the} need of courage and humility to enter {the} Promised Land; all these things {were} written for our instruction, living in the last times: (a) let he who stands take heed lest he fall; {there must be} humility, dependence on grace, *not contemning others* lest we fall into {the} same fault; (b) {there is} no temptation "save that which is human"[198] (some

---

against them, and that I may destroy them, and I will make of thee a great nation. But Moses besought the Lord his God, saying: Why, O Lord, is thy indignation kindled against thy people, whom thou hast brought out of the land of Egypt, with great power, and with a mighty hand? Let not the Egyptians say, I beseech thee: He craftily brought them out, that he might kill them in the mountains, and destroy them from the earth: let thy anger cease, and be appeased upon the wickedness of thy people. Remember Abraham, Isaac, and Israel, thy servants, to whom thou sworest by thy own self, saying: I will multiply your seed as the stars of heaven: and this whole land that I have spoken of, I will give to you seed, and you shall possess it for ever. And the Lord was appeased from doing the evil which he had spoken against his people. And Moses returned from the mount, carrying the two tables of the testimony in his hand, written on both sides, And made by the work of God: the writing also of God was graven in the tables. And Josue hearing the noise of the people shouting, said to Moses: The noise of battle is heard in the camp. But he answered: It is not the cry of men encouraging to fight, nor the shout of men compelling to flee: but I hear the voice of singers. And when he came nigh to the camp, he saw the calf, and the dances: and being very angry, he threw the tables out of his hand, and broke them at the foot of the mount: And laying hold of the calf which they had made, he burnt it, and beat it to powder, which he strowed into water, and gave thereof to the children of Israel to drink. And he said to Aaron: What has this people done to thee, that thou shouldst bring upon them a most heinous sin? And he answered him: Let not my lord be offended: for thou knowest this people, that they are prone to evil. They said to me: Make us gods, that may go before us: for as to this Moses, who brought us forth out of the land of Egypt, we know not what is befallen him. And I said to them: Which of you hath any gold? and they took and brought it to me: and I cast it into the fire, and this calf came out. And when Moses saw that the people were naked, (for Aaron had stripped them by occasion of the shame of the filth, and had set them naked among their enemies,) Then standing in the gate of the camp, he said: If any man be on the Lord's side let him join with me. And all the sons of Levi gathered themselves together unto him: And he said to them: Thus saith the Lord God of Israel: Put every man his sword upon his thigh: go, and return from gate to gate through the midst of the camp, and let every man kill his brother, and friend, and neighbour. And the sons of Levi did according to the words of Moses, and there were slain that day about three and twenty thousand men."

197. "Neither let us tempt Christ: [as some of them tempted, and perished by the serpents]" (1 Cor 10:9).

198. 1 Cor 10:13.

texts {translate}: no trial has come upon you but the normal ordinary ones of men); (c) *God will provide* (N.B. the context—after {verse} 14: {the} question of scandal[199]).

The Spiritual Sabbath—from St. Ailred's *Speculum Caritatis*.[200] St. Ailred wrote {the} *Speculum* as novice master at Revesby.[201] {The} general outline: Book I[202]—"The Excellence of Charity"[203]—{focuses on} the love of God; man {is created in} God's image; {the divine} likeness {was} lost by sin and restored by charity; {the} problem of free will and grace {is considered} (cf. St. Bernard[204]); *all things seek rest* ({the} "*Sabbath*") *in God*—rest {is} not found in worldly *friendship* (why does he take this first?[205]), not found in bodily *pleasure* nor worldly *power*; true rest {is found} in charity; {the} problem—struggle and labor in monastic life; this labor comes from {the} burden of worldliness, {the} self that is in us, not from charity. Book II[206] expands this question of *labor* and *requies*—*labor* arises from *cupiditas*,[207] *requies* from *caritas*[208]—{the} problem {is that} of dryness and temptation in {a} hard life. Then {he discusses} *the graces of prayer*—{the} three kinds of "compunction"—*timor, consolatio, dilectio*;[209] the dialogue with the novice {follows} (cc. 17–20;[210] N.B. {the}

---

199. I.e. the question of eating food sacrificed to idols (vv. 14–33).

200. Migne, *PL* 195, cols. 503A–620D.

201. In fact Ailred (Aelred) wrote the *Speculum* while he was novice master at the Abbey of Rievaulx in 1142–43; in the latter year he became the founding abbot of the daughter house of Revesby, returning to Rievaulx as abbot in 1147; see Merton, *Cistercian Fathers and Forefathers*, 298, 306-7 for the correct information.

202. Migne, *PL* 195, cols. 505A–546C.

203. "*charitatis excellentiam*" (Migne, *PL* 195, col. 505A).

204. See St. Bernard, *De Gratia et Libero Arbitrio* (Migne, *PL* 182, cols. 1001A–1030A).

205. Merton is apparently calling attention to Aelred's most famous work, *On Spiritual Friendship* (*De Spirituali Amicitia* [Migne, *PL* 195, cols. 659A–702B]), which was written after the *Speculum*.

206. Migne, *PL* 195, cols. 545D–576C.

207. See Book 2, c. 4: "*Quod a triplici concupiscentia omnis labor interior oriatur*" (Migne, *PL* 195, col. 549AC) ("That all inner labor arises from a triple concupiscence").

208. "*Inveniemus requiem animabus nostris . . . in dulcedine charitatis [Sabbatum] aeternum et spirituale*" (2.26 [Migne, *PL* 195, col. 576C]) ("We will find rest for our souls, an eternal and spiritual Sabbath, in the sweetness of charity").

209. See Book 2, c. 12: "*Quod in prima visitatione specialiter timor, in secunda consolatio, in tertia sit dilectio*" (Migne, *PL* 195, cols. 556C–557B) ("That fear is particularly present in the first visitation, consolation in the second, love in the third").

210. Migne, *PL* 195, cols. 561D–570A.

final chapter on Cistercian simplicity etc.[211]). Book III[212] {presents a} formal discussion of the *three Sabbaths* (cc. 1–6),[213] {with} technical details on charity {and the} psychology of love: *electio, motus, fructus*;[214] {the} ordo *caritatis*[215] {and the} different kinds of love. {Is there} fruition in this life? How? to what extent?

Ancient Peoples of {the} Palestine Area: (1) *Rephaim* (*Stone Age*)—the "giants," {the} Nephilaim of Genesis; oldest inhabitants {of the land, who} came {in the} mid-stone age; {they} leave cyclopean dolmens etc. (Gen. 6:1-4; Num. 13:33, Deut. 2:10, 20) (oldest type of fossil man—in Galilee). (2) *Canaanites* (*Bronze Age*) came {in the} early bronze age (3000 B.C.)—Semites {of} southern origin, from {the} borders of {the} Red Sea; {they} became navigators {and were the} ancestors of {the} Phoenicians. (3) *Amorrhites* (Bronze Age) {were} closely related to {the} above—*Semites* {who} were there in {the} time of Abraham (Gen. 14:13); {they} lived in {the} highlands and Transjordania. (4) *Hittites* (Bronze Age): {their} empire {lasted} ca. 1500–1200 B.C.; {they} had Hebron in Genesis 23—{a} non-Semitic {people}. (5) *Hurrites* (*Middle Bronze Age*—{the} time of Abraham) {were} non-Semitic ({the name} means cave men in Hebrew); {they} formed part of the Hyksos; intermingled with {the} Edomites {and} formed {the} Amalekites, Gabaonites {and} Pherezites. (6) *Aramaeans* {were} Semites from Mesopotamia, centered around *Haran*, {and included the} Edomites, Moabites {and} Ammonites; {they} took over Palestine after {the} Hittites and Horrites. (7) *Philistines* (*Iron Age*) invaded {the} coast and {were} held back by Egypt in {the} late bronze {and} early iron age; {they came} from {the} Aegean seacoast {and} gave {their} name to Palestine; {they} had {a} monopoly of iron until {the} time of Saul.

---

211. C. 26 (Migne, *PL* 195, cols. 574C–576C).

212. Migne, *PL* 195, cols. 575D–620D.

213. Migne, *PL* 195, cols. 575D–583D.

214. See Book 3, c. 8: "*Quomodo in electione, in motu, in fructu, amoris rectus usus constet, sive perversus*" (Migne, *PL* 195, cols. 584B–585B) ("How the right or wrong use of love depends on the choice, the movement and the enjoyment").

215. "the ordering of charity" (a traditional term not actually used by Aelred here, drawn from Song 2:4: "*Ordinavit in me caritatem*"; on this theme in St. Bernard, see Merton, *Cistercian Fathers and Their Monastic Theology*, Appendix V: "*Ordinavit in me Caritatem*" [338–55]).

LEVITICUS[216] {is} the book of the Levites' duties. Exodus takes us down to {the} erection of {the} Tabernacle. But what do they do *in* the Tabernacle? {They perform} the Hebrew *ritual*. Based on the vocation to be the People of God ({as} described in Exodus), {this book} shows the Jews how they are to live as the ones chosen by a God Who is infinitely transcendent and Who yet lives in their midst. Two main aspects of {the} cult {are described}: (1) *sacrificial worship*, due to God as transcendent {and} signifying obedience and total dedication; (2) *holiness of life*, due to God as present among them. *Outline of {the} Book*—{it is a} collection of miscellaneous rites and laws: {in chapters} 1–7 the focus {is on the practices} of sacrifice; {chapters} 8–9–10 {describe the} ordination of Aaron and his sons {and} the need for priestly sanctity (10); {chapters} 11–15 {explain} cleanness and uncleanness {with the rites of} ritual purification; {chapter} 16 {focuses on} the Day of Atonement; {chapters} 17–27 {consist in} the Law of holiness (various precepts and punishments)— n.b. especially {chapters} 25 ff.: the Sabbatical year and Jubilee year; {see} also {chapter} 26—{a} hortatory speech.

---

216. See Saydon, "Leviticus," 229 [n. 182b-e].

Textual Notes

1   NOTES ... 1957] *handwritten title page*
    salvation, creates] *preceded by x'd out* His
    summarized] *preceded by x'd out* may have
    edited] *preceded by x'd out* order
4   man to multiply] man *interlined above cancelled* all beings
    In connection ... te creavit] *opposite page*
    Psalm 135] 5 *interlined above cancelled* 6
5   cf. Dan.13] *added on line*
6   Evidently ... grown.] *opposite page*
    Two points ... of speech)] *interlined*
    Read Ezech. 31:8 ff.] *added in left margin*
    Read Daniel 4] *added in left margin*
7   Ecclesiasticus 24] *followed by x'd out* Note how the description of the trees and is vers of Paradise is referred directly to God's wisdom, in Ecclesiasticus 24, 25 etc.
    cf. Proverbs 3:18] *added on line*
    read Eccli. 24:17–32] Go on then to read verses 35–37 words of wisdom *added in left margin and cancelled*
8   Note: *Paradise ... Our Lady*] *opposite page*
9   read vv. 16–17 ... for man] *interlined*
10 the privilege of being] *interlined with a caret above cancelled* to be formed] *interlined above cancelled* led
11 goes out ... pleasure"] *interlined and marked for insertion*
11–12 Here read ... realities?] *interlined*
12 *The Creation of Eve:*] *interlined preceded by* In my opinion Paradise was God's creation *in a spiritual mode*, filled with His wisdom + manifesting his love, a "spiritual world" in which Adam lived in union with God, all things sanctified through this union. Adam

fell not only from a mystical condition subjectively, but from an objective mystical realm—not entirely united to any place, nor outside space and time either. This mystical paradise continues to exist – not exactly in a geographical location, not in heaven either. A "spiritual place" to which we do not have access. *on opposite page and cancelled*

Trappists . . . of language.] *interlined*
and of the Divine . . . Trinity] *added on line*

13   the whole] *preceded by x'd out* so mu
The Fall . . . consequences] *altered from* The Fall . . . consequences
denies] *preceded by x'd out* and
The work] *preceded by x'd out* He promi
to divide] *altered from* to divide
opinion and now] *followed by x'd out* at

14   these futile] *preceded by x'd out* an
In Him] *preceded by x'd out* What is
attractiveness.] *followed by x'd out* She sees that
Delightful] *typed interlined above x'd out* desirable
their propensity] *preceded by x'd out* the

15   not naked, and] *preceded by x'd out* naked
clothing] *altered from* clothes
a source of ambivalence] *added on line*
man by virtue] man *interlined above cancelled* him

16   in himself] *altered from* in himself
outside himself] *altered from* outside himself
something to be feared . . . security] *added on line*
within himself] *altered from* within himself
become hostile] *preceded by x'd out* been
above . . . within] *altered from* above . . . within
Creation is] *interlined above x'd out* Paradise
Creation is . . . from Him] *altered from* Creation is . . . from Him
the goodness of] *preceded by x'd out* "good

17   He takes] *preceded by x'd out* He takes the part

18   Eden, in which] *followed by x'd out* no lon
doubt other] *preceded by x'd out* small sins committed
now breaks] now *interlined with a caret*
itself definitively] *followed by x'd out* in

The custom] *preceded by x'd out* How an
His name] *preceded by x'd out* Here begins a
struggle] *preceded by x'd out* twofold
days] *added on line*

19 However, . . . special love.] *interlined*
    Cain's sin] *altered from* Cain's sin
    no pause, . . . into the field] *interlined*
20 business."] *followed by x'd out* As if
21 blood of Abel] *followed by x'd out* the Just
23 compare . . . seed"] *interlined and marked for insertion*
    praising himself] *added on line*
24 *Ethiopic Henoch*] *altered from* Ethiopic Henoch
25 i.e. the Messias] *interlined and marked for insertion*
    he shall . . . their hearts] *altered from* he shall . . . their hearts
    Slavonic Henoch] *altered from* Slavonic Henoch
27 more exactly. . . roof] *interlined and marked for insertion*
    Read 7:1–6] *added in left margin*
28 read here Wisdom . . . cometh"] *added on line*
    Read ch. 7:7 ff.] *added in left margin*
    read 11–16] *added in left margin*
    solemnity of verses 11–16] 16 *altered from* 15
29 16: And] 16 *added on line*
    the outside.] *preceded by x'd out* without
    the chaos has returned] *altered from* the chaos has returned
    all life . . . the ark] *altered from* all life . . . the ark
    abandoned . . . darkness] *altered from* abandoned . . . darkness
    What is . . . taught?] *added in lower margin*
    24: the . . . days] *interlined*
    verse 13] *added in left margin*
30 8:20–22] *added in left margin*
    the most . . . sacrifice] *altered from* the most . . . sacrifice
    Verse 21] *added in left margin*
    remain] *preceded by x'd out* emerge, man
    Hence] *preceded by x'd out* An interesting application
31 a gentle love for] *followed by x'd out* anima
    recedes,] *followed by x'd out* man
    Other Books] *preceded by x'd out* New Testament

TEXTUAL NOTES

32 As in ... not yet] *added in left margin*
to the Gentiles ... Church] *interlined and marked for insertion*
speaking to Gentiles] Gentiles *interlined above cancelled* Israel
Danel ... sage] *added typed in left margin*

33 read Luke 17:22–37] *added in lower margin*
these souls,] *followed by x'd out* sufficiently

34 some were] *interlined with a caret*
he was made] he *interlined above cancelled* and
see 9:22–25 ... by Noe] *added in upper margin and marked for insertion*

34–35 St. Augustine ... in Sion)] *opposite page*

35 especially Ninive.] *followed by x'd out* The cities built by Nemrod are in the plain of Senaar
see Apocalypse ... 47:7–15] *added on line*
(cf. Apocalypse 16:19)] *added on line*

36 2:1–11] *added on line*
the gift ... of God] *added on line*
conclude ... 13:19–22] *added in left margin*
The formation of the] *followed by x'd out* Race of

38 (to the end)] *interlined*

40 the Chaldees] *followed by x'd out* and having
divinely appointed] *typed interlined and marked for insertion*
Ur was ... this time] *interlined*
cf. St. Benedict ... alienum] *interlined*

42 either you] *preceded by x'd out* better look
read Matthew ... 14:25 ff.] *added in left margin*

43 the promises] *preceded by x'd out* to

44 12:7] *added on line*

44–45 read Galatians ... Gentiles] *added in lower margin*
especially ... 26–29] *interlined and marked for insertion*

46 Origen ... the land] *added in lower margin*

47 18 ff.] *preceded by x'd out* 16

49 Abraham will] Abraham *altered from* Abram

50 and justice,] *followed by x'd out* the
Abram had presumably] had *typed interlined above x'd out* then
angel, sometimes] *followed by x'd out* a created
poses] *interlined above cancelled* is

TEXTUAL NOTES 197

51   submit."] *followed by x'd out* Reality is
      an expression] *preceded by x'd out* a knowledge which

52   verse 13] *added in left margin*
      reminiscence] *preceded by x'd out* refers
      line. It was] *preceded by x'd out* life

53   1] *added in left margin*
      2] *added in left margin*
      3] *added in left margin*
      4] *added in left margin*
      5] *added in left margin*
      6] *added in left margin*
      a sign that . . . rites] *added in lower margin and marked for insertion*
      7] *added in left margin*
      Abram is now] *preceded by x'd out* Abraham
      First] *preceded by x'd out* Walk before me and be perfect
      El Shaddai] *altered from* El Shaddai

54   Walk . . . perfect] *altered from* Walk . . . perfect
      (again . . . sees us)] *added on line*
      A very weak . . . is nothing.] *opposite page*
      I establish . . . and thee] *altered from* I establish . . . and thee
      my alliance] *followed by x'd out* with thee
      read . . . page 8] *added on line*

55   A name] A *interlined above cancelled* The
      as opposed . . . meaningless] *added on line*
      especially spiritual . . . ritual] *added on line*

55–56 Read Galatians . . . 6:12–18] *added in left margin*

56   cf. St. Francis . . . purity] *added in left margin*

57   impressive] *followed by x'd out* and
      of the wicked] *preceded by x'd out* by
      falls into several] *preceded by x'd out* has
      Note that . . . Princes of Sodom"] *added on line*

57–58 read Isaias . . . men of Sodom] *interlined*

58   READ John 3:16–21] *preceded by x'd out* (cf. John 3:19—This is the judgement
      in this connection] *added on line*

59   in the tent door] *typed interlined and marked for insertion*

St. Paul] *preceded by x'd out* Obviously
kind of hospitality] *interlined with a caret*
hospitality do not] *preceded by x'd out* his

59–60 this passage ... Abraham] *added in lower margin*

60 a little bread] *followed by x'd out* and water

tinged ... natural spirit] *interlined above cancelled* a sign of disbelief

Sara's laugh] *preceded by cancelled* In fact *and followed by x'd out* Sara's was that of a disbelieving spirit, and this is manifested at once by her fear of having been detected

persons] *interlined above cancelled* bodies

practiced] *preceded by x'd out* of his race and

61 affections] *preceded by x'd out* heart

read Romans 1:18–28] *added in left margin*

62 our own ... sinners] *added in lower margin*

of nature.] *followed by x'd out* and against

63 there is the element] there *interlined with a caret*

future] *added on line following cancelled* past

Luke 17:20 ff.] ff. *added on line*

64 This brings ... of revelation] *opposite page*

66 says BJ] *preceded by x'd out* (so BJ.)

the following facts] *preceded by x'd out* the fact of the fulfilm

or rather ... their lives] *added on line*

67 see 14–16] see *interlined and marked for insertion*

68 man or by] *preceded by x'd out* God or by the will of the

tables] *altered from* table

those who are] *preceded by x'd out* Ismael can be

Isaac – eo quod] *preceded by x'd out* Sara

and St. Paul ... of Abraham] *added on line*

3] *added in left margin*

69 Hebrews] *preceded by x'd out* Romans

70 believing ... recovered] *altered from* believing ... recovered

voice of God] *preceded by x'd out* word of God is

Hence] *preceded by x'd out* Only

like that which] *preceded by x'd out* that

71 After these ... Abraham] *altered from* After these ... Abraham

Abraham ... I am] *altered from* Abraham ... I am

TEXTUAL NOTES

of the name] the *typed interlined above x'd out* his
Ecce adsum] *altered from* Ecce adsum
fullness of spiritual] *preceded by cancelled* a
for his son] *followed by x'd out* by creating in his heart a special lo

72   for the sacrifice,] *followed by cancelled* places it upon Isaac's shoulder, in which we see a deeply moving figure of God the Father laying the wood of the Cross upon the shoulder of His Son.
holy] *added in left margin*

73   can surmise] *preceded by x'd out* must
His Beloved] *preceded by x'd out* the Son I
evident victim.] *followed by x'd out* "After we have worshipped"—but Abraham somehow anticipates returning with Isaac, though he does not understand how.

74   some suggestion] *preceded by x'd out* an adum
By his . . . in Abraham] *altered from* By his . . . in Abraham
On the mountain . . . wills] *altered from* On the mountain . . . wills

75   When we receive] *preceded by x'd out* Either God is direc
our logic we] *followed by x'd out* assign what seems best to us
necessary] *preceded by x'd out* fitting

76   corroborated] *preceded by x'd out* based on reason
We do not . . . he wants.] *added in lower margin*
naturally] *interlined with a caret*
Note the special . . . denied God.] *opposite page*
perfectly] *interlined above cancelled* in this manner
impious] *interlined above cancelled* unjust
(Hittites)] *added in right margin and marked for insertion*
First] *preceded by x'd out* Again

78   will certainly] *followed by x'd out* obey what God wants in His will, but after all the decision rests with Rebecca
Read 24:61–67: . . . narrative.] *added in lower margin*

79   grace of] *followed by x'd out* Scripture which

80   miraculous] *preceded by x'd out* birth
the Word with] *preceded by x'd out* Jesus with the
Here we have . . . processus.] *interlined*

81   ensure] *preceded by x'd out* make Him answer

83   meaning] *preceded by x'd out* value

second degree is then] *preceded by x'd out* This third de

84 Esau and Jacob] *preceded by uncancelled handwritten page:* Jacob + Esau. (1) *outline story*—Discuss St Augustine's interpretation non mendacium sed mysterium. (2) Real meaning of the story—a) Explain hostility between Israelites + Edomites (Arabs) (see in light of Israel—Jordan today) b) Explain *the promise*—to Isaac c) Explain the Biblical theme of the *younger + weaker supplanting the stronger.* d) Show how 12th responsory ties it in with Prodigal Son e) Read with *emphasis on the story* not on the moral point. See contrast between the 2 characters—significant Read *Genesis* 25:21-34 Explain 21-24 (1) Oriental viewpoint—one viewpoint. Sympathy with the simple, rugged country boy.—to be quiet, smart at right time, + to succeed—sign of divine predilection (2) From wider view Esau—*static*—remaining in rut Jacob—*dynamic* —growing, developing—new type of man. 30-34 Ease with which Esau parts with birthright Hebrews 12:16 Romans 9:9-16 (3) Emphasis on freedom of God's choice The incident of the Blessing a) meaning of deathbed blessing—b) The primitive scene—realism (note—eating on deathbed—means what??) c) Rebecca's plan d) The blessing Read Gen. 27: The Dream

85 making little ... birthright] *altered from* making little ... birthright cf. Hebrews 12:16: ... things of God!] *interlined*

85-86 cf. Romans ... moral angle] *interlined*

86 the moral] *preceded by cancelled* it

marks] *altered from* mark

passionately] *altered from* passion *preceded by cancelled* with

87 make his plans] *preceded by x'd out* real

absolute] *preceded by x'd out* what

N.B. he has ... to him.] *interlined*

88 read John 1:47-51] *added in left margin*

Cf. ... prodigal son] *altered from* Cf. ... prodigal son

paternal blessing] *preceded by x'd out* blessing and

90 read 28:10-17] *added in left margin*

workings of] *preceded by x'd out* action of

N.B. ... universe] *interlined*

91 interior ... of God] *altered from* interior ... of God

wherever man may] *followed by x'd out* God,

92 Read 28:18-22] *added in left margin*

TEXTUAL NOTES 201

92–93 The God of the Psalms . . . His power.] *added in lower margin*

93 (Benjamin . . . 35)] *added in upper margin and marked for insertion*
Abraham's] *interlined above cancelled* his
finds] *followed by cancelled* the
gathered] *preceded by cancelled* of his uncle Laban
meets Rachel] *preceded by x'd out* hears that
wedding] *added on line following cancelled* first
Palestine] *followed by cancelled* not so far away as Haran
Jacob comes to] Jacob *added on line before cancelled* he

94 read 29:9–15] *added in left margin*
his flock] *preceded by x'd out* the flo

95 read 30:31–42] *added in left margin*

96 he left for Laban] *added on line*
Read 31:16–27] *added in left margin*

97 cf. Dark . . . Soul] *added in left margin*

98 natural . . . light] *added on line*
in the next] *followed by x'd out* chapter

99 first] *interlined with a caret*
cataract] *altered from* cataracts
fed by] *followed by cancelled* melting snows
summer rains] *typed interlined preceded by cancelled* and
It has . . . succession.] *added on line*

100 probably from Asia] *added on line*
then . . . united] *added in left margin*
Calendars] *preceded by x'd out* But calendars first originated in Upper Egypt.
"sothic period,"] "sothic *altered from* "sothiac *preceded by x'd out* Sothic period.
and we cannot] *preceded by cancelled* since we do not know exactly when Sirius rose each year,
"sothic periods"] "sothic *altered from* "sothiac
short chronology.] *followed by cancelled* (Main problem—when did the new empire begin? If in 1580—then how account for 200 pharaohs in 200 years? Long chronology adds a sothiac period—giving another 1460 years—new dynasty begins about 3000. Short chronology thinks about 4000. In practice, difference of about 1000 years as to the beginning of the new empire. This naturally very important for Joseph.

202   TEXTUAL NOTES

          4241 ... date] *added in right margin*
101   seventeenth] *added on line*
          Hittites? ... infiltration] *added in right margin*
          Hyksos ... feudal lords] *added in right margin followed by cancelled* under Amosis
          Rameses II ... Hittites] *added on line*
          Babylonia, etc.)] *followed by x'd out* Amenophis IV, initiate decadence.
          Assyria ... Egypt] *added on line*
102   broke out] out *altered from* up
          N.B. papyrus ... tax)] *interlined and marked for insertion*
          oranges, lemons, dates] *added in left margin and marked for insertion*
          One tenth ... Pharaoh] *altered from* One tenth ... Pharaoh
          hyenas.] *followed by cancelled* Later
103   abolished] *interlined with a caret above cancelled* ceased
          Isis collects ... of the dead.] *added on line*
104   "Book of the Dead,"] *added on line*
          (in the west)] *added on line*
          Book of ... instructions] *added on line*
          continued existence] *preceded by x'd out* continuance of
          Pyramid texts ... the night] *added on line*
          "Piety ... virtue"] *added in lower margin and marked for insertion*
          "Keep this ... among them"] *added in lower margin*
105   as witnessed] *preceded by x'd out* able to
          Fear not ... people] altered from Fear not ... people
          cf. ... prophecy of Caiphas] *interlined*
106   difference ... the novel.] *interlined*
          psychological] *interlined with a caret*
107   c. 37] *added on line*
108   the dream] *interlined above cancelled* it
109   foreshadowing] *typed interlined above x'd out* all reminiscence
          Joseph has been] Joseph *added in left margin before cancelled* He
          35 ... to Putiphar.] *added on line*
110   "onanism"] *preceded by x'd out* spilling of the seed
          This was ... Messias] *added in lower margin*

Note . . . with Joseph."] *interlined*

Joseph's] *interlined with a caret*

111 How often . . . Lent] *added on line*

Joseph in Prison] *Joseph added in left margin*

112 happy dream.] *followed by x'd out* in

perhaps a ballet!] *added on line*

113 Joseph is summoned] *preceded by x'd out* Note how

for two] *followed by x'd out* year

subordinated] *preceded by x'd out* subservient to

humility] *preceded by x'd out* mock

114 Note—Jacob . . . Isaac.] *added on line*

115 no, he is] *added in lower margin and marked for insertion*

117 Again Jacob's . . . Benjamin] *interlined*

protest] *preceded by x'd out* assure

of the cup . . . his part] *added on line*

118 This throws] This *added on line*

to save Benjamin] *interlined below and marked for insertion*

lifts] *altered from* lifted

is heard] is *added on line following cancelled* was

119 Jacob's reaction] *preceded by x'd out* Joseph

121 concerning Whom] *preceded by x'd out* to whom

122 smiles] *preceded by x'd out* laughs

124 Read 28–34] Read *added in left margin*

see 47:6] *preceded by x'd out* Probably not.

The passage . . . Promise] *altered from* The passage . . . Promise

125 Read 7–10] Read *added in left margin*

126 comes from the fact] *typed interlined above x'd out* is

case of each] *followed by x'd out* tribe

127 tendencies, these trends] *preceded by x'd out* and diluting

prosaic] *preceded by x'd out* rationalistic explanation for everything

128 literal-minded] *preceded by x'd out* a bunch of *and followed by x'd out* and

agree] *interlined above cancelled* admit

129 Gen. 35:22] *followed by x'd out* Hence

mutilated] *interlined below and marked for insertion*

204 TEXTUAL NOTES

    he diminishes] he *interlined with a caret*
129–30 Here, read . . . His Spirit] *opposite page*
131 read St. Paul] *followed by cancelled* Galatians
132 across . . . Jordan] *interlined and marked for insertion*

135 Genesis 1–3] 3 *preceded by x'd out* 11
   15–31] 31 *preceded by x'd out* 24
   4—Numbers] 4 *altered from* 3
   8—Ruth] *preceded by x'd out* 3—Oth
   Exodus: Preamble from . . . prayer.] *opposite page*
136 Preamble: this . . . 10:2–4.] *added in right margin*
137 (a) Moses] Acts 7:23–25 *added in left margin and cancelled*
   Read chapter 3] *added in left margin*
139 cast] *preceded by cancelled* removed
140 heavenly bodies] *preceded by cancelled* lights
140–41 St. Bonaventure . . . meo.] *opposite page*
141 to signify . . . ad {2}] *added in right margin*
143 middle ages] *preceded by cancelled* 10th century
   4–18] 4 *altered from* 5
145 struggle between . . . give!] *opposite page*
   blind alley] *followed by cancelled* based on
146 directly] *interlined with a caret*
   I, q. 105, a. 4] *added in left margin*
   Omnis inclinatio . . . ordinantur] *opposite page*
   I, q. 103, a. 6] *added in left margin*
   I, q. 103, a. 7] *added in left margin*
147 I, q. 19, a. 6: . . . alium.] *opposite page*
   The concept . . . His being.] *opposite page*
   I, q. 19, a. 6, ad 1] *added in left margin*
   19, a. 6] *interlined above cancelled* 6
   ad 1] *altered from* a.1
149 Creation] *added in left margin*
   in creation] *interlined below and marked for insertion*
   Government] *added in left margin*
150 man can attain] *preceded by cancelled* God can attain man + all
   N.B. God's first . . . my causality] *added in right margin*
   from {a} human] *preceded by cancelled* with

	not treat ... SONS] *added in left margin*
152	Pharaoh begins] *preceded by cancelled* Moses
154	READ 12:1–11] *added in left margin*
156	The slaying ... 12:29–39] *added in left margin*
	no explanation] *added in right margin*
156–57	*For special ... then the* Exultet.] *opposite page*
156	universa] *altered from* universum
157	22:14–20] *added on line following cancelled* 18
	Jesus ... sacrificed] *added in right margin*
162	HERE ... cf. Numbers 33)] *added in lower margin*
	first ascent] *followed by cancelled* (further preparations)
	33] *followed by cancelled* 6 [illegible] adverse
	35–40] 40 *preceded by cancelled* 37
	16–17] *added in left margin*
	revolt of ... Abiron] *interlined*
164	death of Moses] *followed by cancelled* 31. Holy War against Madianites. Special purifications
167	manna {is a} type of] *interlined above cancelled* Application to
170	in the midst] *preceded by cancelled* between
172	Read Genesis] *added in left margin*
173	But the Blessed ... souls] *follows* Apoc. 21–22 *and marked for insertion*
178	from contact] *followed by cancelled* with other
179	problem of idolatry ... Exodus 32] *opposite page*
	"exchange"] *preceded by cancelled* Image
181	proscription ... "idols")] *opposite page*
182–83	n.b. 6:13 ... POWER.] *added in right margin*
183	Name of thy God] thy *interlined with a caret*
183–84	N.B. ... silence—read)] *opposite page*
185	N.B. ... blasphemy)] *opposite page*
186	and not a ... vocation] *added in left margin and marked for insertion*
	a fresh] *preceded by cancelled* an
	Pharaoh within ... power] *added in right margin*
187	Sabbath ... 65:16–25] *opposite page*
	The Poor] *preceded by cancelled* Read Lev 25—The Sabbatical Year.

206 TEXTUAL NOTES

   Sabbath ... mercy and charity] *added in right margin and marked for insertion*
189 cf. Psalm 105:28–30] *added in right margin*
190 trial] *preceded by cancelled* tempt
191 oldest type ... Galilee] *added in right margin*
   empire] *interlined above cancelled* came in
   formed] *preceded by cancelled* related
   held] *interlined above cancelled* pushed

BIBLIOGRAPHY

Astrov, Margot, ed. *The Winged Serpent: An Anthology of American Indian Prose and Poetry*. New York: John Day, 1946.
Auvray, P., trans. *Ezéchiel. La Sainte Bible Traduite en Français sous la Direction de l'École Biblique de Jérusalem*. Paris: Cerf, 1956.
Bonaventure, St. *Sancti Bonaventurae Opera Omnia*. Edited by PP. Collegii S. Bonaventurae. 10 vols. Quaracchi: Collegium Sancti Bonaventurae, 1882–1902.
Bouyer, Louis. *The Meaning of the Monastic Life*. Translated by Kathleen Pond. New York: Kenedy, 1955.
———. "La Schékinah: Dieu avec Nous." *Bible et Vie Chretienne* 20 (Dec. 1957–Feb. 1958) 7–22.
Breviarium Cisterciense Reformatum. 4 vols. Westmalle, Belgium: Ex Typis Cisterciensibus, 1951.
Buber, Martin. *I and Thou*. Translated by Ronald Gregor Smith. Edinburgh: T. & T. Clark, 1937.
Catechism of the Council of Trent for Parish Priests. Translated by John A. McHugh, OP, and Charles J. Callan, OP. New York: Wagner, 1934.
Charles, R. H., ed. *The Apocrypha and Pseudepigrapha of the Old Testament*. 2 vols. Oxford: Clarendon, 1913.
Crehan, J. H., SJ. "The Inspiration and Inerrancy of Holy Scripture." In *A Catholic Commentary on Holy Scripture*, edited by Bernard Orchard, OSB, 45–52. New York: Nelson, 1953.
Dyson, R. A., SJ. "The Poetical and Wisdom Literature." In *A Catholic Commentary on Holy Scripture*, edited by Bernard Orchard, OSB, 412–16. New York: Nelson, 1953.
———. "Proverbs." In *A Catholic Commentary on Holy Scripture*, edited by Bernard Orchard, OSB, 474–88. New York: Nelson, 1953.
———. "Some Recent Catholic Viewpoints on the Pentateuchal Question." In *A Catholic Commentary on Holy Scripture*, edited by Bernard Orchard, OSB, 174–77. New York: Nelson, 1953.
Dyson, R. A., SJ, and R. A. F. Mackenzie, SJ. "Higher Criticism with Special Reference to the Old Testament." In *A Catholic Commentary on Holy Scripture*, edited by Bernard Orchard, OSB, 61–66. New York: Nelson, 1953.
Foster, R. J. "The Apocrypha of the Old Testament and New Testament." In *A Catholic Commentary on Holy Scripture*, edited by Bernard Orchard, OSB, 121–26. New York: Nelson, 1953.
Fransen, Irénée. "Cahier de Bible: Jacob l'Avisé (Genèse 25, 19–37, 1)." *Bible et Vie Chrétienne* 15 (Nov. 1956) 66–79.

Fromm, Erich. *Psychoanalysis and Religion*. New Haven: Yale University Press, 1950.
Gillet, Lev. *Communion in the Messiah: Studies in the Relationship between Judaism and Christianity*. London: Lutterworth, 1942.
Gilson, Etienne. *The Mystical Theology of Saint Bernard*. Translated by A. H. C. Downes. New York: Sheed & Ward, 1940.
Grégroire de Nysse. *La Vie de Moïse, ou Traité de la Perfection en Matière de Vertu*. Edited and translated by Jean Daniélou, SJ. Sources Chrétiennes 1. 2nd ed. Paris: Cerf, 1955.
Grignion de Montfort, Louis-Marie. *True Devotion to Mary*. Translated by Frederick William Faber. Bay Shore, NY: Montfort, 1956.
Guardini, Romano. *The Living God*. Translated by Stanley Godman. New York: Pantheon, 1957.
———. *The Lord*. Translated by Elinor Castendyk Briefs. Chicago: Regnery, 1954.
———. *Pascal for Our Time*. Translated by Brian Thompson. New York: Herder & Herder, 1966.
Heinisch, Paul. *Theology of the Old Testament*. Translated by William G. Heidt, OSB. Collegeville, MN: Liturgical, 1955.
Hoever, Hugo H., OCist, ed. *Saint Joseph Daily Missal*. Rev. ed. New York: Catholic Book Publishing, 1959.
Hyvernat, H. "Egypt." In *The Catholic Encyclopedia*, edited by Charles G. Herbermann et al., 5:329–63. 16 vols. New York: Encyclopedia Press, 1917.
Kelly, J. N. D. *Early Christian Doctrines*. Rev. ed. San Francisco: Harper & Row, 1978.
Kierkegaard, Søren. *Fear and Trembling: A Dialectical Lyric*. Translated by Walter Lowrie. Princeton: Princeton University Press, 1941.
Lagrange, M.-J. "Genèse, Ch XLIX, 1–28: La Prophétie de Jacob." *Revue Biblique* 7 (1898) 525–40.
Laudes Vespertinae: seu, Cantus Diversi ad Benedictionem SS. Sacramenti. Westmalle, Belgium: Typis Ordinis, 1956.
Leonard, W. "The Gospel of Jesus Christ according to St John." In *A Catholic Commentary on Holy Scripture*, edited by Bernard Orchard, OSB, 971–1017. New York: Nelson, 1953.
McCann, Justin, OSB, ed. and trans. *The Rule of St. Benedict in Latin and English*. London: Burns & Oates, 1952.
Merton, Thomas. *Bread in the Wilderness*. New York: New Directions, 1953.
———. *Cassian and the Fathers: Initiation into the Monastic Tradition*. Edited by Patrick F. O'Connell. Monastic Wisdom 1. Kalamazoo, MI: Cistercian, 2005.
———. *Charter, Customs, and Constitutions of the Cistercians: Initiation into the Monastic Tradition 7*. Edited by Patrick F. O'Connell. Monastic Wisdom 41. Collegeville, MN: Liturgical, 2015.
———. *Cistercian Fathers and Forefathers: Essays and Conferences*. Edited by Patrick F. O'Connell. Hyde Park, NY: New City, 2018.
———. *The Cistercian Fathers and Their Monastic Theology: Initiation into the Monastic Tradition 8*. Edited by Patrick F. O'Connell. Monastic Wisdom 42. Collegeville, MN: Liturgical, 2016.
———. *The Collected Poems of Thomas Merton*. New York: New Directions, 1977.
———. *Conjectures of a Guilty Bystander*. Garden City, NY: Doubleday, 1966.
———. *Disputed Questions*. New York: Farrar, Straus & Cudahy, 1960.
———. "Guerric of Igny's Easter Sermons." *Cistercian Studies* 7 (1972) 85–96.

———. *The Hidden Ground of Love: Letters on Religious Experience and Social Concerns.* Edited by William H. Shannon. New York: Farrar, Straus & Giroux, 1985.
———. *The Inner Experience: Notes on Contemplation.* Edited by William H. Shannon. San Francisco: HarperCollins, 2003.
———. *An Introduction to Christian Mysticism: Initiation into the Monastic Tradition 3.* Edited by Patrick F. O'Connell. Monastic Wisdom 13. Collegeville, MN: Liturgical, 2008.
———. *Learning to Love: Exploring Solitude and Freedom. Journals.* Vol. 6: *1966–1967.* Edited by Christine M. Bochen. San Francisco: HarperCollins, 1997.
———. "Life and Celebration" [Tape 12A]. *The Merton Tapes.* Series 1. Chappaqua, NY: Electronic Paperbacks, 1972.
———. *The Life of the Vows: Initiation into the Monastic Tradition 6.* Edited by Patrick F. O'Connell. Monastic Wisdom 30. Collegeville, MN: Liturgical, 2012.
———. *Medieval Cistercian History: Initiation into the Monastic Tradition 9.* Edited by Patrick F. O'Connell. Monastic Wisdom 43. Collegeville, MN: Liturgical, 2019.
———. *A Monastic Introduction to Sacred Scripture: Novitiate Conferences on Scripture and Liturgy 1.* Edited by Patrick F. O'Connell. Eugene, OR: Cascade, 2020.
———. *Monastic Observances: Initiation into the Monastic Tradition 5.* Edited by Patrick F. O'Connell. Monastic Wisdom 25. Collegeville, MN: Liturgical, 2010.
———. *Mystics and Zen Masters.* New York: Farrar, Straus & Giroux, 1967.
———. *The New Man.* New York: Farrar, Straus & Cudahy, 1961.
———. *New Seeds of Contemplation.* New York: New Directions, 1961.
———. *Pre-Benedictine Monasticism: Initiation into the Monastic Tradition 2.* Edited by Patrick F. O'Connell. Monastic Wisdom 9. Kalamazoo, MI: Cistercian, 2006.
———. *The Rule of Saint Benedict: Initiation into the Monastic Tradition 4.* Edited by Patrick F. O'Connell. Monastic Wisdom 19. Collegeville, MN: Liturgical, 2009.
———. *A Search for Solitude: Pursuing the Monk's True Life. Journals.* Vol. 3: *1952–1960.* Edited by Lawrence S. Cunningham. San Francisco: HarperCollins, 1996.
———. *Seasons of Celebration.* New York: Farrar, Straus & Giroux, 1965.
———. *Seeds of Contemplation.* New York: New Directions, 1949.
———. *The Seven Storey Mountain.* New York: Harcourt, Brace, 1948.
———. "Silence and Purity of Heart." In *Solitude and Togetherness,* disc 7. 11 discs. Rockville, MD: Now You Know Media, 2012.
———. *The Spirit of Simplicity.* Trappist, KY: Abbey of Gethsemani, 1948.
———. *The Springs of Contemplation: A Retreat at the Abbey of Gethsemani.* Edited by Jane Marie Richardson, SL. New York: Farrar, Straus & Giroux, 1992.
Merton, Thomas, and Jean Leclercq. *Survival or Prophecy? The Letters of Thomas Merton and Jean Leclercq.* Edited by Brother Patrick Hart. New York: Farrar, Straus & Giroux, 2002.
Merton, Thomas, and Robert Lax. *When Prophecy Still Had a Voice: The Letters of Thomas Merton and Robert Lax.* Edited by Arthur W. Biddle. Lexington: University Press of Kentucky, 2001.
Migne, J.-P., ed. *Patrologiae Cursus Completus, Series Graeca* [PG]. 161 vols. Paris: Garnier, 1857–1866.
———, ed. *Patrologiae Cursus Completus, Series Latina* [PL]. 221 vols. Paris: Garnier, 1844–1865.
Missale Cisterciense: Reformatum juxta Decretum Sacrorum Rituum Congregationis Diei 3 Julii 1869. Westmalle, Belgium: Ex Typographia Ordinis Cist. Strict. Obs., 1951.

Missale Romanum: Ex Decreto Sacrosancti Concilii Tridentini Restitutum: S. Pii V, Pontificis Maximi, Jussu Editum: Aliorum Pontificum Cura Recognitum: a Pio X Reformatum et Benedicti XV Auctoritate Vulgatum. 4th ed. New York: Benziger, 1944.

O'Connell, Patrick F. "Awakening in Eden: Thomas Merton and the Recovery of Paradise." *Milltown Studies* 47 (Summer 2001) 77–95.

———. "The Fall." In *The Thomas Merton Encyclopedia*, by William H. Shannon et al., 153–54. Maryknoll, NY: Orbis, 2002.

———. "Paradise." In *The Thomas Merton Encyclopedia*, by William H. Shannon et al., 349–51. Maryknoll, NY: Orbis, 2002.

Origen. *Contra Celsum.* Translated with introduction and notes by Henry Chadwick. Cambridge: Cambridge University Press, 1953.

Peers, E. Allison, ed. and trans. *The Complete Works of Saint John of the Cross.* 3 vols. Westminster, MD: Newman, 1946.

Pirot, Louis, and Albert Clamer, eds. *La Sainte Bible, Texte Latin et Traduction Française d'après les Textes Originaux avec un Commentaire Exégétique et Théologique, Commencée sous la Direction de Louis Pirot, Continuée sous la Direction de Albert Clamer.* 12 vols. in 15. Paris: Letouzey & Ané, 1946–1961.

Pius XII, Pope. *Divino Afflante Spiritu, Encyclical Letter on Promotion of Biblical Studies.* Washington, DC: National Catholic Welfare Conference, 1943.

———. *Humani Generis. Acta Apostolica Sedis* 42 (1950) 561–78.

Pontifical Biblical Commission. *Epistula ad . . . Cardinalem Suhard. Acta Apostolica Sedis* 40 (1948) 45–48.

———. *The Interpretation of the Bible in the Church* (April 15, 1973). *The Bible Documents: A Parish Resource.* Chicago: Liturgy Training Publications, 2001.

Pontificale Romanum Summorum Pontificum Iussu Editum a Benedicto XIV et Leone XIII Pontificibus Maximis Recognitum et Castigatum. Mechlin: Dessain, 1958.

Power, E., SJ. "Exodus." In *A Catholic Commentary on Holy Scripture*, edited by Bernard Orchard, OSB, 206–28. New York: Nelson, 1953.

———. "The History of Israel to 130 B.C." In *A Catholic Commentary on Holy Scripture*, edited by Bernard Orchard OSB, 84–95. New York: Nelson, 1953.

Quenon, Paul, OCSO. *In Praise of the Useless Life: A Monk's Memoir.* Notre Dame, IN: Ave Maria, 2018.

Rituale Cisterciense ex Libro Usuum Definitionibus Ordinis et Caeremoniali Episcoporum Collectum. Westmalle, Belgium: Ex Typographia Ordinis, 1948.

La Sainte Bible Traduite en Français sous la Direction de l'École Biblique de Jérusalem. Rev. ed. Paris: Cerf, 1956.

Saydon, P. P. "Leviticus." In *A Catholic Commentary on Holy Scripture*, edited by Bernard Orchard, OSB, 229–44. New York: Nelson, 1953.

Shannon, William H., Christine M. Bochen, and Patrick F. O'Connell. *The Thomas Merton Encyclopedia.* Maryknoll, NY: Orbis, 2002.

Sutcliffe, E. F., SJ. "Genesis." In *A Catholic Commentary on Holy Scripture*, edited by Bernard Orchard, OSB, 177–205. New York: Nelson, 1953.

———."Introduction to the Pentateuch." In *A Catholic Commentary on Holy Scripture*, edited by Bernard Orchard, OSB, 167–74. New York: Nelson, 1953.

———. "The Replies of the Biblical Commission." In *A Catholic Commentary on Holy Scripture*, edited by Bernard Orchard, OSB, 67–75. New York: Nelson, 1953.

Thomas Aquinas, Saint. *Sancti Thomae Aquinatis Doctoris Angelici Ordinis Praedicatorum Opera Omnia, secundum Impressionem Petri Fiaccadori Parmae 1852-1873 Photolithographice Reimpressa.* 25 vols. New York: Misurgia, 1948.

Trevor, George. *Ancient Egypt: Its Antiquities, Religion, and History, to the Close of the Old Testament Period.* London: Religious Tract Society, 1863.

Vaux, Roland de, OP, trans. *La Genèse. La Sainte Bible Traduite en Français sous la Direction de l'École Biblique de Jérusalem.* Paris: Cerf, 1956.

Wellhausen, Julius. *Die Composition des Hexateuchs.* 3rd ed. Berlin: Reimer, 1899.

Willmering, H., SJ. "The Epistle of St Jude." In *A Catholic Commentary on Holy Scripture*, edited by Bernard Orchard, OSB, 1191-92. New York: Nelson, 1953.

Winzen, Damasus, OSB. *Pathways in Holy Scripture.* Series 1. Bethlehem, CT: Abbey of Regina Laudis, 1948-1949.

SCRIPTURAL INDEX

Old Testament

Genesis

	vii–xi, xlii, 1, 135
1–11	xiv
1–3	135
1–2	xiv
1:1—2:4a	xiv, 3
1:1–2	3
1:2	4
1:26	3
1:27	3, 12
1:28	4, 30
2	4–5
2:1–2	4
2:3	liii
2:4b–25	xv
2:5	6
2:8	4
2:10	11
2:12	11
2:13	11
2:15–17	122
2:16–17	9
2:18–20	12
2:19	12
2:21	12
3	xvi–xviii, 13–17
3:1–11	13–14
3:5	20
3:6	14
3:9	16, 71
3:10	16
3:12–24	17
3:15	17
3:21	84
3:22	9
3:24	9
4–11	135
4	xviii, 18–20
4:1	18
4:7	19
4:8	20
4:9	20
4:10–11	20
4:13	20
4:17–26	22–23
4:20	22
4:21	22
4:23–24	22
4:25–26	23
5:22	23
5:23	23
5:24	23
6:1–4	24, 26, 191
6:2	26
6:5–7	26
6:12–18	56
6:12	27
6:13	27
6:14–22	27
6:19	27
7	28
7:1–6	27
7:2–3	27
7:7–16	28

Genesis (continued)

7:7–10	28
7:11–16	28
7:12	28
7:13	28
7:14	29
7:15	29
7:16	29
7:17–24	xix
7:17	29
7:18	29
7:19	29
7:21	29
7:23	29
7:24	29
8:1	29
8:2	29
8:4	29
8:5	29
8:9	29
8:11–12	29
8:13	29–30
8:18	34
8:20–30	29
8:20–22	30
8:20	33–34
8:21	30, 34
8:22	30
9:1	30
9:22–25	34
9:24–25	43
10:6–20	34
10:9	34
10:10	34
11	35
11:1–9	xx–xxi
11:1	35
11:3	35
11:4	35
11:5	35
11:7	36
11:31	xxii
12–25	135
12	xxii–xxiii, xxvi
12:4–20	45
12:4–5	45
12:7	44
12:8	91
13	xxiii, 46
13:1	46
13:8	46
13:10	60
13:12	46, 60
13:14–18	46
13:14	46
14	xxiii, 47
14:13	191
14:18–24	47
14:18–22	142
14:19–20	47
15	xxiii, 48–49, 151
15:1	48
15:2–3	48
15:4–6	48–49
15:7–11	49
15:7	44
15:9–18	49
15:17–21	49
16	xxiii–xxiv, 49–51
16:3	50
16:7–16	50
16:13	52
17	xxiii–xxiv
17:1	xxv, 53–54, 70, 142
17:3	43
17:4	55
17:5	55
18–19	57
18	xxii, xxv–xxvi
18:1–8	173
18:12	xxvi
18:20	61
18:21	57, 62
18:23	62
19	xxvi, 62–63
19:6–14	63
19:9	63
19:11	58
19:12	63
19:15	63
19:27	63
20	xxvi, 65–66
20:12	66
21	xxvi–xxvii, 53, 66–67
21:6	66

SCRIPTURAL INDEX

21:8	67
21:9–20	67
21:14–16	67
22	xi, xxvii–xxix, 141–42
22:1–14	69
22:1	71
22:2	71–72
22:3	72
22:4	72
22:5	72, 73
22:6	73
22:7	74
22:8	74
22:9	74
22:11	74
22:12	74
22:14	74
22:16–18	75
23	xxix, 76, 191
24	xxix, xxxiii, 76
24:7	76
24:10–33	76–77
24:50	77
24:61–67	78
25–36	135
25	xxix, xxxi
25:2	109
25:12	109
25:21–34	84
25:25	84
25:29	85
25:34	85
26	xxx–xxxi
26:23–25	86
26:29	86
27–37	86
27–35	xxxi
27–28	xxxi–xxxii
27	87–88
27:20	87
27:28–29	87
27:30–45	89–90
27:40–41	90
27:46	90
28:1–4	90
28:10–22	90, 91
28:10–17	90
28:16–17	91
28:17	91
28:18–22	92
29–31	xxxii–xxxiii, 93
29	93–94
29:9–15	94
29:16–21	94
29:20	94
29:32	93
29:33	93
29:34	93
29:35	93
30:1–2	95
30:6	93
30:8	93
30:11	93
30:13	93
30:14–17	95
30:18	93
30:20	93
30:21	93
30:24	93
30:31–42	95–96
30:42–43	96
31	96
31:8	96
31:12–14	96
31:16–27	96
31:32	96
31:34	96, 181
31:36–42	97
32–33	xxxiii–xxxiv
32	97
32:22–32	97
32:31	97
33	97–98
33:1–3	98
33:4–7	98
33:8–11	98
33:12–15	98
33:13	98
34	xxxiv, 98
34:25	129
35	xxxi, xxxiv, 93, 98–99
35:4	45
35:9–15	98
35:16–20	99
35:18	93

Genesis (*continued*)

35:22	xli, 129
36	99
37–50	xi, xxxiv, 135
37	xxxv, 99, 105, 107–9
37:2–4	107
37:2	107
37:5–11	108
37:12–36	108–9
37:12–17	109
37:18–20	109
37:23	109
37:26–27	109
37:31–36	109
37:35	109
38	xxxv–xxxvi, 105, 109–10
38:26	110
39–50	xxxvi
39	xxxvi, 105
39:2	110
39:3	110
39:6	120
39:19–23	111
40	xxxvi–xxxvii, 105, 111–12
40:7–8	111–12
41	xxxvii
41:1–16	112–13
41:16	113
41:25	113
41:32	113
41:37–46	113–14
41:45	120
41:53–57	114
42–45	xxxvii–xxxviii
42	105, 115
42:1–7	115
42:4	115
42:8–25	115–16
42:9	115
42:21	115
42:24	115
42:35–38	116
43–45	105
43	116–17
43:3–15	116–17
43:16–23	117
43:31–34	117
43:33	117
44	117–18
44:4–13	117–18
44:15–34	117–18
45	118–19
45:2–9	118
45:2	118
45:5	xxxiv, 195
45:12	119
45:14–15	119
45:16	119
45:25–28	119
45:26–28	xxxviii–xl, 119–20
45:26	120
45:27	120
46–47	xl
46	123–24
46:1–7	123
46:7–27	124
46:28–34	124
47	124–25
47:6–7	124
47:6	124
47:7–10	125
47:11–26	125
47:27–31	125
48	xl–xli, 105, 114, 125–26
48:4–20	129–30
48:7	126
48:15–16	126
48:16	129
49–50	xlii
49	xli, 105, 126–29
49:3–4	129
49:5–7	129
49:7	128
49:8–12	130
49:12	131
49:13	131
49:14	131
49:16	132
49:18	132
49:19	132
49:20	132
49:21	132
49:22	132
49:25	132
49:26	132

49:29–33	132
50	105, 132–33
50:11	132
50:15–21	132
50:19–20	xxxiv, 105
50:24–25	133

Exodus

	vii–xii, xlii–xliii, 1, 135, 192
1–14	xliii–xliv, 135, 136
1–3	xii
1	xliv
1:1–7	136
1:8–22	136
2	xlv
2:11–15	137
2:15–25	137
2:25	137
3	xliii, xlv–xlvii, l, 137–38, 139, 169
3:1–7	137
3:13–15	138
4–18	xlvii, 143
4	151
4:10–18	151
4:21	151
4:22	151
4:24–26	151
5	151
5:2	151
5:3	151
5:19	151
6:2–3	142
6:3–9	138
6:3	151
6:12	151
6:30	151
7–10	xlvii, 151
7:1–7	151–52
7:3	151
7:4	151
7:10–13	151–52
7:15–25	152
8:1–25	152
8:8	152
8:15	151, 152
8:16–19	152
8:19	152
8:20–24	152
8:28	152
8:32	151, 152
9:1–7	152
9:7	152
9:8	152
9:12	152
9:14	152
9:15–16	152
9:18–26	152
9:23–27	152
9:27	152
9:30	152
9:34–35	152
9:34	151
10:1–2	152
10:4–15	152
10:7–11	152
10:21–23	152
10:24–29	152
11	153–54
11:1	154
11:4	154
11:6	154
11:8	154
12	xlviii, 154–55, 157
12:1–28	143–44
12:1–11	154
12:1	154
12:5	xlviii
12:6	154, 156
12:9–10	154–55
12:11–23	155
12:12–14	155
12:12	156
12:25–28	155
12:29–39	156, 157
12:39	156
12:40	136
12:42	157
12:46	156
13–14	l
13	158
13:1–15	158
13:1–16	144
13:8–10	156
13:9	158
13:17	158

Exodus (continued)

13:19	158
13:21–22	169
14	xlviii, 159
14:5–14	159
14:14	159
14:15–23	159–60
14:19–20	169
14:19	160
14:20	160
14:24–31	160
14:24	169
14:31	xlviii
15–31	135
15–18	135
15	161
15:1–21	xlix, li, 144
15:1–13	161
15:20–21	161
15:22–27	xlix, li, 161, 162, 164
15:27	li
16–19	xlix
16	162, 164, 166
16:1–18	xlix
16:1–12	166
16:1–5	164
16:4	164, 167
16:5	165
16:6–18	165
16:6–7	xlix, 165
16:6	166
16:7–8	165, 167
16:10	l, 165, 166
16:13–36	166–67
16:13	165, 167
16:16–18	165
16:17	167
16:19–20	167
16:27	167
17	176
17:1–7	162, 188
17:8–16	li, 162, 176
18	162
18:13–27	li
19–24	176
19	162
19:3–15	162
19:3–8	176
19:5	176
19:9–14	178
19:16–24	162
19:16–22	178–79
20	li, lii–liii, 162, 175
20:1–17	179
20:7	183
20:8–11	185
20:20–23	160
21–23	liv, 162
23:9–12	186
23:20–33	162
23:23–26	181
24	l, liv, lv
24:9–11	162, 169
24:15–18	169
25–31	liv, 162
25:18–22	181
25:22	170
32–34	lv, 135, 176
32	162, 179, 183
32:1–28	188–89
32:8	189
32:25	188
32:26–29	129
33	162
33:23	52
34	l, 162
34:12–17	181
34:27–35	175
34:28	175
34:29	169
35–40	liv, 135, 162
40:32–38	162
40:32–36	170

Leviticus

	liv, 1, 135, 192
1–7	192
8–10	192
11–15	192
11:47	27
16	192
16:2	170
17–27	192
19:12	183

SCRIPTURAL INDEX

23:1–22	186–87
23:15–16	186
25–27	192
25	188
25:1–7	188
25:8–19	188
25:23–43	188
26	192

Numbers

	xii, xlix, 1, 135
1	162
6:1–21	18
7:89	170
9–14	135
9:15–23	162
9:33–36	162
11–12	162
11:34	162
13	162
13:6	173
13:33	191
13:34	26
14:1–24	189
14:36–45	189
16–17	162
20–26	135
20	162–63
20:14–21	84
21	163, 181
21:9	189
22–23	163
25	163
25:1–9	189
27:12–23	163
31–36	135
32:33–38	129
33	162

Deuteronomy

	xlix, lii, 1–2, 135
1–11	135
5	li, liii
5:6–21	179
5:6–7	175
5:8	175
5:11	175, 183
5:12–15	185–86
5:12	175
5:16	175
5:17	175
5:18	175
5:19	175
5:20	176
5:21	176
6:4–13	182
6:13	182, 183
7:1–24	176
7:1–6	179, 181
7:7–15	180
7:17–26	180
7:25–26	180
8	xlix
8:1–6	164
10:12—11:1	182
10:20	183
12:1–14	184–85
12:2–7	181
12:3	184
12:5	li, 185
12:11	185
14:2–29	188
14:28–29	187
15	187–88
15:1–18	187–88
15:4	188
15:11	188
23:10–15	178
26–33	135
31–34	164

Joshua (Josue)

	xiii, xiv, liv, 1, 135
1–12	135
13:23	129
14–24	135
19:1–9	129
21	129

Judges

	xiii, 135
1–12	135
3:15–30	132

Judges (continued)

5:14	132
5:15	132
8:22	109
8:24	109
8:26	109
13–16	135

Ruth

xiii, xlii, 135

1 Samuel (1 Kings)

	xiii
15:9–23	181
15:22–23	182
28:3–25	lii
28:7–20	181

2 Samuel (2 Kings)

xiii

1 Kings (3 Kings)

8	171
8:1–10	170
8:10–11	l

2 Kings (4 Kings)

2:12	123
18:1–4	181

1 Chronicles (1 Paralipomenon)

12:8–15	132
12:23–40	134

2 Chronicles (2 Paralipomenon)

3:1	72

Job

xiii

Psalms

8	3, 4
13[14]:1–3	145
13[14]:2–7	62
19[20]:2	185
23[24]:1–6	92
32[33]:9	183
33[34]:9	82
44[45]:3	120
50[51]:5	19
52[53]:1–3	145
64[65]	xx, 34–35
64[65]:2	35
77[78]	145
77[78]:12–13	136
77[78]:43–52	152–53
79[80]:2	170
80[81]	92–93
91[92]:8	6
94[95]	164
98[99]:1	170
103[104]	4
103[104]:30	3
105[106]:14	188
105[106]:28–30	189
109[110]	xxiii, 47
123[124]:8	4
135[136]:1–9	4

Proverbs

3:18	7, 9
9:13–18	145
14:1–35	145
18:1–24	145
18:10	185
19:1–29	145
22:17—24:22	104

Song of Songs (Canticle of Canticles)

1:1	xxx, 80
1:2	81
1:3	82

SCRIPTURAL INDEX   221

1:4	82
1:5	82
1:7	83
3:1	83
3:4	83
4:12–13	8
5:2	xxx, 83
8:6	xxx, 84

Wisdom

7–14	23
7:16–21	149
7:30	17
8:1	149
10	64
10:4	64
10:5	69
10:6–8	63
11:16–27	149
14:1–7	28
14:6–7	28
14:6	26

Sirach
(Ecclesiasticus)

	l
16:8	26
18:15–18	145
19:11–12	145
19:22–25	145
20:6–7	145
20:13–22	145
21:11–28	145
24:3–15	172
24:17–32	7–8
24:17	7
24:35–37	12
31:5–7	145
33:1–6	145
44	31
44:16	23
44:17–19	31
49:16	23

Isaiah
(Isaias)

1:2–10	57–58
1:9–10	57
1:9	23
6	l, 170
8:23—9:1	131
13:6	28
13:19–22	36
25:6	131
30:12–18	159
30:15	159
30:27	185
33:19	36
37:16	170
44:9–28	181
44:25	181
47:7–15	35
54:7–14	32
60:15–22	187
65:16–25	187

Jeremiah
(Jeremias)

2:1–10	136
2:1–3	176
4	xxiv
4:4	55
7:3–15	185
35:2–19	18
46:10	28

Baruch

3:26–28	26
6	181

Ezekiel
(Ezechiel)

1	l, 172, 181
10	l
10:1–22	171–72
11:16	172
14:14–22	32
14:22	32
30:3	28
31:8–9	6

Ezekiel (continued)

39:9	187
47	131

Daniel

3:55	170
4:7–25	6–7
13	5
13:1–62	111

Hosea (Osee)

2:8–22	177
2:14	136
9–14	132
10:1	136
11:1–9	176–77
13:4–5	136

Joel

1:15	28
3:16–21	131
3:18	131

Amos

5:18	28
5:25	183
8:11–12	164
9:13–14	131

Micah (Micheas)

6:1–5	161
6:3–4	161

Habakkuk (Habacuc)

3:2	170
3:4	175

Zephanaiah (Sophonias)

1:14	28

New Testament

Matthew

1–3	xxxvi
1:1	xxi, 36
1:3	110
3:9	xxi, 37
4:4	164
4:8–11	183
4:13–16	131
5:4	46
5:6	164
5:33–37	184
6:25–34	167
8:5–13	xxi, 37
10:15	58
10:34–38	42
11:24	58
11:28	82
13:12	132
17:1–8	173
18	xix
18:22	23
19:27–29	133
20:1–16	89
23:29–39	21
24	xix
24:15–35	65
24:36–44	32–33
24:37	32
25:29	132
25:31–46	119
26:15	109
26:26–32	157
28:8–10	119

Mark

3:29	119
4:25	132
14:22–29	157
14:36	74
16:15–18	133

Luke

1:40–41	66
1:46–55	66
2:20	66–67

SCRIPTURAL INDEX

2:23–24	158
10:16	165
10:42	10
11:47–52	20–21
14:25–27	42
15:11–32	88
17	34
17:20–37	63–64
17:22–37	33
17:20	64
17:24	64
17:30	64
17:32	64
17:33–37	64–65
19:41–47	xii
22:14–20	157
22:24	74
23:43	6

John

1:14	173
1:29	145
1:35–39	157
1:47–51	88
1:51	88
3:16–21	58
4	lii, 45, 181
4:1–42	88
4:11	98
6	xlix, 38, 164, 167
6:25–35	167–68
6:47–59	168
7:37–39	xxx
8	xxii
8:31–59	38–39
8:44–59	58–59
8:56	48
11:51–52	105
12:25	80
12:31–36	58
14:23	173
19:14	156
19:31–36	157
19:36	156
20:11–18	119

Acts

2:1–11	36
2:15	131
4:27–28	106
4:35	165
5:29	75
7	xxii, lii
7:2–8	40
7:4–5	40–41
7:47–53	181

Romans

	xxvii
1	61, 69
1:18–28	61
4	xxi
4:1–3	37–38
4:15–25	37–38
4:18	73
4:23–25	38
4:24–25	38
5:1	37
8:28	105
9:7–10	68
9:9–16	85
9:11	85
11:1–22	106–7
11:15	106
12:3	11
12:20	115

1 Corinthians

1:1–3	177
2	189
5:6–8	157
5:7	145, 154
10	liv, 179
10:2–4	136
10:2	188
10:6–13	188
10:6	188
10:7	188
10:8	188
10:9	189
10:13–22	179
10:13	189

1 Corinthians (continued)

10:14–33	190
10:14	190
12:3	130

2 Corinthians

3:7	175
6:16	173
12:4	6

Galatians

	xxvii, 10
3	44–45
3:5–9	45
3:7	37, 68
3:13–18	45
3:26–29	45
4:21	68
5	55–56
5:6	xxii, 38

Ephesians

4:7	133
5:22–33	12–13
5:31–32	12

Philippians

4:4–7	131
4:4	131
4:5	131

Colossians

2:9	173
2:20	65
3:3	34

1 Thessalonians

4:10–11	64

2 Thessalonians

3:10–13	64

Hebrews

2:14	17
3:13	164
4:12	17
7	xxiii
7:1–11	48
7:10	48
9:6–14	170
10:8–25	157
11	xix
11:1–5	21
11:5	23
11:7	34
11:17–18	70–71
11:17–19	69
11:22	133
12	xix
12:16	85
12:22–29	22
12:29	169
13:1–2	59
13:2	42

James

1:17	43

1 Peter

1:17–21	145, 157
2:5–9	177–78
2:11	144
3	xix
3:1–14	139
3:18–22	33

2 Peter

1:17–18	173
2:4–10	34

1 Joh

	xiii, 10
2:27	10
3:8	17
3:12	18

Jude

7–11	22
14–15	24

Revelation (Apocalypse)

2:7	8
3:18	173
3:20	173
7:1–10	133
7:2–12	133
11:3–12	23–24
11:12	24
15:1–8	161
15:3	145
16	153
16:19	35
17	35
18:11–24	36
21–22	xxi, l, 36
21:1–4	13, 178
21:2	xvii
21:2–5	133
21:3	173
21:10–14	133
21:22	l, 174
22:1–3	8

GENERAL INDEX

Aaron, 143–44, 151–52, 154–56, 161–66, 169–70, 175, 189; death of, 163; obedience to, 167; order of, 48; ordination of, 192; punishment of, 163; race of, 134; sons of, 192
abandonment, xx, 31, 151
abbot(s), 134; as sign of Christ, xxx, 78; commands of, 98; consideration of, 98; discretion of, 98; holy, 133; moderation of, 98; prudence of, 98
Abel, xviii–xix, 18–23, 156; as breath, 18; as nomad, 18; as shepherd, 18; as type of Christ, 19; as victim, 19; birth of, 18; blood of, 20–22; city of, 34; flock of, 19; in New Testament, 20–22; murder of, xviii–xix, 20; name of, 18; remnant of, 32; sacrifice of, xviii–xix, 19, 21–22; voice of, 20; works of, 18
Abimelek (Abimelech), xxvi, xxx, 86; marriage to Sara, 65–66
Abiron (Abiram), revolt of, 162
Abiu (Abihu), 169
abomination, xxvii, 124, 180
Abraham (Abram), ix, xiv, xxi–xxx, xl, 36–78, 86, 91, 130, 135, 141–42, 174, 182, 189; alliance with, xxiii, xxxi, 53–56, 86, 135; altars of, 39–40, 45–46; as father of all, 38; as father of elect, 43; as father of multitudes, xxiv, 38, 54–55; as father of People of God, xxi, 36; as father of redeemed, 73; as friend of God, 64, 70; as instrument of divine will, 75; as instrument of salvation, 52–53; as nomad, 76; as rescuer of Lot, xxiii, 47; as touchstone, 43; as transmitter of blessings, 43, 45; as victim, 72; bargaining of, xxv–xxvi, xxix, 62, 76; blessing(s) of, 39, 43–45, 47, 90; bosom of, 43; call of, xiv, xxii, 39–40, 52; charity of, 59; child of, 41; children of, xxii, xxv, 38, 44, 51, 68; Christ as son of, xxi–xxii, 36; commitment of, xxviii; complacence of, 69; confidence of, 48; compassion of, 69; contentment of, 52; contrast with Lot of, 57; country of, 39–40; courage of, xxviii, 70; covenant with, xxiii–xxiv, 49, 137; death of, xxix; death to self of, xxvii, 74; descendant(s) of, xxiii, 37; descent from, xxi; destiny of, 53; discouragement of, 48; enemies of, xxiii, 49;

Abraham (*continued*)
    faith of, xxv, xxvii–xxviii, 37–38, 40–41, 43, 49, 52, 59, 63, 69–72, 74–75, 142; fear of God of, 74; fidelity of, xxvii; gloomy vision of, xxiii, 48–49, 151; God of, 51–52, 90–91, 138; goodness of, 49; guests of, xxv, xxix, 59–60; happiness of, 52; heart of, 71; heir of, 48; hope of, xxi, 73; horror of, 49; hospitality of, xxv–xxvi, 59, 172; house of, 39; humility of, xxix; identity of, 39; in New Testament, 36–39; insecurity of, 40; intelligence of, 49; intercession of, xxv, 57, 60, 62; journey(s) of, xxii, xxvii, 39–40, 45; joy of, 69, 78; justice of, xxiii, 44, 48–49; justification of, 37, 49; kinsmen of, xxix, 39–40, 43; laughter of, xxvi, 56–57, 60; life of, xxv, 49; loins of, 48; love for child of, xxviii, 71–72; love for God of, xxv, xxviii, 54, 60, 72; loyalty to God of, xxvii; marriage of, 66; meeting with Melchisedec, xxiii, 47–48; mystery of, xxix; name of, 71, 130; new name of, xxiv, 53, 55; obedience of, xxvii, xxix, 69–71, 75, 142; optimism of, 48; peace of, 52; piety of, xxv, 60; pilgrimage of, 40; pleading of, 62; politeness of, xxv, 60; posterity of, 44; poverty of, 72; prayer of, 74; promise(s) to, xxi–xxii, xxiv, xxvii, xl, xlviii, 41, 43, 48–49, 51, 53–55, 57, 60, 66, 69, 74, 86, 123; prosperity of, 52; protection of, 66; reasoning of, 49; relationship with God of, xxv; religion of, xxvii; reproachfulness of, 62; rescue of Lot by, xxiii, 47; respect of, 62; revelation to, 62; righteousness of, xxiii; sacrifice of, xxvii–xxviii, 49, 69–74, 142; sanctity of, 49; seed of, xxii, 38–39, 43–46, 48–49, 57, 66, 68, 106, 189; sensitivity of, xxv; separation from Lot of, xxiii, 46; servant(s) of, xxx, 48, 72–73, 76–78; sign for, 49; silence of, 63; sleep of, 49; solicitude of, xxv, 60; son(s) of, xxiii, 36–39, 49, 66, 68–74; soul of, 71; spirituality of, xxiii, 46; submission of, xxvii; subterfuge of, 45; suffering of, ix; tent of, 59; testing of, 41, 70–71; time of, 191; trial of, xxvii, 48, 69–71; trust of, xxvii, 72, 142; vision of, 57, 59–60; visitors of, 57, 59; vocation of, 39–45, 52; wife of, 39–40, 46; will of, 49; work(s) of, 38, 41
abundance, 34
abyss, 3, 29; fiery, 24–25; nether, 28; of darkness, 3; of soul, xiv, 3; of water, xiv; upper, 28
Abyssinia, 99
accuracy, historical, 128
Achor, 177
act(s), creative, xiv, 3; free, 150; of love, xviii; righteous, xxxvi
action(s), 3, 51, 146; doctrine of, xlvi, 140
activity, xxxi, 85; autonomous, 150; creative, xv; immanent, 150
Adam, ix, xv–xvi, xviii, 5, 10–11, 15–16, 20, 23, 73, 84; as arbiter of good and evil, 16; as his own god, 16; as his own judge, 16; as his own master, 16; as namer of creatures, xvi, 5; banishment of, 17; bone of, 5; cords of, 177; creation of, xv, 5;

GENERAL INDEX   229

defense of, 17; descendants of, 16; fall of, xv–xviii, 3, 13–17; flesh of, 5; illusions of, 16; illusory divinity of, 16; parrhesia of, 15; sin of, ix, xvii–xviii, 14, 18; sleep of, 5, 12; sons of, 18, 23, 28
Adama (Admah), 177
administrators, Egyptian, 101–2
adoration, xiv, 3, 54; of God, 175, 179, 183
adulteress, 88
adultery, 175
Advent, First Sunday of, xii
adversity, 40
affairs, temporal, 85
affection(s), 123; human, 77; of heart, 61; shameful, 61
affliction, 50, 116; hopeless, 142
afterlife, 112
agape, 91
Agar (Hagar), xxiii–xxiv, 49–52; as Old Testament, 68; casting out of, xxvi–xxvii, 67–69; child of, xxiv, 52; fertility of, xxiii; sorrow of, 67
age, bronze, 191; iron, 191; messianic, liv; middle bronze, 191; mid-stone, 191; of peace, liv; stone, 191
agents, created, 146
aid, divine, 174
Ailred (Aelred) of Rievaulx, St., liv, 190–91
air, fowls of, 5
Ajax, 132
Alexander the Great, 101
Alexandria, school of, 127
alienation, xvii–xviii
aliens, 124
All Saints, Feast of, 133
allegory, viii
alliance, xix, lii, 32, 176, 179; of Abraham, xxiii, xxxi, 53–56, 86, 135; of Noe, 30; realization of, 177
almonds, 117
aloes, 8

altar(s), 21, 106, 153, 179, 181, 185; of Abraham, 39–40, 45–46; of Isaac, xxx, 86, 123; of Jacob, 98; of Noe, 30
Amelec (Amalek), battle with, li, 162, 176
Amalekites, 191
ambivalence, 15
Ambrose, St., xxix–xxx, 59, 80–84
Amenophis III, 102
Amenophis IV, 103
American, casualsy of, 118
Ammonites, 57, 132, 191
Amon, as sun god, 103; cult of, 103; priests of, 103
Amorrhite(s) (Amhorites, Amorites), 138, 145, 158, 179, 181, 191; iniquities of, 49; war with, 163
anarchy, Egyptian, 101
anathema, 180
Aner, 47
angel(s), xxvi, 3–4, 22, 26, 32, 36, 42, 44, 50–51, 57–59, 62–63, 65, 67, 74, 76–77, 88, 90–92, 160, 183; bread of, 168; evil, 153; fallen, 26; guest as, xxii, 59; hierarchies of, 91; joy of, xxvi, 67; of Lord, xxiv, 50–52; of waters, 153; of Yahweh, 138; protection of, 130; seven, 153; song of, xxvi, 67; vision of, 96; wrestling with, 97
Angelico, Fra, 131
anger, 137; of God, 64, 153, 161–62, 189
anguish, 116
Ani, 104
animal(s), 12, 150; clean, 27; pure, 30; sacrifice of, 49; totem, 103; unclean, 27
antelopes, 102
antichrist, 18, 133
Antioch, school of, 127–28; fear of, 127; literalism of, 127; Nestorianism of, 127
antitype(s), viii, xxviii

anxieties, 95
apostasy, 176
apostles, xxxix, xlii, 4, 20, 41, 120–21, 133, 173; college of, xxxix, 120; twelve, xlii, 133
appearance, 140; of unity, xxi
Aquarius, 129
Aquila, 6
Arabia, 11
Arabs, 54, 84
Aramaeans, 191
Ararat, Mt., 11
archangels, 4
archers, 132
Argonauts, 11
ark, Noah's, xix, xlv, 27–33; building of, 31; darkness of, 29–30; dimensions of, 27; entry into, 28; management of, 31; roof of, 30
ark, of covenant, 170; of testimony, 170
Armageddon, 153
Armenia, 29, 39
arms, nuclear, vii
army, Egyptian, 102, 159–60
arrogance, 35, 62
arrows, 178
art, Christian, ix
Ascension, Feast of, xi, 133
ascent, intellectualist, 173; mystical, 80, 143; negative, 173
asceticism, 150
Asenath, 114
Aser (Asher), 93, 132, 134, 136; as farmers, 132
Ashera, 181
ashes, 152
Asia, 100
Asiatics, invasions of, 101; migrations of, 100
asperges, 131
asps, poison of, 62
ass(es), 57, 72, 96, 118, 134, 145, 158, 186; strong-built, 131–32
Assuan (Aswan), 99
Assyria, 101; king of, 6

Assyrian(s), 5, 34, 177
Astarte, 181
Astrov, Margaret, 183–84
atheists, 51
Aton, cult of, 103
Atonement, Day of, liv, 192
attentiveness, 79
attitude, magical, xviii, 19; pseudo-scientific, 128; rationalistic, 128; religious, xviii
attraction, fatal, 14
attractiveness, 14
attributes, divine, 143
Augustine, St., xvi, xx, xlvi, 9–10, 34–35, 59, 87, 105–6, 141, 150, 159
Australia, 28
authority, 37
autocracy, Egyptian, 102
autonomy, 150; illusion of, xvi
Auvray, P., 32
awareness, 54
awe, 54; interior, 91
awl, 188
Azymes, 155

Baal(im), 106, 177; days of, 177; service of, 177
Babel, tower of: xx–xxi, 34–36, 57; as symbol of pride, 35; builders of, 36; spirit of, 35
Babylon, xx, 32, 34–36, 153, 171; captivity in, 124; citizens of, 35; exile in 124
Babylonia, 2, 101
Babylonians, 34
baker, dream of, 111–12; fate of, 112
Bala (Bilhah), xli, 93, 129; as maid of Rachel, 93; children of, 93
Balaam, 163; error of, 22
balance, threat to, 16
ballet, 112
balm, 8, 108, 117
Bañez, Domingo, 145–46
banquet, eschatological, xxi
baptism, xv, xxv, 4, 38, 92; character of, 55; figure(s) of, liv, 27, 33, 35, 143, 188; image of,

xlvii; institution of, xxiv; seal
of, 55
Barad (Bered), 50
bargaining, oriental, 76
barnfloor, 188
barns, opening of, 114
barrenness, 180
Bashan, 163
Basil, St., Rule of, 125
baskets, 102
Bathuel (Bethuel), xxxii, 77–78, 90
battle(s), noise of, 189; sham, 102
bdellium, 5, 11
bears, 149
beast(s), 5, 7, 25–26, 29, 49, 144,
  155–56, 177, 180, 185–86;
  apocalyptic, 24, 153; clean,
  27–28; dumb, 22, 149; evil,
  108–9; four-footed, 61;
  heart of, 7; kingdom of,
  153; mouth of, 153; naming
  of, xvi, 5; rest for, 186; seat
  of, 153; unclean, 27–28;
  unknown, 149; wild, 7, 109;
  worthless, 149
Beatitudes, 46
beauty, 83, 136; exaggerated, 14;
  illusory, 14; narrative, xxix,
  61, 76, 87
beef, 117
Beelsephon (Baal-zephon), 159
Beersabee (Beersheba), xxx, xl, 86,
  90; sacrifice at, 123
beggar, 187
behaviors, exemplars of, ix
being(s), 55; absolute, xlvi; bodily,
  149; created, 91; depths of,
  15; fallen, 83; fullness of,
  xlvi; living, 19, 31; material,
  150; offering of, 91; spiritual,
  71, 149
bells, 102
Benedict, St., xxii, xxiv, 35, 40, 51,
  60, 98, 125, 164–65, 184
benefits, 67
benignity, 56
Benjamin, xxxiii, xxxvii–xxxviii,
  93, 115–18, 132, 136; as

ravenous wolf, 132; birth of,
  xxxiv, 99; framing of, xxxviii,
  117–18; sack of, 118; sons of,
  134; tribe of, 106
Bernard of Clairvaux, St., xvi,
  xl, 8–12, 80, 83, 122–23,
  190–91
Bethel, xxxii, xxxiv, 40, 90, 92, 96–
  98; as rival sanctuary, 92
Bethlehem, 99, 130
Bible, apocryphal books of,
  xix; *Bible de Jerusalem*
  translation of, xliii, 14,
  45, 55, 59–60, 66, 84–85,
  152, 183; Douay-Rheims
  translation of, xlii, lvi, 14,
  26, 46, 52, 55, 98, 114, 131;
  Vulgate translation of, xlii,
  98, 107, 131
bigots, 85
bird(s), 7, 25, 27–28, 31, 49, 61,
  111–12; mother, 3; of prey,
  xxiii, 49
birth, miraculous, 66
birthright, 84–85, 87
bitterness, 62, 161
blains, plague of, 152
blasphemer, 184
blasphemy, liii, 153, 184; reparation
  for, liii, 185
blessing(s), 67, 88; by Jacob, 126–32;
  deathbed, xxxi, 87; of
  Abraham, 39, 43–45, 47,
  90; of Isaac, xxxi–xxxii, xl,
  89–90; of Jacob, 87–88, 90,
  93, 97; spiritual, xxii, 44–45;
  temporal, xxii, 44
blindness, 58, 63
blood, 24, 62, 153–55; effusion of,
  19; of Abel, 20–22; of Christ,
  xlviii, l, 22, 157, 168; of
  goat, xxxv, 108–9; plague of,
  152–53
boats, 102
body, 84, 149–50; ambivalence
  toward, xvii; embalmed, 104;
  feeding of, xvi; heavenly,
  140; of Christ, 1, 13, 106,

body (*continued*)
123, 157, 173; preservation
of, 112
boils, plague of, 152
Bonaventure, St., xlvi, 140–41
bondage, house of, 144–45, 158,
180, 182; liberation from,
xlviii; yoke of, 56
bondservant, 188
Book of Funerals, 104
Book of the Dead, 104
Book of the Lower Hemisphere, 104
Bouyer, Louis, xii, l, 54, 157, 169–74
bow, 177
boxing, 102
brass, 22
bread, xxiii, xlix, 47, 60, 62, 64,
67, 84, 87, 92, 110, 114,
164–65, 172, 175, 181, 187;
from heaven, 164, 166, 168;
leavened, 144, 155, 158;
living, 168; of angels, 168;
of children, 168; of life,
xlix, 168; unleavened, xlviii,
liv, 144–45, 154–55, 158,
186–87
breath, 18
breezes, 5
brethren, as sign of Christ, xxx, 78
bribes, 182
brick, invention of, 35
bride, Jerusalem as, xvii, 13, 178;
soul of, 8
brother, 187, 189; needy, 188; older,
130; poor, 188; younger, 130
bruises, 57
Buber, Martin, 54
bull(s), white, 25; wild, 102
buns, 112
bureaucracy, theocratic, 103
bush, burning, xliii, xlv–xlvi, lii,
137–40, 169; as symbol of
transcendence, xlv, 139;
unconsumed, 139–40
butler, dreams of, 111–12; fate of,
112; office of, 112
butter, 173

Cabala (Kabbalah), 143
Cades (Kadesh), 7, 50
Cain, ix, xviii–xix, 18–23, 85,
135; anger of, xviii, 19; as
exile, 20; as farmer, 18; as
wanderer, 20; attitude of,
xviii, 19; birth of, 18; city of,
34; contempt of, 20; crime
of, xix; descendants of, xix,
22–23; desolation of, 21;
despair of, 20; envy of, 156;
freedom of, 19; hatred of,
19–20; heart of, 19; in New
Testament, 20–22; ingenuity
of, 19; murder by, ix, xviii,
20; pride of, 20; sacrifice of,
xviii, 19; sin of, 19; sorrow
of, 19; toil of, 19; way of, 22;
works of, 18
Cainites, 22–23, 26
Caiphas, 105
cakes, 112, 172; earth, 156
calendar, Egyptian, 100
calf, 173, 187; golden, liv, 129, 162;
molten, 188–89
Calvary, xxviii, 70, 72, 74; ascent of,
xxviii
Calvinists, li, 175
camels, 76–78, 96–97, 108, 134
Canaan (Chanaan), xxii, xxxiii,
xl, 18, 39, 44–45, 49, 55,
76, 90, 96, 132; borders of,
167; control of, 136; land
of, 115, 118–19, 124, 129;
reconnoitering in, 162;
tribes of, liv
Canaanite(s) (Chanaanites), 34, 39,
47, 101, 132, 138, 145, 158,
179, 181, 191; as navigators,
191
canon, biblical, xi
Capharnaum, 37, 131, 168
captive, 68
captivity, Babylonian, l
caravan, 105, 109
carcasses, split, xxiii, 49
care, divine, xvii, xxxv; for poor, liv,
187–88; providential, xxvi

caritas, xx, liv, 190
Cassian, John, 92, 125
castanets, 102
cattle, 5, 7, 28, 108, 124–25, 152–53, 180; firstborn of, 145, 156, 158; mutilation of, 129; plague of, 152–53
causality, 146; divine, xlvi, 150; personal, xlvi, 150; primary, 150
cause(s), efficient, 150; primary, xlvi, 151; secondary, xlvi, 146, 148–51
census, 1, 162
centurion, faith of, xxi, 37; servant of, 37
cereals, 99
ceremonials, elaborate, 104
ceremonies, 180; cremation, 183; Passover, 144, 155
certitude, supreme, 121
Chaldea, 11
chalice, 74
Cham (Ham), 8; curse of, 34, 43; descendants of, xx; sons of, 34; tabernacles of, 153
Chamina ben Teradion, 172
change, 140
chaos, xix; return to, 28–30
character(s), 124; biblical, viii–ix
chariots, 159
charity, liv, 12, 34–35, 38, 56, 81, 173, 187, 190–91; excellence of, 190; of Abraham, 59; ordering of, 191; perfect, 122–23; sacrament of, 173; supernatural, xxv; sweetness of, 190; works of, xxi
Charles, R. H., 24–25
charm, xxix, 78
chastity, 56
checkers, 102
Cheops, 101
cherubim, 4, 170–71, 181
chess, 102
Chinese, 28
Chobar (Chebar), 171–72
choir(s), angelic, 26; monastic, 185

Christ, Jesus, ix, xxviii, xliv–xlv, li, 3–4, 8, 27, 33, 37, 45, 57, 68, 73, 79, 120, 122, 136, 178; ancestry of, xxxvi; apparitions of, 119; as Bread of Life, xlix, 167–68; as child of Mary, xlvi; as child of promise, xxv, 53, 68; as Epiphany of Father, 52; as eye of soul, 84; as fulfillment of promise, xxi, 38; as gain, 123; as God made flesh, xxxvi; as head, 106; as head of church, 13; as head of soul, 84; as high priest, xxiii; as holy child of God, 106; as incarnate Word, 78; as King of Israel, 88; as Lamb of God, xxix, l, 8, 74, 157–58; as life, 121; as life-giving spirit, 174; as light, 58; as light of soul, 84; as Logos, 50; as Lord of heaven, 120; as mediator, 22; as Messiah, xxxv, 110; as one teacher, 80; as only-begotten Son, xxix, 73, 88; as overthrower of law, 174; as Pasch, 154, 157; as paschal lamb, xlvii–xlviii, 120, 145, 168; as pastor, 168; as redeemer, 17, 106; as resurrection, 121; as Sacred Heart, 184; as sacrificial offering, xxix; as Savior, liii, 13, 18, 45, 88, 120, 185; as seal, xxx, 84; as second Adam, 12; as seed of Abraham, 44, 57, 66; as seed of woman, xviii, 17; as servant, 106; as shepherd, 157; as Son of Abraham, xxi–xxii, 36; as Son of David, xxi, 36; as Son of Father, ix, xxviii, 73; as Son of God, xxii, 41, 48, 88, 106; as Son of Man, 32–33, 64–65, 88, 106, 167; as strength of soul, 84; as tree of life, xvi, 9, 161;

Christ, Jesus (*continued*)
as true bread, 168; as true heir, xxxi; as true temple, l, 174; as truth, 121; as victim, xxviii, 18, 74; as Wisdom incarnate, l, 80, 173; as Word made flesh, 173; as Word of God, 121; baptism of, xxviii, 70; beauty of, 120; belief in, 167; believers in, 157; betrayal of, xxxv; birth of, xxvi; blood of, xlviii, l, 22, 157, 168; body of, l, 13, 106, 123, 157, 173; bones of, 13, 157; charity of, 88; coming of, xxiv; command of, xix; confessing, 185; cross of, xlix, 56, 109, 161; crucified, l, 24, 44, 174; day of, 78; dead, 157; death of, xv, xxii, xxviii, 27, 38, 58, 71, 116, 156; debate of, xxii, 38–39; descent into hell of, 33; desire of, 157; disciple(s) of, 38, 42; divine name in, xlvii; divinity of, 173; divinization in, 88; enemies of, 106; espousal to, 79; faith in, 157, 168; faith of, 44; false, 65; flesh of, 13, 106, 140, 168; following of, xxvi, 65; forgiveness of, xxxviii, 119; genealogy of, xxxvi, 110; giving of, 133; glorified, l, 173; glory of, 119; grace of, 82; healing by, 37; help of, 125; humility of, 119; identification of with least, xxxviii; image of, 84; in desert, 182–83; incarnation of, xxv, xxxii, xlv, 52, 57, 90, 139; knowledge of, 121; lecture hall of, 80; life in, 34; life of, 122; light of, 140, 178; living, 122; love for, 122; love for church of, 13; love of, xxxviii, 119; member of, 43; mercy of, xxxviii, 23, 119, 168; mildness of, xxxviii, 119; Mystical Body of, 76, 88; name of, 130, 143; parables of, xxi, 88–89; Pasch (Passover) of, 143; passion of, xxxi, xxxv, 73, 88, 109, 154, 156; person of, xxii, 168; poverty of, 119; power of, xxi; promises of, 43; recapitulation in, 107; recognition of, 119; redemption in, ix; resurrected, xxxix, l, 38; resurrection of, xv, xxii, xxviii, xxxix, 38, 70–71, 119, 121; risen, xxxix, 120–22, 157; sacrament of, xxx, 78; sacrifice of, xlvii, 47; sanctification in, 88; signs of, xxx, 78; soul of, 106; stripping of, 109; tears of, xii; tempting of, liv, 164, 189; thanksgiving to, 185; throne of, 8; time of, 132; transfiguration in, 139, 173; transfiguration of, xxviii, 70, 173; transformation in, 88; truth of, 140; type(s) of, xxx, 9, 19, 27, 32, 71, 78–84, 106, 120, 133; union of with church, xxx, 78, 80; union of with soul, xxx, 78, 80; union with, xxxix, 79–80; unity in, 91; victory of, 157; virgin birth of, 80, 140; virginal conception of, xlv–xlvi; virtues of, 178; vision of, xxv; visitor as, xxvi; weakness of, 119; will of, liii, 185; word of, liii, 39, 185; work of, xxii

Christian(s), 64; individual, l

Christmas, xxvi, 66; Eve, xlix, 165–66

Christology, Nestorian, 128

chrysolite, 171

church(es), ix, xxii, xxxii, l–li, 8, 13, 32, 34, 41, 43, 47, 91, 122,

GENERAL INDEX   235

177; as people of God, 36, 43; as temple of God,173; dedication of, 91, 133; glorious, 13; Greek, li, 175; history of, 107; holy, 13; Latin, li, 175; minister of, 80; monastic, xlii, 133; of firstborn, 22; Orthodox, 173; union of with Word, xxx, 78, 80
Chus (Cush), 34
cinnamon, 8
circumcision, 37, 53, 55–56; as visible sign, 55; covenant of, xxiv, 53, 55–56; of Sichemites, 98; of son of Moses, 151; rite of, 53; spiritual, 55
Cistercians, as idealistic, 123; as practical, 123
cisterns, 182
city, earthly, xxi; first, 34–35; goodly, 182; great, 153, 182; guardians of, 83; holy, 178; monastic, xxi, 36; of Abel, 34; of Cain, 34; of God, xx, 22, 34, 133; of man, xx; of this world, 34; self-sufficient, 22; two, 35; wickedness of, 62
civilization, 18, 78, 184; Egyptian, 100; highest, xxii
Clamer, Albert, 19, 124
class, poor, 188
cleanliness, personal, 124; physical, 178
cleanness, 192
clergy, Egyptian, 101, 103
clothing, 87, 102, 178; use of, 15
cloud, liv, 165–66, 169–71; baptism in, 188; dark, xlviii, 160; darkness of, 178; luminous, l, 169; pillar of, 160, 172; thick, 178
coasts, Mediterranean, 102
code, covenant, liv
Colchis, 11
cold, 40

color, narrative, 111
Columbia University, xiii
columns, Canaanite, 181; phallic, 181
comfort, 40; lack of, 109
command, divine, 4
commandment(s), lii–liv, 161, 164, 167, 175–76, 179–90; divisions of, li, 175, 179; first, lii, 179–83; great, lii; individual, li; ninth, li; second, lii–liii, 183–85; ten, 162, 175–76, 179; tenth, li; third, liii–liv, 185–90; violations of, liii
commentary, patristic, xix
commiserations, 177
commissioner, special, 113
commitment, of fidelity, li; of love, li
communication, genuine, xx
communion, authentic, xxi; holy, 168; of intelligences, 91
community, as sign of Christ, xxx, 78; authentic, xx
compassion, divine, xxviii
complaints, 83
complexes, guilt, lii, 179
compliance, servile, 150
compunction, 190
concupiscence(s), 14, 56; triple, 190
condescension, divine, xviii
confessors, 4
conflict, xvii, xxi, 147; inner, 16; knowledge of, 14; state of, 10; with serpent, xviii
confrontation, existential, 183
confusion, 34
consecration, of place, xxxii, 91; of self, xxxii, 91; of stone, 91; to God, xxiv, xxvii
consolatio, 190
consolation(s), li, 47, 67, 176, 190
Constantinople, Second Council of, 127
consumerism, vii
contact, 81; sexual, 178

contemplation, 12, 15, 51, 165; depths of, 79; doctrine of, xlvi, 140; infused, 67; settings for, xv, 5
contentions, 56
continency, 56
contingency, 148
contract, xxiii, 49
contradiction(s), apparent, xxvii; internal, 17, 136
conversion, xlviii, 159
cooking, 87
Core (Korah), contradiction of, 22; revolt of, 162
coriander, 167
corn, 89, 115–16, 177, 180, 186–87; new, 144; seven bad ears of, 112; seven good ears of, 112
Corpus Christi, Feast of, 156, 168
cosmos, 90–91
counsel, 62, 118
countryman, 187
courage, 123, 180, 189
court, of temple, 171
courtesy, 78; oriental, 98
courtiers, Egyptian, 101
courtliness, 78
covenant(s), xxiii, li, 32, 55, 137, 170, 174–77, 180; ark of, 170; fidelity to, xlviii; Mosaic, 162; new, li; of circumcision, of, xxiv, 53, 55–56; of peace, 32; ratification of, liv, 162; renewal of, 175; tabernacle of, 170; with Abraham, xxiii–xxiv, 49, 137; with all creation, xix
cow, 49
craftiness, 23
creation, xiv, xxvii, xxxii, xlv, liii, 1, 3–13, 26, 61, 90, 135, 139, 143, 147, 149, 186; accounts of, xiv–xv, 3–5; as place of concealment, xvii, 16; as place of divine encounter, xvii, 16; blessing of, 4; celebration of, xv; covenant with, xix; first account of, xiv, xviii, 3–4; from nothingness, 149; mediators for, xiv; mode of, 149; new, xv, xix, xlv, 4, 30, 34, 65, 134, 139; of Adam, xv, 5; of earth, 3–4, 6; of Eve, xvi, 5, 12–13; primeval, 184; relationship with, xvii; second account of, xv, 4–5; transfigured, 173
creativity, xiv, 150; true, xx
creature(s), 3, 16–17, 29, 61, 90–91, 141, 173; as mirrors, xvii; clean, 27; dialogue with, 183; end of, liii; four living, 171; generosity of, 91; kinship with, xiv, 3; living, 27; love of, 91; new, 56; opaqueness of, 141; perfections of, 141; qualities of, 149; soul of, liii; unclean, 27
creaturehood, 69
Crehan, J. H., 2
crime, wicked, 107
crops, dependency on, 19
cross, xxviii, xlviii, 42, 73, 112; folly of, 55; mystery of, 161; scandal of, 56; sweetness of, li, 162, 176
crow, 29
crying, 13, 178
cult(s), cosmic, xlviii; Egyptian, 103; fertility, lii, 181; nature, xlviii, 174; of departed souls, 104; of gods, 104
culture, 51
cup, of Joseph, xxxviii, 117–18; of Pharaoh, 111
cupiditas, xx, liv, 190
cupidity, 35
curiositas, 83
curse, 18, 44
cursing, 62, 184
Cyril of Alexandria, St., 128

Dan, 93, 132, 134, 136; as tribe of Antichrist, 133
dances, 189

GENERAL INDEX   237

dancing, 102
Danel (Daniel), Phoenician sage, 32
Daniel, 7, 32, 65
Daniélou, Jean, 139
Darius, 101
darkness, xix, xxviii, 30, 58, 62, 67,
    70, 131, 141, 154, 178; abyss
    of, 3; blind, 142; days of, xx,
    31; deep, 154; exterior, 37; of
    hell, 122; of sense, 67; plague
    of, 152; total, 74
dates, 102
Dathan, revolt of, 162
daughter(s), 179, 185–86
David, 107, 132, 134; city of, 170
day(s), for God, 186; holy, 186–87;
    last, 153; light of, 122;
    of Lord, 28; of rest, 186;
    solemn, 187
dead, 38; cult of, 104; dwelling of,
    104; land of, 104; life from,
    106–7; rites of, 104
deal, business, 145
deans, 162
death, 5, 9, 13–14, 21, 23, 27, 29, 39,
    102, 153, 178; actual, xxviii;
    as gain, 122–23; chains of,
    157; divine prerogative over,
    xviii; fruit of, 10; pain of,
    178; power of, 80, 157; realm
    of, 184; shadow of, 131;
    symbolic, xxviii; taste for, 10;
    to self, xvii
decalogue, versions of, li
deception, xxxv, 48, 87
dedication, total, 192
deeds, 149
deep, fountains of, 29
deficiencies, 123
degeneracy, pagan, xxvii, 70
degeneration, moral, 15
degradation, 43
delights, garden of, 9
deliverance, 45
deluge, 26–34, 36, 64, 135; darkness
    of, 29
demands, charter of, 174
descendence, carnal, 68; spiritual, 37

descent, physical, xxi; spiritual, xxi
desert, xxiii, xliii, xlv, xlix, liv, 1,
    18, 50–51, 65, 67, 137, 158,
    176, 188; custom of, 87;
    Egyptian, 99; emptiness of,
    26; innermost, xlvi, 139;
    journey through, xliv, li, 135,
    162–68; of time, xix, 22; trial
    in 164
desire(s), xvii, 14, 16, 35, 38, 63, 69,
    81, 113; evil, liv, 176, 188;
    human, xx; illusory, 14;
    purgation of, 67; subjective,
    14; superficial, xvii
desolation, abomination of, 65
despair, xviii
destiny, 55, 76; evil, 46; human,
    xviii; of chosen people, 75
destroyer, 144, 155, 189; of world, 64
destruction, 62, 159, 183
detachment, 64; monastic, xxvi
detail(s), mundane, viii;
    psychological, 111
de Vaux, Roland, 14, 45, 55, 59–60,
    66, 84–85
devil(s), 13–14, 22, 38–39, 58–59,
    131, 154, 179; as liar, 39, 58;
    image of, 157; power of, 80;
    spirits of, 153; temptation by,
    183; works of, 17
devotion, inward, 85; monastic, liii
dew, 7, 149; manna as, 165–66
dialectic, 15
dice, 102
Diegueño, 183
dignitas, 83
dignity, 78, 83; creative, 150; human
    xiv, 3, 83; ignorance of, 83;
    intrinsic, xxx; supreme, 83;
    of free will, 150
dilectio, 190
diminution, 140
Dina (Dinah), xli, 93; rape of, xxxiv,
    98, 129
Dionysius, Pseudo-, 90–91, 173
discernment, tree of, 10
disciple, life of, xxiii
disinheritance, 43

disobedience, ix, 167; sinful, 10
disorder, 146
dispute, Thomist–Molinist, 145
dissentions, 56
distrust, 38
disunity, xxi
divination, lii, 181
divining, 118
divinity, 61, 139; cosmic, 103; illusory, 16; local, 103
divinization, 91
division, xxi, 10, 13–15; agent of, xvii; from God, 10, 13; from others, 13; from self, 10, 13; inner, xvi; of flesh and spirit, xvii, 14–15; of God, 14; of mankind, 36; source of, xvi
doctors, Egyptian, 103
doctrine, Cistercian, xl, 122; spiritual, 78; traditional, 140
dogs, 102, 168
dolmens, cyclopean, 191
domination, 35
Dominic, St., 131
Dominican(s), xlvii, 131, 146
dominion(s), 187; angelic, 4
door, 188; anointing of, 144, 154–55
Dothan (Dothain), 108–9
doubts, 13
dove(s), 29, 31, 158
dragon, 153
drama, 111
dream(s), xxxviii, 106; agency of, xxxv; happy, 112; interpretation of, xxxvii, 105, 108, 113; of baker, xxxvi, 111–12; of butler, xxxvi, 111–12; of Joseph, xxxv, xxxviii, 105, 107–8, 115; of Pharaoh, xxxvii, 105, 112–13; prophetic, 105; prosperous, 112
dreamer, 120
drums, 102
drunkenness, 56
dryness, 190
dullness, 51
dung, 180

duplicity, xxxi
duties, customary, xxv, 60; to believe, 182
Dyson, R. A., 1–2, 104

eagles, 33, 64–65; face of, 171; wings of, 176
ear(s), 107, 121, 139, 188
earrings, 177
earth, 5, 13, 20, 22–23, 26–27, 35, 47, 89, 149, 172, 176–77, 182, 185; as footstool of God, 184; beasts of, 5; creation of, 3–4, 6; dry, 30; dust of, 90; face of, 165; first, 13, 178; forces of, xlviii; new, 13, 178; tribes of, 65, 90
earthquakes, 153
Easter, xxxix, 119–20; grace of, 121; vigil, xlviii
ecstasy, xvii, 12, 90; contemplative, 12
Eden, 5–6, 15, 18, 20; man in, 4–5
edification, xliv; moral, 87
Edom, xxxi, xxxiv, 90, 99; Arabs of, 54, 84
Edomites, 84, 191; dispute with, 163; hostility toward, 84
effects, contingent, 148; necessary, 148
egg, 120
Egypt, xxii, xxxiv, xlvii, 24, 40, 45–46, 49, 66, 99–104, 108, 114–15, 118, 124, 136, 138, 144, 151, 154–55, 157–58, 164–66, 177, 182, 186, 188–89, 191; agricultural products of, xxxiv, 102; archaic period of, 100; as black country, 99; bondservant in, 188; cult of dead of, xxxiv; culture of, xxxiv; deliverance from, 36, 135–36, 143–61; delta region of, 100; departure from, xliv, li, 1, 157; enslavement in, liii; escape from, xlviii; esoteric texts of, xxxiv; ethnography of, 99–100; exile in, xxiii, 49;

GENERAL INDEX 239

famine in, 113–15, 118, 125; geography of, xxxiv, 99; gods of, 110, 143–44, 155; history of, xxxiv, 100–101; industry in, 102; infirmities of, 180; Jacob in, 123–32; Joseph in, xxxvi–xxxviii, xl–xli, 105, 110–34, 136; king of, 103, 111, 137; kingdoms of, xxxiv, 100–102; leaving, 176; liberation from, 186; lower, 100; Middle Kingdom of, xxxiv, 100–102; moral code of, xxxiv; New Kingdom of, xxxiv, 101–3, 125; Old Kingdom of, xxxiv, 100–101; oppression in, xxiii; prehistoric period of, 99–100; priestly class of, 102–3; races of, 100; recreation in, 102; religious system of, xxxiv, 103–4; river of, 49; royal power in, 102–3; rulers of, xxxiv, 102–3; social strata of, xxxiv; society of, xxxiv, 101–2; spoils of, 138; sports of, 102; tax in, 102; trade in, 102; upper, 100; viceroy of, 120
Egyptian(s), 34, 40, 112, 136, 138, 152, 156, 160, 176, 180; camp of, 160; clamor of, 154; destruction of, 161; hands of, 138, 160; heart of, 160; jealousy of, 125; king of, 159; land of, 125; striking of, 144, 155
elect, 65, 172
electio, 191
election, 86, 88, 106–7
elephants, 102
Elias (Elijah), 24, 106
Eliezer, son of Moses, 137
Eliezer, steward of Abraham, 48
Elim, 164, 166, 176; springs of, li, 161
Elizabeth, St., 66
emanations, 143

emotion, 94, 147
emulation(s), 56, 107
encounter, divine, xxxii; providential, xxix
end, attainment of, 147, 150
Endor, Witch of, lii, 181
enemy, 161, 185, 189
energies, divine, 173; uncreated, 173
Englishman, sangfroid of, 118
enlightenment, xxx
enmities, 56
Enos, 23
enslavement, liberation from, liii
envy, 56, 85, 108
Ephesus, Council of, 127
Ephraim, xl–xli, 105, 114, 129–30, 132–33, 177; adoption of, xl–xli, 125–26; family of, xli; sons of, 134
Ephrata, 99, 130
equality, of men and women, xvii
eros, 91
error, 14, 61, 110; exegetical, 127
Esau, xxxi–xxxiv, 54, 84–90, 97–99; as bustling, xxxi; as busy, xxxi; as glutton, 85; as hunter-farmer, 84; as husbandman, 84; as profane person, 85; as red and hairy, 84; as reprobate, 85–86; as sincere countryman, xxxi, 84; bewilderment of, 97; birth of, xxxi, 84; birthright of, xxxi, 84–85, 87; blessing of, 90; descendents of, 99; flaws of, xxxi; heel of, 84; heritage of, 85; marriages of, xxx, 86; passion of, 85; reconciliation with Jacob of, xxxiii–xxxiv, 97–98; weariness of, 85; wives of, 90; wonderment of, 98; wrath of, xxxii, 89
Escol (Eschol), 47
Esdraelon, plains of, 131
espousal, li; to Christ, 79; to Yahweh, xlviii, 176
essence, divine, 141, 173

estates, Egyptian, 101
estrangement, xviii
eternity, 185
Ethanim, 170
Ethiopia, 5, 11
Eucharist, xlix–l, 168
Euphrates, 5, 11–12, 49, 153
Europe, 100
evangelists, 4
evasion, from reality, 76; speculation as, 76
Eve, ix, xviii, 11–14, 17–18; as type of church, 13; banishment of, 17; children of, 18, 23; creation of, xvi, 5, 12–13; defense of, 17; gnomic pronouncement of, xviii, 18; humility of, xviii, 18; sin of, ix, 14, 18; wisdom of, xviii, 18
Everest, Mt., 28
evil(s), xxvi, 5, 9–10, 14, 16–18, 20, 26, 30, 65, 105, 107, 115, 118, 146, 148, 154, 161, 176, 184, 189; climax of, 62; deliverance from, 130; existence of, 106; experience of, 10–11; kingdom of, 18; knowledge of, xvi, 10, 13, 15; mystery of, 107; of punishment, 148; of sin, 148; power of, xviii; prey of, 73; problem of, xxxv, 105; speaking, 104; taste of, 11; transmutation of, xlii
evildoers, 106
evolution, 3; rationalistic, 2
ewes, 95
excitement, moment of, 112
execution, 3
exegesis, biblical, xiv; medieval, xl; objective, xv; patristic, xl; scientific, 127–28
exegete, 2
exemplar, divine, 141
exile, 155, 172; happiness in, 114
existentialism, xxvii

exodus, xliv, xlviii, liv, 27, 99, 101, 136, 158–61; as revelation, xliv; as sign, xliv; daily, 164; date of, 136
experience, 11; contemplative, xxiii; dark-night, xix; growth in, 81; lived, l; monastic, l; of God, ix, xxiv, 51, 54; personal, xxv; religious, xxiv, 51
exultation, song of, 66
Exultet, xlviii, 156–57
eye(s), 14, 107, 119, 121, 139, 149, 178, 182; of Benjamin, 119; of Godhead, 51; uncircumcised, 151
Ezechias (Hezekiah), 181
Ezechiel (Ezekiel), 32, 171–72; vision(s) of, l, 171–72

faces, four, 171; of cherub, 171; of eagle, 171; of lion, 171; of man, 171
fact, historical, 100
faculty, executive, 147; of love, 147; of will, 147
failure, l, 174
faith, xx, 21, 31, 37–38, 44–45, 56, 68–69, 76, 107, 174, 177; as dark night, 160; community of, lii; deep, 72; eyes of, 70; free, 174; growth in 83; hearing of, 44; hesitation in, 75; icon of, xlviii; in promise, 76; justification by, xxi, 37, 45; lack of, 60; loving, 81; night of, xx, 31; of Abraham, xxv, xxvii–xxviii, 37–38, 40–41, 43, 49, 52, 59, 63, 69–72, 74–75, 142; perfect, 76; perfection of, 75; reparation through, 157; sacrifice of, 21; sign of, 71; spirit of, xxv
fall, xv–xviii, 3, 13–17, 84, 135; cause of, xx; consequence of, xviii; effect of, 15
falsity, 14–15; criterion of, 184

family, foundations of, xvii, 12
famine, xxxvii, 40, 105, 164, 166; Egyptian, 113–15, 119, 125; seven years of, 113–14; terror of, 114
fantasies, xvii
fate, 27; arbiter of, 20; common, 150; of world, 27
father(s), church, xxix–xxx, 3, 5–6, 9, 15, 48, 57, 59, 78–85, 121, 139; Cistercian, 80; earthly, 43
fatherless, 182
fault, 189; happy, xviii
favor, divine, xviii
fear(s), 8, 15, 22, 62, 107, 112, 123, 185, 190; of God, 62, 74, 87, 91, 152, 160, 164, 182–83, 185; of Lord, 160
feast(s), 117, 185–86; family, xlviii, 154; marriage, 95; new, 157
fecundity, 4; importance of, xv
feeling(s), base, 133; compassionate, 12; personal, 133; subjective, xxxvi, 111; wounded, 111
female, 45
fertility, 34; cult of, 19; days of, xx, 31; greater, 31; of Agar, xxiii; promise of, xix
festival(s), 177; paschal, xlviii, 157
fetishism, 104
feudalism, Egyptian, 102, 125
fidelity, 151; commitment of, li; divine, 72; life of, xxvii; of God, xl, xliv, 136, 180, 182
fields, scent of, 87
figs, 102, 134
filth, 180; shame of, 189
fire, xxviii–xxix, l, 57, 73–74, 144, 153, 153–54, 162, 169–70, 179; coals of, xxxvii, 115, 171; column of, 49; consuming, 22; eternal, 22; flame of, 137; lamp of, 49; on ground, 152; pillar of, 160
firmament, 171
firstborn, death of, 154; killing of, xliv, 136; of herds, 181, 185; of sheep, 181, 185; redemption of, 145; sanctification of, 144, 158; slaying of, 144, 153, 155–56
firstfruits, 107, 153, 181, 185–87
fish, 99
fishing, 131; Egyptian, 102
flames, leaping, 183
flax, 177
fleece, golden, 11
flesh, xvii, 14–15, 22, 37, 44, 55–56, 65, 68, 107, 112, 144; desires of, 176; end of, 27; human, 139; of Christ, 13, 106, 140, 168; to eat, 165; unruly, 15; works of, 56
fleshpots, 164, 166
flies, plague of, 152–53
flocks, 46, 93–96, 108–9, 124, 152–53, 180, 188
flood, ix, xix, 26–30, 33, 64; Babylonian story of, 28; Hindu story of, 28; receding of, 29–30; universality of, 27–28; vision of, 25
Florence, 131
flour, 167, 172, 187
flowering, 91
flowers, 5
flutes, 102
folly, xvii, 14, 63, 177
font, baptismal, 4, 53
food, 9, 182; miraculous, 166; of travelers, 168; sacrificed to idols, 190
fool(s), 61, 145
forces, cosmic, 104
foreigner, 187
forest, 177
formation, monastic, xliv; spiritual, xv
fornication, 22, 38, 56, 189; spiritual, 179
Foster, R. J., 24–25
fountain(s), 131; of deep, 29; sealed; twelve, 161
fowls, 5, 26, 28, 177
frailty, xvii, 14

France, southern, 143
Francis of Assisi, St., 56
frankincense, 8
Fransen, Irénée, 87
free, 45
freedom, xxxviii, liv, 3, 17, 71, 83, 119, 151, 174, 187; absolute, 87; authentic, xxvii; complete, xlvii; dignity of, 148; education of, 150; forfeit of, xlviii; human, xlvii, 145; of speech, 15; perfection of, 150; promise of, xlviii
friend(s), 187, 189; abandonment of, 70
friendship, love of, xxxiii, 94; worldly, 190
frogs, plague of, 152–53
Fromm, Erich, 10
fructus, 191
fruit(s), xvi, 99, 153; of land, 180; of love, 8; of tree of knowledge, 13–14; of wisdom, xvi, 8; of womb, 180
fruitfulness, 6; genuine, xx
fruition, 191
frumenty, 187
frustration, xvii
fulfillment, xxii, 3; hope of, xxxvii, 113
furnace, 179

Gabaonites (Gibeonites), 191
Gad, 93, 132, 134, 136; territory of, 132
gain, Christ as, 123; death as, 123; desire for, 123
Galaad (Gilead), 96, 108, 132
galbanum, 8
Galileans, 131–32
Galilee, 131, 191
games, Egyptian, 102
garden(s), 8, 15; Egyptian, 102; of delights, 9; of God, 46; paradise as, xv, 5
garments, 153, 178
gates, twelve, 133

Gedeon (Gideon), 135
Gehon (Gihon), 5, 11–12
generation(s), 4, 68; chosen, 178
generosity, 91
Genesareth, Lake of, 132
gentiles, xxvii, 21, 32, 44–45, 69, 106–7; apostle of, 107; cities of, 153; consorting with, 176; Galilee of, 131; riches of, 107; relations with, 162; righteous, xxi; salvation of, 106–7; separation from 180
gentleness, 47; land of, 47
Gerara (Gerar), 86
Gergezite (Girgashite), 179
Germany, 28
Gersam (Gershom), 137
Gessen (Goshen), xl, 101, 105, 124
Gethsemani, Abbey of, vii, xi, xiii, 148
giants, 26, 28, 191
gibbet, 112–13
gift(s), 93, 117, 181, 185; divine, xiv; of God, xviii, xxiv, xxvii, 53, 167; supernatural, 113; to God, xviii
Gillet, Lev, 169
Gilson, Étienne, 122–23
glory, 38–39, 59, 153, 165, 173, 183; divine, l; of God, l, 19, 149, 165–66, 169–71
gnostics, 22
goat(s), 49, 97; black, 95; blood of, xxxv, 108–9; brown, 95; buck, 187; variegated, 95
God, 8, 14, 111, 136, 184; abandonment to, 49; absence of, 184; act(s) of, xiv, 72, 143, 183; action of, 106; activity of, xv; adoration of, 175, 179, 183; adversaries of, 161; Almighty, 53, 117, 153; alone, 70; angel of, 142, 160, 169, 181; anger of, 64, 153, 161–62, 189; appearance of, xxv; arm of, 149; as Absolute, 51; as Adonai, 142–43; as all-powerful, 151;

as Being, 142; as consuming fire, 22, 169; as Creator, xv, xxvi, 1, 16, 47, 61, 67, 92, 172; as *Deus* (*Theos*), xlvi, 141–42; as El, 142; as El Elyon, 142; as El Roi, xxiv; as El Shaddai, 53, 142; as Elohim, 3, 142; as end of all, liii, 149–50, 179; as enemy, 16; as faithful, 86, 177, 180; as Father, xxviii–xxix, 4, 43, 73, 88, 107, 150; as Father of Lights, 43; as God of gods, 182; as governor, 146; as great, 182; as guide, ix, 40; as healer, 161; as Holy One of Israel, 57, 159; as judge, 22; as life of being, 51; as living Father, 168; as Lord of lords, 182; as man of war, 161; as person, 54; as prime mover, 146; as protector, 48; as *qui est*, xlvi, 142; as reward, 48; as rival, xvii, 16; as salvation 161; as savior, 82; as source of all, liii; as source of being, 51; as strong, 86, 180; as Terror of Isaac, 86; as Tetragrammaton (YHWH), xlvi, 142–43; as Trinity, 3; as true God, 110, 143; as ultimate truth, 140; as witness of acts, 184; as Yahweh, xlvi, 23, 110, 142–43, 167; aspect of, 142; assistance of, 51; awareness of, 54; being of, xxxii, 14, 92, 147; belief in, 37; blessing(s) of, xxxii, 43, 93, 110, 181; bosom of, xxviii, 20, 70; bread of, 168; call of, xlvii, 52, 151; causality of, 146, 150; ceremonies of, 182; child of, 3; children of, 45; choice for, xxvii; choice of, 18, 87; city of, xx, 22, 34, 133; command(s) of, xix, 29, 31, 69, 71; commandments of, 161, 167, 180, 182; communication with, 71; communion with, xxi, 44; concreteness of, xxiv, 51; confession of, liii, 185; confrontation with, xxxiii–xxxiv; consecration to, xxiv, xxvii; considerateness for, 61; contact with, xxxii, 91; contempt for, 20; conversation of, 169, 175; covenant of, 176, 180; creative activity of, xv, 183; creative word of, liii, 17; denial of, 76; dependence on, 29, 113; designs of, 67, 149; division from, 10, 13; duties to, 179; ecstasy of, 91; elect of, xxxv, 105, 107; equality with, xx, 35; essence of, 91; existence of, 140, 142; experience of, ix, xxiv, 51, 54; faith in, lii, 179; favor of, xxxiii, 43, 97; fear of, 62, 74, 87, 91, 152, 160, 164, 182–83, 185; fidelity of, xl, xliv, 136, 180, 182; fight with, 97; finger of, 152; footstool of, 184; formation by, 36; free act of, 19, 149; free choice of, 39; freedom of, xxxi, 148; friend of, 64; garden of, 46; gift of, xviii, xxiv, xxvii, 53, 167; gift to, xviii; glory of, l, 19, 149, 165–66, 169–71; good pleasure of, 148–49; goodness of, 14, 16, 82, 107, 141, 147; government of, 146, 149–50; greatness of, xxiv, 53, 56, 125; grace of, xxi, xxvii, 17, 51, 70, 82, 88, 107, 151; habitation of, 161; hall of, 91; hand(s) of, xxix, 180, 189; hidden, xxii; holiness of, 54, 69, 161; homage to, 110; honoring, liii; house of, xxxii, 90–92, 170–71; identity of, liii, 183;

God (*continued*)
ignorance of, 61; image of, 3, 12, 83, 190; immutability of, 140; incorruptible, 61; indignation of, 153, 189; infinite, xlvi; inheritance of, 172; instructions of, xxvii; instrument of, 126; intentions of, xv; interior action of, xxxv; interior richness of, 3; intimacy with, xx, xxxii, li, 15, 86, 90; Israel of, 56; journey to: ix; judgments of, 153, 182; justice of, xlv, 74, 137, 185; kingdom of, 18, 56, 64, 133; kinship with, xiv, 3; knowledge of, xxii, 44, 54, 59, 166; law of, 44, 145, 158, 164, 166–67; letters from, ix, 35; life in, 23; light of, 51, 139, 152; living, xxiii, lii, 4, 22, 52, 55, 142, 179; love for, xvi, xxv, lii, 35, 54, 60, 87, 123, 174, 179–80, 182, 190; love for Israel of, 180; love for Moses of, 162; love for stranger of, 182; love for world of, 58; love of, xxxi, xxxv, lii, 13, 30, 51, 58, 74, 85, 90, 105, 118, 147, 149, 180, 182; love of for Son, xxviii; manifestation of, 78; mercy of, xix–xx, xxvii, xliv, lii, 4, 17, 22, 29–32, 66, 70, 74, 82, 136, 141, 149, 154, 159, 161, 180, 182, 185; messages of, xxxii, 91; messenger of, xxii; might of, 185; mighty, 180, 182; mind of, 41; most high, 47; mountain of, xlv, 137; mystery of, 12, 52, 56; name(s) of, xlvi–xlvii, l, lii–liii, 4, 21, 23, 40, 50, 52–53, 138, 141–42, 151, 169, 175, 182–85; nature of, liii, 173, 183; oath of, 180; obedience to, xliv, 69, 136; of Abraham, 51–52, 90–91, 138; of exodus, 93; of fathers, 137–38, 161, 184; of heaven, 153; of Isaac, 52, 90, 138; of Israel, 86, 98, 169; of Jacob, xxxii, 52, 92, 138; of Joseph, 93; of judgment, 159; of philosophers, 52; of Psalms, 92; omnipresence of, 91; oneness of, 182; order of, 147–48; peace of, 32; people of, xxi–xxii, xlviii, li–lii, liv, 36, 39, 43, 55, 98, 106, 114, 133, 162, 174, 176, 178, 192; perfections of, 141; personality of, xxiv, 51; plan of, xxiii–xxiv, xxxv, xxxvii, xlv, 13, 49, 53, 105, 113, 124, 138; pledge of, xxvii, xxxiii; possession of, 176; power of, xxv, xxxii, xxxvi, xlvii, 54, 61, 71, 74–75, 91, 93, 143, 149, 152, 154, 172, 174, 184, 189; praise of, 67, 185; precepts of, 161, 182; presence of, xxi, xxiii, xxv, xxxii, xl, lii, 35–36, 51–52, 54, 61, 71, 91–92, 169, 180, 184; priest of, xxiii, 47; promise(s) of, xxiv, xxvii, 17, 30, 37, 41, 43–44, 47–49, 53–55, 69, 71, 107, 142, 151; property of, li, 176; protection of, 125, 158, 176; providence of, xix–xx, 29, 31, 141; purpose of, 86; quest for, 64; reality of, xvii, 14, 51, 54; reconciliation with, 30; redemption by, 180; relationship with, xvii, lii, 151; reliance on, li; request to see, liv; resignation to, 151; respect to, 60–61; rest in, xv; rest of, 3–4, 186; restoration to, 107; revelation(s) of, 52–53, 106, 138; richness of, 3; sacrifice of, 70; sacrifice

to, 138; sanctity of, xxv, 54; search for, 136; self-communication of, 147; self-gift of, 147; separation from, 10–11, 16; service of, 150, 181–83; severity of, 107; sight of, 142; sign of, 20, 152; silence of, 136; simplicity of, 141; son(s) of, xix, 26, 36, 150; sorrow of, 26, 61; spirit of, 4, 113; strength of, 18, 149; subsistence of, 141; substance of, 141; support of, 176; supremacy of, 182; sweetness of, 82, 151; tabernacle of, 13, 178; temple of, 8, 174; tempting of, 188; terrible, 180, 182; thanksgiving to, liii; things of, 85; throne of, 8, 184; time of, xx, xxxvii, 31, 49; transcendence of, 52; transcendent, lii, 192; true, xxii, lii, 43–44, 47, 143, 167, 179; trust in, xliv, xlix, lii, 136, 167, 182; truth of, 14, 51, 61, 140; union with, xxvii, 12, 15, 43, 83, 123; unwillingness to punish of, 61; vision of, 98, 173; voice of, 16, 70, 161, 171, 176, 187; warning of, 19; ways of, 23, 164, 182; will of, xxviii, xxxvii, xl, xliv, xlvii, li, liii, 10, 14, 26, 49, 72, 74–76, 78, 84, 87, 105–6, 118, 138, 145, 147–48, 151, 174, 183; wisdom of, xxxv, 20–21, 28, 30, 49, 75, 105, 149; wonders of, 152, 161; word(s) of, xv, xviii–xix, lii–liii, 14, 21, 41, 48–49, 78, 127–28, 164–65, 182–83; work(s) of, xx–xxi, xxvi, xliv, 3–4, 31, 36, 42, 66, 136, 167, 189; worship of, xxxii, lii, 91, 179; wrath of, 31–32, 61, 153, 177, 188; writing of, 189

god(s), 181, 188; adoration of, 181; earth, 18; Egyptian, 103, 110, 155; false, xvi, lii, 44, 69, 110, 138, 142, 181–82; household, 96–97, 181; little, 76; oneself as, xvi, 11, 13, 20; strange, 179; totems as, 103; worship of, 44, 181, 184
gold, 5, 118, 177, 180, 189; vessels of, 138, 156
Gomorrha (Gomorrah), 22–23, 46, 58, 69; cry against, 61–62; destruction of, xxv, 34; people of, 58
good, 5, 9–10, 14, 17, 20, 86, 105, 107, 118, 146, 148; choice of, 146, 150; communication of, 147; desire for, 147; divine, 11; general, 147; greater, xlii; illusory, 14; knowledge of, xvi, 10–11, 13, 15; particular, 147; specific, 147; universal, 146
Good Friday, 106, 154
goodness, xxxvii, 56, 115; divine, xxx; exaggerated, 14; illusory, 14
goods, material, 176; of neighbor, li; temporal, 87
goose, 117
gospel, ix
grace(s), 8–9, 22, 38, 56, 71, 88, 92, 106, 145, 150, 157, 173–74, 190; containers of, xxx, 78; created, 173; dependence on, 151, 189; divine, xx; efficacious, 146; glory of, 107; likeness as, 3; mystical, 151; odor of, 81; of Easter, xxxix; of God, xxi, xxvii, 17, 51, 70, 82, 88, 107, 151; of prayer, 190; sanctifying, 92; special, 79; struggle of, xlvii, 145; theology of, 173; touch of, 81; vehicles of, xxx, 78
grain, 105
grapes, 102, 111
graves, 159

greatness, 136
Greek(s), 45, 175; rhetoric of, 79
Gregory of Nyssa, St., xlvi, 81, 139–40
Gregory Palamas, St., 173
grief, 123
groves, 179, 181, 185
growth, 140; spiritual, xxiv
Guardian Angels, Feast of, 160
Guardini, Romano, l–li, 52, 141–42, 174
Guerric of Igny, Bl., xxxviii–xl, 119–23
guest(s), as angel, xxii, 42; as messenger of God, xxii, 42; human, 59; of Abraham, xxv, xxix, 59–60
guile, 16
guilty, slaughter of, 162
guitars, 102

Hai (Ai), 40
hail, plague of, 152–53
halo, magic, 184
hand, 187; sign on, 182; strong, 180
handmaid(s), 96, 186
happiness, xxxvii, 15, 113
Haran (Charan), xxii, xxxii–xxxiii, 39–40, 45, 89–90, 191
hardship, xxi
harmony, 149; perfect, 17
harpers, 22
harps, 96, 102
hart, 132
harvest(s), 186; bad, 114; barley, 187; Egyptian, 102, 114; wheat, liv, 187
hatred, 73, 108, 111
head, 57; swearing by, 184
hearing, sense of, 139
heart(s), 7, 24, 35, 57, 69, 77, 81, 83, 92, 106, 121, 187–88; affections of, xxvi, 61; desires of, 61; direction of, 92; foolish, 61; foreskin of, 182; hardness of, xxxviii, xliii, xlvii, 119, 145, 151–52, 159; human, xxxv; intimacy of, xviii; of slave, 69; of son, 69; one, xxi, 35; purity of, xviii, 19; sorrow of, 26; whole, 179, 182
heat, 40, 153
heaven(s), xxvi, 22, 24, 33, 41, 47–48, 51, 57, 65, 67, 88, 90, 92, 123, 169, 172, 177–78, 180, 182, 185; as throne of God, 184; assault on, 35; bread from, 164; circuit of, 172; creation of, 3–4, 6; dew of, 7, 89; door to, 92; fields of, 88; first, 13, 178; gate of, xxxii, 90–92; kingdom of, 37, 89; liturgy of, 145; new, 13, 178; powers of, 65; sanctuary of, 170; starry, 49; stars of, 182, 189
Hebrews, land of, 111
Hebron, 46, 108, 134, 191
Hector, 131–32
Heinisch, Paul, 50
heir(s), 45, 48, 69
Heliopolis, 100–101, 103, 114
hell, 109; darkness of, 122; judgment of, 21
helplessness, xvii, 14
Hemor (Hamor), 98
Henoch (Enoch), xix, 21, 23–26; age of, 23; apocalypses of, 24–26; assumption of, 25–26; Ethiopic (1 Enoch), 24–25; Slavonic (2 Enoch), 25–26
Henoch (Enoch) son of Cain, 22
herb, 5
herds, 124, 156, 173, 180–81, 185, 187; of Pharaoh, 124–25
herdsmen, 22, 46
hermeneutics, xi
hermits, 4
Herod Antipas, 106
heroism, 151
hesitations, 15
Heth, sons of, 76
Hethite (Hittite), 138, 145, 158, 179, 181
Hevilath (Havilah), 5, 11

Hevite (Hivite), 138, 145, 158, 179, 181
hierarchy, 91; angelic, 91
highlands, 191
highwaymen, 132
hill(s), 131, 181, 184; ensign on, 159; eternal, 132
Hillary of Poitiers, St., 59
hippopotamus, 102
hireling, 188
history, Christian, viii; monastic, xi
Hittites, 76, 86, 101, 136, 191
hoarfrost, 153; manna like, 165–66
holiness, 157; laws of, liv; of life, 192
holocaust(s), 73, 181, 185, 187
holy of holies, 143, 170
Holy Spirit, xiv, xxx, 3–4, 10–11, 44, 130, 150; action of, 121; as inheritance, 133; descent of, 36; fire of, 74; gift of, xxxix, xlii; infusion of, 81; kiss of, 81; life-giving, 122; person of, 173; presence of, 121; promise of, 44; sin against, xxxviii, 119; temple of, l; waters of, 78; witness of, 121
homage, xxxiii, xxxv–xxxvi, 94
home, abandonment of, 70; true, 40
homeland, love for, ix, 35; spiritual, 41; true, xlii
Homer, 132
homosexuality, 61
honesty, xxxiv, 117
honey, 8, 117, 167; land of, 137–38, 145, 158
honeycomb, 8
honor, 8
hope, xvii–xviii, xx–xxi, xxv–xxvi, 8–9, 25, 31, 35, 37–38, 53, 56, 62, 65, 78, 81, 112, 123, 159, 177
Horeb, Mt., 138, 170
hornets, 180
horse(s), 159, 161
Horus, as falcon, 103; identified with Ra, 103

hospitality, xxxiv, 42, 104, 172; duty of, 62–63; mystery of, xxii, xxix, 42, 77; refusal of, 84
house(s), li, 181–82; doors of, 182; spiritual, 178
household, 42, 136
humanity, xvii, lii; corruption of, xix; degeneracy of, xix; divided, xxii; divine image in, 4; fallen, xviii; reunification of, xxii; sinful, ix
humility, xx–xxi, xxix, 31, 35–36, 51, 75, 113, 184, 189
hunger, for justice, 164; for word, 164; in spiritual life, 164; spiritual, xlix
hunting, Egyptian, 102
Hurrites (Horrites), 191
husband(s), 12; as head of wife, 13; Yahweh as, 177
hyenas, 129; trained, 102
Hyksos, 100–101, 191
hymns, eucharistic, xlix
hypothesis, documentary, xiv, 1–2
hyssop, 144, 155
Hyvernat, H., xxxiv, 99–104

Ice Age, 100
idealism, 94
identity, communal, xxiv; mystery of, 184; personal, liii; spiritual, 83
idol(s), lii, 96, 169, 171, 179–81, 185; burial of, xxxiv, 45, 98; Egyptian, 103; names of, 185; possession by, 179; sacrifice to, 177; service of, 182; world as, 183
idolatry, lii, liv, 56, 61, 167, 174, 179, 188–89; exclusion of, 181; temptation to, lii, 179
ignorance, 83
illumination, xvii; higher, 13
illusion(s), xvi, xx, l, 16, 145, 174
image(s), 175, 182; as nature, 3; divine, xiv, xvii, liii, 3–4; graven, 175; of false gods, 181; of God, 3, 12, 83, 190;

image(s) (*continued*)
  prohibition of, lii, 181;
  worship of, 181
imagery, nuptial, xvii
imagination, 121, 128
Immaculate Conception, Feast of, 8
immodesty, 56
immortality, 9
imperfections, 123
impulses, selfish, xviii
incantation, magic, 184
incense, 177
incredulity, 57
independence, xl, 124; economic, liv, 187
Indians, 183–84
indignation, 153
Indus, 11
infidelity, xlviii, 63; reparation for, liii, 185
infirmities, 180
infusion, 81
inheritance, 41, 88; divine, xxxi, 88
iniquity, 57, 62, 149, 159; mystery of, 42
injustice, xxxvii, 50, 61, 86, 88, 110; racial, vii
insecurity, 112
insensibility, spirit of, 107
insight, l, 174
inspiration, xliv; biblical, xi
instrument(s), divine, xxxi; of God, 126
insults, 122
intellect, surrender of, xxiii
intelligence(s), 150; communion of, 91; loving, 91; world of, 90
intermediaries, 180; angelic, xxxii
interests, individual, 113; of whole, 113
interpretation(s), allegorical, xxix–xxx; biblical, vii; freedom of, 127; historical, viii; literal, 127; literary-critical, viii; methods of, vii–ix; mystical, 127; of texts, vii; patristic, ix, xxix–xxx, 3; principles of, xi; spiritual, x, xxxix, 120, 127

intimacy, relationship of, xx; with God, xx, li, 15
invaders, Ethiopian, 101; Libyan, 101
iron, 191
irony, xxxii; dramatic, xxxvii, 115; effectiveness of, xxxvii, 116
Isaac, xxix–xxxi, 37, 66–84, 86, 89–90, 114, 123, 130, 135, 174, 182, 189; altar of, xxx, 86, 123; as fulfillment of promise, 66; as laughter, xxv–xxvi, 56, 66; as sacrament of Christ, xxx, 78; as sole heir, 67; as type of Christ, xxx, 71, 78–84; birth of, xxv–xxvi, 66–67, 80; blessing of, xxxi–xxxii, xl, 89–90; blindness of, xxxi; circumcision of, 66; conception of, xxv; covenant with, 137; death of, xxxi, xxxiv, 99; deceiver of, 109; descendants of, xxvii; God of, 52, 90, 138; growth of, 78; in Gerara (Gerar), 86; love for, 71; marriage of, xxx, 78, 80; meeting with Rebecca of, 78; name of, xxv, 56, 66, 80, 130; mourning of, 78; sacrifice of, ix, xxvii–xxix, 41, 69–76, 109, 156, 168; sons of, 68; trust of, 72; weaning of, 67; well of, 123; wife of, xxix, 76–80
Isaias (Isaiah), 57, 131, 172; inaugural vision of, l, 170
Ishmael (Ismael), xxiii, 50–51, 53–54; birth of, 49–50, 52; casting out of, xxvi–xxvii, 67–68; daughter of, 90; name of, 51; rejection of, 68
Ishmaelites (Ismaelites), 108–9
Isis, wife of Osiris, 103
island, 153
Israel, xxxi, 18, 43, 57, 62, 90, 136, 138; affliction of, 138, 164; ancients of, 138, 144, 155,

GENERAL INDEX   249

169–70; apostasy of, 135; army of, 144, 151, 155; as child, 177; as chosen, 181; as consecrated, 181; as holy, 176; as northern kingdom, 92; as settled people, 171; as sinful nation, 57; as son, 150; as wicked seed, 57; as unfaithful spouse, 177; as ungracious children, 57; assembly of, 155, 165; camp of, 160, 162, 165–66, 178, 189; chariot of, 123; children of, xl, xlviii–xlix, 136–38, 143–44, 151–52, 154–61, 164–67, 169–70, 175–76, 178, 186, 189; cities of, 57–58; congregation of, 165, 175; cry of, 138; deliverance of, xlvii, 138, 143–45, 151–61; elders of, 162, 169, 176, 178; escape of, xlix; faith in, 37; fathers of, 164, 182; fidelity of, xlviii; future of, 25; God of, 86, 98, 169; greatness of, 43; hardness of heart of, 162; heart of, 164; horseman of, 123; house of, 167; ignorance of, 57; in desert, 162–68; infidelity of, l, 135; inheritance in, 172; journey of, xlix–l, 162–64; joy in, 134; king of, 177; leaders of, 57; murmuring of, xlix, liv, 161–62, 164–66, 189; nation of, xli; people of, 106, 151, 158; persecution of, 137; pilgrimage of, xlix; prayer of, xlv, 137; prevarications of, 188; priests of, 57; proving of, 164; rebellion of, 166; return of, 177; rulers of, 175; salvation of, 62; sins of, 183; sons of, xlii; sorrow of, 138; tribes of, xlii, 93, 126, 133–34, 181; vocation of, li, 135, 138

Israelite(s), lii, 175; as aliens, 124; as nomads, 124; as shepherds, 124–25; belief of, 161; character of, xl; faithful, l, 172; hostility of toward Edomites, 84; house of, 167; independence of, xl; journey of, xlii–xliii, liv; Paul as, 106; persecution of, xliv; reveling of, 163; struggles of, liv; temptations of, liv; without guile, 88
Issachar, 93, 131–32, 134, 136; as farmer, 131; as laborer, 131; sons of, 134; territory of, 131
Issus, Battle of, 101

Jabbok (Jaboc), xxxiii, 97
Jabel (Jabal), 22
Jacob (Israel), ix, xxxi–xxxiv, xxxviii–xlii, 37, 45, 62, 84–99, 115–17, 119–33, 135–36, 172, 174, 182, 189; achievement(s) of, 98, 125; adoption of sons of Joseph by, xl–xli, 114, 125–26; adventures in Mesopotamia of, xxxii–xxxiv, 93–97; aged, 126; altar of, 98; anger of, 87; as ancestor of chosen race, xxxi, 86; as bedouin, 92; as city-slicker, xxxi, 84; as divine instrument, xxxi, 126; as elect, 85; as energetic, 86; as father, 126; as fighter, 86; as figure of Christ, 85, 133; as Israel, xxxiii, 86, 98–99; as man of God, xxxi, 86; as meek, 85; as patient, 86; as peaceful, 85; as plain man, 84–85; as predestinate, 85; as prophet, 126; as prudent, 86; as quiet, xxxi, 85–86; as reflective, xxxi; as shepherd, 86; as thoughtful, 85–86; as trickster, xxxii–xxxiii; as useless servant, 125; as younger son, 84–85, 88;

250 GENERAL INDEX

Jacob (Israel) (*continued*)
birth of, 84; blessing by, 126–32; blessing of, 87–88, 90, 93, 97; burial of, xl, 105, 125, 132–33; care of, 97–98; change of name of, xxxiii–xxxiv, 97–99; children of, xxxiii, xli, 93, 95, 97; confidence of, 86; covenant with, 137; curse of, 129; death of, xl, xlii, 132; deathbed blessings of, xli–xlii, 105, 126–32; deception of by Laban, xxxii–xxxiii, 94–95; deception of by sons, xxxv, 109; deception of Isaac by, xxxi–xxxii, 87–90, 109; deep sleep of, 119–20; desperateness of, 116; discretion of, 98; disillusionment of, 125; divine favor toward, xxxiii; dream(s) of, xxxii, xxxiv, 90–92; dying, 126; enmity of Esau for, xxxi, 89–90; etymology of name of, xxxi, 84; eyes of, 130; family of, 124; flocks of, xxxiii, 95–96; funeral procession of, 132; God of, xxxii, 52, 92, 138; greatness of, xl, 125; heart of, 93; historical, xli; house of, 176; in Egypt, 123–32; interests of, 93; intimacy with Yahweh of, 86; journey of, 93–94; joy of, 124, 126; ladder of, 88, 90, 92; love for Benjamin of, 93; love for Joseph of, xxxiv–xxxv, 93, 105, 107; love for Rachel of, xxxiii–xxiv, 93–95; magnanimity of, xl, 125; manipulative behavior of, xxxi; marriages of, xxxii–xxxiii, 94–95; maturity of, xxxi, 86; meeting of with Pharaoh, xl, 124–25; name of, xxxi, 84, 130; nobility of, xl, 125; piety of, 86; pilgrimage of, 125; prophetic oracles of, xli; prosperity of, 131; prudence of, 86; punishment of, xxxii; rash promise of, 96; reconciliation with Esau of, xxxiii–xxxiv, 97–98; reconciliation with Laban of, xxxiii–xxxiv, 96–97; reunion with Joseph of, xl, 120; sacrifice of, 123; seed of, 90–91; sensibility of, 86; servants of, 97; simplicity of, xl, 125; sons of, xli–xlii, 86, 93, 117; sorrow of, 109; soul of, 86; spiritual maturity of, xl; strength of, 97; struggle of, 93; stubbornness of, 97; subtlety of, 86; sufferings of, xxxii, 86, 93; tact of, 97–98; tears of, 94; thigh of, 97, 136; toil of, xxxii, 93; traditions of, 87; trickery of, xxxi–xxxii, 87–88, 93, 95–96; vineyards of, 131; vow of, 92–93; well of, xxxii, 45, 88, 98; wives of, 93–98; works of, 125; wrestling of, xxxiii–xxxiv, 97

James, St., 43
Japanese, 28
Japeth, 28
jasper, 32
jealousy, 125
Jebusite, 138, 145, 158, 179, 181
Jehovah, 143
Jeremias (Jeremiah), xxiv; Letter of, 181
Jericho, 1, 7
Jerome, St., 6, 96
Jerusalem, xii, xx, xxiii, 21, 32, 34–36, 47, 170, 172; as city of great king, 184; as city of peace, xxiii, 47; desolation of, 21; earthly, 68; heavenly, xxi, 22, 36, 68; New, xvi–xvii,

xlii, l, 13, 133, 178; temple
of, 72
Jesuits, 146
Jethro (Raguel, Reuel), 137; as priest
of Madian, 137; daughters
of, xlv, 137, 139; meeting
with, 162
Jew(s), 21, 37–39, 43, 45, 58, 68,
101, 106, 116, 126, 136,
142, 152, 156, 174, 192;
deliverance of, 154; fear
of, 159; pious, 172; prayers
of, 172; salvation of, 106;
spirituality of, 157
jewels, 177
Jezrahel (Jezreel), 177
Job, 32
John Damascene, St., 142
John of the Cross, xxvii, 8, 42, 67–
69, 97, 159–60; as mystic,
xlviii
John the Baptist, St., xxi, 66;
preaching of, 37
John the Evangelist, St., 81, 133, 178
Joiada (Jehoiada), 134
Jordan, xxiii, 12, 46, 97–98, 131–32,
134, 185
Joseph, ix, xii, xxxiii–xlii, 93,
98–99, 101, 132–33, 135–36;
affection for brethren of,
119; as elegant, 110; as father
to Pharaoh, 118; as feeder
of the land, 114; as fertile
branch, 132; as governor,
113–15, 118; as handsome,
110; as interpreter of
dreams, xxxvii, 105, 111–13;
as redeemer figure, xxxv; as
savior of the world, 113–14;
as tale-bearer, 109; as type
of Christ, xxxviii, 106, 116,
120; at court of Pharaoh,
112–15; attempted seduction
of, xxxvi, 110–11; birth of
xxxiii, 95; blessing of, 132;
bones of, 158; brothers of,
xxxiii–xxxiv, xxxvii–xxxviii,
93, 105, 107–8, 114–19;

chariot of, 124; charity of,
xlii, 133; contentment of,
114; death of, 133, 136;
divining cup of, xxxviii,
117–18; dreams of, xxxv,
xxxviii, 105, 107–8, 115;
enslavement of, xxxv,
105; exile of, 114; faith
of, 133; forgiveness of,
xxxviii, 119; game of, 105,
114–19; glory of, 119; God
of, 93; happiness of, 114;
identity of, xxxviii, 118;
imprisonment of, xxxvi–
xxxvii, 105, 111–13, 120;
in Egypt, xxxvi–xxxviii,
xl–xli, 105, 110–34, 136;
ingratitude toward, 113;
jealousy toward, xxxv,
107–8; love for Benjamin of,
xxxiii, 93; love of Jacob for,
xxxiii, 105, 107; mildness
of, xxxviii; mother of,
108; motivation of, xxxvi;
narrative account of,
xxxv–xxxvi; new name of,
113–14; oppressors of, xxxv;
plot against, xxxv, 108–9;
presence of, 115; prudence
of, 120; reconciliation of
with brothers, xxxvii–
xxxviii, xlii, 118–19, 132–33;
resentment toward, xxxv;
reunion with Jacob of, xl,
120; revenge of, xxxvii,
115; seed of, 130; sold by
brothers, xxxv, 107–9; sons
of, xl–xli, 105, 114, 125–26,
129–30; spiritual insight
of, xxxviii; sufferings of,
xxxv; tears of, xxxviii, 117,
119; testing of brothers by,
xxxvii–xxxviii, 115–18; tunic
of, xxxv, 107, 109; unknown
identity of, 115; wife of, 114;
wisdom of, 114

Joseph, St., 114–15; as instrument of divine providence, 115; as provider for church, 114–15; as provider for Holy Family, 114; as provider of poor, 114
Josephus, Flavius, 143
Josias (Josiah), King, 2
Josue (Joshua), 164, 189
journey, xxii, xxvii, 41, 182; apostolic, ix, 41; back to God, ix; mystery of, xxix, 77; of Israelites, xlii–xliii, liv; of servant, xxix, 76–78; spiritual, vii
joy(s), xxv–xxvi, xxxix, 5, 56–57, 66–67, 80, 95–96, 122–23, 131, 134; of messianic times, 131; of Spirit, 131
Jubal, 22
jubilee, liv, 188
Juda (Judah), xxxv–xxxvi, xxxviii, xli, 93, 105, 108–10, 116–18, 124, 129–31, 136; as ancestor of messiah, 130; as lion, 130; as powerful, 130; as prosperous, 130; as victorious, 130; sons of, 109–10, 134; wife of, 109
Judaism, Sephardic, 143
Judas, xxxv, 109
Judea, 65, 131
judge(s), li, 137, 162; Egyptian, 103; first, 135; institution of, 176; time of, 132
judgment(s), 24–25, 27, 56–58, 104, 108, 126, 144, 151, 155, 161, 177, 180, 182, 184; final, xxv, xxxviii, xlvii, 24, 33–34, 57, 64, 119, 143, 157; human standards of, xxix, 75; night of, 143; of God, 153, 182; practical, 76; prophecy of, 24; speculative, 76
just, 57, 62; monuments of, 21; trials, of, 34
justice, xxiii, xxxiv, xxxvi, 28, 34, 38, 44, 48, 50, 56, 95, 104, 110, 177; heir of, 34; hunger for, 164; king of, xxiii, 48; of God, xlv, 74, 137, 185; thirst for, 164
justification, xxi, 38; by faith, xxi, 37, 45
Justin Martyr, St., 50

Karkhemish, 101
Kelly, J. N. D., 128
Khons-Hotep, 104
Kierkegaard, Søren, xxvii
kine, seven fat, 112; seven lean, 112
king(s), 153, 180; deceased, 104; four, 47; of Gomorrah, 47; of justice, 48; of peace, 48; of Salem, 47; of Sodom, 47
kingdom(s), glory of, 183; immoveable, 22; of God, 18, 56, 64, 133; of world, 18, 183; priestly, 176, 178
kinship, physical, xxiv
kiss, of mouth, xxx, 81; of Word, 80–81
knowledge, 64, 80; book, 140; divine, 81; existential, 11; intellectual, 81; interior, 121; key of, 20; mother of, 8; mystical, 121; of evil, xvi, 10, 13, 15; of God, xxii, 44, 54, 59, 166; of good, xvi, 10, 13, 15; of Jesus, 121; of reality, 140; of theories, 140; of truth, 140; of words, 140; speculative, 81; sure, 140; tree of, xvi–xvii, 9–12; unitive, xvi; worldly, xlvi, 140
Kush, 11

Laban, xxxii–xxxiii, 77–78, 89–90, 93–97; as pragmatist, 94; character of, 94; craft of, 93; daughters of, xxxii–xxxiii, 93–97; dream of, 96; idols of, 96–97, 181; mercy of, 93; power of, 93; reconciliation with Jacob of, xxxiii, 96–97

GENERAL INDEX 253

labor, xliv, 18, 186, 190; Egyptian, 102; hard, xliv, 136; inner, 190; prohibition of, 155
labor, liv, 190
laborers, Egyptian, 101–2
ladder, Jacob's, 88, 90, 92
Lagrange, M. Joseph, 128–29
lamb(s), 25, 187; blood of, 144, 154; bone of, 156; paschal, xlviii, 143–44, 154, 156–57, 168; slaughter of, 156; without blemish, x, lviii, 154, 187
Lamech, xix, 22–23
land, arid, 46; desolation of, 63; division of, 135; of living, 168; of milk and honey, 138, 145, 158; of promise, xxxii–xxxiii; possession of, 164; promised, xiv, xliv, xlviii–xlix, 1, 41, 76, 84, 105, 133, 135, 156, 164, 181, 189; rest for, liii, 188
language, abandonment of, 70; devaluation of, xvi, 12; mystery of, xvi, 12; respect for, liii; reverence for, liii
Latins, 175
laughter, xxv–xxvi, 67
law(s), l–lii, 1, 37–38, 44, 48, 56, 135, 144, 158, 161–62, 174, 176, 179; as burden, l, 174; as charter of rights and demands, li, 174; as pedagogue, 44; as heavy yoke, 174; book of, 1; curse of, 44; debtor to, 56; function of, 174; giving of, liv; human, li, 174; Mesopotamian, 49; miscellaneous, 192; Mosaic, 1; New, 47, 181–82; of holiness, liv, 192; of God, 44, 145, 158, 164, 166–67; of Lord, 145; of nature, 62; of purification, liv; of sabbath, 186–87; old, 135; perversion of, 174; reaffirmation of, 1; recall of, 1; reception of, 158; re-promulgation of, 1; second, 1; tablets of, liv; versions of, 179; works of, 44
lawyers, 21
Lax, Robert, 148
leaven, 56
Leclercq, Jean, xi
legends, resonance of, 183
legislation, Sinaitic, 2
leisure, liii, 186
lemons, 102
Lent, 111, 120
lentils, 84
Leonard, W., 45
lesson(s), moral, ix; spiritual, xxxvii
lettuce, wild, 144, 154
Levi, xli, 48, 93, 98, 126, 133, 136; condemnation of, 129; fidelity of, 129; inheritance of, 129; sons of, 48, 134, 189; violence of, 129
Levites, 170, 185; duties of, liv, 192
Lia (Leah), xxxii, 93–96, 98; as blear-eyed, 94; children of, 93, 98; fruitfulness of, 93; marriage of, 93–95
liar, 39, 88
Libanus (Lebanon), 7
libations, 187
liberation, xlviii; from bondage, xlviii, liii; from Egypt, 186; mystical, xxv, 57; true, 157
liberator, 186
liberty, xlviii, liii, 56, 67, 69, 177, 186; bond of, xlviii; carnal, xxvii, 68; hope for, 35; human, 147; love of, 174; of desire, 68; of spirit, 68–69; principle of, 146; spiritual, 68; talent of, 150
Libyans, 103
lie, 39, 87
life, xxxix, 27, 122; angelic, 157; book of, 8; breath of, 5; Christian, viii, xxii; common, 165; consciousness of, xxiv, 51; contemplative, xxvi, 65, 146, 148;

254 GENERAL INDEX

life (*continued*)
crown of, 8; development of, xxiv, 51; divine, 143; divine prerogative over, xviii; essence of, 30; eternal, 168; everlasting, 8, 58, 168; from dead, 106–7; gift of, xiv; goal of, viii-ix; hard, 190; holiness of, 192; human, ix, xlvii; inexhaustible, 3; inner, 51; interior, 51; liturgical, xiv, 3; Logos of, 157; long, 6; meaning of, xxiv, xl, 51; monastic, xiv, xxxix, 122, 190; mystery of, xx, 31; mystical, 80, 82; new, xxxix; of disciple, xxiii; of prayer, 51, 165; ordinary, 64; pattern of, xiv, 3; present, 173; reality of, xxiv, 51; religious, xxii, xxix, li, 176; routine of, 64; Spirit of, 3, 24, 171; spiritual, x, xxiii, xliv, xlix, 46, 159, 161, 164; state of, 147; surrender of, xxiii; tending of, xxiv, 51; tree of, xvi, 5, 8, 161; value of, xxiv, 51; water of, 8

light, 58, 74, 141, 172–73; beauty of, 139; children of, 58; divine, 10, 140, 173; field of, 139; great, 131; inaccessible, 70; Logos of, 157; mysticism of, 173; of column, 157; of mind, xvii, 13; rays of, 139; right to, 10; voice of, 139; uncreated, 173

lightning(s), 153, 178, 183; flashes of, 175

likeness, as grace, 3; divine, xiv, xvii, 3, 190

limitation, human, xxviii

linen, 171

lion(s), 102, 149; face of, 171

lips, 121

liturgy, xlviii–xlix, 40, 65, 91; cosmic, 3; of Christmas Eve, xlix; of heaven, 145

livestock, li

loaves, 112

locusts, plague of, 152–53

Logos, image of, 157; of life, 157; of light, 157

longanimity, 56

loss, 122

Lot, ix, xxiii, xxvi, 33–34, 39, 45–47, 57, 59, 62–64; as ancestor of Moabites and Ammonites, 57; daughters of, 57, 63; flight of, 57; rescue of, xxiii, 47; struggles of, 57; wife of, 33, 63–64, 69

love, xvi, xxv, xxxix, l, 10, 19, 81, 85, 122, 190; act of, xviii; as act of willing goodness, 147; as answer, xiv, 3; bands of, 177; bond of, xlviii; carnal, 111; capacity to, 83; choice of, 191; commitment of, li; degrees of, 123; divine, xvii, 12, 91; eagerness of, 94; ecstatic, 91; enjoyment of, 191; faculty of, 147; for bodies, 149–50; for friend, 54; for God, xvi, xxv, lii, 35, 54, 60, 87, 123, 174, 179–80, 182, 190; for homeland, ix, 35; for neighbor, lii, 56, 179; for self, 179; for souls, 149; for world, 58; freely given, 123; fruits of, 8; human, 12, 77, 151; in Christ, xxxix; just, 123; kinds of, 191; living by, 151; mature, xxxiii, 94; mode of, 151; mother of, 8; movement of, 191; mutual, xvii; mystery of, xvii, 12; mystical, 173; of creatures, 91; of darkness, 58; of friendship, xxxiii, 94; of God, xxxi, xxxv, lii, 13, 30, 51, 58, 74, 85, 90, 105, 118, 147, 149, 180, 182; of scripture, li, 176; of superiors, 91; of world, 35; perfection of,

122–23; psychology of, 94, 191; pure, xl, 122–23; purity of, 123; reparation through, 157; Trinitarian, xvii; unconditional, xxviii; unitive, 10; use of, 191; value of, 94; work of, 149
lovers, 177
loyalty, xxxvi, 110, 174
lust(s), 61; graves of, 162
Lutherans, li, 175
luxury, 56
lying, 176
lyres, 102

Mackenzie, R. A. F., 1
Madian (Midian), xlv; Moses in, 137; priest of, 137; war against, 135
Madianites (Midianites), 108–9
magic, 181
magisterium, 2
maidservant(s), 185–86
majesty, 65, 129
Mal'akh Yahweh, xxiv, 50
male, 45
malice, xviii, 17; deliberate, xxxviii, 119
malicious, 106
Mambre (Mamre), 47
Mambre (Mamre), Vale of, xxv–xxvi, 46, 172; vision at, 57, 59–60, 172–73
man, 3; as arbiter of good and evil, 10; as attuned to reality, 15; as high priest of creation, 3; as image of God, 3; as king of creation, 3; as mediator, 3; as simple, 15; change in, xvii; city of, xx; civilization of, 22; corruptible, 61; despiritualization of, 42; extinction of, 26; formation of, 5; fossil, 191; free, 69; insufficiency of, 16–17; just, 44, 64; pious, 172; rest for, 186

Manasses (Manasseh), 105, 114, 129–30, 132, 134; adoption of, xl–xli, 125–26
mandrakes, 93, 95
mankind, corruption of, 26; destiny of, 1
manna, xlix, li, 162, 164–68, 176; gift of, xlix, 156
manservant, 185–86
Mara, li, 161, 164, 176; waters of, xlix, 161–62
Maritain, Jacques, 148
marriage(s), xxx, 3–4, 33, 98, 179; importance of, xv; spiritual, xxx, 83
martyrs, 4, 106
Mary, Blessed Virgin, 8–9, 138, 148, 172; as Mother of predestinate, 85; as *theotokos*, 127; Child of, xlvi; Magnificat of, 66; mediation of, xxxi–xxxii; office of, 8; paradise as type of, 8; Rebecca as type of, xxxi–xxxii, 85, 88; salutation of, 66
Mass, 131; readings of, ix
Massa (Massah), 176
massebah, 181
Massoretes, 143
Mattiawit, 183
Maximus Confessor, St., 173
McCann, Justin, 36, 40, 51, 60, 98, 125, 164–66, 184
meal, 111, 134, 156; paschal, xlviii, 156
meaning, hidden, ix; literal, xix, 30; sources of, xvii
means, human, 112
measure, 149
measurements, viii
meat(s), 89, 111, 156, 167–68, 177
mediator(s), 44; humans as, xiv, 3
meditation, x, liii, 185; material for, xxvii
Megiddo, 101
Melcha (Milcah), 77

Melchisedec (Melchizedek), xxiii, 47–48; as king of justice, 48; as king of peace, 48; as king of Salem, xxiii, 47; as priest of most high God, xxiii, 47; blessing of, xxiii, 47; mystery of, 48; order of, xxiii, 47–48
memorial, 145
memory, 121
Memphis, 100–101
men, cave, 191; children of, 62; daughters of, xix, 24, 26; impious, 76; primitive, 34
mentality, magic, 179
mercy, xviii, liv, 56, 77, 86, 111, 177, 179, 187; divine, xx, xxx, 70; loving, xxviii, 70; of God, xix–xx, xxvii, xliv, lii, 4, 17, 22, 29–32, 66, 70, 74, 82, 136, 141, 149, 154, 159, 161, 180, 182, 185
Meriba (Meribah), 163–64, 176
merit, 126
Merton, Thomas, as artist, vii; as biblical interpreter, vii; as master of novices, xi, xliv, lv; as master of scholastics, xi; as photographer, vii; as poet, vii; as spiritual leader, vii; as teacher, vii; audience of, xxii, xxiv, l; baptism of, xlviii; conferences of, vii, xi–xiii, xv, xxi, xxxiv, xxxviii–xxix, xlii–l, lv–lvi, 135; depth of understanding of, vii; hospitalization of, xii; insights of, vii; legacy of, x; methodology of, xv, xxii; novices of, vii, xxx, xxxiv, xxxix, xlii, li, lv; spiritual teaching of, xvi; WORKS, *Bread in the Wilderness*, 127; *Cassian and the Fathers*, xi, xliii, xlvi, 81, 92 *Charter, Customs, and Constitutions*, xi; *Cistercian Fathers and Forefathers*, xxxix, 119–20, 123, 190; *Cistercian Fathers and Their Monastic Theology*, xi, xiii, 80, 83, 123, 191; *Collected Poems*, xx–xxi, xxxii; *Conjectures of a Guilty Bystander*, xlviii; *Disputed Questions*, xvi, 173; *Hidden Ground of Love*, 10; *Inner Experience*, xvi, xxvii; *Introduction to Christian Mysticism*, xi, xlvi, 81, 90–91; *Learning to Love*, 52; *Life of the Vows*, xi; *Medieval Cistercian History*, xi; *Monastic Introduction to Sacred Scripture*, xi, xxxix, xli, 120; *Monastic Observances*, xi, 157; *Mystics and Zen Masters*, 173; *New Man*, xiv–xviii, xlviii, 10–11, 15; *New Seeds of Contemplation*, xv; *Pre-Benedictine Monasticism*, xi; *Rule of Saint Benedict*, xi, 36, 40, 51–52, 60, 164, 166, 184; *Search for Solitude*, xii–xiii, xv; *Seasons of Celebration*, xlvi; *Seeds of Contemplation*, vii; *Seven Storey Mountain*, xlvi, xlviii; *Solitude and Togetherness* [CD], 148; *Spirit of Simplicity*, xvi; *Springs of Contemplation*, 148; *Survival or Prophecy*, xi; *Tower of Babel*, xx; *When Prophecy Still Had a Voice*, 148
Mesopotamia, xxxi–xxxii, 35, 76, 90, 96, 129, 191; upheavals in, 100
message, appropriation of, xxiv
messias (messiah), 25, 47–48, 126; as judge, 130; as king, 130; strength of, 131; worldly, 58
metals, 99
methods, democratic, 10; rational, 10
Michael the Archangel, St., 22
midwives, Hebrew, xliv

GENERAL INDEX   257

mildness, 56
milk, 67, 131, 173; land of, 138, 145, 158
mimicry, demoniacal, 143
mind, 13; Jewish, 50; light of, xvii; one, xxi, 35; submission of, xxvii
minerals, 99
ministers, angelic, 92; Egyptian, 103; sacred, 91
ministry, 107
miracle(s), xxi, 44, 162, 167
Miraculous Medal, Feast of, 158
mirth, 177
Miryam (Mary), 161–63; death of, 163; leprosy of, 162
misdemeanors, xxxv
mission, divine, 1
Moab, desert of, 163
Moabites, 57, 163, 191; women of, 163
modesty, 56, 131
Molina, Luis de, 145–46
monastery, xxi; as sign of Christ, xxx, 78
money, purchase, 116; return of, 117–18
monk(s), xxv, xxxix, 4, 64, 122; average, 123; good-living, 125; ill-living, 125; negligent, 125; newly professed, xi; obedient, 125; slothful, 125
monkeys, trained, 102
Montfort, St. Louis de, 85
moon(s), dream of, 108; new, 177
morality, 50; Egyptian, 104
Moré, oak of, 45
Moriah, 72; ascent of, xxviii
mortality, xxviii
Moses, ix, xlv–xlvii, liv, 27, 52, 86, 135–40, 142–45, 151–68, 175–79, 188–89; adoption of, xlv, 137; anger of, xlv, 137, 162; as answer to prayer, xlv, 137; as author of Pentateuch, xiv, 1–2; as contemplative, xlv–xlvi, 137; as god of Pharaoh, 151; as lover of justice, xlvi, 139; as lover of solitude, xlvi, 139; as man of God, 137; as prophet, 137; as servant of Lord, 160; as slayer of Egyptian, xlv, 137; birth of, xlv, 137; body of, 22; call of, xlv; canticle of, xlix, li, 144–45, 161, 176; character of, xlv; death of, xlix, 1, 135, 164; desire to see God of, liv, 162; diffidence of, 151; divine encounter of, xlv, li; face of, 175; failure of, xlv, 137; five books of, 1; flight from Egypt of, xlv, 137; greatness of, xliv, 136; hand of, 160; horns of, 169, 175; intervention by in quarrel, xlv, 137; loftiness of, 136; marriage of, xlv, 137; maturity of, 136; miraculous powers of, xlvii, 151; obedience to, 167; prayer of, 136; preparation of, 137; punishment of, 163; reproaches of, 135; return to Egypt of, xlvii, 151; revelation to, xlv, 137–40; rod of, 160; shoes of, 137, 139; sister of, 161; son(s) of, 137, 151; struggle of, 151; sublimity of, xliv, 136; veil of, 175; vision of, 139, 162; vocation of, xlv
Moses de Léon, 142
Moslem (Muslim), 127
mosquitoes, plague of, 152
motus, 191
mountain(s), l, 63, 65, 96, 131, 153, 162, 176, 178, 181, 183–84, 189; ancient, 132; ascent of, 162; Egyptian, 99; highest, 29; mast upon, 159; of God, 137–38
mourning, 13, 178
mud, alluvial, 99
mules, 134
mummy, xxiv, 104

murder(s), 56, 175; of Abel, ix, 20
murmuring, xlix, liv, 161–62, 164–66, 189
music, Egyptian, 102; modern, 112
musicians, 22
myrrh, 8, 108, 117
mystery, xxiv, xxix, xli, liv, 3, 9, 12, 40, 51, 55, 72–73, 87, 127, 142, 187; incomprehensible, xxviii; of cross, 161; of God, 12, 52, 56; of hospitality, xxii, xxix, 42, 77; of identity, 184; of iniquity, 42; of journeys, xxix, 77; of language, xvi, 12; of life, xx, 31; of love, xvii, 12; of Melchisedec, 48; of purification, 158; of redemption, xlviii; of scripture, 81; of stranger, xxii, 42; of travel, 42; paschal, xxxix
mysticism, Jewish, 172–73; Russian, 173
mystics, xlviii, 173
myth, origin, 183
mythology, North American, 183; pagan, 26

Nabuchodonosor (Nebuchadnezzaar), King, 6–7; dream of, 6–7; madness of, 7
Nachor (Nahor), 76–77
Nadab, 169
nakedness, xvii, 14, 17, 189; original, 15
name(s), viii, 130; abstract, 141; concrete, 141; divine, xlv–xlvi, 141–42; mystique of, 184; of Creator, 5; of God, xlvi–xlvii, l, lii–liii, 4, 21, 23, 40, 50, 52–53, 138, 141–42, 151, 169, 175, 182–85; positive, 141; power of, liii; profanation of, 183
Napoleon, 150
narrative(s), balance of, xxxvi, 112; beauty of, xxxvi, 112; biblical, ix; contrast in, xxxvi, 112; creation, 3; movement of, xxxvi, 112; vividness of, xxxvi, 112
Nathanael, 88
nation(s), 24, 84; blessing of, 44; consecrated, li, 176; great, xxvii; healing of, 8; holy, 176, 178; hostile, 36; power over, 8
nature(s), 15, 61, 69, 147, 151; cycle of, xlviii; demands of, 149; divine, xlvi, 121, 142; human, ix, l, 61, 150, 174; image as, 3; laws of, 62; level of, 69; mode of, 151; prisoner of, lii, 181; religion of, 104; respect for, 149
Nazareth, 131
Nazarites, 18
Nazism, 136
necessities, 188
necromancy, 181
need(s), 165, 188; greater, 165; lesser, 165; of whole, 113
neighbor, xxv, 137, 187, 189; love of, lii, 56, 179
Nemrod (Nimrod), xx, 34–35
Nephelim, 26, 191
Nephtali (Naphtali), 93, 131–32, 134, 136; as hart, 132; as terebinth, 132
Nestorianism, 127–28
Nestorius, 127–28
neurosis, 179
neurotics, 17
New Testament, viii, xiii, xix, xxi, xxviii, xlviii, l, liv, 13, 20, 22, 32, 37, 71, 88, 131, 136, 150, 173, 188; Abel in, 20–22; Abraham in, 36–39; Cain in, 20–22; sabbath in, 188–90; texts of, xlviii
New York City, xxi, 35
night, 183; dark, xxvii, xlviii, 67, 160; enlightening, 160

Nile, xlv, 11, 102; delta of, 99, 136; flood of, 99; valley of, 99; waters of, 99
Ninive (Nineveh), 35
Ninivites, 34
Nisan, 154
nobles, deceased, 104
Noe (Noah), ix, xix–xx, 26–34, 36, 43; alliance of, 30; altar of, 30; as builder, 31; as heir of justice, 34; as just man, 27, 31; as mediator, 31; as perfect, 31; as preacher of justice, 34; as protector, 31; as provider, 31; as representative of God, 30; as savior, 31; as type of Christ, 27, 32; care of, 31; curse of, 43; days of, 64; faith of, 34; love of, 31; sacrifice of, xix–xx, 30–31, 34; sons of, 28; wife of, 28, 30
nomads, 124; as barbarians, 124
nome, Egyptian, 103
nothingness, xvii, xix, 14–15, 17, 22, 73, 83; creation from, 149
nourishment, 20, 120; spiritual, 168
novel, style of, xxxv, 106
novice, dialogue with, 190
novitiate, 176
Nubia, 99, 101–2
number(s), viii, 149
nut, 120

oasis, 5
oaths, 184; silly, 184; thoughtless, 184
obedience, ix, xlix, 75–76, 182, 192; as test, 167; blind, 69; perfect, 76; to Aaron, 167; to Moses, 167; words of, 165; yoke of, 150
obligation(s), objective, xxxvi, 111; pressing, liii, 186; reality of, xxxvi, 110
observance(s), 174; everlasting, 144, 155; perpetual, 155; vain, lii, 181

O'Connell, Patrick F., x, xv–xvii, xx
odor(s), 5; of fields of heaven, 88; sweet, 8, 88, 187
offense, infinite, 36
offering(s), 92; burnt, 187; peace, 187
Og, King of Bashan, 163
oil, 57, 91–92, 134, 177, 180, 187
ointments, xxx; perfumed, 81
Old Testament, viii–ix, xiii, xix, xxi, xxvii, xxxvii, xlii–xliii, xlvi, xlviii, l, 3, 35–36, 68–69, 101, 115, 137, 157; Agar (Hagar) as, 68; fulfillment of, 158; names of God in, 142; sapiential books of, 145; Septuagint translation of, xvi, 4–5, 96; spiritual interpretation of, 120; theme of, 159
oliveyard(s), 182, 186
omnipotence, divine, 17
Onan, 105, 110
onanism, 110
onyx, 5, 8
operations, divine, xlvi, 141; immanent, 150; spiritual, 150
opinions, 13
oppression, 101, 159
optimism, false, xxi, 35
oranges, 102
orchards, Egyptian, 102
order, 91; divine, 146; gift of, xiv; natural, 18
ordinance, 161; everlasting, 187
ordination, priestly, 71, 192
ordo caritatis, 191
Origen, xxix–xxx, xliv, 27, 46–47, 78–81, 121, 127, 136, 161
origins, human, 3
Osee (Hosea), 132
Osiris, as god of death, 103; as god of vegetation, 103; as enemy of Seth, 103; as husband of Isis, 103; as king of dead, 103; killed and revived, 103; kingdom of, 104

ostrich, 102
owls, 129
ox(en), 7, 25, 57, 129, 134, 170, 186

pact, xxiii, 49
paganism, 18, 69, 181
pagans, 34, 55, 69
pains, 153
Palestine, 41, 47, 93, 191; peoples of, liv
pantheism, 92
paper, 102
papyrus, 102
paradise, 4–8, 18, 23, 90, 185; as type of Mary, 8; definition of, 4–5; earthly, 8; expulsion from, xviii, xxxii, 9; middle of, xvi; rivers of, xvi, 11–12; setting of, xv, 4–6; symbolism of, xv; trees of, 9–11
parents, honor of, 175
parrhesia, 15, 71
Pascal, Blaise, 52
Pasch (Phase, Passover), xlvii, liv, 143–45, 151, 154–56, 186; in desert, 162
passion(s), xvii, xxxvii, 16, 61, 69, 111, 147; control of, 147; incontrollable, 17; intensity of, 116; ordering of, 147
patience, xx, xxxvii, 31, 51, 56
patriarch(s), xxi, xxix–xxx, xxxv, xxxix, xlii, 1, 4, 44–45, 66, 133, 142; as forebears of Israel, xiv; blessing(s) of, 126–33; twelve, 126, 133
Paul, St., xxi, xxvii, xxxvii, l–li, liv, 13, 37–38, 48, 56, 59, 68, 81, 106–7, 131, 174–75
peace, xii, xxvii, xxix, 4, 42, 54, 56, 77, 159, 165; age of, liv; city of, xxiii, 47; king of, xxiii, 48; reign of, 187; sign of, 97; vision of, 34; way of, 62
peasants, Egyptian, 101–2
pedagogue, 45

Peers, E. Allison, 8, 42, 67, 69, 97, 160
penance, xx, 31, 153
Pentateuch, xiii, xlix–l, liv, 1–2
Pentecost, xi, xxi, xxxix, xlii, liv, 121, 131, 133–34, 187; Last Sunday after, 188; Ninth Sunday after, 65
people(s), 24; abandonment of, 70; ancient, 191; chosen, xiv, xxix, xxxv, 1, 27, 36, 41, 43, 54, 75, 109; great, 41; holy, 179; of God, xxi–xxii, xlviii, li–lii, liv, 36, 39, 43, 55, 98, 106, 114, 133, 162, 174, 176, 178, 192; persecuted, 137; purchased, 178; shameless, 36; stiff-necked, 188
peoplehood, xxiv
Peor, 163
Perez, xxxvi, 110
perfection(s), 91; analogical, 141; formal, 141; image of, xv; liturgical, 103; moral, xxv; of creatures, 141; of God, 141; ritual, 103
period, archaic, 100; prehistoric, 100; sothic, 100; transition, 100
persecution, xxiv, 51, 56; beginning of, 136
Persia, 101
person(s), divine, 12; structure of, xiv
perspectives, individual, xxxvii, 113; personal, xxxvii, 113
Phanuel (Peniel), 97
Pharaoh(s), xxvi, xliv, 45, 101–2, 105, 109, 111, 115–16, 118–19, 124, 137–38, 143, 152, 160, 180, 186; army of, 159–61; as figure of devil, 154; as god(s), 102, 145; as head of priesthood, 102; as head of state religion, 102; ancestors of, 102; attitude of toward Hebrews, xliv, 136; attraction to Sarai of, xxii–xxiii, 40,

45; baker of, xxxvi, 111–12; butler of, xxxvi–xxxvii, 111–12; chariots of, 159–61; confrontation with, xlvii, 151–52; daughter of, xlv, 137; demoniacal character of, xliv, xlvii; dreams of, xxxvii, 105, 112–13; hand of, 137, 180; hardness of heart of, xliii, xlvii, 145, 151–52, 159; health of, 115–16; heart of, xlvii, 145, 151–52, 159; horsemen of, 160; horses of, 159–60; host of, 160; increase of sin of, 152; inner, liii, 186; meeting with Jacob of, xl, 124–25; power of, 186; pride of, 151; reigns of, 100; resistance of, xlvii, 151; tyranny of, xliv, 151; worship of, xxxiv, 102
Pharisees, 21, 37, 58, 64, 109, 174
Pherezites (Perizzites), 138, 179, 181, 191
Phihahiroth (Pihahiroth), 159
Philip, 88
Philippe, Paul, 148
Philippe, Thomas, xlvii, 148–51
Philistines, xxx, 132, 191; land of, 158; rivalry with, 86
philosophy, 91, 173; scholastic, 121
Phineas (Phinehas), 163
Phison (Pishon), 5, 11–12
phobia, 184
Phoenicians, 191
piety, xxxii, 54, 104; practice of, xxv
pigeon, 49
Pilate, Pontius, 106
pilgrimage, of Israel, xlix
pinball, 102
Pirot, Louis, 19, 124
pit(s), 108; bitumen, 47
Pius XII, Pope, 3, 120; *Divino Afflante Spiritu*, 120; *Humani Generis*, 2–3
place(s), consecrated, 92; hallowed, 92; holy, 90

plague(s), xlvii–xlviii, 24, 143–44, 151–54, 180; final, 154
plan, divine, xxvii, xxxi, xlii, 133; of God, xxiii–xxiv, xxxv, xxxvii, xlv, 13, 49, 53, 105, 113, 124, 138; providential, 119
plant(s), 4–5; creation of, 6
pleading, confident, xxv
pleasure, bodily, 190; divine good, 69; paradise of, 5
poems, Japanese, 18
poet, inspired, 126
poetry, xli, 128–29
policeman, 42
polygenism, 3
Pontifical Biblical Commission, ix, 2
poor, 62, 114, 186–88; care for, liv, 187–88; wanting, 188
posterity, 44
potassium, deposits of, 99
pottage, 84; mess of, xxxi, 85
poverty, 122, 187; interior, xxix, 76
power(s), 65, 121, 129; angelic, 4; eternal, 61; of God, xxv, xxxii, xxxvi, xlvii, 54, 61, 71, 74–75, 91, 93, 143, 149, 152, 154, 172, 174, 184, 189; of prayer, li, 176; symbol of, 6; worldly, 190; worship of, 183
Power, E., 136, 175, 181, 186
practices, ecclesial, xv; monastic, xi
praise(s), xiv, 3; divine, liii, 185; of God's name, liii, 185
prayer(s), vii, xlvii, 81, 92; answer to, xxxvii, 113; Cistercian, xl, 122; for dying, xv, xxii, 4; for travelers, xxii; graces of, 190; interior, 168; life of, 51, 165; power of, li, 176; spirit of, xliv
precepts, 161, 180, 184, 192
predilection, divine, 85
pre-history, xiv, xx
prelacy, xxvii, 68
preparation, time of, 136
prescriptions, priestly, 1; ritual, 162
presence, divine, xvi, xxiv–xxv, xxxi–xxxii, xlvi, l, lii, 51;

presence, divine (*continued*)
    holy, 92, 173; impersonal, xxxii, 92; of God, xxi, xxiii, xxv, xxxii, xl, lii, 35–36, 51–52, 54, 61, 71, 91–92, 169, 180, 184; religious, xxxii, 91–92; vague, xxxii, 92
preservation, 118
presumption, 62
pride, xviii, xx–xxi, 23, 35, 83; of impious, 76; of tyrants, 76
priest(s), 47, 134, 156, 170, 179, 186; assistants of, liv; duties of, liv; high, 143; kingdom of, li, 176
priesthood, holy, 178; kingly, 178; Levitical, 48; of old law, 135
princes, 137; Egyptian, 103
principalities, angelic, 4
principles, abstract, 75
prison, 116; Joseph in, 105
probity, xxxvii
problems, 15
prodigy, 152
produce, 113
productiveness, 19
promise(s), xxiv–xxv, 17, 86, 124, 135, 162, 174; accomplishment of, xxiv; child(ren) of, xxiv–xxv, 44, 68, 86; confirmation of, 123; divine, xl–xli, 60, 70, 72, 124, 126; faith in, 76; fulfillment of, xxiii, 48, 66, 76; kingdom of, 41; land of, xxxii–xxxiii; meaning of, xxiv; of God, xxiv, xxvii, 17, 30, 37, 41, 43–44, 47–49, 53–55, 69, 71, 107, 142, 151; of victory, xxxiii; renewal of, xxiii, 57, 60, 75, 98, 151; to Abraham, xxi–xxii, xxiv, xxvii, xl, xlviii, 41, 43, 48–49, 51, 53–55, 57, 60, 66, 69, 74, 86, 123
propagation, 53
prophecy, xxvi, xli, 49, 129; deathbed, xlii; divine, xli, 126; messianic, 24, 130–31; of Caiphas, 105; of judgment, 24
prophet(s), xlviii, 4, 20–21, 32, 39, 51, 59, 106, 174; blood of, 20–21, 153; false, 65, 153, 181; nuptial theme in, 13; oracles of, 181; sepulchres of, 21
propitiatory, 170
proprietors, Egyptian, 101
prosperity, xxi, 35, 43, 136
protection, 40; divine, xviii
Protestants, 37–38
proto-evangelium, xviii, 17
proud, sin of, 20
providence, 145, 148–51; divine, xix, xxxv, xxxvii–xxxviii, xlii, xlvii, 66, 68, 90, 105, 113, 115, 118; of God, xix–xx, 29, 31, 141; ordinary, 126–27
punishment(s), xviii, 10, 22, 35, 88, 116, 192; evil of, 148; sevenfold, 21
purification, from sin, 30; laws of, liv; mystery of, 158; ritual, 192
purity, 91; of victim, xlviii, 154; spiritual, 56
Putiphar (Potiphar), xxxvi, 101, 105, 109; house of, 110; wife of, xxxvi, 105, 110–11
Putiphar, priest of Ra, 114
pyramid(s), xxxiv, 36, 101, 104
pyre, 183

quails, 162, 165–66
qualities, human, 78
quarrels, 56
quarries, 99
Quenon, Paul, xiii
questions, 15
quietude, aversion to, 184; education in, 184

Ra, as sun god, 103; gift of, 114; priest of, 114; worship of, 101

GENERAL INDEX 263

race, human, 77; Mediterranean, 100; mixed, 100; Semitic, 100
Rachel, xxxii–xxxv, 93–96, 98, 126, 181; barrenness of, 93; beauty of, 94; children of, 93, 98, 107; death of, xxxiii–xxxiv, 99, 126, 129; goodness of, xxxiii, 94; love of Jacob for, xxxiii, 93–95; marriage of, 95; reality of, xxxiii, 94; sepulchre of, 99
rage, 149; human, 61
raiment, 92, 138, 156, 164, 182
rain(s), 27, 29, 40; tropical, 99
rainbow, 32, 183
raisins, 134
ram(s), xxviii, 49, 74, 95, 187
Ramesse (Rameses), 156
Ramses II, 101, 136; temple of, 102
Ramses IX, 103
rank, seating by, 117
Raphidim (Rephidim), desert of, 162
reach, highest, 141
reading(s), contemplative, xix; eschatological, xix; ethical, xix; sacramental, xix
realism, xxvi, 60; narrative, 87; psychological, xxxv, 106
reality, xxix, 15–16, 140; awareness of, xvi; control of, 147; divine, xlvi, 81; eschatological, xxi; external, xvi, 147; finding, xxiv; ineffable, 81; invisible, xxx; ordering of, 147; sign of, xxx
reason, 14, 76; autonomy of, 10; use of, 10
reassurance, divine, xxiii
Rebecca, xxix–xxxii, 77–90, 94; as favoring Jacob, 85; as patience, 79; as type, xxix–xxxii, 80–84, 88; children of, 84; family of, xxix, 77; marriage of, xxx; meeting with Isaac of, 78; plan of, 87
rebellion, 14

rebirth, symbolic, xxviii
Rechabites, 18
reckoning, eschatological, xxv
recognition, gesture of, 31
recollection, 131
reconciliation, 31; sacrifice of, xlviii
rectitude, moral, xxxi
redemption, xiv, xviii, 145; mystery of, xlviii; promise of, 17
refreshment, spiritual, 82
reign, of peace, 187
rejection, xxviii, 43, 122
relationship, genuine, lii
relaxation, 186
religion, 104, 179; animistic, 103; beginning of, 23; biblical, 10; Egyptian, 100, 103–4; essence of, 69; exterior, 103; pagan, 69; polytheistic, 103
remission, 187; year of, 187–88
remnant, 32, 34, 36, 106; faithful, 172; of Abel, 32
renewal, 183; covenant, 176
renown, men of, 31
renunciation, principles of, 64
reparation, act of, 157; vicarious, 57
repentance, xxxii, 149; sincere, 88
Rephaim, 191
repose, liii, 186
reproach, unbearable, 17
reproachfulness, xxv, 48, 62
requies, liv, 190
resistance, demoniacal, 143; of Israel, 151; of Pharaoh, 151
respect, xxv–xxvi, xxxiii, 54, 60, 62, 94
responsibility, li, 71; personal, 32; sharing of, 176
rest, xx, 3, 31, 172, 190; day of, 186; divine, 3; for man, 186; for stranger, 186; in God, xv; mystical, xxx, 83; of God, 3–4, 186; sabbath, 167; true, 190
resurrection, xxviii; effects of, 121; general, 143; spiritual, xxxix, 121; truth of, xxxix, 121; witnesses of, 122

GENERAL INDEX

reticence, education in, 184
retirement, 85
revelation, xxxii, xxxviii, xlvi, 90; at Sinai, 143; biblical, xvii; Christian, xxvii, 69; deepening of, 64; direct, xxxv; divine, 138; exodus as, xliv; literal, xv; of God, 52–53, 106, 138; poetic, xv; symbolic, xv; to Abraham, 62; to Moses, xlv, 137–40; true, xv
revellings, 56
revenge, xxxiv, xli, 22, 111
reverence, 22
reverses, 48
Revesby, Abbey of, 190
revolt, 162
revolution, Egyptian, 101
rewards, 126
rhinoceros, 102
Rice, Edward, 148
riches, 44; eternal, 22; immovable, 22; of mercy, 22
rider, 161
Rievaulx, Abbey of, 190
righteousness, xxiii; Lord of, 25
rights, charter of, 174; marriage, 95
rising, 182
rite(s), 37, 91; fertility, 53, 55; funeral, 104; miscellaneous, 192; of circumcision, 53; pagan, xxiv, 53; Passover, xlviii; sacred, 145, 158; sacrificial, xxviii
ritual(s), Hebrew, 192; Mosaic, 55; Passover, xlviii; pathological, lii, 179; sacrificial, liv
Ritual, Cistercian, xxii
river(s), 5, 8, 153; legendary, 11; of paradise, xvi, 5, 11–12; real, 11
robbers, tomb, 104
rock, water from, 162–63
rod, 152
Rome, 142–43
ropes, 102
rose, 7

royalty, Egyptian, 103
Ruben (Reuben), xli, 93, 108–9, 115–16, 118, 126, 129, 133, 136; hostile neighbors of, 129; incest of, 129; inheritance of, 129; sons of, 134; territory of, 129
Rule, Benedictine, xxii, xxiv, xlix; c. 4, 40, 164; c. 5, 164; c. 7, 35–36, 51–52, 184; c. 23, 164; c. 31, 60; c. 32, 60; c. 34, 164–66; c. 35, 60, 164; c. 36, 60; c. 37, 60; c. 38, 60; c. 40, 164; c. 41, 164; c. 48, 60; c. 53, 164; c. 57, 60; c. 64, 98; c. 73, 125
ruse, 96

sabbath(s), xv, liii–liv, 3–4, 65, 167, 175, 177, 185–89; annual, liii; blessed, 186; consecrated, 186; eternal, 190; great, 157; in New Testament, 188–90; institution of, 162, 165; law of, 186–87; keeping of, liii, 185; of weeks, 187; of sabbaths, liv; of years, 186; spiritual, liv, 190–91; three, 191; weeklong, xlviii, liii–liv, 155; weekly, liii
sacrament, 9, 13; as visible sign of invisible reality, xxx; blessed, 167–68, 173; of charity, 173
sacrifice(s), xx, 21, 31, 47, 104, 135, 145, 162, 182, 185–86; at Salem, 98; bloody, 19; community, 154; human, xxvii, 70; in wilderness, 151–52, 156; new, 187; odor of, 30; of Abel, xviii–xix, 19, 21–22; of Abraham, xxvii–xxviii, 49, 69–74, 142; of Cain, xviii, 19; of Isaac, ix, xxvii–xxix, 41, 69–76, 109, 156, 168; of Noe, xix–xx, 30–31, 34; of reconciliation, xlviii, 154; ominous, 48–49;

paschal, 154; place of, xxxii; practices of, 192; selfish, 19; spiritual, 72, 178; true, 47; unacceptable, 182
sacrilege, 63
sadness, 123
Sadoc (Zadok), 134
St. Marco, Convent of, 131
saints, xxiii, 4, 46, 64, 177; blood of, 153; hearts of, 121
Salem, 98; Melchisedec as king of, xxiii, 47; sacrifice at, 98
salt, pillar of, 63
salvation, xxxv, xlvi, 9, 42, 64, 90, 174; drama of, xi, xlii, 1; gift of, xxiv, 53; history of, xxii, 36; of gentiles, 106–7; of Jews, 106; of sinners, 64; of soul, 53, 140; of wicked, 57; promises of, 1; story of, xxvi
Samaritan(s), 39, 59, 132, 143
Samson, 132, 135
sanctity, 131; gift of, xxiv, 53; priestly, 192
sanctuary, 170, 181; of heaven, 170; rival, 92; special, 92
sanity, threat to, 16;
sapphire(s), 32, 169, 171
Sara (Sarai, Sarah), ix, xxvi, xxx, 38–40, 45, 49–51, 60, 65–66, 68–69, 78, 85–86, 172; as mother of kings, 56; attraction of Pharaoh to, xxii–xxiii, 40, 45; beauty of, 66; burial of, xxix, 76; cruelty of, 67; death of, xxix, 76, 78; disbelief of, 60; fear of, 60; jealousy of, 67; joy of, 66–67; laughter of, 57, 60, 66; marriage to Abimelek of, 65–66; new name of, 53, 56; repentance of, 60; resentment of, xxiii, 50, 67; servant of, 49–50; son of, 53, 66–67; song of, 66; tent of, 78
Satan, xlix, 183
satisfactions, 95; worldly, xxvii

Saul, King, lii, 134, 182; brethren of, 134; house of, 134; kingdom of, 134; mentality of, 182; sacrifice of, 181–82; time of, 191
savages, 34, 85
Saydon, P., 191–92
scandal, question of, 190; rock of, 178
scepter, 130
scholars, biblical, vii–viii, x, xli; Catholic, xli
scholarship, biblical, viii, xli
scientia, 83
scientists, Egyptian, 103
sciniphs, 152
scribes, 21, 174
scripture(s), 79; application of, 120; approaches to, vii; as letters from God, ix, 35; conferences on, xi; de-spiritualization of, 127; dilution of, 127; letter of, 161; love of, li, 176; mysteries of, 81; reading of, 80; well of, xxx, 78
scruples, 179
sea, xlix–l, liv, 13, 28, 153, 161, 178, 185; baptism in, 188; passage through, xlvii–xlviii, 160–61; Red, xlviii, 157, 159, 161, 169, 176, 191
seacoast, 131; Aegean, 191
season, paschal, 121
Seboim (Zeboiim), 177
seclusion, reticent, 184
sects, 56
security, 16
seduction, attempted, 111
sefirot, ten, 143
Segor (Zoar), 57, 63
Sehon (Sihon), 163
self, as center of life, xvii; death to, xxvii; false, xvi; genuine, xvii; in Christ, xxxix; inmost, 51, 141; inner, xvii; perception of, xvi; relationship with, xvii;

266 GENERAL INDEX

self, as center of life (contiinued)
    tree of, xvi; true, xvi, xxiv,
    xxxix–xl, 51
self-deception, xvii
self-interest, xxi, 35
selfishness, 77
self-knowledge, 83
self-sufficiency, xviii, 23
self-surrender, xxvii
Sem (Shem), 28, 39, 43
Semites, 191
Senaar (Shinar), 35
sense(s), carnal, 81; common, 121;
    exterior, 121; interior, 121;
    mystical, 121; outward, 121;
    religious 127–28; spiritual,
    81–82
sense(s) of scripture,
    accommodated, xxxix;
    allegorical, viii–ix, xxxix,
    6; anagogic, viii; literal,
    viii–ix, xxix, 77–78; moral,
    viii; spiritual, viii, xxx,
    6, 127; tropological, viii;
    typological, viii–ix
sensuality, renunciation of, xlvi
separation, mystery of, 73
Sephora (Zipporah), xlv, 137
sepulchre(s), 21, 24; open, 62
seraphim, 4
Seraphim of Sarov, St., 173
serfs, Egyptian, 101–2
Sermon on the Mount, 167
serpent(s), xvi, 13, 183–84, 189;
    as agent of division, xvii;
    as creator of song, 183–84;
    as ruler of death, 183; as
    ruler of life, 183; as symbol
    of devil, 13; brazen, 156,
    163, 181; cleverness of,
    132; condemnation of, 17;
    conflict with, xviii; craftiness
    of, 13; death of, 183–84;
    dumb, 149; fiery, 189; rod
    into, 152
servant(s), xxx, li, 79; civil, 103;
    head, 112; of Abraham, xxx,
    48, 72–73, 76–78

services, synagogue, 143
Seth, 23
Seth, Egyptian deity, 103–4
Sethites, xix, 22–23, 26, 32
sex, 14; power of, 14
shade, 40
shame, 125
sharecroppers, Egyptian, 101, 125
sheaves, 186–87; dream of, 108
sheep, 24–25, 94–97, 134, 137, 145,
    156, 158, 170, 180–81, 185;
    brown, 95; flocks of, 107,
    180; lord of, 24–25; people
    as, 153; sacrifice of, 145;
    variegated, 95–96; white,
    95–96
sheepfolds, 132
shekinah, l, 162, 165–66, 169–74
Shela (Shelah), xxxv, 110
shelter, 40
shepherd(s), 94, 137; Abel as, 18;
    hearts of, xxvi, 66; seventy,
    24
shield, 134
Shimon bar Yohai, 143
shipwreck, 40
shoes, 102; of Moses, 137, 139
shrines, pagan, lii
shrubs, 5
Shua, 109
Siberia, 28
Sichem (Shechem), xxii, xxxiv, 39,
    45, 98, 108–9, 132
Sichem (Shechem) son of Hamor, 98
Sichemites (Shechemites), 98
sickness, 180–81; mental, 15
Sidon, 131
sight, spiritual, 121
sign(s), 138, 145, 151–52, 167–68,
    138, 180, 182; heavenly, 25;
    invisible, 55; spiritual, 55;
    visible, xxx, 55
silence, 30, 62, 64, 83, 154, 159, 184;
    aversion to, 184; mystery
    of, xx, 31; mystical, xxx, 83;
    power of, 184

silver, 118, 177, 180; thirty pieces of, 109; twenty pieces of, xxxv, 108–9; vessels of, 138, 156
Simeon, xli, 93, 98, 126, 129, 133, 136; as hostage, 116; inheritance of, 129; sons of, 134; violence of, 129
simplicity, xxvii, 16, 79; Cistercian, 191; narrative, xxix, 76
sin(s), xiv, xviii, 10, 14–15, 17, 26, 33, 38–39, 61, 63, 73, 77, 82, 118, 147, 149, 174, 187, 189–90; actual, xviii, 19; arrogance of, 63; darkness of, 157; destruction of, 31; detachment from, 80; deterrent from, 51; evil of, 148; experience of, 11; gloom of, 157; history of, 18; inclination to, 19; mortal, 51; of Adam and Eve, ix, xvii–xviii, 14, 18; of proud, 20; of world, 74; offense of, 148; original, xviii, xx, 10, 19, 140; purification from, 30; reign of, 18; servant of, 38
Sin, desert of, 162, 166
Sinai, 101, 138, 164, 166, 169; alliance at, 135; ascents of, 162; desert of, 162, 169; Mount, xlv, xlvii, xlix–l, 1, 169, 175, 178–79; peninsula, xlii; revelation at, 143
sincerity, 122; growth in, 83; naïve, 16
singers, 189
singing, 102
sinners, xxviii, xxxi, 73, 88; intercession for, xxvi, 62; salvation of, 64
Sion (Zion), 4, 7, 22, 35, 62, 170, 172, 178; daughter of, 57
Sirius, rising of, 100
Sisara (Sisera), 132
skill, xxxi, 18, 85
skins, garments of, 84, 140
sky, xxiii, 183

slave(s), 45, 117; base, 68; Egyptian, 101–2
slavery, 68–69; Egyptian, xlviii; perpetual, 157
sleep, 12, 83; deep, 119–20; of Abraham, 49; of Adam, 5, 12; of Jacob, 119–20
sleeping, 182
smoke, 149, 178–79
snake, 183–84; mythical, 183
sobriety, 78
society, American, vii; atheist-materialist, 51; business, 42; challenge to, vii; Egyptian, 124; human, 12; primitive, 78; totalitarian, 42
Socoth (Succoth), 98, 156
Sodom, xxiii, xxv–xxvi, 22–24, 33, 57–65, 69; cry against, 61–62; destruction of, xxv, 34, 57, 46, 64; intercession for, 57, 60–62; king of, 47; people of, 58; princes of, 57; punishment of, 57; rulers of, 58; survival of, xxv
Sodomites, arrogance of, xxvi; insolence of, xxvi; lust of, xxvi
soldiers, 37, 132
solemnity, 145, 158, 177
solitude, xlv, 82–83; preparation in, 137; ways of, 184
Solomon, 170; power of, 43
son(s), 185–86; elder, 18, 86, 88; of bondwoman, 69; poorer, 18; prodigal, xxix, xxxii, 73, 88; stronger, 18; weaker, 18; younger, xviii, xxxi, 18, 85–86, 88
song(s), 96; creation of, 183–84
sonship, divine, 88, 157; true, xxvii
sores, swelling, 57
sorrow(s), 13, 83, 95, 178
soul(s), xxiv, xxvii, xxxix, 51, 67, 70, 84, 104, 120–23, 150, 160, 165, 182; abyss of, xiv, 3; beauty of, 83; Christian, 4; dark night of, xxvii;

268   GENERAL INDEX

soul(s) (*continued*)
    dignity of, xxx; fecund, xxx; fruitfulness for, 84; healing of, 148; human, vii; humble, 82; indeliberate passion of, 82; kindred, 77; liberation of, xxii; living, 5; love for, 149; meeting of, xxiv; nature of, 83; obligations of, 82; patient, xxx; poor, 82; salvation of, 53, 140; simple, xxx; sin of, 82; solitude of, 83; teaching for, 78; thirst of, 79; union of, 12, 80; whole, 182

soup, red, 85
sources, Deuteronomic, xiv, 2; Elohist, xiv, xxvi, xliii, 2, 66, 125; Priestly (Levitical), xiv, xix, xxix, xliii, 2, 27–28, 30, 76, 125; Yahwist, xiv, xix, xxvi, xliii, 2, 28–29, 125
sovereignty, divine, xlvii
space, 65
Spain, 96, 143, 145
sparks, 149
spear, 134
speculation, 76
speech, 36, 184; free, 15; hortatory, 192; profound, 36
spices, 5, 108
spies, 115–16
spirit(s), xvii, 15, 56, 81, 150; angelic, 50; as universe, 150; depths of, 81; fallen, 33; feeding of, xvi; fruit of, 56; human, 9, 60; imprisoned, 35; Lord of, 25; lost, 15; loved, 150; missionary, 77; natural, 60; of Babel, 35; of prayer, xliv
spirituality, 85; as guided by God, ix, xxiii, 46; Benedictine, xxvi; Cistercian, xl, 122; high, 69; monastic, xi, 65; of Jews, 157; ordinary, ix, xxiii, 46
staff, 40; for just, 25
stag, antlers of, 132

stars, xxiii, 24, 48, 65, 182–83; dream of, 108
state(s), fallen, 83; interior, xvii
statues, 179, 181, 185
Stephen, St., xxii, lii, 40–41; martyrdom of, lii; speech of, lii, 181
stock, 153
stock-raising, Egyptian, 102
stone(s), 39, 59; consecrated, 91; corner, 178; elect, 178; foundation, 133; living, 178; precious, 32, 178; rejected, 178; stumbling, 178
storax, 8, 117
stranger(s), 63, 97, 185, 187; as consumer, xxii; as customer, xxii, 42; as escapee, 42; as threat, xxii; defenseless, 63; hearts of, 186; love for, 182; mystery of, xxii, 42; rest for, 186; to world, 40
strength, 159; human, xx; spiritual, 184; whole, 182
strikes, Egyptian, 102
struggle(s), liv, 17, 95, 190
stubbornness, 152
students, Egyptian, 103
study, xliv; scientific, 127
stupidity, 51
subconscious, 179
subjection, 151
sublimity, 136
submission, 10
substance, divine, 142; infinite, 142; ocean of, 142; unlimited, 142
success, temporal, xxvii
suffering, xxiv, xxviii, xxxvii, 51, 73, 83
Suhard, Cardinal Emmanuel, 2
sun, 25, 65, 153; dream of, 108
superior, desire of, 75; love of for inferiors, 91; religious, 75–76; will of, 75–76
superstition, lii, 181
support, natural, 40
supremacy, divine, 182
Sur (Shur), 50, 161

GENERAL INDEX   269

surrender, interior, 179
Susanna, 111
Sutcliffe, E. F., 1–2, 5, 18, 26, 45, 50, 52, 72, 74, 93, 96–98, 107, 109, 114, 117, 124, 127, 129–32
sweetness, 131, 161; inner, 81; of sense, 67
sword, 25, 42, 73–74, 89, 96, 161, 177, 189
symbolism, religious, 100
symbols, fertility, 181
Symmachus, 6
synagogue(s), 21, 143, 168
Syria, 90, 99, 101
system, religious, 174

tabernacle, l, 162, 165, 169, 172; construction of, liv, 135, 162; erection of, liv, 192; manna in, 167; of covenant, 170; of God, 13, 178; of testimony, 170
tablets, stone, 170, 175
Talmud, 10
Tanis, 152
taste, spiritual, 121
tax, 113
Tcikumat, 183
teaching(s), incorruptible, 139; patristic, xiv; pure, 139
tears, 13, 56, 178; of Joseph, xxxviii, 117, 119
temperance, xxxvi, 110
temple(s), lii, liv, 21, 39, 59, 131, 153, 169, 171, 173, 185; dedication of, 171; destruction of, 171; Egyptian, 102–3; eternal, 174; of God, of, 8, 174; of stone, 174; profanation of, 171; true, 174
temptation(s), liv, 164, 181, 189–90; fundamental, xvi; sexual, xxxvi
tendency, proper, 146
tenderness, natural, 72
tent, 169, 173

tent-dwellers, 22, 165
Terah, 39
teraphim, 96, 181
terebinth, teacher's, 45
terror, xxi, 16
testament, 44
testimony, 21; ark of, 170; tabernacle of, 170; tables of, 169, 175, 189
testing, place of, xlix
text(s), biblical, viii, xi, xv; ecclesial, xv; interpretation of, vii; New Testament, xlviii; understanding of, viii
Thabor (Tabor), Mt., 173
Thamar (Tamar), xxxv–xxxvi, 105, 109–10; children of, xxxv–xxxvi, 110
thanksgiving, xix, 31
thearchy, 91
Thebes, 100–101, 103
theft, 95, 117, 175; accusations of, 117–18
Theodore of Mopsuestia, 127–28
Theodoret, 143
Theodotion, 6
theologians, 2; Orthodox, 173
theology, apophatic, 173; Egyptian, 104; Jewish, 173; image-likeness, xiv; medieval, 173; mystical, xxiv, xxx, 52, 80; negative, 173; oriental, 173
theophany, xxxii, xxxiv–xxxv, xliii, xlv, 106, 137–39, 175, 178
thief, 153
things, bodily, 121; created, 78; creeping, 26, 61, 177; divine, xxvi, 65; evil, 188; exterior, 150–51; graven, 180; material, 80; spiritual, 136
Thinis, 100
thinking, magic, lii, 179
Thomas Aquinas, St., xlvi–xlvii, 141–42, 145–48
thorns, 131
Thoth, as god of writing, 100
thought(s), 51; wicked, 187
threat, 152

throats, 62
throne(s), 153, 171–72; angelic, 4; twelve, 133
thunders, 153, 178
Tigris, 5, 11–12
timbrels, 96
time(s), 65, 185; desert of, xix, 22; fullness of, xlviii; God's, xx, xxxvii, 31, 49; messianic, 131; paschal, 131
timor, 190
Titans, 26
tithe(s), 47–48, 92, 181, 185, 187
tongues, 24, 36, 62, 153; gift of, xxi, 36
Torah, xiv, 1–2, 172
touch, spiritual, 121
tower(s), leveled, xxi; of Babel, xx–xxi, 34–36, 57
traders, 105
tradition, genuine, 98; Jewish, 6, 24; legal, 76; monastic, xxxix; oral, 1; sapiential, 172; written, 1
training, 79; place of, xlix
tranquility, 54
transformation, xx, xxv, xlvi, 31, 173; perfect, xxx, 84
transgression(s), 38, 44
Transjordania, 191
Trappists, xvi, 12
travelers, Mass for, 91
traveling, mystery of, 42
treasurers, Egyptian, 103
tree(s), xvi, 5, 7, 161, 172, 183; almond, 95–96; as symbols, 6, 9; branches of, 107, 132; cedar, 6–7; cypress, 7; fig, 65, 88, 177; fir, 6; fruits of, xvi, 6; mulberry, 153; of discernment, 10; of knowledge, xvi, 5, 9–12, 14; of life, xvi, 5, 9; of paradise, 6–7, 9; of self, xvi; olive, 7, 23–24, 107; ordinary, 6; palm, 6, 161; plane, 6–7, 95; poplar, 95–96; roots of, 107; shady, 5, 181, 184; sycamore, 6, 96; turpentine, 8, 98; wild olive, 107; without fruit, 63
Trevor, George, 99
trial(s), xlix, 72, 83, 161; greatest, xxvii; normal, 190; ordinary, 190
tribe(s), 24, 185; Arab, 51, 132; desert, 26; double, xli; future role of, xli; of earth, 65; princes of, 170; twelve, xlii, 133–34
tribulation, final, 153; great, 65
Trinity, Blessed, 74
triumph, song of, 66
trombones, 102
trouble, 153
trumpet(s), 102, 178–79
trust, xxvii, xxxvi, xlix, li–lii, 110, 174, 180
truth, xviii, 14, 38–39, 58, 77, 118, 146; criterion of, 184; divine, 139; encounter with, xlvi; fruits of, 8; infinite, xxiv, 52; knowledge of, 140; real, 141; respect for, 184; search for, 13; spiritual, xix, 29–30; testimony of, 63; ultimate, 140
truthfulness, 104
Tubal Cain, 22
tumult, 159
Turin, 102
turmoil, inner, 16
turpentine, 117
turtledove, 49
Tutankhamen, 101
Tuthmes (Tutmose) III, 101
type(s), viii, xxviii
typology, viii
tyranny, 136
tyrants, pride of, 76

unbelief, 107
uncertainty, state of, 10
uncleanness, 56, 61, 180, 192
underprivileged, 188
understanding, grace of, 79; lofty, 136

underworld, 184; powers of, 183
ungodliness, 61
unhappiness, 62
union, divine, 68–69; of souls, 12; of wills, 83; Trinitarian, 12; with God, xxvii, 12, 15, 43, 83, 123
uniqueness, personal, 151
unity, xxii, xxix, 41, 77; fragile, xxi, 35; in Christ, 91; pretense of, xx; return to, 42
universe, xv, 149–50, 173; order of, 149; hierarchical, 90–91
unknowing, darkness of, xxvii
unreality, 11, 17
Ur, xxii, 39–40, 76; as center of civilization, xxii, 40

vainglory, 56
Vanier, Jean, 148–49
vapor, 149
vegetables, 99
vegetation, 6, 29
veil, of ark, 170; of Moses, 175
vengeance, xix, 149
venison, 89
vessels, 138, 154; of sanctuary, 170; potter's, 159
vials, seven, 153
vice(s), viii, 56, 62; of world, 157
victim(s), 144, 177, 181, 185; Abel as, 19; Abraham as, 72; purity of, 154; sacrificial, 73, 188
victory, final, 17; Old Testament, 157; temporary, 157
view, dim, 127; modernistic, 127; pedestrian, 127
vigil, Easter, xlviii
vigilance, 32
vine(s), 177
vinedressers, 177
vineyard(s), 57, 82, 153, 182, 186; parable of, 88–89
vintage, 180
violence, 23; sublimation of, xxxvii, 115
virgins, 4
virtue(s), viii, 47, 54; heights of, 125; practice of, xxv; subjective, xxxvi, 110; tools of, 125
virtus, 83
vision, land of, 72
visir, Egyptian, as administrator, 103; as judge, 103; as overseer, 103; son of king as, 103
visitations, 190
vitality, xiv
Viviano, Pauline A., vii–x, lvii
vocation, xxii, xxvi, xxxi, 41–42, 62, 85, 159, 186, 192; discovery of, xlviii; monastic, xlii, 133; pattern of, 42; religious, 41
voice(s), 153; of God, 16, 70, 161, 171, 176, 187
vows, 181, 185

wagons, 119, 123
war(s), 177; armor for, 134; fratricidal, 20; horror of, vii; Egyptian, 101; Jewish, 142
warden, 111
warfare, atomic, xxi; bloodthirsty, 36
wastelands, 85, 87
watchers, 7; angelic, 24
water(s), 131, 137, 144, 154, 160, 175, 183; angel of, 153; bitter, 176; blessing of, 181; fountains of, 153; into blood, 152–53; laver of, 13; living, xxx; mighty, 161; of baptism, 34; of flood, 29, 34; struggles for, 86; troughs of, 95
way(s), 40; monastic, xx; of world, 40; unknown, 42
weak, craft as defense of, 132
weakness, 18, 165
weapons, 187
weariness, 40
weeks, sabbath of, 187
weight, 149
well(s), xxx, 77–78, 86, 93–94; dried-up, 109; of Isaac, 123; of Jacob, xxxii, 45, 88, 98; of scripture, 78

Wellhausen, Julius, 1–2
wheat, 102, 115–16
wheels, 171; of chariots, 160
wicked, 62
wickedness, xxxviii, 26, 69, 119, 189
widow, 182
wife, 178; head of, 13; love for, 13; of neighbor, li
Wild Cat, 183
wilderness, 138, 151, 153, 159, 161, 164–67, 177; dreariness of, 158
will(s), 14, 62, 75, 150; concept of, 147; conformity of, xxx; created, 145–46; divine, xxix, xxxv, xlvii, 75, 147; faculty of, 147; free, 83, 150, 190; human, 145; limited, 145; object of, 146; of another, 76; of flesh, 68; of God, xxviii, xxxvii, xl, xliv, xlvii, li, liii, 10, 14, 26, 49, 72, 74–76, 78, 84, 87, 105–6, 118, 138, 145, 147–48, 151, 174, 183; of good pleasure, 148; of man, 68; submission of, xxvii; surrender of, xxiii; union of, 83
Willmering, H., 24
wind, 161; burning, 160; strong, 160
wine, xxiii, 18, 47, 89, 112, 131, 134, 177, 187; of indignation, 153
winepress, 188
wings, 171
Winzen, Damasus, 23
wisdom, xviii, l, 6–9, 11, 13, 17, 36, 63–64, 69, 172; as mother of fear, 8; as mother of hope, 8; as mother of knowledge, 8; as mother of love, 8; deep, 174; disciplines of, 81; enlightenment of, xxx; fruit of, xvi, 8; heights of, 125; inner, l; mystical, 81; of God, xxxv, 20–21, 28, 30, 49, 75, 105, 149; proud, 79; spiritual, xxix; symbolic, xvi; work of, 149; worldly, 79

Wisdom of Amenomope, 104
wise, 21
wishes, illusory, 14
witchcrafts, 56
witness(es), 3; false, 176; interior, 121; of resurrection, 122; two, 23–24
wives, 33
wolf, ravenous, 132
woman, 3, 14, 61; as equal of man, 12; as subject to husband, 12–13; creation of, 5, 12; free, 69; Hittite, 86; Samaritan, xxx, xxxii, 45, 79, 88, 181; seed of, 17; serving, 49
womanservant, 188
wonder(s), xxv, 57, 151, 180; of Lord, 159
wood(s), xv, xxviii, xlix, 5, 28, 99; for holocaust, 72–73; sweetening, 161
wool, 177
Word, 81–84; action of, 81; as spouse of soul, 123; chamber of, xxx, 82; encounter with, xxx; epiphany of, xlvi, 139; kiss of, 80–81; marriage with, 79; presence of, 80; storerooms of, 82; union with, xxx, 80
word(s), 183; as coin, 184; as tool, 184; as weapon, 184; consoling, 47; creative, liii, 183; ineffable, xlvi; inflation of, 184; mystique of, 183; of God, xv, xviii–xix, lii–liii, 14, 21, 41, 48–49, 78, 127–28, 164–65, 182–83; power of, 183; prophetic, 79; reverence for, 184; value of, xvi, 12, 184
work(s), liii, 37–38, 65, 106, 109, 153, 167, 185–86; evil, 58; just, 18; of God, xx–xxi, xxvi, xliv, 3–4, 31, 36, 42, 66, 136, 167, 189; of law, 44; servile, 186–87; wicked, 18

world, xvii, xxvi, 65, 149, 185; as idol, 183; broken, xxviii; condemnation of, 34; created, xxvi, 67; destruction of, 64; fallen, 90; fate of, 27; history of, 107; inner, xiv; judgment of, 58; kingdom(s) of, 18, 183; leaving, li, 176; love of, 35; materialistic, 42; of intelligences, 90; outer, xiv; place in, xxiv; power of, lii; prince of, 58; reconciliation of, 106–7; riches of, 107; totalitarian, 42; vices of, 157; ways of, 40
worldliness, burden of, 190
worm(s), in manna, 166–67
worship, xiv, lii, 3; Canaanite, 91; in spirit, lii; in truth, lii; object of, lii; of false gods, 44, 181, 184; of God, xxxii, lii, 91, 179; place of, 181; sacrificial, 192
wounds, 57, 153
wrath(s), 38, 56
wrestling, 102
writing, hieroglyphic, 100

year(s), church, 65; good, 113; jubilee, liv, 188, 192; lean, 113; of plenty, 114; of scarcity, 114; sabbatical, liii–liv, 188, 192
yoke, 177; of bondage, 56; of law, 174; of obedience, 150

Zabulon (Zebulon), 93, 131, 134, 136; territory of, 131
Zacchaeus, 79; humility of, 79
Zacharias, blood of, 21
Zara (Zerah), xxxvi, 110
zeal, 83
Zelpha (Zilpah), 93; as Lia's maid, 93; children of, 93
ziggurat(s), 36, 90
zodiac, patriarchal alignment with, 129
Zohar, 143